THE
RAVENS

Books by Christopher Robbins
Assassin
Air America

THE RAVENS

THE MEN WHO FLEW IN AMERICA'S SECRET WAR IN LAOS

CHRISTOPHER ROBBINS

CROWN PUBLISHERS, INC., NEW YORK

For the Ravens who never flew home,
and the Hmong who can never return.
And in memory of my father.

Published by Crown Publishers, Inc., 225 Park Avenue South, New York, New York 10003 and represented in Canada by the Canadian MANDA Group.

CROWN is a trademark of Crown Publishers, Inc.

Manufactured in the United States of America

CONTENTS

Chronology

LAOS—THE WAR YEARS

1960 Capt. Kong Le's coup in August returns power to Souvanna Phouma. Gen. Phoumi Nosavan, backed by the CIA, forms opposition faction in Laotian panhandle.

John F. Kennedy elected president of the United States in November.

General Phoumi attacks Vientiane in December, creating a crisis in the country. The Soviet Union launches massive airlift to support the neutralist faction.

1961 Eisenhower warns the young president-elect that Laos is a major crisis, the first "domino" in Southeast Asia.

The CIA begins the covert build-up of Meo forces under Gen. Vang Pao at the beginning of the year.

At the same time the U.S. sends the rightist forces in Laos six AT-6 Harvard trainer aircraft armed with machine guns and equipped to fire rockets and drop bombs.

The covert PEO infantrymen are replaced by 400 clandestine U.S. Special Forces personnel known as White Star Mobile Training Teams.

Kennedy announces U.S. support for the sovereignty of Laos in March, directly confronting the Soviet Union.

Geneva conference on Laos opens in May.

1962 An agreement on Laos is finally reached in Geneva and accords are signed in July.

American Military Assistance Command formed in South Vietnam. Advisers grow from 700 to 12,000 in less than six months.

1963 President Kennedy assassinated in Dallas in November. He is succeeded by Lyndon Johnson.

American military advisers in South Vietnam number 15,000.

1964 In response to a request from Prime Minister Souvanna Phouma for assistance in training the Royal Lao Air Force, the U.S. Air Force deploys Detachment 6, 1st Air Commando Wing to Udorn, Thailand, in April. Code-named Waterpump, it also provided Air Commandos as forward air controllers.

A spring attack by Communist forces against Neutralists on the Plain of Jars prompts Kong Le to request air support. Leonard Unger, the U.S. ambassador in Vientiane, releases the fuses to bombs previously delivered to the Royal Lao Air Force.

Prime Minister Souvanna Phouma agrees to low-level reconnaissance by U.S. "Yankee Team" jets in June.

Barrell Roll, a bombing program to complement Yankee Team reconnaissance missions, is approved by the National Security Council and gets under way in December.

William Sullivan arrives in Vientiane at the end of the year, replacing Leonard Unger as American ambassador to Laos.

1965 Headquarters 2d Air Division/13th Air Force is established at Udorn to serve as focal point for support of the air war in Laos.

The first night bombing mission is flown over the Ho Chi Minh Trail in April—the beginning of Operation Steel Tiger. By midyear, Air Force and Navy planes are flying 1,000 sorties a month.

Prairie Fire teams, dropping special forces troops onto the trail, are introduced.

The North Vietnamese set up a special unit, Group 565, to secure the vital Ho Chi Minh Trail from ground attack.

B-52s strike Mu Gia pass on the Ho Chi Minh Trail on December 11, the first time the bomber is used in Laos. Two marine battalions land in Vietnam, America's first combat troops. By year's end troop strength is nearly 200,000.

1966 Udorn headquarters redesignated 7th/13th Air Force in April 1966 following the establishment of 7th Air Force at Tan Son Nhut airbase near Saigon, Vietnam.

The Steve Canyon Program, as part of Project 404, replaces non-pilot, Air Commando–enlisted Butterfly FACs flying in the right seat of Air America planes, with pilot officers using the call sign Raven.

The U.S. Air Force installs a tactical air navigation system on the mountain of Phou Pha Thi—"The Rock" or Lima Site 85.

American combat troops in Vietnam reach 400,000 by year's end.

1967 The original navigation equipment at Phou Pha Thi is replaced with an all-weather system, operated and maintained by Air Force personnel "in the black."

American troop strength in Vietnam now reaches almost 500,000 as antiwar protest grows.

1968 The North Vietnamese and Pathet Lao launch their attack on Phou Pha Thi in January.

Richard Nixon elected president of the United States in November. Henry Kissinger chosen as national security advisor in December.

Gen. Vang Pao launches a counterattack against Phou Pha Thi and briefly recaptures the air strip.

American troop strength in Vietnam reaches its peak at 540,000.

1969 The Communists threaten Lima Site 36 in late February, and after fierce fighting it is abandoned on March 1.

Secret bombing of Cambodia using B-52s begins in March.

As the Communists push toward Long Tieng, Gen. Vang Pao launches a counterattack on March 23. At the end of the first week in April he storms Xieng Khouang.

Ambassador Sullivan leaves Laos in March.

A Communist offensive against the town of Muong Soui on the Plain of Jars results in its loss in late June. A counterattack led to heavy fighting throughout July, when government forces were again overrun.

Ambassador G. McMurtrie Godley III arrives in Laos in July.

Gen. Vang Pao launches his highly successful "Operation About Face" in August, routing the enemy.

Kissinger meets secretly with North Vietnamese negotiator in Paris in August.

Xieng Khouang is reoccupied by government forces on September 12; Muong Soui is retaken on September 28.

Ambassador Sullivan and Air Attaché Robert Tyrrell give testimony in October before a Senate subcommittee investigating the U.S. role in Laos.

American troop strength in Vietnam drops for the first time, reduced by 60,000 men.

1970 North Vietnamese forces capture Phou Nok Kok, the northeast entry point to the Plain of Jars, on January 12.

Xieng Khouang and its air strip falls in February.

The B-52 is used in Northern Laos for the first time on February 17–18.

The enemy move on Muong Soui on February 24, and the town falls.

Kissinger begins secret talks in Paris with Le Duc Tho in February.

The enemy attack Sam Thong on March 17.

The United States and South Vietnam invade Cambodia in April.

American troop level in Vietnam at year end: 280,000.

1971 Lamson 719, the invasion of Laos by South Vietnamese troops supported by U.S. air support and Army helicopters, jumps off on February 9.

The St. Valentine's Day Massacre on February 14 at Long Tieng when U.S. fighters bomb Raven FACs and friendly Meo during an enemy attack.

American troop level in Vietnam at year end: 140,000.

1972 Prime Minister Souvanna Phouma proposes a new effort at peace negotiations in a letter in July to his half-brother Prince Souphanouvong, chairman of the Pathet Lao.

Peace talks begin in Vientiane in October.

1973 The Vietnam peace agreement takes effect January 28 (January 27, Washington time).

A peace agreement for Laos signed in Vientiane on February 21, providing for a cease-fire, an immediate end of U.S. bombing, and formation of a new coalition government.

Bombing operations are renewed on February 23 at the request of the Vientiane government after Communist ceasefire violations. B-52s strike enemy positions near Paksong.

Last American troops leave Vietnam on March 29.

Repeated enemy cease-fires bring back the B-52s on April 17, the final combat sortie by the U.S. Air Force after nine years of operations.

U.S. Congress in November overrides Nixon's veto of law limiting the president's right to wage war.

1974 New coalition government finally formed in Vientiane in April.

House Judiciary Committee opens impeachment hearings on Nixon in May.

Communist buildup of men and supplies in South Vietnam and Laos.

U.S. reconnaissance flights, monitoring the preparations for the Communist offensive, halted on June 4 when the Senate approved a bill, endorsed by the House of Representatives, to block funds for any U.S. military activities in Indochina.

Nixon resigns in August, replaced by President Gerald Ford.

1975 Pathet Lao attack Vang Pao's forces in March.

North Vietnamese and Pathet Lao troops seize government-held positions north of Vientiane in March and April.

Saigon falls in April.

Pathet Lao openly announce a future program of genocide against the Meo (Hmong) in an article in their party paper on May 9.

The CIA convince Gen. Vang Pao to withdraw from Long Tieng. He leaves Laos on May 15 after a lifetime at war, never to return.

Communist troops enter Luang Prabang and Vientiane in August.

Prime Minister Souvanna Phouma resigns on November 28.

The ancient Lao monarchy is abolished in December, together with the 600-year-old system of village autonomy. The People's Democratic Republic of Laos is proclaimed and the country becomes a Communist state.

1977 The Hmong's last stronghold, the Phu Bia massif, is besieged by Vietnamese troops and shelled by 130mm artillery. Unable to penetrate the defenses from the ground, the Vietnamese resort to aerial bombardment of napalm and possibly gas and chemical weapons.

1979 By the end of the year the exodus of the Hmong reaches its peak with 3,000 crossing into Thailand each month. A total of 300,000 Laotians have fled the country's increasingly totalitarian regime, with at least 20,000 remaining "officials" interned in remote jungle camps for reeducation. Tens of thousands of North Vietnamese move into northern Laos as permanent colonizers, while 50,000 North Vietnamese soldiers remain scattered throughout the country.

1987 Thai security forces raid Ban Vinai refugee camp just south of the Mekong, and detain more than one hundred Hmong at gunpoint, the first batch of refugees to face the harsh fate of forcible repatriation to Laos.

Prologue:

MYTH

As the war dragged on, so the myth grew. It started in the mid-1960s as a mix of gossip and bar talk among a battle-hardened elite who told stories that seemed fantastic to everyone who heard them. Apparently, there was another war even nastier than the one in Vietnam, and so secret that the location of the country in which it was being fought was classified. The cognoscenti simply referred to it as "the Other Theater." The men who chose to fight in it were hand-picked volunteers, and anyone accepted for a tour seemed to disappear as if from the face of the earth.

The pilots in the Other Theater were military men, but flew into battle in civilian clothes—denim cutoffs, T-shirts, cowboy hats, and dark glasses, so people said. They fought with obsolete propeller aircraft, the discarded junk of an earlier era, and suffered the highest casualty rate of the Indochinese War—as high as 50 percent, so the story went. Every man had a price put on his head by the enemy and was protected by his own personal bodyguard. Each pilot was obliged to carry a small pill of lethal shellfish toxin, especially created by the CIA, which he had sworn to take if he ever fell into the hands of the enemy. Their job was to fly as the winged artillery of some fearsome warlord, who led an army of stone-age mercenaries in the pay of the CIA, and they operated out of a secret city hidden in the mountains of a jungle kingdom on the Red Chinese border.

It certainly sounded farfetched, yet the talk emanated from people who commanded respect. Men like the Special Forces soldiers who fought behind enemy lines, CIA case officers who lived in the field year after year, and the fighter pilots who flew over North Vietnam. The pilots spoke of colleagues who had vanished into a highly classified operation code-named the Steve Canyon Program.

When such men reappeared they had gone through a startling metamorphosis. In the military world of spit, polish, and crewcuts, they stood apart: some sported long hair and muttonchop whiskers or curling, waxed mustachios, and many wore heavy gold bracelets and GMT Master Rolex watches with wide gold bands. If they happened to be on the edge of a combat zone they carried a 9mm pistol in a holster, the preferred weapon of the professional soldier of fortune. And, like a caste mark, each wore a 22-karat gold ring that had an oriental royal crest set into a red cloisonné top, with a roughly cut piece of locally procured diamond at its center.

The greatest change of all was not in their appearance, but in their manner. Self-confident to the point of arrogance and disdainful of anyone outside of their own group, they had the distant air of people inducted into a powerful and mystical secret society.

Insiders who worked with them knew these pilots as the Ravens. It was only natural that such a romantic group should generate talk. That almost all of it was true, in one form or another, was never established at the time. The secrecy of their activities, and the very fact of their actual existence, was guarded throughout the war. Even the Air Force colonels whose job it was to interview new pilots for the program had no clear idea of what the mission involved.

The secret is still guarded today. A large number of the documents and oral histories relating to the activities of the Ravens during the Indochinese war will remain classified until after the year 2000. An official history of the war in which the Ravens fought, prepared by Air Force historians with Top Secret security clearances, will not be released for publication within the lifetime of anyone reading this.[1]

The legend has become hazy, a half-remembered war story known only to a few veterans of Vietnam. "The Steve Canyon Program? Yeah, I remember. The Ravens—a weird bunch of guys who lived and fought out there in the jungle in the Other Theater somewhere. Hell, what was the name of the country?"

PART I

PART I

1

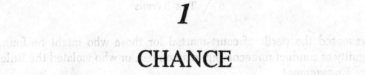

CHANCE

"Want to take a chance?"

The men who found themselves in the secret war had first chosen to draw the Chance card in Vietnam. Later it would all seem part of the peculiar nature of things that their very first experience of war should be the board of a Monopoly-style game.

It was the brainchild of an enterprising officer who briefed newly arrived young pilots assigned to Vietnam as forward air controllers (FACs), whose job was to direct fighter-bombers onto targets from small, vulnerable spotter planes. He had organized an elaborate and complex briefing into a more readily remembered game patterned on Monopoly. Laid out on the board for the newcomer was his year's tour. A small model plane was moved square by square around the board, while the briefing officer explained what to expect in the months ahead. Instead of moving from Broadway to Boardwalk, the FAC was taken from Day One to DEROS (date of eligible return from overseas).[1]

The first moves on the board covered such dull stuff as aircraft maintenance, radio procedures, and the Rules of Engagement. The briefing officer attempted to enliven his description of the first few weeks of technical drudgery with a spirited talk on the art of living in a war zone, as the model plane was moved onto squares marked "Life on Base" and "Indigenous Population." The Monopoly briefing took newcomers through the gradual process where an FNG (fucking new guy) developed into an "old head." Instead of acquiring houses or hotels the players won experience, promotion, and medals. Jail represented the perils of court-martial for those who might be found guilty of conduct unbecoming to an officer, or who violated the Rules of Engagement.

The briefing officer moved the model plane around the board, explaining the various jobs which might be assigned. At one base a FAC would be working with American troops in the field—a very high priority; at another he might be working with Vietnamese or Korean troops, and adapt accordingly. There were FACs who flew over the Ho Chi Minh Trail, others who only worked at night. From time to time a FAC would be called in to oversee a search-and-rescue (SAR) mission for a downed fighter or helicopter pilot.

The pilots were not actually asked to throw dice, but halfway around the board at the point representing the six-month mark of the tour, they were invited to take a chance. The briefing officer took on a mischievous, secretive look. The plane had been moved onto a square marked "Chance." He looked up at his audience, pausing for dramatic effect. "Anyone want to take a chance?"

The group's reaction was always interesting. A couple of the new FACs frowned, uncertain how to take this unmilitary levity; others shrugged or grinned sheepishly, waiting for the briefing officer to take back the initiative and explain the next move; but occasionally there would be someone who would answer the question almost before it had been asked. Want to take a chance? "Sure!"

The briefing officer picked up the Chance card, the only one lying on the board, and held it up for everyone to see. It read: "Steve Canyon Program."

The pilots waited to hear what the officer had to say about the Steve Canyon Program, but he just kept grinning at them crookedly and cultivating the look of mischief and mystery, until someone inevitably asked, "Well, what is it?"

It seemed for a moment as if the officer was going to say nothing at all. "I can't tell you much about it," he allowed finally, enjoying the intrigue, "but if you are on the adventuresome side and something like this might interest you, we can have *certain people* talk to you. *After* you've been here six months."

"Yeah, but what is it?"

The briefing officer stopped smiling. "When you've been here six months, come and talk to us again, *if* you're still interested." The card was placed back on the board and the model plane moved into the squares denoting the second six-month segment of the tour, until finally it reached the safety of home. (There was, of course, a missing

Chance card the briefing officer failed to mention which the pilots joked about among themselves—Do Not Pass Go, Do Not Collect $200. It was marked KIA—killed in action.)

In a long and complex briefing, even one so cunningly fashioned as this, the small joke of the Chance card and the single tantalizing mention of the Steve Canyon Program did its work. Everyone was fascinated, but to men who had just arrived fresh in Vietnam there seemed to be plenty of war to go around without volunteering for some comic-strip mission no one was going to say anything about for six months. Within days they would be shot at for the first time, and six months seemed like eternity. The general consensus after the briefing when the pilots discussed it with one another was: "Bull-shit—I'm not volunteering for anything named Steve Canyon."

Everyone in America had heard of Steve Canyon, the comic-strip flyboy created by Milton Caniff. The strip was syndicated to more than two hundred newspapers throughout the country and had a readership of thirty million people a day. Canyon was a Gary Cooper type, with a shock of slicked-back blond hair and a pipe clamped in his jutting jaw. He dressed in flying coveralls, always carried a 45mm automatic in a shoulder holster open to sight, and traveled the world undertaking "any assignment as long as it's perilous, exciting, and decent."

Steve Canyon came into being, significantly, in 1947—the same year that the Air Force and the Central Intelligence Agency were created. The fictional hero was a product of Middle America. A college football player on the team of Ohio State University in 1941, his red-blooded patriotic instincts overrode his academic ambitions and made him volunteer unhesitatingly to fly in the war. "I stopped some enemy ordnance (nothing compared to what happened to some of the guys)," Canyon wrote in a supposed letter to a friend about his war experiences, "but it gave me the chance to . . . say to the officer passing out medals, 'Just give me some aspirin—I already have a Purple Heart!' "

On his return from the war, Steve Canyon set up a one-plane air taxi service, Horizons Unlimited, adopting a Navajo double-eagle design as its symbol. He flew everywhere, had friends in all the right places, and was dedicated to bachelorhood, with a girl in every airport. He was always broke and often slept in his cubbyhole office, which was equipped with blankets stored in the filing cabinet—the files were kept in his pocket. Adventure followed adventure, year after year, in one exotic locale after another, as Steve Canyon enjoyed a nonstop life of action and excitement. But then, in the 1950s, he turned his back on this carefree, adventurous existence and settled permanently in the Orient—to be on guard against the new "invader from the north." He opted for responsibility and reenlisted in the military. But above all else, whether as freelance adventurer or committed military volunteer, Steve Canyon was a man who could keep a secret.[2]

He was also dated. The young pilots thought of Steve Canyon as a bit much. John Wayne looked battered and cynical beside Canyon with his breathless and unquestioning patriotism, hunk's courage, clean-cut good looks, and Boy Scout philosophizing. The young forward air controllers, unbaptized by fire as yet and uncertain of what the realities of war had in store for them, laughed off Steve Canyon and concentrated on steeling themselves against flying in Vietnam.

Later, as the months went by, a small number of them would increasingly wonder about the Steve Canyon Program. What sort of outfit in such a straitlaced and bureaucratic service as the United States Air Force could possibly be modeled on a character like Steve Canyon? The pilots joked about Canyon's old-fashioned virtues— honesty, patriotism, bravery, adventurous spirit, and general all-round copper-bottomed Americanness—although they were the qualities which most hoped to emulate. The Air Force wag who gave the program its name could not have dreamed how accurately he had described the sort of man the mission needed, or how many potential Canyons there would be willing to join it.

The young pilots who went to Vietnam to fly as forward air controllers arrived pumped up and ready for action. They had a wide range of training behind them and were convinced of their status as an elite. They had not been unwillingly drafted and rapidly processed into some ground-pounding grunt, but were volunteers who had survived the stringent weeding-out processes of pilot training.

The most romantic and adventurous of those who had volunteered to fly were certain that the ultimate manner in which to pursue the war was as a fighter pilot, a figure who had emerged from World War II as the most glamorous in the air—the very top of the pilot pecking order. The fighter pilot was viewed as a man with dash, derring-do, and a special edge of courage that singled him out from all others. The young trainee at pilot school yearned for the day when he would be allowed to sit on the bar of the officers' club and sing:

> *There are no fighter pilots down in hell.*
> *The place is full of queers, navigators, bombardiers,*
> *But there are no fighter pilots down in hell.*

Fighter pilots possess an overweening arrogance, an almost messianic egocentricity and self-confidence that borders on the obnoxious. This can be tedious for anyone not committed to the system of narrow absolutes that constitutes the fighter pilots' world. But then, by definition, such a person has no value. To those steeped in the lore of flying, especially those who go through the intense indoctrination of the Air Force Academy, these things are carved as if in stone.

The dream of young romantics destined for the war was to earn an opportunity to duel with a Russian MiG, one on one and head to head, up in the wild blue yonder over North Vietnam. But it is the fate of romantics to be disillusioned, and most would-be pilots were soon forced to accept that being given a fighter was little more than a dream.

Anyone who had survived the obstacle course of pilot training recognized the statistical improbability of becoming a fighter pilot. The trainee pilot lives in perpetual fear of being washed out for the most minor infraction. The first obstacle on the course is a flight physical, which claims its quota of victims. This is followed by the Air Force Officers' Quotient Test, in which a potential candidate for pilot training has to convince his examiners that he is both officer *and* pilot material (only *rated*—that is, *pilot*—officers count). Of those who go forward into pilot training, a high percentage flunk in the very early stages, doomed by persistent airsickness, a slowness in acquiring the ability to read aerial maps, or a hundred other possible failings. The entire year of training is one long, uphill haul, with casualties and failures throughout.

At the end of it all the survivors earn their wings. The very top students are given fighters—if luck is on their side and there are aircraft available. The others have to settle for the despised transport or bomber—not as bad as navigating, but the terms fighter pilots use for those who fly bombers for Strategic Air Command (SAC pukes) and transports (trash haulers) indicate their disdain.

The disappointment a young pilot feels—especially if he has passed out as a distinguished graduate—when he fails to get a fighter is crushing. His aspirations have relegated him to a world that by his own definition is perpetually second-rate.

But during the Vietnam War the word went around that a pilot who had not received a fighter assignment could volunteer for another combat flying job that was rapidly gaining the reputation of being as righteous, dangerous, and terrifying as a fighter pilot's. The job was that of forward air controller. Combat FACs were easy targets for the enemy and suffered high casualties, and as a result there was always a slot for any young pilot who wanted to volunteer.

A FAC did not have the glamour of flying a high-tech jet, but his role was dignified by danger. He took enormous risks to coordinate air support for ground troops, working with slow, low-flying aircraft (described by the Air Force as "noncosmetic"). Of the twelve Medals of Honor awarded to Air Force personnel for bravery in the Vietnam War, two went to forward air controllers.

A good FAC needed a fighter pilot's mentality but was obliged to operate at the pace of a World War I biplane. Until as late as 1971 the FACs flew Cessna O-1 Bird Dogs, fore-and-aft two-seater, high-wing monoplanes, most of which had been built for the Army in the early 1950s, although production continued until 1961. The Air Force felt the plane was inadequate for its task in Vietnam. The plane had no armor, lacked self-sealing fuel tanks, its range was only 530 miles, it carried too few marking rockets, and its maximum speed was 115 mph (although 60 knots was more likely when configured for combat). In addition, its ground-looping characteristics made it unforgiving to the uninitiated on the taxiway. (Pilots did not like to turn their backs on the O-1 until it had been taxied to a halt, the engine turned off, and the wings tied down.) Eventually, the Cessna O-2 was introduced to replace the older plane. This was a modified business aircraft with double the range of the O-1 and the ability to carry twice as many rockets. Although it too was insufficiently armored, the Air Force felt it could serve as a stopgap until enough North American OV-10 Broncos were available. The Bronco had been specially designed for the job, with a glass canopy providing excellent visibility, armor, rockets, bombs, and machine guns.

The FAC was essential to every aspect of the military operation in Vietnam. It was his job to find the target, order up fighter-bombers from a circling airborne command and control center (AB Triple C) or ground-based direct air support center (DASC), mark the target accurately with white phosphorus smoke rockets (Willy Pete), and control the operation throughout the time the planes remained on station. And after the fighters had departed, the FAC stayed over the target to make a bomb damage assessment (BDA), which he relayed to the fighters and airborne command. Putting in a strike meant that you were busier than a one-legged man in an ass-kicking contest, the pilots said.

The FAC also had to ensure that there were no attacks on the civilian population, a complex and constant problem in a war where there were no front lines and any hamlet could suddenly become a part of the combat zone. As early as 1961 it became established policy that all tactical strike aircraft—fighters, fighter-bombers, and gunships—would be under the control of a FAC, who cleared combat strikes with local civilian officials. FACs worked in every one of Vietnam's forty-four provinces and became a prime source of combat intelligence. When major U.S. ground combat units were first sent to Vietnam in 1965, each battalion was assigned a number of FACs, whose role became that of local air commander.[3]

The initial training of the FACs was undertaken by the Air Commandos, and young pilots were sent to the base at Hurlburt Field, Fort Walton Beach, Florida. The Commandos flew all the special-operations airplanes—old prop fighters and adapted transports with not a cosmetic one among them—and performed a wide variety of strange missions not usually associated with the Air Force. The Air Commandos were given the clandestine, classified operations, and their school was designed to put a young FAC through his paces.

A FAC also had to know how the Army worked. At the Air and Ground Operations School he was taught the difference between a platoon and a brigade, how soldiers operated in the field, the way artillery was used, and so on. The Army had insisted that any FAC working fighters near troops be fighter-qualified himself, believing that such a pilot would be safer and more competent. It was the Army's illusion that the Air Force would respond to this requirement by filling all the FAC slots with old-time combat-experienced fighter pilots. Instead, the Air Force took the young FAC, gave him eighty hours of flying time in a fighter, trained him in fighter-weapons delivery to give him an idea of what it was like to deliver ordnance from a high-performance airplane, and then declared him fighter-qualified. At first the FACs were trained in Phantom F-4s, but the expense proved to be prohibitive, so they were relegated to T-33 Shooting Stars, the cheapest jet fighter-trainer available. Pilots thus qualified were "A" FACs, the only group allowed to direct ordnance near American troops. "B" FACs were not required to be fighter-qualified, but could direct ordnance near South Vietnamese, Korean, or Australian troops. It is unlikely the Allies were aware always of these distinctions.

Survival schools came next. At water survival in Homestead, Florida, a pilot learned what to do if he was shot down over the ocean and was left to bob on the waves in a one-man boat. Scooped from the sea, the FAC was sent to Fairchild Air Force Base, Washington, where he was subjected to interrogation in conditions replicating a North Vietnamese prison camp.

After Fairchild he was sent to the Far East for the final and most challenging survival training—Snake School. This was the Jungle Survival School in the Philippines. There were lessons in recognizing edible and inedible jungle roots and berries, how to deal with the sort of medical problems that might be encountered, and E&E—escape and evasion. (One instructor urged his students to imagine themselves as so much 10-weight motor oil, effortlessly slipping downhill through grass.)

Clear distinctions began to emerge among the pilots during the courses at the various survival schools. There were those who treated the whole thing as a prank, something to be endured and shrugged off, while others went through each stage of the training as if their lives depended on it. The second group began to take pains, almost without knowing it, to distance themselves from the first. War was still only a word to all of them, but there were those who intended to be fully prepared when it became real.

Once in Vietnam there was one final step before being allowed to join the war—the in-country checkout at FAC-U (FAC University) in Phan Rang, headquarters of the 14th Air Commando Wing. A combat tactics instructor sat in the backseat on the local area checkout rides. The FAC would be given a set of military grid coordinates—two letters and six numbers, which came over the radio in the form "X-Ray Uniform 436457"—check his map, fly to the area, and orbit. He would then stand by to receive a "two-ship" (pair) of fighter-bombers. Once the fighters arrived, the pressure was enormous. Handling the radio traffic alone would fray the average man's nerves to breaking point: the FAC maintained constant radio contact not only with the airborne command post but with the unit on the ground and each of the individual fighters. In a large operation he might be talking to a couple of other FACs as well and to as many as five sets of air—pairs of fighter-bombers—stacked in layers above him awaiting their turn.

The FAC would then roll in and mark the target with smoke—which had to be accurate—and direct the fighters onto it: "Cleared in hot—hit my smoke." ("Hot" meant that the guns and ordnance on a fighter should be armed; the "smoke" came from the FAC's marking rocket.) Technique apart, the instructor was watching the new FAC to see if he could operate under pressure. After a few dummy tree-busting runs a FAC was supposed to be ready for the real thing, known in the trade as the "dollar ride."

After what seemed to be a lifetime of training flights, the day arrived when the FAC took off in his spotter plane to go out and find the enemy, to kill or be killed. Suddenly it was real, the war at last, and almost always it came as a surprise. The FAC would be out with an instructor in the backseat as usual, honing his technique in some area or other, when the airborne command and control center would come up on the air to give the radio frequency of a certain ground unit and the coordinates of its location.

The first time it happened for John Wisniewski he was sent over to a South Vietnamese Army commander who had a target of Vietcong troops. Beside him, in the right seat of the O-2, the instructor was rubbing his hands together. "Got something now!"

The SVA commander described the target over the radio. "I've got this house and it's full of VC." Wisniewski checked his maps and circled the house beneath him. "See it?" the commander asked. "You got it? I want you to kill them."

Wisniewski felt the breath leave him as if he were winded. "Now it was no longer in the jungle blowing trees away. It was people. I could see them. I didn't know what the hell I was doing. What is this? Some guy I can't see is telling me those figures running around down there are VC. I don't know who they are."

The Vietnamese commander grew impatient. "Bad guys. *I want you to kill them!*" he repeated.

Wisniewski orbited and brought the plane down low, trying to take a closer look. He was operating as coolly as he knew how, but his mind was in turmoil. "Shit, what do I do? Live people down there. Fuck." An AC-47 gunship had come on station and was standing by. It was the war at last.

The instructor was as impatient as the ground commander. "He was so excited he was almost jumping up and down, the son of a bitch. The instructor was yelling, 'Do it! Do it! You got real guys. A real target! See where it is? Hit it with a rocket. Do it!' "

Wisniewski took a deep breath. He was so nervous he felt he would never be able to get it right. He rolled in on the house and fired a marking rocket. It was right on target and hit directly in the center of the house. People began to run out in every direction. He hesitated for a moment before keying the radio mike and talking to the gunship. "Hit my smoke!"

The AC-47 banked lazily into position. It took only seconds. The Dragonship—known by the grunts as Puff or Spooky—was equipped with three rapid-fire Gatling guns, each capable of pouring down six thousand rounds a minute. When it opened up the tracers alone made it look as if it were hosing the earth with fire. The house dissolved in seconds. One moment Wisniewski had looked down and the house was there, the next it had disappeared as if it had never existed. "Thanks," the ground commander said over the air. "Bad guys all dead."

Wisniewski flew home feeling nauseous and very confused. It had not happened as he had imagined it would, and the enormous step of killing people for the first time had seemed so arbitrary and ordinary. Nothing had really blown up; he had seen no blood nor heard any human cries. There had also been the instructor watching the whole operation, which allowed Wisniewski to say to himself, "It was *not quite* just me."

Two days later, in a firefight on the banks of the Mekong, Wisniewski put in an air strike on his own. Friendly ground forces had called for air support to destroy enemy troops who had stationed themselves in a group of houses that straggled along the bank of the river for a mile or so. Wisnieswski arrived and worked five sets of fighter-bombers, loaded with a variety of ordnance, onto the target. "The people on the ground said there was nothing there but bad guys. I smoked the houses, an easy target, working the air up and down, back and forth. I blew them all up. Everything burned. Somebody had told me it was all bad guys, but I have no idea who was in there. And when I left I looked back into the sunset—everything was burning. And that was when I really got sick—I felt fucking terrible about that shit."

Back on the ground the moral question became very simple— either one did it, or one didn't do it. It was not a job that permitted fence-sitting, and no one who had struggled for so long through the pilot hierarchy to arrive at some point of combat respectability was going to quit. "I was in a situation where if I didn't like what I was doing I could quit. That decision took about thirty seconds. I wasn't going to quit. And if I wasn't going to quit I was going to do it right."

* * *

There is no training in the world that quite prepares a soldier for the realities of the battlefield. The moral question for a FAC soon receded into the background as friends and colleagues were routinely killed by an enemy who had demonstrated a willingness to shoot them out of the sky without any qualms at all.

A word the FACs used a lot when talking about their initial stint on the job was "tense." Contemplating the hidden mysteries of an imminent combat mission made them tense; getting shot at made them tense; taking the plane down low to look under the trees for antiaircraft guns made them tense. In conversation over a beer, safely back at the hootch, FACs would swap stories about the day's tense moments. Nobody spoke of being "scared"—except in the sense that somebody had made them jump: "Got down there under the trees and that goddam 37-mike-mike AA gun opened up right in front of me—scared me shitless." The FAC would laugh and chug his beer. Combat has its own etiquette, and a soldier does not have the poor taste to talk about fear. Fear followed its own immutable logic, and once it was admitted, disintegration was bound to follow: a FAC began to fly too high to be effective, or became so cautious he was a hazard to himself.

Death was the same, a taboo subject too serious for serious discussion. If a FAC was good and was killed, his friends said he had the worst sort of luck. It was a damn shame. But if he had made a mistake, or had never really had what it took in the first place, then he had fucked up or was a damn fool. Either way, none of the survivors, drinking beer around the bar, was going to have luck that bad or be so dumb as to fuck up.

So the FAC moved inexorably through the first six months of his tour, coping with each experience as it came. Two stood out: being shot at, especially for the first time (although a real hosing was always a nasty surprise), and trolling for ground fire.

"Trolling" involved flying over an area known to be infested by the enemy, and then deliberately taking the plane down low to draw ground fire. Circling as if he had found something and was waiting for fighters, the FAC tempted the enemy to break fire discipline and give away their position. It was an act which went against every instinct of survival and all of a pilot's training.

But real as the war in Vietnam was, it proved to be something of a disappointment. Sometimes it seemed as if it was spread so thin there wasn't enough to go around. Seasonal, sporadic, and scattered all over the country, it erupted in one area for a brief spurt of furious action before relapsing into long periods of inactivity. Having geared themselves up for combat, many FACs were disappointed to find themselves flying only fifteen days a month. The free time led to intense boredom and endless opportunities for getting into trouble with senior officers, military policemen, and downtown bar girls.

There were plenty of FACs who were very pleased to be reducing the arithmetical risk by flying so little; they further minimized it by finessing their way into quiet areas where they flew high or at night, and were careful not to look too hard for the enemy. There were others, who called themselves "the Shooters," who felt that every day out of the war was a waste of time.

It soon became clear to the more aggressive pilots that Vietnam was a war in which the Shooters were out of place. They were forced to operate under extraordinary restraints, and praise and promotion were more likely to be awarded to those among the horde of rear-echelon types. Although the sky was dense with the machinery of war, often the most dangerous part of any mission was getting back into the traffic pattern. FACs and fighter pilots both bemoaned the fact that the greatest risk in the war in South Vietnam was not enemy action but a midair collision.

Too much free time, endless stretches of boredom spent in the hootch drinking beer instead of flying in the war, led to flights of subversive fancy. Most of the FACs had gone to Vietnam willingly enough—jumped at the opportunity, almost—and accepted their role as a duty demanded of them by their country. But after a few months all sorts of questions began to arise about the quality of leadership, the motives of the politicians, the way the war was being conducted— "fought" was dismissed as too strong a word—and the South Vietnamese themselves. Anyone with eyes to see could not help noticing that while all the young Americans in the country were in uniforms of one sort or another, a great many of the young Vietnamese were riding around on mopeds with stereos blaring western rock hitched to their shoulders. By definition a FAC is a hawk—and the Shooters were the most hawklike of them all—but even they had second thoughts about the war in Vietnam.

From his very first day in-country the FAC came up against the Romeos—the Rules of Engagement.[4] They had become enormously complex and almost incomprehensible as the war progressed, elaborated upon and changed at will by political decisions made in Washington, until they had become an end in themselves. There were rules for every part of the country, all of them different and forever changing. There were rules to cover every type of activity, and different sets of rules for every service—the Army, the Marines, the Navy, and especially the Air Force. One of the commanders of the 7th Air Force, Gen. John D. Lavelle, gave a graphic description of their bulk: "We finally found out why there are two crew members in the F-4. One is to fly the airplane and one is to carry the briefcase full of the Rules of Engagement."

Rules to cover FAC activity were legion, and each new pilot spent the first two days of the war in Vietnam learning them. Every month afterward a FAC had to take a multi-question written exam—the Romeo exam—for each of the political areas he worked. The bailiwick of Lew Hatch, who would become a Raven to escape the rules, was spread over three military areas, and he spent a significant amount of his time preparing for exams. "I would go in to the intel folks a couple of days before the exam and get the ROE out and study them. You had to know everything—the start and end coordinates of free-fire zones, which LOCs (lines of communication) we could hit without political clearance. In Cambodia we couldn't hit within a thousand meters of a pagoda—in III Corps, in South Vietnam, it was five hundred meters. If you didn't pass the written test you were decertified and couldn't go out on air strikes, and would have to be in the intel shop studying for several days. Some of the rules were asinine. I ended up taking a Romeo exam on three sets of ROE every month. I spent all my time sweating the exams."

The rules were impossible to memorize in their entirety, and sometimes even to understand, and were open to different interpretations. Huge sanctuary areas were granted to the enemy. A fighter pilot could not attack a North Vietnamese MiG sitting on a runway until it was in flight, identified, and showing hostile intentions (the possible peaceful intentions of an enemy MiG were left undefined). In some regions enemy trucks could avoid attack by simply driving off the road. SAM missile sites could not be struck while under construction, but only after they became operational. Limited extensions of target areas would be arbitrarily declared, only to be unexpectedly canceled and withdrawn later.

The Romeos were classified as Top Secret throughout the war—right up until 1985—but the enemy gained a close and detailed knowledge of them, which they used to their great advantage. The

Americans ruled that pagodas were not to be struck: the enemy stored ammunition, sheltered troops, and set up antiaircraft guns in them. Field hospitals were not to be struck: the enemy moved its casualties onto ammo dumps and supply caches and called them hospitals. And after every major action the enemy could always slip back into clearly defined sanctuaries where their safety was assured.

The FACs fully understood the need to control bombing in a war without front lines, but the rules governing forward air control missions severely hampered them from doing an effective job. The Air Force demanded that a FAC fly at a minimum altitude of fifteen hundred feet, putting him out of the range of small-arms fire. It was also often too high to be able to spot the enemy. To get the job done there were times when fifteen hundred feet was too low, or five hundred feet too high—what a FAC really needed was to be allowed to make a judgment based on experience and the actualities of the battlefield, rather than follow a rigid set of rules. Any FAC who broke the rules, in whatever circumstances and however effective the results, was liable to court-martial. So FACs ended up either doing a really poor job or breaking the rules.

Flying at fifteen hundred feet, they would find a target, peering with difficulty through binoculars. The next step was to call it into the direct air support center (DASC) or the orbiting airborne control and command center (ABCCC) for approval. Each target took between ten and fifteen minutes to approve, if the system was working smoothly, although there could be a wait of a half hour or more.

The frustration of being unable to operate freely enough to take the war to the enemy mounted daily among the FACs, and the bureaucratic illogic of the Romeos was reflected in their clashes with rear-echelon administrative officers.

"Major, can I ask you something?" Fred Platt, a FAC destined to become a Raven, asked one such officer after being refused permission to put in an air strike on Vietcong who had been shooting at him in open country.

"Go right ahead, captain."

"We're over here to fight a war. Fighting a war means killing the enemy before he kills you. I can find the enemy okay, and he's sure as hell trying to kill me. Why can't I kill him?"

"You have to wait for permission."

"If he's shooting at me can I shoot back—because then I'm sure he's a bad guy?"

The major sighed. "No. You have to wait for permission."

"What if he shoots and hits me?"

The major smiled in quiet triumph. "You'd be violating the Rules of Engagement by flying too close to him."

So Fred Platt adjusted the rules. "I said, fuck it, shot them wherever I saw them and just didn't report it." Instead of protecting the lives of innocent civilians, the Romeos turned honest men into liars. "Don't get the wrong impression—I wouldn't go out and get some peasant walking with his buffalo. But I can tell between VC firing AK-47s at me and some old peasant with a water buffalo."

While the rules often forbade a FAC to act in the face of the enemy, the system similarly demanded action when there was clearly no hostile activity whatsoever. FACs who flew the OV-10 over the Ho Chi Minh Trail usually operated at ten thousand feet, one hand on the stick and the other holding binoculars. In the wet season, which was six months of the year, they could often see nothing. A FAC walled in by solid undercast was obliged to stay on station hour after hour, regardless of being unable to put in air strikes. The only enemy was boredom. "I used to do spins—spin the plane just to stay awake," Terry Murphy said. "Take the airplane up, kick the rudder and stall it, spin it for a couple of thousand feet, and then recover it. Hour after hour."

The realities of the battlefield demanded again and again that the rules be broken. FACs would find mortars dug in around fortified pagodas which had been converted into antiaircraft bunkers, but would be refused permission to put in a strike even after they had been shot at. Some risked court-martial by concocting phony coordinates and calling in fighters anyway.

There were times when a refusal to authorize an air strike met with appalling consequences. Douglas Mitchell was flying OV-10s over Cambodia late in the war as a Rustic, the only armed FACs in Southeast Asia. The OV-10 carried two pods of high-explosive rockets—nineteen in each pod—a smaller pod carrying six flechette rockets, six Willy Pete rockets, and two thousand rounds of strafe. Vietnam was drawing most of the air support, and Rustic FACs had a capability to provide immediate air support when everything else was unavailable. Mitchell flew up to a small river town north of Phnom Penh, the capital of Cambodia, after a report from a ground commander that the Khmer Rouge had taken it the previous evening. When he arrived and swooped low over the town, he could see soldiers in the process of slaughtering the townspeople. Beneath him in clear view, villagers were being dragged from their houses by the Khmer Rouge and shot.

As Mitchell had already been fired upon, and taken a hit that had ricocheted off the nosewheel strut, he asked for permission to fire his own ordnance. He added a graphic description of the horror he was being forced to witness below him.

He was told to stand by. As he waited for an answer, he made a low orbit, watching the slaughter with a mounting sense of fury. Twenty minutes later permission was refused.

Disgusted and enraged, he flew back to base and immediately called a friend at Air Force HQ in Saigon who had influence over the selection and transfer of FACs into other units. The inside word on the FAC circuit was that you never had to go through this sort of thing in the Steve Canyon Program. And any program less bound by the Romeos began to seem like a very attractive alternative. "Goddammit, send me to the Steve Canyon Program," Doug Mitchell told his friend. "I want to go where I can fight."

There was only one thing more galling than the Romeos, and that was the REMFs (pronounced *remfs*). They arrived in the aftermath of battle, once the enemy had slipped away and the dead and wounded had been removed, swarming out of Saigon like locusts. They vastly outnumbered the men in combat units in the field, and all too often contrived to smother any enterprise or initiative the warriors of their group might show. They were known, with a dismissive contempt that masked a burning loathing, as the REMFs—rear-echelon motherfuckers.

There had never been an American army so burdened with rear-echelon personnel as the one fielded in Vietnam. At the height of the war only 67,000 to 90,000 men were assigned to front-line units, while the remainder of the 540,000-man force formed a huge logistical tail. For every man at the front there were six to eight others behind him. Less than 20 percent of the U.S. Military Assistance Command, Vietnam, was made up of infantrymen.

There is power, as well as safety, in numbers, and this great host of REMFs inevitably came to dominate the war. The longer it continued, the stronger their influence became. Life for the REMFs, with its barbermobiles, mobile dentistry units, air-conditioned clubs, in-country rest and recreation (R&R) centers, and Saigon nightlife, was often more comfortable than back in the States. The Vietnam War was the only one the military had, and a tour in the combat zone was essential for a career officer's advancement. Vietnam, for many ambitious officers, became just another rung on the way up the ladder.

The enemy did things differently. Their ratio of men in the field to support troops was almost the opposite to that of the U.S. Army, thus enabling them to outnumber U.S. forces with fewer men. But the American fighting man not only had to face the enemy, he also had to deal with the combination of the Romeos and the REMFs, one feeding off the other in a deadly symbiosis which was impossible to overcome or circumvent.

After a little more than one month in Vietnam, and after being on a front-line base during a period of great enemy activity, Craig Morrison—another FAC who would become a Raven—visited a rear-echelon HQ in Nha Trang. On his return to the front he wrote in his journal: "Jesus but I am *so* glad to be here and not down there. All the BS experts and useless straphangers are all there shuffling papers etc. They never come up here, for this is easily the hottest place in II Corps. This war grows on you, and I'd sure hate to get pulled out and have to go down there. I would *so* much rather put up with mortars and rockets than headquarters. Mortars and rockets are exciting and can only kill you, but those guys can frustrate and bore you to death which is a damned sight worse. The home of the useless regulations!!!"[5]

It is the first reference in the journal to a frustration which was to become unbearable within a few short months. At Pleiku, Morrison slept under his bed clutching an M-16, a flak jacket tossed over him as a blanket, and surrounded by empty ammo boxes full of sand for protection. He was often awakened by enemy attacks so close he could hear the mortar shells coming out of the tubes. In such circumstances he was entirely safe from REMFs. But once the enemy offensive was over they arrived in force.

One colonel lectured FACs and fighter pilots on the length of their hair, their slack dress code, and their ungentlemanly behavior in the officers' club. The colonel then cleared his throat, as he came to the important part of his talk. It had come to his attention, he said, that the proper respect was not being accorded to rank. He had noticed that officers did not salute his staff car when it passed them. It did not matter whether he was in it or not, there was a principle involved, and the pennant of his rank flew clearly from the fender. There was a moment's incredulous silence, broken by an exasperated stage whisper from the back of the hall: "I'm not saluting a fucking empty car!"

The more REMFs and combat personnel came into contact, the worse the atmosphere of mutual suspicion and incomprehension became. They lived in different worlds, used different vocabularies, and measured the progress of the war in different ways. Front-line troops wanted to hurt the enemy; REMFs wanted to keep U.S. casualties and loss of equipment to a minimum.

Such fundamental differences led to serious disagreements, and confrontation was inevitable. The conflict was symbolized at Pleiku at a USO show. The original intention of these shows—to reduce the awful tension of combat—had become lost in a welter of petty regulations governing their conduct.

A bespectacled Army warrant officer, who flew "Dustoff" helicopter medical evacuation missions, took his seat in the front row. (Dustoff pilots, who spent their lives in the midst of the worst battles, were considered to be a combat elite.) A Filipino stripper on the stage danced up to the pilot, playfully snatched his glasses, and draped them across her small breasts. She wiggled her hips provocatively, moved the spectacles to her panties, and gyrated her hips directly in front of the chopper pilot. Egged on by the audience, the young man removed the glasses with his teeth and then whipped the girl's panties down. There was a roar of approval.

Unfortunately, the Army pilot was not fully conversant with the nuances of USO show regulations. In the Army, strippers were allowed to remove their panties, but at an Air Force show this was forbidden. The officer in charge, outraged at this breach of the rules, climbed over the tables and chairs to reach the offending Army pilot. To an uproar of boos and abuse he publicly reprimanded the man and ordered him from the club.

The pilot left, and the show went on. It was interrupted some time later when the screen door at the rear of the club was flipped open. Slowly, the doorway was filled with the gun barrel of a 155mm howitzer, carefully backed into position by a jeep. The attention of every man in the audience shifted from the stage at the front of the club to the massive cannon commanding the rear, and an expectant silence fell over the room. Two Army colonels jumped from the jeep, accompanied by the Dustoff pilot. One stood by the gun, while the other marched through the club until he found the officer in charge, a lieutenant colonel he outranked.

"Colonel, our friend here flies a rescue helicopter and he was sitting in the front row. You are going to give him his seat back and you are going to apologize to this entire group or my friend, the colonel over there, is going to pull the string and blow the top off the whole of this fucking officers' club."

Pandemonium broke out. Combat people separated from REMFs as oil from water. While the former yelled "Pull the string, fellas," REMFs climbed under tables and looked for places to hide. The lieutenant colonel apologized stumblingly to the chopper pilot and gave him back his seat, although there was no act in the show which could possibly compete with such excitement. The colonels turned on their heels, hopped in their jeep, and drove off into the night with their howitzer.[6]

But such moments of combat justice were rare, and mostly it was the REMFs who triumphed. It was not unusual for a senior officer, whose experience might have been in transports, to be put in command of a large group of junior combat FACs. The senior officer naturally held the keys to the young men's advancement, and promotion depended on the Effectiveness Reports (ERs) he wrote on them. Men at the front, who were superb in combat, might be given a poor ER by the REMF commander for unruly behavior in the officers' club as they unwound after battle, while deskbound officers far to the rear, who were in no danger and under no pressure, routinely earned exemplary ERs. This meant that a combat FAC often came out of the war with a worse record and less chance of promotion than the lowliest and safest of the REMFs. It was a situation as intolerable as it was absurd, and it sapped morale.

The REMFs and the Romeos brought a petty, nagging quality to life in Vietnam. It was to avoid this, rather than a lust for glory, which motivated most of the men who eventually became Ravens. The absurdities of military life in Vietnam combined to tempt them to take the Chance card first heard of in the Monopoly briefing.

Somehow the word always seemed to reach the right people. "The reason I joined the Ravens was because there appeared to be some awfully good flying," Mike Byers said. "I didn't know a goddam thing about it."

"I heard it was on the other side of the fence with none of the Vietnam bullshit," Terry Murphy said. "That guys got shot down a lot, but it was a lot of fun." His group commander tried to talk him out of it, saying that he understood there was an unacceptably high loss rate. "When your buddy says there's less bullshit, it's more attractive than your commander saying it's high-risk." One of Craig Morrison's

FAC friends had volunteered for the program ahead of him and sent letters postmarked Udorn, Thailand. In essence they said, "Come on over, it's dangerous as hell but NO REMFS!!"

Everybody had a different reason, but one by one, from units all over South Vietnam and throughout the war, FACs found themselves inexorably drawn to the mysterious mission they had heard all the rumors about—the Steve Canyon Program.

Raven was the radio call sign which identified the fliers of the Steve Canyon Program. As a symbol of intelligence gathering and aerial control of ground combat, no name could have been more fitting for the men of the secret war. The raven is the bird of the gods. In Nordic mythology, two ravens, Huyin (Thought) and Munin (Meaning), perch upon the shoulders of Odin, lord of gods. Each day they fly to the ends of the earth and return to their master at night to whisper in his ears the world's news. The Vikings believed that the excited birds soaring above a battle were the gods in the guise of ravens.

On the practical side the raven is extremely clever and brave, the bird with the highest mental development, with more than thirty distinct calls with which to convey information to its fellows. With its four-foot wingspan and deadly three-inch beak, it is magnificent, and flies for the sheer delight of its mastery of the air, soaring to great heights, and tumbling earthward in extraordinary displays of prowess.

To certain American tribes the raven could do anything simply by willing it; it created sun, earth, moon, and stars, and also the people of the earth. Indians admire the raven's sagacity, but fear its ruthless opportunism and wily trickery. Men of many cultures have attributed a conflicting duality of nature to the raven, and its harsh cawing has for centuries been interpreted as the harbinger of death. All of which was very apt for the job in store.

In the early days, when the program was haphazard in its methods, a standard form of recruitment was for a Raven already in the program to approach a like-minded colleague still in Vietnam. Later, things became more structured, but the type recruited never really altered. They were always men who enjoyed a maximum of flying and a minimum of administration, and they tended to be the very best pilots. By definition this meant that most of the Ravens were mavericks, never really comfortable in a conventional military organization, and considered too wild by the mainstream military establishment. The sort of men, in short, needed in a war.

2

ACROSS THE FENCE

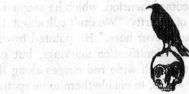

Curioser and curioser!
—Lewis Carroll,
Alice's Adventures in Wonderland

Once a volunteer was accepted into the Steve Canyon Program
he immediately began to notice a change in his status. Even in Vietnam, waiting to cross the border, there was a marked difference in
the way he was treated by senior officers. It was the first indication
that the Ravens seemed to enjoy a unique position of some power and
importance.

The program itself, however, remained a mystery. Fred Platt
presented himself at Bien Hoa for the final, in-country briefing. It
was no more informative than any of the others, its only novel feature
being an explicit statement that this was the last opportunity for
anyone to change his mind. Ravens called it the "back-out briefing."

Almost everyone had had second thoughts now and again. The
advice of senior officers did not count for much, but there were
certain FACs in South Vietnam who had earned a reputation among
their peers for courage. Sy Margolis, a FAC who had flown through
some of the most intense ground fire in South Vietnam and whose
colleagues believed he deserved the Medal of Honor, was one of
them. In a card session Platt thought to impress him by announcing
that he had volunteered for the Steve Canyon Program. According to
Platt, Margolis was appalled. "Are you nuts? This is the last time I'm
ever going to see you alive. You've volunteered to go and die."

It was disconcerting but thrilling too, and the challenge of a
dangerous adventure always overcame good sense in a Raven. New
Ravens saw the back-out briefing as yet another peculiar step on the
way to wherever they were going. Once the briefing was over, Platt

was sent to a hangar on the airfield at Bien Hoa, where he was met by a colonel. "Are you the guy who's getting the airplanes?"

"What airplanes?"

The colonel ignored Platt's incomprehension, which he seemed to dismiss as an exaggerated sense of security. "We can't talk about it, I know, but these are your airplanes over here." He pointed toward three O-1s, stripped of their unit identification markings, but still carrying tail numbers and painted with wide red stripes along the entire length of the white upper wings, to enable them to be spotted more easily by high-flying jets. "Do you want to sign for them?"

"I'll take them," Platt said, flowing with the tide.

"You've got to give me one dollar for each airplane."

"It's a deal." Platt was enjoying himself, happy to have joined a program so novel it sold its pilots airplanes for a dollar each. He took out three one-dollar Military Payment Certificates.

"That won't do. It has to be U.S. currency." The colonel exchanged the scrip for three dollar bills from his own pocket and recorded their serial numbers in a notebook. He then took Platt by jeep to the group HQ, where he signed a set of papers which stated that Platt had purchased the aircraft. The planes were removed from the official records of the USAF, written off as surplus equipment sold to a civilian pilot. Platt was the temporary proprietor of three airplanes.

He was told to deliver them to Detachment 1 (whatever that was) at Udorn, Thailand. HQ had mapped out an air route allowing for an overnight stop in Pleiku for a maintenance check. Two other new Ravens were to accompany him on the trip. Never a man to pass up the chance of making an eccentric and extravagant gesture, Platt hired a taxi to pick up his fellow Ravens and took them out to the flight line. The taxi pulled up in front of three O-1s.

"Take your choice, fellas," Platt told his colleagues. "These are my airplanes. I don't know quite how or why, but I own these airplanes and we've got to take them to Udorn."

The three Ravens flew to Pleiku, where they were met on the tarmac by a full colonel. He saluted them as if greeting general officers. A bevy of mechanics fell onto the aircraft, and it seemed that the entire maintenance section of the base intended to work on them through the night. Platt noticed the O-1s were taxied to secure steel revetments usually reserved for multimillion-dollar jet aircraft. A staff car and driver took them to spacious quarters, where they were met by another respectful, saluting colonel. "With full colonels meeting me everywhere, and seemingly prepared to run errands, I was firmly

convinced I had joined a kamikaze corps and was going out to die,"
Platt says.

Once over the border in Thailand—anywhere outside of Vietnam
was "across the fence"—the status continued to improve, but the
secrecy remained. Udorn was the final gathering spot. Sometimes the
planes carrying Ravens landed in the middle of the night and remained at the end of the runway until a jeep came out to meet them
and they were driven to a house off the base in the town. Several of
them thought it was carrying the cloak-and-dagger aspect of the
operation a bit far.

Ravens who came in on their own, having hitched a lift on a
military transport, were not so fortunate. Questions about the location of Detachment 1 were often met with blank looks and shrugs.
(One Raven, desperate after a dozen fruitless inquiries, was finally
given directions by a Thai waitress who worked in the officers' club.)

Detachment 1 was set apart from the main section of the base and
housed in an upstairs office to one side, where Air America, the CIA
airline, operated. The colonel in charge kept his welcoming speech
short. "I am supposed to be your commander. Your records will be
kept here and our admin people will try and take care of you. I don't
really know what the hell is going on and I don't have control over
you. Goodbye."[1]

When Mike Cavanaugh first arrived in Thailand, after living in
Vietnam in a filthy hut without windows, he was most impressed by
the luxury of the base. He sat in the cool, comfortable office of an Air
Commando colonel, who asked him, "What do you think of coming
over to this dangerous business?"

"Pretty good so far," Cavanaugh replied, a cold beer in his hand.
"Looks like an air-conditioned war to me."

The colonel laughed, but as he bade Cavanaugh farewell and
wished him luck, he looked grave. "Air-conditioned war, huh? Not
where you're going, son."

The Ravens soon discovered they were not going to be working in
Udorn at all. Special orders were issued to them assigning them to
temporary duty (TDY) at a classified location. All uniforms and military ID were handed over to a staff sergeant, who stored them in a
large Container Express (CONEX). They were given various shots,
issued with blood-chits, and told that all their records would be kept
at Udorn, which was also where they would draw their pay.

But no one was able to tell them what to expect from the job. "We
don't really know what you guys do. We're just your front," said the

sergeant who asked them to sign for a weapon, a helmet, and a survival vest. The final formality was a blank on the form for an address in the States: "Wherever you want your body shipped."[2]

It came as no surprise that the next stage in the process should be an informal approach by a mysterious civilian. "Let's go over to the club," the latest stranger said to Craig Morrison. He expected to go to the O club—the officers' club—but found himself in the Air America club, a very different establishment run on highly informal lines. The clientele was exotic and somewhat rowdy.

Morrison was taken over what had become familiar ground. "What do you know about this program?"

"Very little."

When the waitress brought drinks the civilian fell silent. He took the clandestine nature of his calling seriously and stopped talking every time somebody passed by the table. Morrison was still naive enough about his new covert status to look puzzled when the stranger shut up in the middle of a sentence. The secrecy of it all was beginning to get on his nerves. The stranger kept talking about the need to "maintain a low profile." Morrison nodded. The man leaned forward, his mouth against Morrison's ear.

"You're going up-country."

"Oh." Up to which country, Morrison wondered—Burma, India, Cambodia, Laos?

"Until you know what's going on, until you get your feet on the ground, don't say anything to anybody about anything. Tomorrow come out here and get on an airplane."

"I probably shouldn't ask what kind of airplane."

"Just come out here."

The stranger dissolved into the crowd, leaving Morrison to nurse his drink. He began to feel uncomfortable. They had taken everything from him: personal belongings, uniforms, dog tags, and even his Air Force ID card. The loss of the ID card made him feel especially vulnerable. It was the open sesame to military life in Southeast Asia, necessary to get on and off U.S. bases, and was checked a hundred times in the course of a week. He wondered if they would serve him a drink in the O club in civilian clothes without ID. It was early, so he decided to give it a try.

At the club he was in luck. A friend he had known in Vietnam had brought a plane into the base for maintenance and was staying overnight. The friend took him into the club and bought him a drink. The first thing Morrison noticed was four men in their flight suits sitting *on* the bar. It seemed incongruous in the semiformal atmosphere of the officers' club.

His friend explained: it was combat prestige, yet another gradation in the fine shading of fighter-pilot superiority. Transport pilots, navigators, and administration and maintenance officers were obliged to stand at the bar like ordinary mortals, but fighter pilots sat on it.

Morrison was introduced as the newest Raven. He felt awkward and out of place standing in civilian clothes amid a combat elite. At the word "Raven" the fighter pilots immediately jumped down and grabbed Morrison underneath the arms and hoisted him up to sit alongside them. "You don't know it yet," he was told, "but this is where you belong."

The next morning at 7:00 A.M. he presented himself at Air America operations, a one-room building which was little more than a shack with a desk and counter. The people who worked in it were men of few words. Morrison wore a T-shirt, jeans, and flying boots, and had a duffel bag slung over his shoulder containing overnight gear. He carried his precious 9mm Browning, wrapped in newspaper, under his arm. "Hi. I'm supposed to be the new Raven."

"What's your name?"

"Morrison."

"Okay, wait there." He joined two other men seated on a bench. No one spoke.

An Air America C-123 landed on the runway and taxied up to the building. It turned around and waited with one engine running. The man at the counter jerked a thumb toward it. "Get in."

The three new Ravens trooped across the tarmac to the plane. It took off, flew for twenty minutes, and landed. Again, no one spoke. During the trip the landscape beneath them did not change, except for a wide, slow river which came into view on final approach. (One Raven was flown up in an Air America plane that stopped off at various sites all along the way. Throughout the circuitous trip he thought he was heading directly north, and calculated with increasing unease that he must be deep in Red China.)[3]

But as Morrison landed he finally knew where he was. After weeks of intrigue and mystery, he had arrived to fly combat in a country he knew nothing about. He was now a part of the secret war in Laos.

He walked over to the Air America shack, where he picked up a jeep lift into Vientiane, the country's capital. On the way, various landmarks were pointed out to him in the sleepy riverside town. The river the road followed, which he had seen from the air, was the

Mekong. Except for numerous wooden pagodas and a monument in the style of the Arc de Triomphe built from diverted U.S. AID cement meant for a runway, there was not much else to see. After the long, exciting buildup, the final moment of arrival was anticlimactic. The place was a peaceful backwater, seemingly untouched and untroubled by the ravages of war.

It gave Morrison a strange feeling to see the embassies of the Chinese, Russians, and North Vietnamese open for business as if the war next door did not exist. The American embassy was among the largest buildings in town, situated only a few hundred yards from the legation of the enemy, the Communist Pathet Lao. (In the monsoon season the Americans and Pathet Lao joined in a work detail to clear shared drains blocked by leaves.)

The Ravens reported to the air attaché's office, where they had their photographs taken and were issued with a U.S. AID card and a Laotian driver's license. (It was the second time that day their photographs had been taken. Communist Chinese agents, using high-powered telephoto lenses, routinely took pictures of all newly arriving westerners from the raised ground near the runway at Wattay airport.) They were given their cover stories, which were extremely weak: officially, they were forest rangers attached to U.S. AID—the Agency for International Development.

Nobody was ever to refer to anyone by rank. However, for reasons of discipline, lower-ranking officers were told to call their seniors Mister, while the seniors called their juniors by their first names. Special blanket orders were issued to allow unrestricted access in and out of Thailand. They were given strict instructions not to indicate their whereabouts in letters home—all mail was to be sent out of Udorn, Thailand, and was to be received there.

During the day's cursory briefing the new Raven learned there were almost as many different wars in Laos as there were Military Regions. In Military Region V (MR V), the neutral zone around Vientiane, the war was pursued in the abstract from the embassy compound, far from the noise and heat of battle; in Military Regions III and IV, in the Laotian panhandle, the Royal Lao Army attempted to keep the conflict to a minimum by avoiding contact with the enemy, except for periods when the North Vietnamese Army was especially active in maintaining the flow of arms and supplies for their operations in South Vietnam. These were transported down the Ho Chi Minh Trail, which drove through the edge of both regions and was the target of a massive U.S. bombing campaign. In MR I the

Royal Lao Army battled the North Vietnamese who infiltrated troops into the region via Communist China, threatening the royal capital of Luang Prabang; but the real battleground was in MR II, where the Special Guerrilla Units of Gen. Vang Pao's Meo* slugged it out with large forces of NVA coming in from North Vietnam itself for the annual seasonal offensive across the strategic Plain of Jars. Ravens were sent to each of the Military Regions, but the posting everyone considered to be the plum, carrying with it equal amounts of glamour and dread, was Long Tieng—Gen. Vang Pao's top-secret base in MR II.

The new Raven also understood, after his first day in Vientiane, that he was at the end of an extremely convoluted command structure.

Ravens were issued orders in Vietnam which put them under the formal command of the 56th Special Operations Wing based at Nakhon Phanom, Thailand, and their records and pay were taken care of by Detachment 1 of this wing at Udorn. All U.S. air in Thailand came under 7/13th Air Force—a hybrid of 7th Air Force, Vietnam, and 13th Air Force, the Philippines—both controlled by CINCPAC, Hawaii. But they had been loaned to the air attaché in Vientiane, Laos, who became their operational Air Force commander. Out in the field they were, for all practical purposes, under the command of the CIA and native generals. At the same time, overall command of all U.S. forces in the country came under the ambassador.

The endless tug-of-war for control between the various agencies, old head Ravens explained, worked in their favor: the beauty of the arrangement was that so many people owned them, no one was really in charge.

In the early days of the program, after a full day of in-processing, the Ravens were housed overnight in two old French chalets: Ice

---

*This proud, mountain, warrior people have always called themselves Hmong, meaning "Mankind" in their own language, which is of the Tibeto-Burman group. However, until the midseventies they were always known by the non-Hmong inside Laos, and by all foreigners, as Meo. This is a contraction of the Chinese Miao, which means "Barbarian." Neither the French, nor the Americans who came after them, were aware of this ancient slur. It was only after 1972, when Dr. Yang Dao, the first Hmong to gain a PhD from a French university, returned to Laos and began to insist on the universal use of the term, that the name Hmong was used by other than his own people. The Ravens and other Americans who worked with the Hmong, including sympathetic journalists and writers, used the term Meo in complete ignorance of any derogatory connotation. Dr. Yang Dao agrees with the author that in the historical context of this book, when Meo was the only word used (even by Gen. Vang Pao himself when in conversation with non-Hmong), the term Hmong would be anachronistic. The term Meo is therefore used throughout, until it began to be replaced in general use by Hmong.[4]

House One and Ice House Two, so called because they were situated on either side of a building the French had used to store ice. Later, more elaborate accommodation was provided at Lan Xiang 9, an architecturally eclectic structure. In both places Ravens briefly rubbed shoulders with administration officers from the air attaché's office and various State Department officials working in the embassy.

The new man was taken out on the town in a tradition known as "nubie night." This was an extended period of debauchery which included heavy drinking at the Purple Porpoise, an Air America hangout run by a genial Australian alcoholic named Monty Banks; more drinking at the White Rose, a favorite girlie bar; and a final round of drinking at the Les Rendezvous des Amis, an establishment specializing in warm beer and oral sex, and presided over by the distinguished Madame Lulu, famous throughout the Far East.

Mercifully, the stopover in the drowsy capital was brief for Ravens eager to be in the thick of things. After only a day and a night, the new Raven was taken back to Wattay airport, where he was met by a CIA case officer. For most it was their first encounter with the clandestine, and they relished the aura of the secret agent on a dangerous mission into the unknown. The moment was ruined for Karl Polifka by an American schoolteacher waiting for a plane to go south. She explained that she was flying to Bangkok to get her teeth fixed. Polifka said nothing and attempted to look mysterious. The teacher looked him up and down. "You must be a new Raven going to Long Tieng, huh?"

The planes arrived and they went their separate ways. The schoolteacher flew south to keep her dental appointment, while the Raven boarded a C-123 transport plane to take him north to the war.

PART II

PART II

3

THE SECRET CITY

He came from the right place, he was one of us.
—Joseph Conrad,
Lord Jim

The new Raven flew to war over terrain unlike anything he had ever seen before. Mountains erupted out of a sea of green jungle, some shaped like cones with sharp jagged edges, others thin as knife blades. Towers of limestone stood sentinel on the banks of rivers which twisted between them. From the air the countryside took on the shapes of fantastical animals. No one could fail to recognize that this was a place of very great beauty.

During the monsoon season, in the biting cold of the first light of dawn, the valleys swirled with wisps of white fog and every mountain seemed wrapped in its own ominous black cloud. In the dry season the valleys filled with a milky froth in the early mornings, which the French, when they had fought in this country, had called *crachin*—spittle. Crouched in the back passenger seat of an O-1 spotter plane, snaking along a river valley, or straining to climb a mountain ridge, the new Raven looked upon the landscape in awe, as if flying into an exquisite Chinese scroll painting, backdrop to a dream.

There seemed very little of anything resembling civilization below. Occasionally the plane flew over a small village perched on a mountaintop, connected to the valley beneath it by a path so sheer it looked like a hanging thread. It was a sobering thought that the months ahead would be spent searching for enemies hidden in the endless emptiness of this unfamiliar landscape.

The new Raven's unknown destination was the secret city of Long Tieng. This was the hub and nerve center of the clandestine war in the Other Theater. It appeared on no maps but had grown to be the largest city in the country after the capital. Insiders never referred to it by name, but further shrouded the town in mystery by calling it Alternate. (Towns and villages all over the country had been numbered, each one indicating a landing strip—a Lima Site. Lima Site 20 was Sam Thong, the U.S. Agency for International Development [AID] showcase with its hospital and school, and lay twenty kilometers over the zigzag mountain road to the northwest. Long Tieng, which dwarfed it, was 20 Alternate. The idea was that any visiting dignitary, or prying journalist, would naturally assume that Site 20 was the bigger operation, and Alternate merely a secondary emergency landing strip.) Outsiders who had never visited Long Tieng but had heard of its existence called it Spook Heaven because of the number of CIA agents who lived there. For a period in history it was the most secret spot on earth.

Long Tieng had been built in a valley which lay in a perfect bowl. It was surrounded by mountains on three sides, while a gently rolling hill fell away on a fourth. A runway had been built in the valley, which made it look as if an aircraft carrier had been beached more than three thousand feet up in the mountains after some cataclysmic flood. A traditional thatched village was dotted over the foothills, while on the other side of the runway the corrugated iron roofs of thousands of new buildings glittered in the sun.

Once upon the ground the new Raven climbed from the plane, stood on the ramp, and looked around at his new home. The first impressions of arrival would never be forgotten. Certain images, so strange and new, entered the memory forever: a tiny child, barefoot and in black pajamas, smiling broadly as he skips across the runway, a high-explosive rocket perched on his shoulder; a native fighter pilot, slight as a jockey, pulling back the canopy of his cockpit; a burly American dressed as if for a game of golf in a yellow cap and polyester slacks, yawning in a doorway; two red sacks of strangers' mail leaning against the side of a building.

The town of Long Tieng itself took longer to assimilate. In the monsoon season it was thick with sticky red mud, and the craggy limestone rock known as karst was covered with moss and green slime. Everything was wet and shrouded in gray fog. Trees somehow grew from the cracks in the limestone, clinging to the mountainside like gnarled old hands. The landscape was primeval, a million years out of its time, the setting for a pterodactyl to come flapping out of the dripping rocks.

After the monsoon the whole area blossomed. A thousand different kinds of wild flowers carpeted the valley. There were giant yellow daisies as tall as a man, and acre upon acre of white and red poppies. Whatever the season, Long Tieng resembled nowhere on earth as much as the mythical paradise of Shangri-La.[1]

It was a curious city, a contradictory mixture of ancient and modern. Dirt streets lined with native huts, built in the style traditional since people had first inhabited these mountains, were hung across with a web of cables. Naked toddlers played outside of front doors and pigs rooted in the gutters, while in the background the antennae of sophisticated telecommunications equipment rose like stands of spruce. There were no paved streets of any kind, no sewers, no private cars, and yet planes and helicopters landed and took off without pause. Meo women in traditional dress—a black costume brightened with highly colored sashes and headdresses, and adorned with beautifully crafted silver jewelry—thronged the market. Military jeeps and trucks and small buses crammed with people crisscrossed the base.

Walking from the runway to the Raven hootch, the newcomer had various landmarks pointed out to him. The great mountain which rose vertically at the end of the runway was known as the Vertical Speed Brake (for reasons which would become obvious); two moundlike hills beside it were known as Titty-karst; the range to the northwest was Skyline Ridge. The house on the slope that looked like a suburban bungalow—except it was surrounded with sandbags instead of hedges, and had the burned-out hulk of a T-28 fighter at the bottom of the garden—was the king's palace (which he had used only once). The somewhat garish modern concrete construction with the captured enemy antiaircraft guns in front of it and the 12.7mm on the roof was the home of the warlord himself, Gen. Vang Pao. The compound which housed the CIA men was discreetly pointed out, together with the barracks they shared with pilots of their proprietary airline, Air America. (Nobody ever referred to the CIA by name, the preferred euphemism being CAS—Controlled American Source—a term the Agency used to apply to assets or agents.)

In the field, operations were run by the CIA. Most of the war was actually being fought by the Meo, who were under the command of Vang Pao, who was officially under the command of the chief of staff of the Royal Lao Army. For the Ravens, the CIA and Gen. Vang Pao added the final convolutions to their eccentric command relationship, to the point that it defied analysis.

Everywhere was the furious activity of war, an endless traffic of men and aircraft. Pilots walked back and forth from the ramp to the operations shack. Troops milled around at the edge of the runway waiting to board helicopters. Mechanics checked airplane engines, and armorers loaded bombs. Soldiers came and went, carrying their wounded and their dead.

There seemed to be a great many children everywhere. Tiny imps, no more than six years old, ran errands for armorers hanging loads on the wings of fighters of the Royal Lao Air Force. The ten-year-old males wore combat fatigues, carried grenades looped in their belts, and were dwarfed by the antiquated American carbines, M-16s, and captured enemy AK-47s they carried.

Every day just before dusk, Long Tieng went through the combat equivalent of rush hour. Planes and choppers began to come in every few seconds, making their final landing of the day before dark. Large, silent, unsmiling Americans in fatigues led files of small, exhausted men from the runway. The native fighter pilots, stiff with cramp after ten hours of combat in the cockpit, were lifted gently from their planes by helpers. Interspersed in the traffic were the Ravens' O-1 spotter planes, known as Bird Dogs, returning from all points of the compass.

If Steve Canyon could step from his cartoon strip, accompanied by Terry and the Pirates, this would surely be their home. "It was such an exotic place," Fred Platt said. "It really had the feel of some pirate hideaway, with guys with tattoos and daggers clutched between their teeth. I felt the moment I set foot there that I had found home."

At the bar of the Raven hootch the newcomer was introduced to the men he would be working with. Nobody made much of a fuss—a welcoming grunt, a quick handshake, maybe a half-smile. But it was a wonderful moment. Almost always there was an instant empathy, the first experience of the mystical bond of fellowship the Ravens shared. "It's difficult to explain, but after all the crap and bureaucracy of the military it was magic," Craig Morrison said. "The *guys!* Even though you didn't know the individuals you were instantly one of the troops. I had never met any of them but felt I knew all of them. It was almost *déjà vu.*"*

---

*The six-month tour meant a rapid turnover as Ravens completed their duty and returned home, or were wounded and killed before their time. Some extended their tours, but for most the war in Laos was a flood of impressions condensed into a brief period. The narrative of this book is punctuated, sometimes with an abruptness that is jarring, by their arrivals and departures. Quite simply, this was the way it was. While the author has avoided logging each and every Raven in and out of the country, he has imposed an order and continuity on events that were often experienced at the time as an incomprehensible chaos of incident. An overview of the war is provided by a chronology of events at the front of the book.

Things were done differently at Long Tieng. There seemed to be no overt recognition of rank and no military bureaucracy whatsoever. War planning for the whole military region was decided each evening over dinner with Gen. Vang Pao. Various Meo military officers, CIA case officers, intelligence people, and the senior Raven went to the general's house every night to dine off the local food, washed down with shots of White Horse whisky.

The newcomer would accompany the senior Raven to the dinner to meet the general. The meal was friendly but almost formal, with Vang Pao seated cross-legged on the floor at the center of the table, his advisers and officers sitting next to him. In person, VP—as he was called by the Americans—did not look so formidable. His round moon face was usually lit with a smile, and his dark eyes twinkled. He was very fond of his Ravens and treated them almost like sons. Bamboo baskets full of hot sticky rice were placed at intervals along the table together with bowls of different vegetables. Meat was rare. A chicken would be a treat, pork a luxury. (Neither was necessarily a welcome sight for westerners. To Americans the local pigs seemed to have no meat on them whatsoever, only gristle. It was also the Meo custom to honor guests by offering them the chicken head—it was traditional to suck out the brains—or the gnarled ear of a prized razorback pig, or a glass of tepid blood.) The Meo did not use chopsticks but dipped their fingers into the communal baskets of sticky rice, rolling a handful into a ball which was then dipped into various spices and sauces before being popped into the mouth. The favorite vegetable was an unrecognizable leaf, a type of chewy spinach that was more stalk than leaf. The cuisine at the general's house was known to the Ravens as "gristle, grass, and rice."

After eating, the ensemble retired to an operations room in the rear of the house. (However, one major offensive was aborted before dinner was over when cooked chickens were carried to the table with their legs crossed in a manner Vang Pao interpreted as a particularly bad omen. From then on the CIA paid one of the cooks to uncross chicken feet and generally keep an eye out for any other indications of bad luck.) The general gave a nightly postprandial briefing: the location and number of enemy forces, the condition of his own men, and what was likely to happen the next day. The senior Raven would then return to the hootch and assign his half-dozen colleagues areas in which to direct air strikes the following morning.

On the way back to the hootch the senior Raven took the newcomer into the CIA bar for a drink. Just outside the entrance on the second floor, built into the side of the mountain, was a large cage that housed the spooks' pet bears. Floyd was a seven-foot-high black Himalayan mountain bear with a striking white V on his chest; he lived with his slightly smaller mate, Mama Bear. Floyd had developed a taste for American beer, which was handed to him through the bars by well-wishers. It was possible to stand in the CIA bar, pop the cap on a can of beer, and pass it through the window to set it on top of the cage below, where Floyd hung from the bars. He had been known to consume beer by the case and on wild nights could get alarmingly drunk. Floyd suffered from these excesses with superhuman hang-overs the next day, and would retreat into the dark cave at the rear of his cage in a black sulk.

Inside the bar the newcomer was awed into silence by the company. The lineup changed every night, but the flavor remained the same: Air America pilots like Art Wilson, who had flown the Hump from China into Tibet in the '40s, nicknamed Shower Shoes because of the thonged rubber sandals he always wore during a flying career in which he had accumulated 25,000 hours in C-46 transports; "Weird" Neil Hansen, dressed in Texan boots and Stetson, who was . . . well, weird; Pop Buell, the lean old Indiana farmer who had made the secret war his life since the death of his wife and ran a hospital and AID operation over the hill in Sam Thong. And then there were the nameless men of the CIA, "the CAS guys": Mr. Clean, Hog, Black Lion, Igor, Kayak. Some of them had the hard, lean faces of Special Forces soldiers, while others looked as if they had stepped from the golf course, complete with loud check pants, short-sleeved nylon shirts, baseball caps, and middle-aged spread. Their talk was of towns and battles and women the newcomer did not know, and he could only nurse his drink and listen.

Later, lying on the bed in his room in the hootch, the new Raven ran over the day's impressions in his mind. It was everything he had hoped for. There had been moments when he had questioned and almost regretted volunteering for the Steve Canyon Program. Those who had stayed in Vietnam had said he was crazy to volunteer for an undefined mission—rumored to have a 50 percent casualty rate—in an unknown location. He was still apprehensive about the type of war that lay ahead, but one day in the secret city had convinced him he had made the right choice. At last he was among a different breed. He had come to the right place and found his own. Reviewing the last six months of his life in Vietnam, he was not sorry he had drawn the Chance card. And at daybreak he would fly into battle.

4

THE SACRED MOUNTAIN

The mountain of Phou Pha Thi was a sacred place for all of the Meo, revered even by those who had never visited it but only heard the stories told by village elders and holy men. It was also of vital strategic importance to the Americans, who called it the Rock and considered it one of their most closely kept secrets. This powerful combination of sanctity and secrecy attracted the attention of the enemy, and led to one of the most curious battles of the war.

A natural fortress, the Rock was a razorback ridge 5,600 feet high, sheer on one side and heavily fortified on the other. A dirt landing strip seven hundred feet long had been cleared in the valley below, designated on aerial maps as Lima Site 85. The Rock held a number of secrets: three hundred Thai mercenaries and Meo guarded it, while Americans "in the black"—that is, on a clandestine posting—from the USAF and Lockheed Aircraft Systems manned highly sophisticated navigational equipment which not only guided American bombers in northern Laos, but led them directly to downtown Hanoi.[1]

On paper it looked like the ideal spot. It was higher than anything around it and only 160 miles west of Hanoi. Although deep in enemy territory and only twenty-five miles from the Communist Pathet Lao capital of Sam Neua, it was considered impregnable to anything except a massed helicopter assault, which was beyond the enemy's capabilities.

The Air Force had first installed a tactical air navigation system on top of the Rock in 1966, despite the objections of Ambassador William Sullivan, who thought the installation extremely unwise—an invitation to disaster. The men manning the site were in a location where they could not possibly be rescued if they were overrun, while the Rock's proximity to the Vietnam border, combined with its role in directing bombing raids on the capital itself, was a constant provocation, possibly even a justification, for an overt North Vietnamese invasion.

In 1967 the Air Force upgraded the original navigational equipment with a much more elaborate system using the latest radar that enabled U.S. aircraft to bomb at night and in all weather; 150 tons of equipment was airlifted in by a top-secret Air Force helicopter unit based in Udorn and code-named Pony Express.[2]

The contingent guarding the Rock was strengthened. The site now needed a weekly resupply of three tons of petroleum products, spare parts, and food and water. The increased activity on the peak provoked the enemy and tipped the balance. They began to feel that the Rock had become important enough to risk an attack.

On January 12, 1968, in one of the most peculiar air actions of the war, the North Vietnamese Air Force launched an attack on the site using Soviet-manufactured single-engine, fabric-covered biplanes. These were Antonov AN-2 Colts, which had enclosed cabins and wooden scimitar propellers. The planes dived at the Rock, while the crews fired machine guns out the window and dropped mortar shells as bombs. The outdated, lumbering aircraft were so vulnerable that an Air America chopper took them on. The crew chief fired an Uzi machine gun out the door and shot one down, and the chopper then chased a second until it forced it down eighteen miles north of the site. A third plane crashed into the mountain, brought down by either gunfire or pilot error. (A piece of the wreckage bearing the tail number of the plane, 665, was later recovered and hung in the Air America bar in Long Tieng as a war trophy.)

The downing of three Russian biplanes flown by North Vietnamese was too good to keep quiet and was released to the press, although the location was given as Luang Prabang—a story CIA director William Colby stayed with in his 1978 memoirs.[3]

Despite the failed aerial attack it became clear that the North Vietnamese intended to take the Rock regardless of the cost in men or effort. And despite a stream of reliable intelligence over three months reporting enemy plans to attack, the work at the installations was deemed so important, it was decided to leave U.S. personnel in place until the Rock was in immediate danger of being overrun.

With deliberate and deadly intent, the enemy began to build a road from the Communist Pathet Lao capital of Sam Neua toward the base of the mountain. Their actions were interpreted as a plan to knock out the airstrip on completion of the road, bring in artillery, and bombard the mountain in preparation for a massed attack. Raven FAC Art Cornelius first spotted the construction from the air and logged its inexorable progress. CIA ground teams reported thousands of coolies pushing the road toward Phou Pha Thi at the rate of a kilometer a night.

Bombing proved ineffective. The coolies worked at night and merely mended the road where it had been cratered, and day after day the road kept advancing. Marching down with it were three battalions of the 766th Regiment of the North Vietnamese regular army.

The attack began at 6:15 P.M. on March 10, 1968. Sappers took the airstrip in the valley while artillery opened up on the southeast side of the Rock, where Thai mercenaries and Meo guerrillas prepared for a long night of bombardment. They were dug in well enough to withstand the heaviest artillery barrage and could easily hold out until daybreak, when T-28 fighters and Raven-directed U.S. aircraft could bomb and strafe the artillery positions. On the peak of the mountain the Air Force personnel crouched in a trench as rockets slammed into the ground around them.

But the enemy did not intend to wait until daybreak. They launched a frontal assault, fighting their way up the defended slopes in hand-to-hand combat. Meanwhile, North Vietnamese commandos attempted the impossible—to scale the sheer side of the mountain and swarm the peak. And somehow they pulled it off.

The Americans were taken by surprise from their undefended rear. Most of them managed to drop down the side of the mountain, lowering themselves on ropes and taking refuge in one of the many grottos which pockmarked the karst. Maj. Stanley Sliz, together with two of his men, slept fitfully in the mouth of one of the grottos. At about 4:15 A.M. they were awakened by gunfire and exploding grenades, and heard strange voices above them.

Sliz and the two airmen crept fifteen yards farther into the grotto, where two more Air Force personnel were already hiding. A sergeant, armed with an M-16 and grenades, kept watch at the entrance. Suddenly he saw six enemy soldiers above him.

"Wait until they get close enough and shoot them," Sliz said. The sergeant opened fire, giving away their position. From then on the group was relentlessly bombarded with hand grenades. As technicians, the men had only the most rudimentary training in combat. With the death of the second airman and the sight of a North Vietnamese soldier atop a rock firing into the position, Sliz resigned himself to death.

"The boy on my right died almost instantly," Sliz said. "The boy on my left had a broken leg from a bullet." He died in the major's arms a short time later. "There were at least half a dozen grenades tossed in through a small cavernous hole. . . . We had no way of defending against it except when the grenades came bouncing on in they would land in my proximity and I could just grab them and throw them down the hill. Each time they fired into that grotto the bullet shattered and the rock shattered, so we were taking constant gashes and hits from this stuff."

A group of Meo, led by Huey Marlow, a partially deaf former Green Beret seconded to the CIA, counterattacked. Armed with an automatic shotgun and with a score of grenades strapped around his waist, Marlow battled his way up the mountainside together with a handful of Meo. A machine-gun nest, which had been set up by the North Vietnamese the moment they took the peak, was destroyed. Marlow shotgunned the crew and managed to rescue an American forward air guide who had been in hiding on the mountaintop. They retreated back down the hill in the face of brutal hand-to-hand combat. (Marlow was awarded the Intelligence Cross, the CIA's highest award, for his night's work.)

The battle continued through the night. Back at Long Tieng the Ravens heard the news over the radio and rose from their beds at 4:00 in the morning to take off in the dark and fly up to Lima Site 36, at nearby Na Khang. At daybreak they were on station at the Rock, ready to direct a combination of Laotian T-28 fighters and U.S. jets against the enemy, while Air America helicopters flew in to lift out the surviving Thai mercenaries and Meo guards. "The Air America guys were going in and landing and taking off in single-pilot helicopters," said Art Cornelius, who was directing air from a Bird Dog, "while these armed, two-pilot Jolly Greens were extremely reluctant to go in. They stood there, hovering on station, and even though they could see what was going on their HQ kept holding them back."

It was exactly as Ambassador Sullivan had feared. The Air Force, which had been quick to commit men to the Rock over all objections, was proving extremely reluctant to commit its own rescue helicopters to get them out. The political consequences of a USAF Jolly Green shot down over Laos, a country in which U.S. military forces were absolutely forbidden to operate by international treaty, would be enormous. So the Jolly Green, manned by crews reputed to be among the bravest of the war, was ordered to hover timidly beyond the range of the guns. The rescue relied on the raw courage of the Air America pilots, sneered at by the unknowing among the military as overpaid mercenaries.

Sliz had abandoned all hope of survival until he saw an Air America chopper directly over him. He was hauled up into it. "My mind was still active in spite of everything, and then I saw a drop of blood and there was this sergeant keeling over." The sergeant had been shot as he was being rescued and died before the helicopter landed back at its base.

The Ravens directed air strikes all day, flying until they ran out of marking rockets or gas, when they returned to Site 36 to swap airplanes. They flew until 8:00 at night, when it was time to count the dead. Reconnaissance pictures of the site showed from between seven and nine men hanging from the mountain in web strapping, apparently having tried to lower themselves down the side. The whole operation has been so shrouded in secrecy that even today the final tally of American dead is uncertain. Only four Air Force personnel were saved, which left twelve unaccounted for, while the number of CIA paramilitary officers on the Rock remains classified. Relatives of the dead were told they had been killed "in Southeast Asia."[4]

In the face of such a reversal it only remained to knock out the radar on the Rock to deny it to the enemy. "They bombed that sucker for a week, trying to destroy the radar so the enemy wouldn't have it," Art Cornelius said. "It broke my heart."

The loss of the Rock, unremarked and unreported back in the States, was a serious setback for the Americans. One quarter of all bombing missions over North Vietnam had been directed from it. (The loss may have been a factor in President Johnson's decision to declare a bombing halt, on March 31, 1968, of the northern two-thirds of North Vietnam, the area in which the Rock had been so effective in directing all-weather strikes.) But for the Meo the loss of the sacred mountain was more than a military reversal, it was a spiritual calamity with complex psychological consequences. As the news that Phou Pha Thi had fallen passed from village to village along the mountain grapevine, the morale of half a million Meo slumped.

It heralded the beginning of a terrible period for Gen. Vang Pao. In the five years since 1963, he had fought a seesaw war. During the dry season, December through May, when the roads were passable, the enemy took the offensive, only to fall back into a defensive position in the months of the monsoon, when the Meo usually regained lost ground. The margins of land between the opposing forces sometimes changed hands twice a year. Even during this period of comparative balance there was a creeping escalation as the enemy fielded more troops and weaponry each year and the Meo strengthened their defensive positions and launched stronger offensives backed by ever-increasing air power.

In the dry season of 1967 the Pathet Lao and the North Vietnamese began to build all-weather roads. This enabled them to extend the period in which they were effective, dependent as they were on wheeled vehicles to haul supplies and munitions, and to bring up heavy weapons. Perhaps provoked by the installation of radar on the Rock, they undertook a major push throughout the region of Sam Neua, involving eleven battalions of North Vietnamese reinforcements.[5]

The effect of this new strategy and escalation by the enemy had already been felt before the attack on the Rock. Government forces defending the royal capital of Luang Prabang had been chopped to pieces, while two provincial capitals in the Laotian panhandle had come under heavy attack. Both the Royal Laotian Army and Gen. Vang Pao's forces began to rely increasingly on U.S. air power.

The partial bombing halt over North Vietnam meant there were idle U.S. jets and a surplus of bombs available, and these were immediately switched to Laos.[6] But bad weather made even the increased air power ineffective. Fighters remained unable to get off the ground, friendly outposts fell one after another, and Vang Pao's forces were swept from the province. With the loss of Site 85 at the foot of the Rock, the Ravens fell back to staging out of Site 36 at Na Khang, now their most northerly base, defended by fifteen hundred Meo.

The enemy, under the cover of the poor weather, had amassed five battalions by early May with which to challenge the Na Khang garrison. But just when things looked most bleak the weather changed. The Ravens began a frantic effort from dawn to dusk to direct air to beat back the massed enemy army. Hundreds of sorties of U.S. jet fighter-bombers blunted the enemy thrust.

The commander of Na Khang was Lt. Col. U Va Lee, a close relative of Vang Pao, one of his most trusted field officers and a very tough soldier indeed. Known among the Americans as "the Indian," thirty-five-year-old U Va Lee had spent most of his life fighting, and he carried an M-16 about with him as a businessman might carry a briefcase. He had an intimate knowledge of the area, and when he was not fighting on the ground he flew in the backseat with a Raven to validate targets. (Vang Pao had provided a whole squad of men, known as Backseaters or Robins, who could advise the Ravens on the terrain and differentiate between friendly and enemy areas. This was the only targeting authority the Ravens had to consult in the area of northern Laos. All other targets in Laos had to go through the embassy and were cleared by the ambassador himself.)

John Mansur had heard all the stories about the Indian, and was pleased to have him as his Backseater on his first strike mission in the country. "I had heard he was the John Wayne of the Meo and that if he told you to hit a target—hit the target."

They flew north to a valley that seemed as empty as it was peaceful. U Va Lee jerked his thumb downward. "That's where we drop bombs."

"Why, what's there?"

"Just drop bombs."

It was Mansur's first solo strike mission in Laos, and, wanting to be sure, he made a couple of low passes through the valley, but could see nothing. He needed reassurance and once more asked, "What's there?"

"Just drop bombs."

Having been told by the CIA he could trust U Va Lee without reservation, Mansur proceeded to direct a set of U.S. jet fighters which dropped deadly antipersonnel cluster bomb units (CBU) in the valley. When they landed back at the strip, Mansur wanted to know what they had bombed. "Okay, I did what you told me, now you tell me why."

The Indian laughed, and slapped Mansur on the back. "All my life I have fought here," he explained. "When we fought the Vietminh they would push us south and we would plant there in that valley. When we would push them north we would harvest. Now we fight the Pathet Lao Communists and when they pushed us south they planted. Today they harvested."

Mansur was routinely flying six to eight missions a day. "My all-time record for being in the air in one day was eleven hours and forty-five minutes. That's a long time in an O-1." The enemy were only two miles from Na Khang, so a Raven spent almost all of the time he was airborne over the target area, constantly exposed to ground fire. "You get to the point when you are flying that much that it's no longer like flying an airplane but just an extension of your body. You never look at the airspeed indicator, but judge the speed by the sound of the wind in the wires."

War was a vocation for U Va Lee, and he had dedicated his life to it, twenty-four hours a day, seven days a week. Now, with the Meo stretched to breaking point, regional commanders were under enormous strain. Their men had taken a terrible beating, after eight years of unrelenting combat against the NVA and Pathet Lao, and the natives were abandoning their villages in droves to escape the war. Some soldiers, exhausted and outdistanced by the enemy, had gone over to the other side. Among such a tight and clannish society as the Meo, a betrayal of this sort was considered the worst sort of crime. And to a man like U Va Lee, who considered hatred of the enemy a given and battling him a constant, a Meo defector was a creature who had automatically forfeited all rights.

The Indian dealt with such men ruthlessly, as Mansur witnessed one afternoon. Walking toward U Va Lee's bunker, he saw a small Meo soldier come tumbling head over heels out of the entrance, closely pursued by the Indian himself.

The Meo soldier lay on the ground, his hands over his head and his legs drawn up into his groin. He made no movement and no sound. U Va Lee stood over him, his eyes bulging with fury and hate. "This man is enemy," the Indian explained. "*A Meo who is enemy*." The Indian took his revolver from its holster and handed it to Mansur. "You shoot him."

"Not me."

U Va Lee waved aside the objection. "Okay. He enemy."

"No, I can't do that."

U Va Lee was genuinely confused. "You drop bombs on them all day."

"That's different."

"But he *enemy!*"

"Look, I can't just shoot a guy lying there like that."

U Va Lee nodded. He barked a command at the prostrate figure. The soldier dragged himself to his feet and stood with head bowed. U Va Lee looked expectantly at Mansur, who dangled the revolver idly at his side.

"Why not? *Enemy!*"

"He's just standing there."

U Va Lee barked another order at the soldier, who began to run. "Now okay?"

Mansur shook his head. U Va Lee snatched back the revolver, raised it toward the fleeing figure of the soldier, and shot him dead. He turned to look questioningly at Mansur, whose scruples were incomprehensible to him. Shaking his head, U Va Lee holstered the revolver and walked back toward the bunker.

The control of air power in Laos had evolved on a trial-and-error basis without much planning. In the early days of the war it was managed by half a dozen sheep-dipped*, nonrated Air Commandos, who flew with Air America pilots in Pilatus Porters and marked their targets with smoke canisters dropped out of the window. Often they did not mark the targets at all, but talked fighters onto the target by describing the scenery: "Drop your bombs two hundred yards north of that gnarled tree."[7]

This small group was given the radio call sign Butterfly (rapidly changed from Wetback, which was not considered a good code name for men who were illegal aliens operating in the black across the Mekong). The program had proved remarkably effective, but its existence had been abruptly terminated by Gen. William M. Momyer, a commander of the 7th Air Force in Vietnam and deputy commander of U.S. Military Assistance Command Vietnam (MACV). An officer in the Prussian mold, he was not predisposed to the unconventional methods of the Air Commandos. Momyer wanted an ultramodern, all-jet Air Force. When he heard his precious high-tech jets were being controlled by ruffians who were neither pilots nor officers, he reportedly threw one of the more impressive temper tantrums of the war.

The result was the creation of the Ravens in 1966. The new FACs were rated Air Force officers with at least six months of experience in Vietnam. It was a breed he might have strangled at birth if he could have envisioned its maverick future. The general was an old World

---

*Sheep-dipped: A complex process in which someone serving in the military seemingly went through all the official motions of resigning from the service. The man's records would be pulled from the personnel files and transferred to a special Top Secret intelligence file. A cover story would be concocted to explain the resignation, and the man would become a civilian. At the same time, his ghostly paper existence within the intelligence file would continue to pursue his Air Force career: when his contemporaries were promoted, he would be promoted, and so on. Sheep-dipped personnel posed extremely tricky problems when they were killed or captured. There would be all sorts of pension and insurance problems, which was one of the reasons the CIA found it necessary to set up its own insurance company.

War II fighter pilot, an ace (he shot down eight enemy aircraft over North Africa) and a brave man (he was awarded three Silver Stars for his courage), but he was unsympathetic to counterinsurgency dogma in general and the Air Commandos in particular. He considered Laos a dubious backwater operation.

Ambassador Sullivan and General Momyer conducted a long duel through numerous jovial telegrams (Sullivan signing his "Sopwith Camel Company," Momyer signing his "20th Century Avionics") which masked a more serious difference of opinion.

The Ravens, like the Butterflies before them, sided with Sullivan—which was not what the general had intended when he created them. The air attaché's office in Vientiane also supported the ambassador, answering to him directly in the chain of command, although they were careful to pirouette gracefully on behalf of the Air Force from time to time in the interests of diplomacy.

The period of 1967, and early 1968, was one in which the Ravens suffered uncomfortable growing pains. There were never enough men or aircraft to manage the ever-increasing use of U.S. air. (There had been only four Butterflies to control the whole of Laos up to 1966, and even by 1968 there were only half a dozen Ravens. This number slowly grew, but even at the height of the war there were never more than twenty-two Ravens at any one time.)

In the early days of the Ravens' evolution its pilots were still essentially in the military mold. That is to say, while they bucked the system of conspicuous waste in Vietnam and were more than willing to take it on themselves to break the Rules of Engagement when they felt the situation justified it, they still lived, behaved, and thought like soldiers. The era of the swashbuckling air pirate, hung with gold jewelry and eccentrically garbed—an image largely borrowed from their Air America colleagues—was still to come. But Sam Deichelman was ahead of his time.

He arrived at Long Tieng during the height of the new push, trudging up the road from the airstrip to be met by Art Cornelius at the door of the Raven hootch. Deichelman was deeply tanned and had a shock of blond hair bleached white by the sun and tied at the back into a nineteenth-century sailor's pigtail. He wore a Waikiki Beach surf shop T-shirt, faded Levi's, and sandals, and carried a beat-up alligator bag with a tennis racket sticking out of it. A surf bum had stepped into the middle of the jungle war. "What have they sent us?" Cornelius asked himself, as he first regarded the apparition with the deepest skepticism. "What *have* they sent us?"

But the moment Sam Deichelman took to the air he proved himself a highly effective FAC, and the Ravens were a pragmatic enough group not to bother about his surfer style. He always wore a big lopsided grin, and there was something so open and honest in his blue eyes that people soon found themselves won over. He had a personal magic which charmed everyone. Women loved him because he was gentle, sensitive, and good-looking without vanity; men loved him because he could be trusted with the most intimate confidences, and seemed to be without fear.

Deichelman was an Air Force brat. His father was a general, and while Sam was in high school the family had been posted to the Air War University at Maxwell Air Force Base, Montgomery, Alabama. The general had wanted his son to follow in his footsteps and go to the Air Force Academy, but Sam rebelled. He packed a bag and left home and spent a happy period in the late '50s living a hobo life in Cuba. Later he worked his passage on a schooner bound for the South Pacific, sailing through the Panama Canal and across to Hawaii. Honolulu suited him; he left ship and became a first-rate surfer. He also enrolled in the university, where he took a degree in philosophy.

But a yearning to fly was in his blood, and after a period climbing mountains in New Zealand, he returned to the States to join the Air Force and go through pilot training. His father, the general, must have been gratified, for his younger son, Sam's brother, had gone to the Air Force Academy. Both of them ended up in Vietnam. Sam became a Blindbat pilot, flying a C-130 gunship at night, which used a starlight scope to spot trucks going down the Trail. As soon as he had accumulated thirty days' leave he used it to train and check out as a FAC. If ever there was a man destined for the Steve Canyon Program it was Sam Deichelman.

He was very happy in Laos. It was as if, deep in the jungle and in the midst of war, he had at last found home. He grew to adore the Meo, who looked upon him as a friendly and amusing god. He flew long hours, always thrusting himself into the white-hot center of battle. On his return to base he would trudge up to the orphanage with a bag of candy and spend his evenings playing with the kids. There was something good and innocent about Sam Deichelman, everyone agreed, and yet he was a fierce and fearless warrior.

If there was one thing Long Tieng abounded in, it was orphaned children. When one of Vang Pao's soldiers was killed in battle the general became directly responsible for the man's surviving wife and children, who were relatively well cared for in the circumstances. The children had to be very young indeed not to be drafted into the army in one way or another. Six-year-olds humped rockets and pumped gasoline for the armorers and maintenance men, while their older brothers fought the war.

By early 1968 the war had already decimated the Meo. Pop Buell described it graphically: "A short time ago we rounded up three hundred fresh recruits. Thirty percent were fourteen years old or less, and ten of them were only ten years old. Another thirty percent were fifteen or sixteen. The remaining forty percent were forty-five or over. Where were the ages in between? I'll tell you—they're all dead."

The children of the town liked the Ravens and ran after them for small change and chewing gum. Despite the war they were delightful, happy children who were always smiling. The shy little girls attempted to teach the Ravens how to flick their hand-painted wooden tops—without much success—while the boys noisily jostled for attention. The U.S. AID school built for the Meo was down the road from the Raven hootch, and the children waved and shouted in the mornings on their way to school. One four-year-old in particular began to stop by the hootch when school was over. Both parents had been killed in the war, and he was one of numerous waifs fed and haphazardly cared for by Vang Pao.

When the little boy discovered the Ravens screened films in the evenings, he attended regularly, sitting on the floor between their chairs to watch wide-eyed what was, for him, the extraordinary vision of Hollywood. He would watch until he grew sleepy, then doze quietly on the floor under the couch. When it grew late one of the general's people would come to fetch him and take him back to the compound. The child came back night after night until it became such a routine that the general, knowing he was safe, stopped sending for him.

Without planning or intent, the Ravens had adopted a son. At a loss for a name, they called him Oddjob. He attached himself in particular to Larry Clausen, the radio operator, and a small bunk bed was built for him. It was eventually discovered that his Meo name was Lor Lu, so he was formally known as Lor "Oddjob" Lu. In a world of war, the orphaned child became the focus of the Ravens' gentler side. Everyone mentioned the chirpy four-year-old in letters home. John Mansur wrote to his wife: "He is hell on wheels, but what a neat little guy. In a couple of months his emotions have developed to where he can really relate to the guys."

Ravens recounted Oddjob anecdotes in their letters like fathers doting on their firstborn, mentioned his size—about two-thirds the height of an M-16—and the fact that he had no clothes. As a result, when one of the Ravens returned from Udorn on the next mail run, his O-1 was crammed with care packages. Unused to children, they made the mistake of giving the four-year-old everything at once.

The next morning the Ravens left the hootch to fly as usual. When they returned Lor Lu was dressed in a neatly pressed pair of tiny jeans, a Mickey Mouse T-shirt, and a pair of thongs. He was asked where the rest of his considerable wardrobe had gone.

Lor Lu smiled from ear to ear and produced a small box stuffed with *kip* currency notes. He had taken the clothes down to the market and sold them. The houseboy counted the money in Lor Lu's box and nodded appreciatively—the child was a natural trader and had done well.

The Ravens were hopelessly overworked by the war. The Air Force insisted that an O-1 should return to Udorn for maintenance every hundred hours, which was often less than ten days. In the meantime, bullet holes were patched with 100-mph typhoon tape, a strong fabric which was simply slapped over the holes. Spare parts were slow to arrive, meaning that sometimes planes were forced to sit on the ramp when they were desperately needed at the front. Fuel on the mountain and jungle sites was often contaminated by dirt and rust. Maintenance was sloppy, and it was not unusual for planes to return from Udorn with water in the gas tanks. It became so bad that the Ravens felt they were fighting on two fronts—one against the enemy in the north, and the other against the air attaché's office and the embassy in the south.

"Not one time while I was a Raven did any of the embassy staff come up to Alternate," Tom Shera said. "They were afraid to come up. They had no feel at all for the conditions we were flying under. They had no appreciation for our daily life at all. We lived in a house on stilts; our bunks were on the porch. Up there in the mountains it went below freezing in the winter. There was no heating, except log fires. It was cool even in the summer. We had open hall latrines. Our showers consisted of four fifty-five-gallon barrels on a platform with immersion heaters in them. You broke the ice on them in the morning and started the heater up. We bought our own food, did our own cooking, and washed our own dishes."

The radios used were obsolete and often went on the blink. FACs in Vietnam had the most up-to-date radio equipment, but in Laos the

Ravens were expected to cope with antiquated, clumsy sets, which greatly complicated an already difficult situation. Radio contact with everyone involved in an air strike was vital for a FAC to be effective. He needed UHF, VHF, and FM radios: UHF to talk to the fighters, VHF to talk to Cricket and to Air America, and FM to talk to troops on the ground. The UHF was a multichannel radio, but the four-channel VHF receiver had to be tuned manually. The FM radio was an Army backpack type that was strapped into the O-1's rear seat. To talk to the troops on the ground a Raven had to swivel in his seat to reach the hand-held cup phone behind him. In addition, the VHF antenna was on the bottom of the airplane, which meant that when a Raven needed to talk to Cricket he had to gain altitude, turn the airplane around, and drop the wing in order to position the antenna toward orbiting airborne command. In combat, when a Raven might need to talk to several sets of fighters, another FAC, and the troops on the ground as well as Cricket, this maneuver was not always convenient.

Support for the Ravens often relied on a conspiracy of the like-minded. The chronic lack of radios came to the attention of an unorthodox senior NCO, Patrick Mahoney, who worked in the Combat Command Center in Blue Chip, 7th Air Force HQ at Tan Son Nhut airbase in Vietnam. Senior Master Sergeant Mahoney—a veteran of World War II, in which he had won three Bronze Stars—had a penchant for people involved in special operations and unconventional warfare. It was his conviction that they received short shrift in the war in Vietnam, and he had set himself the task of equalizing the situation.

He had arrived in Vietnam as a volunteer in 1966 and had flown 250 medevac helicopter missions before being shot down four days before Christmas the same year. As a little extra duty on the side he liked to accompany Green Beret teams on operations thirty miles behind enemy lines, and had been awarded a Combat Infantryman's Badge at a Special Forces camp—a highly unusual distinction for an airman.

Mahoney was moved to Combat Command Center, where he was given the job of noncommissioned officer in charge of combat operations for the 7th Air Force. He was also the top-secret control officer for the out-country war in Laos, Cambodia, and Thailand. The general in charge had picked Mahoney because of his experience with unconventional warfare, and gave him his first briefing on Laos: "Now you are *really* going to find out where the unconventional war is."

Just to enter the office of the Combat Command Center a man needed Top Secret security clearances—sometimes Special Intelligence clearances as well—and no "foreigners" were allowed in the area (foreigners in this case meaning non-Americans). "I began hearing about VP and the Raven forward air controllers—and then I heard they were short of radio equipment," Mahoney recalled.

Mahoney's methods of procuring equipment were as unconventional as the war to which it was destined to be sent. He had once dressed up as a lieutenant colonel and taken a team of men to a downtown Saigon hotel, used primarily by State Department people, where he told the staff on the desk that he was there to check the air conditioning, because some of the striped-pants set had complained of unacceptable stuffiness in their rooms. He walked out of the hotel with fifteen units, which were loaded on a plane and were on their way to a Special Forces camp later the same day.

Grateful Green Berets reciprocated with gifts of captured Russian war supplies, which Mahoney in turn took down to the docks in Saigon where he traded for food with war-souvenir-hungry, rear echelon supply personnel. It took several cases of A3 steaks—each one containing 150 one-inch-thick filet mignons—to procure the radios, which were sent up to the Ravens at Long Tieng.

After the radios arrived the word spread throughout Laos that if you wanted something done behind people's backs, and you wanted it done expediently, Patrick was the man. He was given a clearance to visit the secret base to see firsthand what was needed.

Mahoney was appalled by the Meo guerrillas' equipment. The young soldiers looked a ragged bunch and had only antiquated carbines with which to go up against an enemy armed with AK-47 automatic weapons, B-40 rockets, and heavy artillery. Mahoney began to run guns and uniforms to the base, a back-channel supply line of equipment pilfered from the overstocked warehouses of Vietnam.

Tiger fatigues began to arrive in Long Tieng by the hundred, and the occasional planeload of unconventional weapons (Mahoney was almost caught loading up a T-39 with British Sten guns fitted with silencers, M-16s, and 9mm pistols destined for Laos). The Mahoney back-channel supply line even ran to artillery. "I had found a sergeant running a reclamation artillery yard. I told him the sort of food I could get and his eyes bugged out. He delivered ten pieces in good working order in four days."

Mahoney slowly developed an alternative supply system. "It was taking care of people, and others saw it. When they started talking to some of the Ravens who had walked in the valley of the shadow of death, then they began to understand themselves. The Ravens were the best. Selfless. They were an inspiration.

"And people who met them said, 'To hell with the bureaucrats over us—we'll take care of people like that.' We were building a system that *worked*."[8]

In the meantime the Ravens flew ten-hour combat days, uncertain in bad weather if they would be able to get back in or be forced to divert to another strip. Unreliable aircraft were a final, unacceptable hazard. Properly maintained airplanes are not only necessary equipment for a pilot, but part of his psychic confidence, the central prop of his courage. A single error can be fatal to a pilot flying a small airplane over dangerous mountain terrain in bad weather, and he reaches out instinctively for anything that increases his chance of survival. He can control the risk much of the time, and even manage the fear unlocked by sudden explosions of gunfire, but faulty equipment saps this vital confidence.

The pilot of a single-engine plane is always alone, with only his skill and resolution to fall back on. Once airborne he can rely on no general to lead him, no colleagues to give him advice, and there are no comrades-in-arms to help bolster his courage in critical moments. In battle he has only his airplane to rely on.

It is bad enough to fly into combat, prepared to be shot at, without having to cope with the constant subconscious fear that the engine might quit. So the message which went down to the embassy in Vientiane, in a hundred different forms, was always the same in essence: Give us some support or we are going to kill ourselves.

It was ignored, and the Ravens awaited the inevitable. It happened at Na Khang, when the enemy were almost drawn up to the perimeter of the airfield. Tom Shera had just taken off in a U-17, a Cessna 185 modified by the Air Force to carry rockets. Pilot and passenger sat side by side, which made it a difficult plane to FAC out of. Shera had a Thai mercenary in the passenger seat and intended to fly north. He began to lose power almost immediately after takeoff, because of fuel contamination, and knew that he would never make it over the ridgeline.

The strip at Na Khang was in a bowl, and Shera tried to bring the plane around full circle to land but didn't make it. The plane stalled, the left wing tip touched the ground, and the U-17 crashed into a minefield, snapping off both wings and the tail. Miraculously, swamp vegetation eight feet deep absorbed the shock of the crash and the plane hit no mines. The Thai became hysterical and Shera had trouble making him understand they could not move a single step from the plane.

The minefield into which they had crashed had originally been laid by the French in the 1930s, reseeded by the Japanese in the '40s, mined again by the French in the '50s, and mined yet again by the Americans in the '60s. The pattern was entirely haphazard, and no one knew where early mines had been laid, except when an occasional drunken villager strayed from the path and set one off. Shera waited, bruised and shaken, until an Air America helicopter came to pull them out.

He was given the next day off, which he spent resting quietly in the hootch at Alternate. Meanwhile, maintenance crews were instructed to run every drop of gasoline through chamois in an attempt to sieve out the dirt and rust. The usual complaints were made to the embassy and 7/13th Air Force at Udorn.

The next day Shera was back in the air. This time he took a single round through the cowling, which went into the engine and knocked a lead off a spark plug. The engine began to vibrate, the plane lost altitude, and Shera was forced to make a crash landing. He was shot at all the way down, but managed to slam the aircraft onto a seven-hundred-foot strip scratched onto the top of a ridgeline.

It was a short, rocky downhill strip, meant only for the use of Air America's fleet of STOL (short takeoff and landing) aircraft. The landing had been difficult; takeoff would be well-nigh impossible. An Air America helicopter flew in with a flight mechanic, who fixed the damage done to the O-1's engine. All loose parts, including the radios, were stripped from the plane to make it lighter. Shera pointed the aircraft downhill and had Meo soldiers hold on to the struts and tail until he had revved the engine to full power. He signaled to the Meo to let go, roared down the strip until he had run out of runway, lowered the flaps, and staggered off across the trees under enemy small-arms fire.

In World War I the saying was that a man twice burned was finished. In the Raven program, Shera was given a week off. This was considered just long enough for a pilot to pull himself together—any longer might result in a permanent loss of nerve. Shera, understandably shaken after two bad crashes in as many days, went down to Bangkok to recuperate.

* * *

The crashes had brought the Ravens' dissatisfaction to a head, and they were in open rebellion against the "Downtowners," as they contemptuously called the embassy staff. The air attaché's office was forced to act. They created a new position—Head Raven—in the hope of bridging the ever-widening gap growing between embassy staff and policy, on the one hand, and the Ravens and the war on the other. It was hoped that a Raven with a staff position would know the realities of the job and also command the respect of the FACs.

The man picked for the job was Tom Richards, who had joined the Air Force to keep warm. Originally a ground-pounding grunt in the Army, he had fought in some of the worst campaigns of the Korean War and worked his way up to first sergeant. One day, sitting in a freezing foxhole waiting to storm a position across the valley, he watched the planes roll in on their target. The sun was beginning to come up, but it did nothing to relieve the aching cold Richards had felt in his bones for months. "If those guys get killed, at least they're warm," he thought. "They're going to go back to Japan, they're going to drink a martini, sleep in a comfortable bed tonight, and fly back to the war tomorrow. If I get killed my body will be frozen solid in some dirty hole." He decided right there and then to go back to college and join the Air Force. A passion for flying developed later.

Richards *looked* like Steve Canyon. Tall, trim, and handsome, he radiated command presence and led by example. He had cut his teeth as a Raven during a six-month period in Pakse, in the Laotian panhandle in the south. Pakse had the reputation of being a country club, a quiet area where the corrupt and ineffective Royal Lao Army and Air Force allowed the enemy easy pickings. Richards, using the cover of a civilian engineer, joined one other FAC and three mechanics in civilian clothes. The first thing he did was to write to a friend, Dale Richardson, stationed in Vietnam as a FAC with the 101st Airborne, to volunteer for the program and join him in Laos. Together they worked at taking the war to the enemy.

Richards found the situation in Military Region IV "loose." The Royal Lao Air Force had a wing of T-28 fighters on the base, but the major in charge flew only when he felt like it. Richards would plan a mission and lead the fighters to a target, only to watch them bomb miles away if they even suspected the presence of antiaircraft guns. Sometimes he would arrive on the flight line in the morning to find that no one had shown up. When the commander finally arose from his bed at 10:00 he explained that one of his pilots had come to him the previous night and related a dream. Buddha had told the pilot in the dream that the following day was particularly unlucky for flying. The mission commander had thanked the pilot and given the order "No fly today."

The Lao preferred to use the most expensive ordnance, ordering CBU-25 canister bombs as often as possible. It was a weapon which needed to be delivered in a low-altitude dive, but the Lao pilots dropped it from a great height and brought the empty canisters back to sell the aluminum, having already snipped off the umbilical cords to sell the wire. With uncommitted commanders and lazy fighter pilots, it was only natural that the local Backseaters were equally ineffective. It was exactly the opposite to the situation in MR II, where the Meo fought so hard.

"The Lao Air Force used military aircraft to ferry passengers and refugees for money, to haul gold and opium," Richards said. "I just had no respect for them at all. I did my own thing. I was not there to help that establishment. I felt a lot of sympathy and compassion for the people, especially the Meo in the mountains battling against unbelievable odds."

Richards recognized a situation where the rules made no sense, and did not hesitate to break them. "Theoretically you were supposed to have a Laotian in the backseat to validate targets. They were a pain in the ass. If you went low they panicked. If you got shot at they went absolutely crazy. So I never took one. I got to know the country better than they did anyway."

Ravens were absolutely forbidden to fly the T-28 in combat, but with the Royal Lao Air Force in bed at worst and ineffective at best, Richards broke that rule too. He would find a target in the O-1 Bird Dog only to have the Lao refuse to hit it. He would then return to base, climb into the T-28, and fly out to bomb it himself.

The enemy were everywhere and were used to passing through Military Region IV with impunity. Richards found whole truck convoys on the edge of the Trail, and boats loaded with supplies on the rivers. Targets he hit would blow for half a day. Later he would return in an O-1 to make a bomb damage assessment. "I ran the air war in southern Laos. I could do almost anything I wanted to. The CIA took good care of us. Anything you asked for, they would provide. Ordnance came out of the embassy, shipped in by Air America. After Vietnam the freedom was unbelievable."

Once Richards became Head Raven he went wherever the action demanded, flying support in battle and filling in for anyone on leave.

Things began to change. As a result of lobbying the air attaché's office constantly, maintenance began to improve and more planes were promised. The Ravens began to believe they had someone batting for them.

The CIA personnel could be very good but suffered from an excessive leaning toward the clandestine. As close as Richards worked with them, they rarely confided in him, and it seemed that intelligence was a one-way street. They received information without ever giving any back. At the office in Pakse—a big operation run by Dave Morales, a hard-drinking paramilitary officer with a taste for pornography, whose boast was that he had been present during the assassination of Che Guevara—CIA personnel covered all the papers on their desks every time Richards walked in. "It's nothing personal—just policy," a CIA officer explained.

Richards put up with it for two months before his patience ran out. "The next time you do that—cover a paper on the desk when I come into this office—I'm through working for you."

One of two things happened to Ravens, as they logged an increasing number of combat missions and took their share of groundfire: they became either overcautious or reckless. The first merely made them ineffective, but the second risked their lives. The inclination to duel with a gun in a fixed position, or settle a score after their aircraft had been peppered with ground fire, led them to take risk after risk. Sam Deichelman became one of the worst offenders. Richards thought he was becoming too blasé and had reached the point where he believed himself immortal. Ironically, Deichelman's first intimation of mortality came when he was behaving himself and flying at what was considered a safe altitude.

It was just one of those things. His plane took the Golden BB. Pilots knew from experience that it was possible to fly directly through a cloud of flak or a hail of small-arms fire at point-blank range and come out unscathed, and also possible to be cruising far from the enemy at five thousand feet and be killed by a single stray round—which they called the Golden BB. It was part of their folklore and contributed to their fatalism. They might not have respected the Lao who refused to fly on a certain day for superstitious reasons, but they understood him.

Deichelman had flown his C-130 out of Vietnam over the Trail at night as a Blindbat pilot at ridiculously low altitudes and never taken a hit. Then, flying over Route 4, southeast of the Plain of Jars, accompanied by Vong Chou—yet another close relative of Vang Pao—they took a single round. The shell ripped through the skin of the plane, hit Vong Chou in the arm, and came out of his chest, slamming into the bulkhead and missing Deichelman's head by a hairbreadth. Vong Chou was critically wounded, and losing blood fast. Deichelman immediately turned the plane around and raced home.

The single shell had left two terrible wounds in Vong Chou's arm and chest, and his chances of survival seemed negligible. But he survived the trip, and for the next three days Deichelman was at his side, willing him to live. The Backseater, perhaps sensing his friend's anguish, pulled through against all odds.

Deichelman was shattered by the experience. He somehow felt that he should have taken the round, as commander of the aircraft, and he suffered agonies of guilt. All attempts to reassure him were futile.

He now entered a highly dangerous phase. He had cheated death and dodged the Golden BB, but it had wounded his friend, and he felt honor-bound to embark upon a course of reckless revenge. He was still badly shaken, but undeterred in his resolve to fly in combat as soon as possible.

In the circumstances, the air attaché's office thought it wise to remove him temporarily from the picture. The Air Force had agreed to give the program another O-1, and Deichelman was chosen to return to South Vietnam and ferry it to Laos. In September he left for Bien Hoa, where his younger brother was stationed. He planned to spend a few days of leave with him and then bring the O-1 back.

Deichelman reached Vietnam without incident, and the brothers enjoyed a pleasant reunion. He mentioned a desire to see the great Cambodian lake of Tonle Sap, an illegal but easy detour on the journey back. He boarded the new Bird Dog and took off from Bien Hoa and headed back toward Laos. He was never seen again.[9]

Sam Deichelman's disappearance was deeply mourned at Long Tieng and cast a pall over everyone who knew him. Among those it affected most was Art Cornelius, who had regarded the blond surfer with such skepticism when they had met. That first impression had soon changed, and an easy, respectful friendship had followed.

Cornelius admired the man as a first-rate pilot and FAC, but especially for his humanity. He had seen his friend's genuine compassion as he played with the village children, and his anguish as he sat with Vong Chou, the wounded Backseater. It was difficult not to be attracted to Deichelman's obvious honesty, good-hearted openness, and warmth.

Cornelius first heard the news of his friend's disappearance at the embassy in Vientiane while he was writing his end of tour report before returning home. The war was over for both of them. But Cornelius could not accept that Sam was dead, convinced that he had been forced to make an emergency landing somewhere in Cambodia. One day he would show up, give his lop-sided grin and a deprecating account of yet another escape from death. Cornelius had assumed he had made a friend for life in Sam, not someone who would disappear within a few short months.

But Sam never returned and Cornelius was forced to accept the fact that his great friend was lost forever. (The tragedy was compounded when Sam's younger brother was later killed in a midair collision in Vietnam. The general had paid a terrible price to see his sons follow in his footsteps).

In his role as go-between, Tom Richards fought the war at the front and in staff meetings at the embassy in Vientiane, and at 7/13th Air Force HQ in Udorn, Thailand. A chasm yawned between the different worlds of the Downtowners and the Air Force REMFs, and the Ravens at the edge of battle. While the Ravens' experience of the war might be narrow and parochial, the staff officers' was remote. Richards spent considerable time on the impossible job of bridging the gap, a frustrating and unrewarding task, but he occasionally scored a point for the men in the war.

In his position as Head Raven he sat in on staff meetings at both the embassy and Air Force HQ in Udorn, flying down to 7/13th HQ in the embassy C-47 to bring back the commander, Maj. Gen. Louis T. Seith. On the return flight to Vientiane he sat in the back of the plane briefing the general on the real picture of the war in Laos, "before he got to the embassy and got their version," Tom Richards explained. "Nobody seemed to understand how the enemy thought."

Air Force intelligence was mulish and painfully slow to learn the most basic lessons. The Trail had been bombed regularly since 1965 (with great effect by the Air Commandos and their outdated aircraft; with much waste and noise by the jets and B-52s of the regular Air Force), but the enemy's resilience continued to puzzle Air Force intelligence. At one meeting an exasperated intelligence officer wondered aloud that, as much as they bombed the fords, the enemy still kept coming.

"I can't believe you guys are doing that," Richards said, who had seen the results firsthand. "You're just making gravel for them. They roll a bulldozer out of a cave and fill it in and roll the trucks down at night. When there's a cut, coolies unload supplies and ammo from one set of trucks and carry it to the next."

"Impossible."

"You don't understand the power of thousands of coolies. They can carry more on their backs and their bicycles than you ever thought of. If they don't have a bulldozer they get a thousand people to carry a thousand baskets of rocks for as long as it takes to get the job done."

Those who did learn by the end of their one-year tour were replaced by new men who began the cycle of self-delusion all over again. Throughout Vietnam, and over the whole of Indochina, the one-year tour locked the military into a perpetual cycle of repeating the same mistakes over and over again. The wheel was reinvented every twelve months.

At least in Laos there was a certain amount of continuity. Some of the contract agents with the CIA spent more than a decade in the country, and so had many of the pilots who flew with Air America. The ambassadors spent substantial periods, and Gen. Vang Pao, who was there at the very beginning, would remain long after the end.

But most people passed through, a serious flaw in the case of photo intelligence. Reconnaissance planes crisscrossed Laos daily and returned with high-definition photographic blowups of every square mile of the country. These were scrutinized by photo interpreters, none of whom had ever flown over the battle areas personally, and who might have been put on the job only the previous day. It was sometimes difficult to distinguish a truck from a burned-out hulk or wooden decoy. (On the Trail itself, photo interpreters would rediscover convoys of trucks which had been destroyed the previous year. By the end of the war some trucks had been bombed again and again.)

Richards tried to see photo recon as often as possible, pointing out the more glaring errors. He would pick up a photo which had been designated as a target and already had a set of fighter-bombers scheduled to hit it the following day, and announce, "This is not a target."

"It's obviously a target," the photo interpreter would argue. "Symmetrical patterns along the side of a road. It must be."

"What that is really is some old asphalt that was piled along the road many years ago and is now overgrown by brush and vegetation."

He was ignored. The planes would be sent in on the target. Perhaps the first set would miss, and another would be sent. The old asphalt would be destroyed, making a decent enough fire to record on yet another photo recon flight as a secondary explosion, thus justifying the whole pointless, wasteful, and expensive operation.

The Ravens naturally provided some of the best intelligence of the war in Laos. They knew the terrain and in flying over it every day noticed the slightest change. By listening to the FACs and channeling their intelligence through Udorn, Richards managed to take the fighters off bogus targets and put them on the real thing. "They would have knocked the hell out of half of Laos if it hadn't been for us." Meaning that it was important to knock hell out of the right half of Laos.

One night at dinner at Vang Pao's house, where John Mansur had gone as usual to be briefed for the following day's missions, the general shocked the young Raven. The talk had been about the poor way the war was going, and Vang Pao was arguing for a big push, a quick victory before it was too late. Mansur had made earnest, naive assurances that the Americans could always be relied upon, whatever might happen. They would stick by the Meo through thick and thin. Vang Pao sighed and shook his head. "John, you don't understand."

"What don't I understand?"

"One of these days your people—the American people—will make the American military quit helping us. And as soon as that happens the Communists are going to take my country."

Mansur could not believe his ears. "General," he said emotionally, "we will *never* do that."

Vang Pao smiled. "You do not understand, John."

The leadership of the Lao military were lazy and corrupt, and as a result their men were useless in the field. Traditionally, the lowland Lao looked upon the Meo as their social and cultural inferiors, which created a strain in communications between them. No lowland Lao was going to die defending a Meo village; no Meo was going to trust his life in the hands of a lowland Lao.

Thai pilots, hired as mercenaries, were reluctant to press in on a target, precisely because they were mercenaries. Ethnically they were of the same stock as the lowland Lao—even speaking the same language if they were from northeast Thailand—but the motivation of money took them only so far. A soldier can be bribed with gold to go to battle, but he cannot be made to fight.

For all of these reasons Vang Pao wanted his own Meo fighter pilots to fly a squadron of T-28s. This was a tall order. Technologically, the Meo were in the stone age. Because of the rocky mountain terrain they were a people who had never developed the wheel, and did not even have iron tips on their wooden plows. When the Americans had first built landing strips in the country in the early 1960s, villagers had peered under the fuselages of the planes, anxious to discover their sex. In one remote province, near the Chinese border, so many man-eating tigers roamed the strip at night that Special Forces people were flown in to kill them, using chickens stuffed with grenades as bait.

A certain number of promising young men, handpicked by Vang Pao himself, were sent to Udorn to be trained in a program, known as Waterpump, which the Air Commandos had set up to teach Thai, Lao, and Meo to fly. In the case of many of the Meo they were taken from the backs of water buffalo one day and placed in the cockpit of a fighter the next. The commando instructors were sensitive and pragmatic when faced with native idiosyncrasies, and regularly used a local bonze (Buddhist monk), at $7.62 a session, to exorcise aircraft possessed of bad *phi* (spirits)—the cost included such items as herbs and powder for the ceremony, plus cigarettes, toothpaste, and soap for the monk. Similarly, the Meo's grasp of western medicine was scanty—opium served as their only powerful medication. (As the Meo had built up no resistance to drugs, up-country medics found that antibiotics cleared up a multitude of ills so quickly it seemed like magic.) But despite the enormous cultural and technological gaps, the Meo proved amazingly adaptable, and Vang Pao had his first batch of fighter pilots within six months.

The attrition rate was high. The first two weeks a new pilot was exposed to combat flying were the most critical. It was a period in which many died. Those who survived were expected to fly combat mission after combat mission, until they became among the most experienced fighter pilots in the world. There was no "tour" to complete, no rest and recreation in Hong Kong or Australia, no end in sight to the war. "Fly till you die," the Meo pilots said cheerfully.

One man stood out among all the others. Lee Lue, a cousin of Vang Pao, had originally been a schoolteacher to the Meo children in Long Tieng. He became the first Meo fighter pilot, and his instructor at

Waterpump declared him to be a natural. Experience had made him superb. "He was the best fighter-bomber pilot I have ever encountered," John Mansur said. "That includes Americans or anybody."

Lee Lue was a quiet but immensely personable man, with the definite strut of the fighter pilot. No mission was too dangerous for him, no weather too bad. "He was one of the bravest men I've ever known," said Howard Hartley, a lieutenant colonel with the Air Commandos. "He was a splendid pilot, excellent—so vastly exceptional to all the Lao pilots who came before him there was no comparison. He was very bold, very reckless, extremely courageous. He became squadron commander at Vientiane, and the younger Lao pilots resented the fact at first that a Meo was their commander. He would go anywhere against all odds, and most of them would follow for fear of losing face."[10] His example forced his pilot colleagues to extraordinary levels of achievement which sometimes put even American pilots to shame.

"The first time I worked Lee Lue he came right down the chute with two seven-hundred-and-fifty-pound bombs—which most of the Lao would not carry," Art Cornelius said. "And he got down so low that he was never going to miss by far. But this was unbelievable— just spot on target." Cornelius was so impressed he made a special flight down to Vientiane to meet the man himself.

Lee Lue flew so low in attack missions on enemy troops in the open that maintenance men sometimes found blood on his plane's propeller. When he was shot down on the Plain of Jars and an Air America H-34 helicopter could not land because of the terrain, he clung to the wheel strut until the pilot found a place it could. He took it in his stride and scarcely mentioned it, except in a handwritten note to Raven Jim Baker, asking for a replacement parachute. "MR. BAKER. PLEASE. YOU HAVE FOR ME ONE NEW PARACHUTE. BECAUSE I HAVE NOT MORE. LEE LUE."[11]

Ravens loved to work with him, even more than American Air Force colleagues. John Mansur had found a small gun emplacement and was attempting unsuccessfully to knock it out with a set of Phantom F-4s when Lee Lue flew into the area. The gun had made the Phantoms exceedingly cautious, and they were dropping from such an altitude that Mansur could hardly see them. The F-4s had already made several passes and dropped their entire bomb load. Lee Lue circled the gun site in his T-28 and watched the sorry spectacle for several minutes before calling Mansur on the radio. "What you have for target?"

"A twenty-three position." Mansur had no intention of putting a lone, slow-flying T-28 prop plane onto a 23mm antiaircraft gun emplacement, but Lee Lue was insistent. "Let me bomb. No problem."

Figuring Lee Lue was going to do it anyway, Mansur gave him the go-ahead. He called the lead Phantom. "Hold high and dry. Watch a real fighter pilot."

Lee Lue positioned himself for a run against the gun emplacement. He dropped down in a vertical dive, pickled off a single five-hundred-pound bomb, and blew the gun out of existence. It was as impressive a display of aeronautical skill as anyone could ever hope to witness. The job done, Lee Lue banked his fighter and flew off in search of other prey.

The lead Phantom keyed the microphone to his radio. "Say, Raven, who was that masked man?"

After his second crash, Tom Shera had been sent up to the royal capital of Luang Prabang, a comparatively quiet posting. He was to replace Marlin Siegwalt, who knew the area well but had only a week to go. The two men flew north to where Route 19 came out of Dien Bien Phu. Shera was in the backseat while Siegwalt, whom Shera had met only three days earlier, piloted the plane. They were flying over a ridgeline, high in the mountains, when a single bullet entered the plane. It came through the right side, hit Siegwalt in his right arm, and traveled through to his chest. As he was hit he pulled back on the stick, and the plane went straight up into the air and almost stalled.

In the backseat Shera realized his colleague was unable to fly the airplane. A second control stick was stored in the rear of the O-1, and he fought to connect it while the plane sputtered and coughed. He jiggled the stick into position and regained control of the plane, pushed the nose over, and headed back to Luang Prabang.

The forty-five minutes that followed were an eternity. He called Cricket over the radio to request medical facilities to stand by, but there was nothing else he could do. He droned back to the base at ninety-five knots, flying the plane from the backseat, while Siegwalt lay slumped over the stick in front of him. As he touched down he saw an Air America C-123 waiting on the ramp with its engines running, ready to rush the pilot to hospital in Udorn. A medic ran out to the plane the moment it came to a stop, but it was too late. Siegwalt had been hit by the Golden BB, which had clipped the aorta, and there was no hope of saving him.[12]

The word went around the Ravens that Tom Shera was plagued with bad *phi*, the spirits that were a part of all life for the Meo. They wondered whether he was a marked man to have had three such experiences one after the other, or extraordinarily lucky to have survived them. Shera himself felt strangely removed and unaffected by his experiences. He suffered no post-crash trauma or delayed shock, and slept like a baby. He continued to fly without incident or further misadventure.

Then one morning he walked across the ramp to his plane and found himself frozen to the spot. He had stopped by the tail of the O-1 and found it physically impossible to move around to climb into the cockpit. After several moments he walked back to the operations shack and threw his stuff into the locker.

He had succumbed to one of the occupational hazards of the Raven—combat burnout. Shera was now thrice burned. After a few days' respite he continued to fly, but felt he was too cautious and should not be in the theater at all. It was never the same again. "It didn't get worse. I just didn't want to fly. I had to drag myself out every day."

Siegwalt had been killed with only a week to go. It was a damned shame, his colleagues agreed, for an old head Raven like Siegwalt to buy the farm at the very tail end of his tour. The Golden BB too! It was a bitch. The Ravens talked about luck and fate, the law of averages and mathematical probability, and fingered their Buddhas—which almost all of them wore around their necks as talismans—more than usual as they drank their beer.

Siegwalt was replaced by Charles Ballou, who arrived in Long Tieng five days after the pilot's death. For some reason, from the very first day, everyone called him Bing. The new Raven seemed in a hurry to fight the war. He was so keen to hurt the enemy that he indulged in extracurricular after-hours missions. He would take out an O-1, together with a like-minded mechanic, and fly low over the enemy firing machine guns out of the window. He was a little too gung ho for his own good, the others thought, but he would soon settle down.

He had scarcely been in the war long enough to find his way around when he limped back to Alternate in a Bird Dog after taking small-arms fire. The engine was cutting in and out badly, as if the plane were out of gas, and he was forced to attempt a bush-pilot landing just short of the strip. Unable to raise the nose of the O-1 high enough, he crashed into the side of the mountain. The Backseater survived, but Bing was killed instantly. He had been in Laos five days.[13]

Sam Deichelman had been replaced by Ron Rinehart. On the face of it they could not have been more different: Deichelman, with his blond hair and golden good looks, was seen among the Ravens as a surfer version of a Greek god; Rinehart had red hair and freckles and was a down-to-earth Ohio farm boy whose language was as bad as his manners. He had already completed a year's tour in Vietnam before volunteering for the Steve Canyon Program. During the course of his Air Force career he had picked up the unfortunate sobriquet "Pig Fucker," by which he was known throughout Indochina. The embassy, which made a habit of logging nicknames in its computer, drew the line at Pig Fucker and sanitized it to Papa Fox. (The genesis of Rinehart's nickname is a source of much speculation among Ravens even today: "Ron likes to go ugly early," is one explanation, or "Ron's definition of a Perfect Ten is five Twos." Raven mythology apart, the name has nothing to do with Rinehart's sexual predilections, but hails from the early days of Vietnam when fighter pilots called each other by it as a form of affectionate combat abuse. Rinehart had bought two suckling pigs, dressed them up in blue ribbons, and presented them to a group of F-105 pilots during the O club's happy hour, bearing the Latin tag *Ad Fornicatorum Porci*—"To the Pig Fuckers." The joke boomeranged when Rinehart got stuck with the name for the rest of his Air Force career.)

Like every other boy of his generation in the Ohio farm belt, Rinehart always dreamed of becoming a soldier. He liked to play the country-boy role to the hilt, but behind it there was a shrewd intelligence and a sensitivity he was careful not to show. Papa Fox had more in common with the man he followed than appearances indicated. Among other things, he was fearless.

Apart from Papa Fox's warlike qualities, he could also cook like a dream. Instead of downing their indigestible diet of greasy hamburgers, or the gristle, grass, and rice dinners at the general's house, the Ravens now began to feast on lobsters, homemade spring or cabbage rolls, wonderful baked pies, and lavish Chinese dinners—all supplemented with delicacies stolen from the CIA kitchen. Although Papa Fox flew combat all day, he never shirked cooking dinner—on the single condition that he not be expected to do dishes. The Ravens considered this an excellent arrangement, happily donning the washing-up apron on a rotating basis. (Papa Fox also excelled at combat fire-starting. This consisted of filling a mail sack with wood stolen from Air America, spilling liberal amounts of aviation fuel—av gas—onto it, and then lighting the explosive combination with a match thrown from four feet. The shutters of the windows would shake and the door fly open, and people would pour into the street thinking the hootch had exploded. "It impressed the Thai pilots.")

Papa Fox had arrived at the beginning of Gen. Vang Pao's new push to retake the mountain of Phou Pha Thi. The general felt that the entire future of the Meo depended on the recapture of the mountain, and he intended to commit more than half his army to the task. His closest counselor, Pop Buell, advised him against such a course, arguing that his soldiers were bone-tired and their morale was so low "a dog couldn't sniff it."

But the general remained adamant. "I must have a big victory to stop the Vietminh now, before they take everything. My people need a victory. The Rock is important to them."[14]

Dick Shubert was now FAC commander at Long Tieng, and Rinehart joined John Mansur and Paul Merrick to make the fourth Raven. After a single day's flight around the surrounding countryside, he was let loose with a Backseater. The push to retake Phou Pha Thi became his responsibility and was code-named Operation Pig Fat.

The Meo staged out of Na Khang (Site 36) and moved into attack positions on three sides of the mountain. Jets pounded the enemy with endless sorties and vast amounts of bombs, but they did not budge. The Meo attempted to move artillery into firing positions and prepared for a coordinated air mobile and Special Guerrilla Unit ground assault, but came under heavy mortar attack. There were no more than three hundred enemy soldiers on the mountain, but while bombing kept their heads down momentarily, they would emerge from their bunkers and machine-gun pits after every raid to drive back wave after wave of Meo infantry.

Rinehart put in more than a thousand air sorties of U.S., Lao, and Meo air in a month, logging 280 combat hours. Some days he spent as much as fourteen hours in the cockpit. Fighters came on station in waves, and would be stacked above him in a holding pattern six layers high. The windows on both sides of the Bird Dog were covered in grease pencil where he had tried to keep track of the ceaseless strikes, fighter call signs, and bomb damage. Back at Na Khang, between missions, he helped pump his own gas and load rockets.

The North Vietnamese held on. Meo casualties were appalling. Air losses seemed to be concentrated into black days: in one four-hour period a Phantom flew straight into the mountain in a screaming forty-five-degree-angle dive, a Skyraider was hit by antiaircraft fire, and a helicopter attempting to rescue it was shot down. On another day two Thuds (F-105s) and a helicopter were lost to enemy action.

Rinehart himself was forced to stay overlong on station to direct the stacked fighters until he almost ran out of gas. He nursed the spluttering O-1 back to Na Khang, while U Va Lee cursed him from the backseat. Rinehart had waited until the last moment to return, and as he touched down on the runway the engine quit. The men were forced to push the plane off the runway and into the gas pit.

It was the third time a plane had stalled on Rinehart when U Va Lee was in the backseat, and the Indian had had enough. He refused to go up the following day. "I no fly with you. You try kill me."

Rinehart began to work with another Backseater nicknamed Scar— so called because of the long, jagged scar down his neck. Scar had a deep voice and a throaty chuckle. Together they worked an area to the east of Long Tieng, where Lee Lue liked to fly, and the trio became a close team. But however much they flew, and however many air strikes were put in, the Meo made no headway.

Back on the ground, base commander U Va Lee was at his most unforgiving. A young Meo commander, no more than twelve years old, staggered into Na Khang from the field, leading a dozen of his surviving troops, who were even younger than he was. He had lost his outpost during the night, and U Va Lee berated him in a furious tirade which made the boy cringe. Two Pathet Lao prisoners were interrogated and then summarily executed.

Rinehart continued to fly. During one flight a bullet came through the floor of the plane, directly in front of the stick and between his legs: "It got my attention." It was a close call, but he continued to zig-zag through small-arms fire at three hundred feet, impervious to danger, a habit which made Backseaters extremely reluctant to fly with him. Only Scar would accompany him, chuckling to himself amid the bullets and smoke of battle, which seemed to appeal to some dark sense of fun.

At the end of the month, Papa Fox was given two days off and flew down to Udorn to relax. Ravens never had to buy a drink at the O club, and the F-4 jocks threw a party for him. Papa Fox's dress for the evening was exotic: alligator shoes, sharkskin pants, and an embroidered *Farang Tagalog* Filipino dress shirt. "A nice outfit."

Drink followed drink, until Rinehart was linking arms with the Phantom jocks to make a MiG sweep along the bar. This consisted of yelling "MiG sweep" very loudly, charging along the face of the bar, and running over anyone who stood in the way. A colonel who was slow to move was trampled underfoot. He did not appreciate being knocked to the ground by a drunken redheaded civilian dressed like a Filipino pimp. The colonel wanted Rinehart thrown out of the club, until someone muttered in his ear, "He's a Raven, sir." The colonel grunted and let the matter drop. Exceptions were made for people whose behavior was warped by a solid month of twelve-hour days in the combat zone.

The following morning Papa Fox was on his way to reintroduce himself to the Thai girls who worked in his favorite bathhouse when there was an urgent call for him to return to Alternate. A new Bird Dog, earmarked for the Ravens, was sitting on the ramp at Udorn and was needed at the front. Papa Fox was ordered to ferry it back immediately. Still dressed in his fashionable attire, he boarded the O-1 and flew up to Long Tieng, only to find the base weathered in. He made a detour and landed at Na Khang to pick up a Backseater. Scar was unavailable, and those who knew Papa Fox were in hiding. U Va Lee refused to go himself, but provided an unsuspecting and smiling innocent who clambered into the plane.

They flew up to an area in northwest Laos, near the Chinese border, where they were fired upon. Papa Fox spent the morning putting in strikes on the gun. On the way home he took the plane over a mountain ridge where a single shell ripped into the engine. It stopped dead. The Backseater began to moan quietly to himself in terror. Papa Fox looked below him for somewhere to crash-land and spotted two small rice paddies at the end of a valley. He began to spiral down toward them, while the procedures learned at the various survival schools clicked into place. He immediately called Cricket, giving his position and where he intended to put the plane down. Then he called Air America and gave them the same information.

The Backseater had become absolutely quiet, resigned to his fate, convinced that when a plane crashed life ended. He had abandoned hope the moment the engine quit. Papa Fox concentrated on the landing and slammed the Bird Dog into the paddy. It was too short; the landing gear hit the dike and the nose lifted high into the air. Rinehart's legs flew up and hit the instrument panel, cutting him in several places.

The plane settled back into the paddy. Both men were alive. The Backseater was rapturous and now looked upon Papa Fox as a man before whom Death itself had retreated. He threw his arms around

Rinehart and began to hug and kiss him. "You number one. You Buddha."

The excitement was short-lived. A large number of enemy troops opened fire from a treeline only a quarter of a mile away. Papa Fox grabbed hold of the Backseater and together they ran into the jungle, where they fought their way through the undergrowth.

After running wildly for several minutes, Papa Fox took hold of his companion by the shoulders and made him sit down. They were both breathing heavily and adrenaline was pumping through their bodies. It was important to calm down and form a plan. In the distance they could hear the enemy shooting, but Papa Fox knew they were firing blindly.

He examined the circumstances. Dressed in his Sunday best, he was stranded in the middle of the jungle without maps, a gun, a survival kit, or a radio, and only a pair of alligator shoes to get him out. The Backseater carried a handgun but nothing more. Both men emptied their pockets: a belt buckle, a watch, and a few coins—scant defenses against a battalion of North Vietnamese. They also had no food and no water.

Papa Fox could hear the enemy moving up the trail behind them, and the sound of gunfire grew louder. The two men picked their way painfully through the trees, edging toward the top of the mountain. Papa Fox caught sight of the search-and-rescue aircraft overhead— two A-1 Skyraiders and a Jolly Green rescue helicopter—but knew the Air Force would never undertake a pickup without proper radio contact to establish the authenticity of codes. Their only hope was Air America.

About a quarter of a mile from the top of the mountain the terrain changed suddenly from thick forest to open, head-high elephant grass dotted with clumps of tall bamboo. It was slow work pushing through the bush. After twenty minutes Papa Fox stopped beside a clump of bamboo which had grown to a height of thirty feet. He took off his exotic shirt and made a bamboo frame over which to stretch it. He pulled the tall bamboo cane down and attached his shirt to the end, then hoisted it like a flag on a pole. An Air America chopper was continuing to scour the mountains around the downed plane, half a mile away, while the Skyraiders droned up and down the valley.

"See him?" Papa Fox said to his companion. "He find us. No problem."

The Meo looked at Papa Fox, now stripped to the waist to expose a creamy white torso speckled with ginger hair and freckles, and nodded without conviction. The two men took it in turns to wave the bamboo from side to side in an attempt to attract attention.

They waved their makeshift flagpole for thirty minutes without result, until at 6:00 the sun began to set. A Skyraider was still in the valley, then turned and flew by their mountaintop. Papa Fox's spirits rose, only to slump further when the plane passed overhead without seeing them.

The planes had been searching for an hour and a half and had not found them. The sun had set and it was beginning to grow dark. Papa Fox began to accept that they would not be rescued and to formulate another plan of escape. As an old farm boy and a survivor, he told himself, he could walk the three hundred miles back to safety. Once it was truly dark he would climb to the top of the hill and keep on going, traveling by night and navigating by the stars. They could sleep in hiding during the day.

"Don't you worry," Papa Fox assured his Meo companion. "I'll get us out of here."

Just when hope was failing with the last light, the Air America chopper flew over the mountaintop on its way home. Papa Fox waved the flagpole in a final desperate effort to attract attention. The chopper banked steeply, and turned around on itself. They had been seen. The Meo was ecstatic, cured of his temporary lapse of faith in his ginger godhead, and threw himself on his savior, kissing and hugging him.

The Air America pilot hovered overhead and signaled for them to head up to the very top of the mountain. They battled through the elephant grass, which was eight feet high, wide as a man's hand, and sharp as a knife. It was a punishing last haul. Papa Fox could see nothing, but kept climbing toward the noise of the rotors. At the top of the mountain they were rewarded by the wonderful sight of the Air America chopper dropping into the grass. The pilot brought the aircraft down slowly, the pressure from the rotor blades partially flattening the tall grass, until he hovered only a couple of feet from the ground. Papa Fox clambered aboard, hauling his Meo companion up after him.

"Number one," the Meo cried with tears in his eyes, hugging Papa Fox close to him. "Buddha."

The chopper lifted into the dark and headed back to Na Khang. Papa Fox drank two full canteens of water on the trip. Back at the site he prepared to hop off. "You okay, Raven?" the pilot asked.

"Yeah. Thanks."

Papa Fox jumped down from the aircraft, accompanied by his worshipful companion. The Air America bird lifted off to fly south and had gone before Rinehart was able to ask the name of the man who had saved his life. He was never to learn it.

He hitched a lift on a plane heading back to Alternate. Once in the Raven hootch he decided he would write down every detail of his experience and sat at a table, pencil in hand. It had been quite a day, and he wondered where he should begin. Without warning, he began to shake uncontrollably. Until that moment he had felt in complete command of his actions and had been too busy to be scared. Now he could not even hold a pencil.

He got up and went to the bar, where he poured himself a stiff whisky. Two Ravens sitting by the fire, unaware of what had happened, wondered why dinner was behind schedule. "It's kind of late. Aren't you going to cook?"

"I guess so," Papa Fox said, and went into the kitchen to prepare supper.

At the beginning of Operation Pig Fat, President Johnson had announced that as of November 1, 1968, "all air, naval, and artillery bombardment of North Vietnam" would be stopped. The partial bombing halt in March had already made more sorties available for Laos, but now U.S. airplanes arrived in swarms.

There was no lack of targets, but with only four Ravens to cover the whole of northeast Laos it was impossible to control the number of airplanes. "They had all that capacity in Thailand, so they put it to use in Laos," Tom Shera said. It was as if a business decision had been made to use idle assets. "There were plenty of targets, but we didn't have enough FACs to use that much air. Many times we got so much air we couldn't handle it at all. Even before the bombing halt there were times when the weather was so bad over North Vietnam that they would come back in waves. They were damn near out of gas and they wanted to make one pass and get rid of their bombs. You would try and pre-position yourself, but often you ended up doing saturation bombing in the area you happened to be at the time the first flight got in. Because you might not have had time to get to where you *really* wanted to be.

"It seemed like there was always a conflict for the air. When the ground forces were moving and we needed air to support them often we didn't get it."

On one occasion Shera put in forty-eight sorties on one marking rocket. The instructions from Cricket had been explicit. "Launch Raven, the weather's bad and we've gotta dump this stuff. We gotta get it in someplace."

Shera headed north to a place he thought really needed it, but the fighters came on station before he arrived. He ended up putting strike after strike every five hundred meters along a ridgeline dotted with enemy reinforcements. "I could really have used those fighters if I had been in position and wrought havoc. I was completely out of position. The alternative was that those guys would go and dump those bombs on the range in Thailand."

The few Ravens available to control the air war were further hampered by not having enough planes. If an O-1 was down from battle damage or in for maintenance, Ravens flew as copilots in Air America or Continental Air Services aircraft, a procedure so illegal it would have given the Downtowners conniptions.

Maintenance and support were still only mediocre at best. Papa Fox, who by now had become chief Raven at Long Tieng, attempted to continue the work begun by Tom Richards (who had left the country on completion of his tour) in gaining increased recognition and support for the program. But where Richards had used his comparatively high rank, combined with a sophisticated, diplomatic approach, Papa Fox resorted to nose-to-nose confrontation and the raised voice.

Persistent engine failures had continued to undermine Raven confidence. Almost every day there was a story of some pilot coaxing a plane back into a remote strip. Papa Fox's patience finally ran out when he had four engine failures in a week. "We had a U-17 that every time you turned around you were horsing into another field. It would run and then quit, run a little bit more, and so on. And the O-1s, some of which were almost twenty years old, were doing the same thing." The mechanics who worked on them were passing them after a ground-check inspection—instead of a test flight, which involved a certain amount of risk. The corner-cutting resulted in further engine failures.

"That's it," he announced furiously. "I'm grounding the airplanes."

In effect, the Ravens were on strike and the air war in Laos came to an abrupt halt. Papa Fox went back to the hootch and spent the rest of the afternoon reading. The next morning the Ravens would have been in the air by 6:00, but Papa Fox advised his colleagues to sleep late and enjoy the sumptuous breakfast he intended to prepare. Late in the morning a message came through from the embassy demanding to know why the Ravens were not in the air.

"Be advised airplanes grounded," Papa Fox replied.

A terse message came back from the assistant air attaché, Lt. Col. Gus Sonnenberg—the air attaché himself was still unaware of the problem at this stage—that Rinehart did not have the authority to ground the airplanes. "If I don't have the authority to ground the airplanes, why aren't they flying?" Rinehart replied.

There was no more cable traffic. Things became very quiet. The Ravens stayed in their hootch throwing darts and reading magazines. That night Papa Fox spoke to Vang Pao and explained what was happening: the indifference of the embassy, the negligence of the Air Force in Udorn, and the poor maintenance provided by Air America were going to result in getting Ravens killed. Therefore, the airplanes were grounded until the Ravens received the support they needed. The general listened and nodded.

To Papa Fox's amazement he was supported in his action by the air attaché himself, Col. Robert Tyrrell, who ordered him to attend a meeting in Udorn to present his case. It was an intimidating group to face: twenty high-ranking officers, including two generals, were seated around the table.

Papa Fox listed the twenty-six engine failures which had occurred in the previous three months, and explained what he felt was needed to correct the haphazard maintenance. He complained of a complete lack of logistical support from the embassy.

The assistant air attaché, Sonnenberg, interrupted to assure everyone that the air attaché's office in Vientiane gave every assistance in its power to the program at all times. His speech was cut short by an emotional Papa Fox: "You're full of shit!"

A general raised his voice to suggest that there was nothing wrong with the airplanes, and that Air America maintained them just fine—it was the way these cowboy FACs flew the damn things.

"You don't know what you're talking about," Papa Fox exploded. "You want to come up and fly with us sometime and see how we do things. We are in enemy territory ninety-nine percent of the time that we are airborne. You can't expect people to fly around in that environment with airplanes that are cutting in and out all the goddam time."

People began to shout, including the Air America maintenance manager imprudently defending the record of his mechanics. Papa Fox continued to dominate the meeting by shouting louder than anyone else. As the battle raged, Colonel Tyrrell sat quietly to one side, saying nothing. By the time the meeting closed, Papa Fox had made his point—and annoyed a great many senior officers.

* * *

Improvements were made in the program. All of the Raven air-planes were rotated through Udorn and properly overhauled. Many of the O-1s had come from the Army, where they had been out in the field for years accumulating dirt in the fuel tanks. Some planes had two cups of mud extracted from each of their bladder tanks. New fil-ters and chamois strainers were put on the fuel buggies out in the field.

Most important of all, one of Air America's very best mechanics was permanently assigned to Long Tieng. Stan Wilson was a man after the Ravens' own heart—a mechanical whiz, with a wicked chuckle and a dry sense of humor. His idea of an afternoon off was to fly in the backseat of a T-28 on a combat mission. The Ravens called him "Clean" Stanley because he always seemed to be covered from head to foot in black grease. It was said of Stan Wilson that given a data plate, a set of knitting needles, and a ball of steel wool, he could knit an airplane.

He was working as Air America's chief mechanic at Savannakhet, in southern Laos, maintaining every type of airplane, when he received the call from Udorn to drop everything and join the Raven program. "We'll have a Volpar pick you up—you're going to Long Tieng to maintain O-1s."

"O-1s—what the hell for?" It seemed to Wilson that the O-1 could not possibly pose any special maintenance problems calling on his canny skills. But he flew up to Long Tieng and within hours had isolated the problem. Every one of the spotter planes had been tuned to fly out of Udorn—which is at sea level—while in northern Laos they operated out of strips three thousand to four thousand feet high. Although a pilot could adjust the mixture manually to some extent, a further carburetor adjustment was needed. It was a simple enough procedure. Wilson also found out that the mechanics who had been assigned to work on the Raven Bird Dogs had previously maintained B-52 bombers.

It took Clean Stanley an afternoon to overhaul the nine planes used by the Long Tieng Ravens, and when he was finished he took each one up for a test flight. The program never had to worry about faulty maintenance again. If Stan Wilson signed his name in the log book, he was prepared to fly the plane. The team of mechanics eventually gathered to work on the Ravens' planes was first rate. (Frank Shaw, a twenty-year-old Air Force enlisted man in the "black," became "line chief." He was discovered on several occasions by the Ravens, as they went to their planes at dawn, asleep uncovered on the gravel beneath the wing of an O-1 to be there at takeoff to check that all the birds were ready to go. He worked for a year straight with no time off, refusing all offers of R&R, and saved at least one Raven's life when he disarmed a sabotaged T-28.) Superb maintenance gave the Ravens back their confidence.

The air attaché's office also responded to Papa Fox's emotional plea by imposing more rules. Combat-fatigued Ravens who shouted down generals were a rude shock to the tranquillity of life behind the lines, so new limits were set on the hours they were allowed to fly. No Raven was to be permitted to fly more than 180 hours a month (although this was considerably more than the standard 80 hours a month permitted by the Air Force for pilots outside of Laos; a pilot was allowed to fly 110 hours with a waiver, as long as he did not exceed 240 in a quarter). The rule was more or less ignored from the very first day until the end of the war.

After the Udorn meeting, Papa Fox reported to the air attaché's office in Vientiane on his way back to Alternate. "Listen, we've been doing some thinking," he was told by Gus Sonnenberg. "You're a little bit tired and we're going to switch you around. Why don't you go on up and get your stuff and come back down and we'll decide what to do with you."

Fuck it, Papa Fox thought to himself, I'm fired. He flew to Alternate, arriving at the base at 5:00 in the evening. He figured he just had time for one last mission. He took an O-1 out to the east, where he found two trucks and a bulldozer. He called Cricket for air, only to be told that nothing was available. "I'll see you at first light," Papa Fox said. "Have two sets of fighters ready and waiting."

The next morning the mission went like clockwork. Papa Fox put four sets of fighters on the target and destroyed the trucks and bulldozer. Cricket fed the bomb damage assessment through to the air attaché's office, and within minutes the wires began to burn. "Tell Raven 44 he is to land *immediately*. He is to report to this station *immediately*."

Papa Fox returned to Alternate and closed down the O-1 and did not fly again. That night he was guest of honor at dinner with Gen. Vang Pao, who sat him on his right in recognition of destroying the bulldozer. Papa Fox pointed out the irony of the honor to the general, telling him that he had been called back to Vientiane. "Because of what happened they make me go down now. Fly for you no more. They take me away."

"Aah, Raven 44—you worry too much," the general said jovially. "You go down. I take care of you."

"I don't think it's going to work, sir."

"No problem. You go down. Enjoy little bit. I take care of you."

The general sliced off the ear of the pig and handed it to Papa Fox as guest of honor. He spent the entire dinner cutting off small pieces and nibbling them for several minutes before subtly disgorging them into his napkin. ("The more you chew on a pig's ear, the bigger it gets.")

The next day he returned to Vientiane and went to stay in the Ice House. He was largely ignored by the Downtowners who gathered for dinner. No one seemed interested in the war, and the conversation was about promotion possibilities, laced with mildly bitchy gossip about colleagues. Papa Fox, who had been flying for twelve hours a day and whose only subject of conversation was the war, said nothing. The Downtowners suffered his company, and charged him seven dollars a day for bed and board. At dinner on the third day Sonnenberg turned to him and said, "We've been thinking about all this. We're going to send you back to Alternate."

The general had his way, and Papa Fox returned to Long Tieng.

By Thanksgiving of 1968, despite all of Vang Pao's most confident predictions, the Meo had still not taken Phou Pha Thi or even managed to scale the lower reaches of the mountain. The plan itself was a disastrous departure from the type of war they excelled in. Instead of damaging the North Vietnamese in hit-and-run guerrilla operations, they had become conventional infantry, attempting to attack well-fortified and heavily defended positions. They proved unequal to the task, and casualties were high.

On Thanksgiving Day itself, Papa Fox returned to Alternate, after flying only six hours of combat, in order to prepare dinner. He had already baked homemade pumpkin and mince pies, and now set to work cooking the turkeys, which had been sent up from the commissary in Vientiane and would be served with mashed potatoes, scalloped corn, and gravy. The Air Commandos had sent up two jeroboams of champagne with which to wash the feast down. Bob Tyrrell, the air attaché, flew up to join the Ravens, expecting a meager battlefront lunch, only to find himself feasting as if he were at home in the States.

Gen. Vang Pao stayed at the front. He had originally resisted moving six thousand refugees of his own people, afraid that if his soldiers saw the evacuation they would interpret it as acceptance of defeat. Now, although still speaking of victory, he asked Pop Buell to go ahead.

The war was going badly, and morale among the Meo was low. The Ravens began to believe that skill counted for little in the face of the endless hours they were obliged to fly. They were in the power of sheer, blind luck. Each flight was another exhausted spin of war's wheel of fortune, and every extra day shortened the odds of survival.

The endless combat flying was taking its toll on one Raven after another. It was usual to send a pilot suffering from burnout south. After months of hard flying at Alternate, Ed McBride, known as "Hoss" because of his huge, lumbering, Mississippi country-boy frame, had retired to Savannakhet, a quiet provincial capital situated on the Mekong, just across from the Thai border.

It was thought he needed an extended period of comparative calm to wind down. After Alternate, Savannakhet was the next best thing to R&R the program had to offer. Although the Royal Lao Air Force was headquartered in the town, there was not much war to speak of. Ravens stationed there never went as far east as the Trail. The Royal Lao Army and their Pathet Lao enemy seemed to acknowledge an unwritten gentlemen's stand-off.

Hoss, who wore a ten-gallon hat and carried a guitar, was a favorite among the locals, not least because of his famed "candy" runs. Flying over a village, he would bring his plane down low and buzz the main street, tossing candy and gum out the window to the kids. Bored patrols of friendly troops, meticulously avoiding the enemy, had their day brightened by one of Hoss's candy runs.

To the east of the city there was a large collapsed bridge that had once spanned the river and carried a major north-south highway. Traffic now forded low-water crossings on either side of the bridge, and Hoss often flew out there, together with a Backseater, to check for possible enemy truck tracks. Close to the bridge he saw a large column of troops crossing a field. The fact that they were in the open and did not scatter at the sight of a plane strongly suggested they were friendly. Hoss flew by and waved, and, sure enough, the troops waved back. He picked up the large sack of chocolate, hard candy, and gum and placed it on his lap so he could throw candy out the window by the fistful. He was perfectly positioned for a run, which would take him directly over the soldiers' heads.

It all happened so quickly that perhaps Hoss McBride never realized the troops below him were North Vietnamese regulars. Droning a few feet above them, one hand in the bag of candy, he was a sitting target. The soldiers opened fire and a single round of .30 caliber hit Hoss in the armpit and traveled through to his chest. The plane crashed upside down in a nearby river. Hoss's death, the Ravens agreed, was sheer bad luck.[15]

Luck follows no logic, a circumstance which creates faith or anxiety. There were Ravens who flew through clouds of flak unscathed, and who walked away unharmed from the burning hulks of crashed planes. Other men, flying high in a quiet area, were killed by a single bullet. Some were reckless to the point of absurdity and never took a hit; others were killed while religiously following all of the rules. Experienced old heads got killed in their last week; FNGs got killed in their first. Luck began to seem as mysterious as the spark of life itself.

John Mansur had become almost punch-drunk from flying combat missions out of Alternate and had begun to feel impervious to danger, but some hidden fear suddenly made him decide to wear his helmet. Ravens never wore the armored helmets they were provided with, partly because they were awkward and heavy, but mostly because it was impossible to hear ground fire in one. But Mansur, who had never worn one before, arbitrarily decided that for this particular mission he would wear the helmet.

He flew to Roadrunner Lake to check out the Chinese Cultural Mission at Khang Khay. The CIA had received ground team reports that the enemy had moved large, heavy artillery pieces into town as a prelude to moving them into position under cover of darkness, and wanted the intelligence checked. The high-level recon planes that flew out of Udorn were not available, so Mansur decided to go in low and have a look himself. It was a foolhardy decision, but he knew the positions of the various 37mm antiaircraft guns and calculated he could fly so low that the gunners would be unable to depress their weapons sufficiently to shoot at him. He rolled the plane up to the edge of the town, and as he banked and peered down, he felt a terrific blow to the helmet. He had forgotten the most obvious thing in his foxy calculations—he was so low a soldier with a pistol could hit him.

A single bullet had come through the open window of the cockpit and entered Mansur's helmet. Suddenly he couldn't see, and his first thought was that he had been shot in the eyes. He raised the visor of his helmet and felt blood pour down his face. "Oh my God, I'm blind."

Instinct alone had kept him from losing control of the plane in the first seconds of his blindness and crashing into the ground in what was known among pilots as a graveyard spiral. He rolled out and began to climb, making himself an even easier target for the enemy, whom he could now hear shooting at him. Fighting off panic, and deathly afraid, he called Air America and said he had been hit and could not see. Almost immediately the pilot of a Pilatus Porter came up on the frequency. He was calm and soothing, and his voice amid the gunfire was balm to Mansur's shot nerves. "Well, hello, Raven—looks like you've got yourself a real problem."

The Porter was only a mile away and flew toward Mansur until the plane was on his tail. Then with a casual, almost jovial sangfroid, the pilot talked him away from the danger of the enemy guns and put him on a course for Alternate. "Turn right—little bit more—stick forward—easy, easy—that's it."

On the approach to the strip at Alternate, Mansur could dimly make out shapes from one eye, although the pain was as if they had both been scoured with fine sand. The Porter pilot talked him down, and he made a good landing. His crew chief and the radio operator who had monitored his flight back were on the strip to meet him in a jeep. They dragged him from the plane, thinking he had been shot and wounded in the torso, and raced to a Jolly Green helicopter that was waiting at the end of the runway with its engine cranked, ready to medevac him to Udorn. Throughout the short trip a medic continually bathed his eyes with water.

On arrival he was rushed to hospital, where he was placed in a dentist's chair and a doctor picked splintered glass from his eyes for an hour. He could scarcely see and was in great pain, but knew he was not blind.

During his recuperation the various fighter squadrons on the base treated him like a hero, and pilots volunteered to act as guide dogs and lead him around. The bullet had entered the helmet, traveled around the inside of the visor, shaving glass fragments into both his eyes, and come out the other side. The concussion of the bullet hitting the helmet had blacked both his eyes.

The helmet was brought down and presented to him as a war trophy. When he placed it on his head a pencil could be passed through one bullet hole to the other so that it touched the hair on the bridge of his nose. Had he leaned forward one thousandth of an inch during the moment the bullet hit it would have taken his nose off; any more and he would have been killed outright. But, as the other Ravens never tired of telling him, if he had not been wearing the damned silly helmet in the first place, everybody would have been saved an awful lot of trouble.

The patches remained on his eyes for a week. After a second week he reported to Vientiane for duty. The staffers in the air attaché's office were sympathetic. "Do you want to go back north or do you think you've used up your luck up there?"

"I guess I've used up my luck."

The Meo attack on Phou Pha Thi, despite the massive bombing campaign to support it, finally floundered and failed. Bombing had destroyed the guns defending the airstrip at the base of the mountain, which the Meo subsequently recaptured, but after three weeks of constant fighting only one company had managed to gain a foothold on the middle slopes. They lasted a day and withdrew under withering fire from the stone bunkers at the crest of the mountain.

The six thousand refugees had already been evacuated, a considerable feat in itself, but Gen. Vang Pao stubbornly continued to launch wave after wave of his men against the Rock. He still spoke of victory, but now admitted it would take time.

On Christmas Day, 1968, three fresh Communist battalions launched a counterattack and the Meo fell back to Na Khang. Vang Pao had gambled so heavily on winning back the sacred mountain, staked so many of his men's lives, and his own reputation as a leader and general, on victory, that the defeat was devastating. Its effect on the morale of the Meo and the Ravens was terrible enough, but on the general himself it was catastrophic.

Pop Buell drove over the mountain from Sam Thong to Alternate to join Vang Pao for dinner. Instead of the usual great gathering of officers and elders in the large dining room, Pop found the general quite alone. He was dressed like a derelict in rumpled clothes.

"Where is everybody?" Pop asked.

"They are afraid to come here. Afraid to be with me. I have lost face with my people. I have lost face with the world."

Pop tried to comfort Vang Pao with his usual brand of homespun philosophy and earthy optimism, but the general was beyond consolation. The best of his men were dead, he said, his army was mostly made up of twelve-year-olds. Many of his soldiers did not live long enough even to learn fear. After nine years of constant war, victory was as far away as ever. It was an age-old Meo saying that there was always another mountain, but they were running out of mountains, and Vang Pao foresaw a day when his entire people would be forced to flee the country to live as unwanted refugees.

"I am the Meo general Vang Pao. The king of Laos believed in me. Prince Souvanna Phouma believed in me. They took me, a Meo peasant, into the king's own council. Now I have been defeated. I am no longer the great Meo general." For the first time in his adult life, Gen. Vang Pao wept.

5

THE BIG PICTURE

A Raven viewed the war through the narrow windows of his airplane. Hung above the battle, he observed a larger scene than the fragmentary chaos seen by the soldier on the ground, but fundamentally shared much the same experience of it: smoke and noise, gunfire and flame, underpinned by a constant dull fear, occasionally relieved by rushes of intense excitement or moments of terror. At the end of a day of battle he was left with an overwhelming sense of universal muddle.

It was with a somewhat patronizing air that the Ravens' ideas for improving performance, or complaints about the way things were being done, were met by those higher up the chain of command. The men at the air attaché's office in Vientiane, the CIA planners, and the hordes of noncombatant Downtowners at the embassy all had the same answer when confronted by exasperated and exhausted Ravens: they simply did not understand the Big Picture.

It was true enough. All of the killing and being killed clouded their perspective. The endless demands of combat limited their vision so that the Ravens never did get a clear look at the Big Picture.

This was, at best, a surreal dreamlike work; at worst it was a nightmare piece in the style of Hieronymus Bosch. The Americans looked upon the Big Picture from afar—and Washington, D.C., was about as far away from the mountains and jungle of Laos as it was possible to be. There had been a period when trouble in this tiny country had moved it briefly to the center of the picture, when the superpowers clashed, but this had been resolved by the Geneva

Accord of 1962, which recognized the neutrality of Laos and forbade the presence of foreign military personnel in it.

The North Vietnamese, being closer, had a different view of the Big Picture. Like the Americans, they saw it in a gallery of distorting mirrors, for they too had agreed to the terms of the document drawn up in Geneva, in which they solemnly pronounced they had no troops fighting in Laos. At a stroke, tens of thousands of their regular soldiers were turned into phantoms. The principal difference between these two adversaries was that the North Vietnamese had a very clear view of exactly what the Big Picture would look like when the mirrors were removed. They intended to fight the Americans as they had fought the French before them, across the whole of Indochina—with the ultimate aim of installing Communist regimes in South Vietnam, Laos, and Cambodia (a goal set by Ho Chi Minh when he founded the Indochinese Communist Party in Hong Kong in 1929, and which the West had confirmed at least as early as 1952, when the French Expeditionary Corps captured secret Vietnamese Communist Party documents).[1]

The Ravens knew nothing of all this. In Vientiane the war was seen by foreign diplomats as a Chinese opera: often violent, somewhat amusing, and altogether mystifying. In an attempt to supplement the original sketchy briefing, new Ravens picked up what they could about Laos from colleagues, and a handful read the few works written in English about the country, a narrow shelf of books indeed.

It was in keeping with the arbitrary nature of things in Laos, however, that one or two Ravens who passed through Vientiane were given the lengthy and luxurious education of a Jungle John briefing. Jungle John was the nickname of Maj. John Garritty, one of the intelligence officers in the air attaché's office, a member of the so-called Gray Team. (The White Team consisted of Americans officially assigned to the country; the Black Team was made up of those men who were not supposed to be in Laos at all; the Gray Team consisted of Air Force and other military personnel who ran the operations command post.) Garritty, an Air Commando who had been posted to the country as one of the original Butterfly FACs preceding the Ravens, had been in Laos for many years. Although not a pilot himself, Garritty was the onetime world record holder for an altitude parachute jump, an achievement which earned him the respect of fellow adventurers. He loved Laos and its people and felt the battle to save it from the North Vietnamese Communists to be a crusade of the righteous. The briefings he gave were off-the-cuff, impromptu talks of an informal, highly personal nature, but if he saw he had captured the imagination of his audience they could last three hours.

Garritty conducted the briefings in his own way and at his own pace, his feet up on his desk and a cigarette in his mouth. Once he began, the only other sound in the room was the rattle of the air conditioning. As the briefing progressed through the hot afternoon, sunlight filtered through the shuttered blinds at such an angle that it threw beams of dust particles across the room—a setting which might have been especially designed to enthrall young romantics. However jaundiced a pilot might have become through his experience in Vietnam, by the time he left Jungle John's office he wanted to put on a Laotian uniform and go to war.

"Welcome, gentlemen, to the Kingdom of Lan Xang—the Land of a Million Elephants," Major Garritty began. "You have stepped through the looking glass into a magical place inhabited by a gentle race sadly trapped in a life-and-death struggle not of your making. Imagine, if you will, a comic opera by Gilbert and Sullivan, with splashes of blood." What came next was a lyrical description of the country and its people, a capsule version of Laotian history, and an honest attempt to explain the convoluted, mad-hatter politics of the place.[2]

It was the misfortune of weak, landlocked, peaceful Laos to lie between powerful, perpetually warring neighbors. It holds a key position in Indochina—a Yale key, Ravens thought, looking at it on the map. In the north its borders are merely the work of a cartographer, for its wild mountain terrain is not policed and its people wander across the international borders with Burma and China unaware of their existence. To the south is Cambodia, to the west Thailand, and to the east the country shares a 1,324-mile-long border with Vietnam.

The border with Thailand is largely drawn by the Mekong, which flows from the high Tibetan plateau in China down through deep gorges and into the plains. It is here that more than half the population live, the lowland Lao or Lao Loum, who are ethnically indistinguishable from the population of northeast Thailand and who also follow the same gentle teachings of Theravada Buddhism. The remainder of Laos's population is made up of a variety of tribes who are animists.

The war the Ravens were about to join was the latest chapter in a story of conflict spanning a thousand years. It was a case in which a superpower, ideological conflict had become imposed on an historical one. The battle, beneath all the complex and tortured politics, was over land. Indochina was locked into a continual struggle between the Indian-influenced kingdoms to the south and west of the Annamite mountains and the sinicized Vietnamese. The tolerant, gentler people exposed to Hindu culture were forced to resist the austere, expansionist Vietnamese who had forever been pressing forward from the overcrowded delta of Tonkin in search of new lands. Driven by the needs of a large population and the logic of geography, the Vietnamese clamored ceaselessly for living space. They were resisted by neighbors who feared domination and possible extinction. After thirty generations the enmity was set.

Laos became a political entity in the ninth century and reached its apogee in the eighteenth century, when the kingdom of Lan Xang included regions of Yunnan (China), the Shan States (Burma), parts of the Vietnamese and Cambodian plateau, and large stretches of modern northeastern Thailand. But in less than a century, feudal rivalries, fed by the outside, split the country into three kingdoms: Luang Prabang in the north, the country around Vientiane, and Champassac, in the southern panhandle.

The mountain chains and jungle of Vietnam shielded Laos for a while from her expansionist neighbor, already pushing westward, however. But the open plains of the Mekong valley were an open invitation to the attackers from the growing Siamese state, which also wanted control over Laos to defend itself against Vietnam. The Siamese destroyed the kingdom of Vientiane in 1828, and soon afterward the whole of Laos was split between Siamese and Vietnamese spheres of influence. By the middle of the nineteenth century the peoples of Vietnam and Siam faced each other across the territory that is now Laos and Cambodia. The old Meo mountain states, such as Xieng Khouang, maintained a subject independence by paying tribute to both of their mighty neighbors.

But in 1832 Xieng Khouang was annexed by the Vietnamese when an armed force seized the king and took him back to Hue, where he was publicly executed. The little kingdom became a prefecture of the Empire of Annam, and its people were even forced to wear Vietnamese dress. Its rule was so harsh that there was a revolt in which the Vietnamese governor was killed. Order was soon restored, but hatred of the Vietnamese lingered.

The French conquest of Indochina brought an uneasy peace to the area, at a price. The Laotians greeted the new rulers with relief, and the imposition of French rule in 1887 guaranteed the country's

continued existence. Largely through ignorance, the French accepted the Mekong as the international boundary, with the result that the
most fertile part of the country became a permanent part of Thailand.
French colonial rule did little for the economic development or
education of the country outside of the cities, but it was largely
benign. There were only six hundred Frenchmen in Laos by 1940,
and the single action on their part that fomented rebellion was the
collection of taxes. Laos was allowed, for a brief spell in its troubled
history, to enjoy the drowsy, unworldly torpor of peace its people
seemed created for. Laos was poor—but it was a country where
poverty, not wealth, was admired. (The accumulation of wealth for
selfish ends results in a *loss* of prestige in Laos, so that it is not the
millionaire who is respected but the austere, spiritual man who
willingly embraces the most abject form of poverty.)

French colonial administrators sent to Laos felt they had been
posted to an earthly paradise. The tolerant, easy habits of the native
people and the slow, casual way they lived their lives had a charm
impossible to find anywhere else. The most commonly used phrase in
the language, *Bo pen nhang*, meaning "It doesn't matter," was spoken
with conviction as an article of faith. The women were beautiful,
warm, and uninhibited. In the hot summer months the whole country
sank into a siesta that lasted from after the midday meal until 5:00 in
the evening. Frenchmen who became immersed in Laotian life became a recognizable type. Their quiet, undemonstrative voices, calm
manner, and gentle, rapt expressions reminded one visiting writer
of the victims of successful lobotomy operations—untroubled and
mildly libidinous.[3]

French rule was interrupted by World War II, when—from the
Laotian point of view—the Japanese merely took the place of the
French for an interlude in which they were similarly benign in their
treatment of the subject nation. The defeat of Japan brought back
French colonial rule and also created a power vacuum they were
unable to fill, while the Vietnamese, more aggressive and ambitious
than ever, and doubled in number, once more became the danger.

In 1951 a new service was created by Marshal Jean de Lattre de
Tassigny, the best commander in chief of French forces in Indochina,
who planned to turn the Vietminh's skill in fighting behind the lines
against the Vietminh themselves by implanting anticommunist guerrillas deep inside enemy territory.

During a 1921 uprising of the Meo, which the French crushed, one
of the chiefs told a missionary: "They say we are a people who like to

fight, a cruel people, enemy of everybody, always changing our region and being happy nowhere. If you want to know the truth about our people, ask the bear who is hurt why he defends himself, ask the dog who is kicked why he barks, ask the deer who is chased why he changes mountains."[4]

The French began to understand that the best way to control the Meo was to leave them alone, or to help them actively defend themselves from their enemies. The French accurately saw the Meo as a kind of *maquis,* the French resistance movement that fought the Germans in occupied France in World War II. "A *maquisard* is an inhabitant who takes up arms in the region he lives to defend himself, his family, and his property," explained Colonel Roger Trinquier, the man chosen to recruit and lead these native movements.[5]

Although the *maquisards* were recruited from a variety of hill tribesmen, the greatest warriors were the Meo, a Mongolian race originating from China. They are the most mysterious of the twelve principal races of Indochina, because they have the least written about them and the least reliable history. Depending on an oral storytelling tradition—since they had no written language until recently—the Meo are content to propagate legends such as that they are a people who came out of China on a flying carpet. Other folk stories of eternal snows and arctic nights suggest they are of Eskimo origin. They have also been happy to allow outsiders to believe that they are werewolves, or can turn into tigers at will, and that they eat the livers of their slain enemies.

The first written reference to the Meo is in a Chinese text more than four thousand years old. The Chinese called them Miao, which means "barbarians" (the Meo returned the compliment by referring to the Chinese as "sons of dogs"). Revolt against imposed Chinese rule resulted in displays of the decapitated heads of the insurrectionary Meo leaders in wicker baskets. A large number of Meo moved into Laos in the mid-nineteenth century, driven south by competing Chinese opium farmers who destroyed their poppy fields. The Meo, who believed the world reached only as far as a man could walk, expanded their knowledge of the universe through these forced migrations.

The Meo inhabited only the mountain tops and, when forced to travel, moved through the lowland valley and plateaux without stopping. Obliged to move every ten to fifteen years because of their slash-and-burn style of agriculture, they edged slowly south, sweeping across the mountains like a blight. After first tasting the soil of a chosen site to see if it was sweet on the tongue—a test for lime content—the Meo were said to plow with fire and plant with the spear. By the time the Americans arrived in Laos, the Meo population—estimated to be between 300,000 and 500,000—were burning four hundred square miles of land a year, a figure which experts calculated would destroy the country's forests by the end of a century.

A Meo village is an authoritarian hierarchy, headed by the eldest male, although decisions are made after consultations with family heads. Their houses are primitive wooden structures, dark and airless, although tradition demands that a distant mountain be in view from the entrance. Meo women each wear several pounds of elaborately crafted silver, making them the most elegantly dressed but worst-housed people in the world. Babies wear silver necklaces after birth to indicate to the spirit world that they belong to a family and are not slaves.

The spirit world was enormously important to the Meo, who as animists believed that spirits—*phi*—lived in everything—mountains, rivers, animals, and people. Rainbows represent the spirit of the sky bending to drink; lightning occurs when the same spirit of the sky is angry. There were both good and bad *phi*, and a great deal of the Meo's time was spent consoling them with gifts of rice and elaborate rituals and taboos.

Evil spirits could enter a man's home in the form of a bird roosting in the roof or a pregnant woman of another clan. A provoked trail spirit could sprain ankles or break limbs. There were strong taboos to avoid offending the spirits, such as only bathing during certain times of the year and not wetting the body above the knees or below the shoulders at any other time lest enraged water *phi* cause sickness. All illness was the result of evil spirits luring the soul from the body, and death resulted when it failed to return. Any sickness demands an elaborate ritualistic ceremony of exorcism, in which a shaman, wearing a black mask over his head, gathers up friendly spirits to lead the lost soul back to its master's body.

Magic apart, the Meo relied upon opium as medicine—accepted socially by the Meo only for use by the old and chronically infirm—and exotic substances traditionally associated with promoting health and long life: such as skin of gaur (wild buffalo), deer's soft horn, marrow of tiger bone, gall of bear and python. As they had built up no resistance to drugs, the Meo responded to the smallest doses, and CIA medics reported that a single shot of penicillin brought results that were nothing less than miraculous. American medicine was so effective that even Band-Aids were revered, which the Meo thought were applied by Americans because they contained some magical power which drew out bad *phi*. (Meo fighter pilots would sometimes show up on the flight line after a heavy night with a Band-Aid firmly affixed to the middle of the forehead as a cure for the headache of a hangover.)

Most of the Meo have a deep, traditional loathing of the Vietnamese. "The Meo were not so much pro- or anti-French as against the Vietnamese," Trinquier explained. "They were the most undisciplined people in the world, against all authority. And the French thought it was best to let them handle things in their own way. We didn't make them pay any taxes or do anything they didn't want to. Naturally, they were against the Vietminh, who were trying to organize them. So the Meo were the best because they resented the Vietminh the most."

(They also resented, to a lesser degree, the lowland Lao, who, like the Chinese, looked down upon them. A minority of the Meo, hostile to the traditional leadership mostly because of clan rivalries, fought on the Communist side throughout the war.)[6]

Trinquier himself was an unconventional officer, a scholarly warrior of peasant stock, and he knew and understood the Meo after spending six years in the 1930s in command of an outpost in the wildest and most isolated part of the Sino-Tonkinese border region, known without exaggeration as One Hundred Thousand Mountains. Initially, he recruited two thousand *maquisards* but within eighteen months he had a force of twenty thousand. Each unit of a thousand men was commanded by a French officer, each one a bachelor to enable him to marry a local girl to secure good relations. (Trinquier married the daughter of a regional chief—"a highborn girl, not a whore. She was the go-between. I went to all the weddings and the holidays, and she told me how to behave.")

These early efforts were crowned with success, and team after team was dropped into enemy territory, where they lived off the land and fought a guerrilla war. The CIA took an early interest in Trinquier's force, and after he gave the Agency's then director, Allen Dulles, a complete report, the Americans provided a generous amount of weapons and assigned a case officer to him. The rapid growth of the program led to enormous logistical problems in feeding this army of *maquisards*.

In order to raise cash, Trinquier instigated an ingenious scheme, called Operation X, involving the Meo cash crop—opium. French intelligence had reported that the Vietminh were financing the arms for a division a year from the profits made from the Meo's opium. The intention of Operation X was for the French to deny the Vietminh the opium by buying it themselves, and to use the profits to finance *their* war.

Unknown to the government in Paris, or even the French authorities in Hanoi, Trinquier bought the entire Meo opium crop and transported it to Saigon at eight hundred kilos a time and sold it to the Emperor Bao Dai for fifty thousand francs a kilo. The profits were used to finance the *maquisards'* war. "It was strictly controlled," Trinquier said, "even though it was outlawed."

Later, the Americans chose to turn a pragmatic blind eye to the opium trade—never illegal within the borders of Laos itself—instead of becoming directly involved as had the French, which meant they lost control to a group of high-ranking Laotian military officers who became immensely rich international drug peddlers. Early efforts to contain the trade, by attempting to limit the high command's use of aircraft, was a failure, as was a later clampdown, and the actual outlawing of the trade in 1971 after intense U.S. pressure. In Laos opium was an inescapable fact of life.[7]

As the *maquisards* grew under the French, Touby Lyfoung—the nominal head of the Meo, known to foreigners as the "king" of the Meo—presented twenty young men to Colonel Trinquier whom he considered exceptional. Among them was Vang Pao. "And he was the best," Trinquier said. Vang Pao was sent for officer training to the French military school of Cap St. Jacques, near Saigon, where he earned a commission in the regular French Army. Vang Pao, whose original home was the 4,500-foot-high plateau of Nong Het, had been at war since the age of thirteen, when he acted as interpreter to a small group of Free French officers and men who had parachuted onto the Plain of Jars to stir up resistance against the Japanese. His first experience of actual battle came after the Japanese surrender when local Vietnamese residents tried to gain control of Xieng Khouang Province before French occupation troops arrived. Battle followed battle; the young Vang Pao helped clear Chinese Nationalist troops out of one province, and fought continually in harassing actions against the Vietminh in the mountains of northern Laos.

Perpetual war turned the stocky five-foot-four peasant into the natural leader of the Meo. His power grew out of the early support of the French, but he also commanded the respect of the Laotian leadership, under whom he quickly rose to the rank of major. No Meo had ever reached such a high rank in the Royal Lao Armed Forces before. The massive resources later put at his disposal by the Americans enhanced his prestige among his own people, while his ability to supply rice and medical supplies at will, move villagers by helicopter on command, and control U.S. air power gave him the status of a minor deity. But mostly his leadership rested on the force of his own personality, which was energetic, volatile, direct, and fearless. He carefully chose each of his six wives from large, prestigious families, so that he might cement or extend his influence among the various Meo clans.

He could also act like a warlord: one of his officers, caught selling Air America rice to the Pathet Lao, was found dead with a bullet between the eyes, and prisoners were often executed. As the war continued, without any apparent end in sight, the loss of life among the Meo led to some resistance to his leadership, and certain village headmen refused to fill their quotas of young men for the army. Vang Pao could respond ruthlessly by cutting off such villages from American rice drops, and would not hesitate to order his own T-28s to bomb and strafe villages that collaborated with the enemy. (At the same time, by Meo custom, Vang Pao became responsible for the widows and orphans created by the war, doling out money and favors to those who approached him.)

Despite his commitment to the war he was also dedicated to the progress of his people. A visit to the States in the late 1960s had turned him into something of a visionary. He saw the automobile factories in Detroit and the Saturn rocket at Cape Kennedy, but was most inspired when he visited the section of Williamsburg, Virginia, which was preserved in its original colonial state. He noticed that even the Americans had used wooden plows and weaved on hand looms—and that their muskets were inferior to those used by the Meo (beautiful copies, which took two years to make, of the guns first supplied by the Jesuits to the Chinese). If the Americans had used such primitive tools only two hundred years before, and were now putting men on the moon, what might the Meo achieve in the next two hundred years?

He attempted to curb his people's poetic but superstitious view of the world by holding seminars in Vientiane for hill tribe leaders in which they were given talks on technical subjects, medicine, and history. He deplored his people's primitive methods of slash-and-burn agriculture. "In one year a single family will chop down and burn trees worth six thousand dollars and grow a rice crop worth two hundred and forty dollars. Our people must come down from the mountains. We must demand our share of fertile, irrigated land."[8]

By Meo standards, Vang Pao was a wealthy man. This was partly as a result of his control of his people's opium crop—although even by 1972 a Meo farmer received only fifty dollars a kilo for opium that would retail in New York, as refined heroin, for twenty thousand dollars. His wealth also stemmed from the unlimited funds at his disposal from his American patrons. This has led to charges of corruption.[9] But personal gain was not a priority for Vang Pao, who never shirked the dangers of the battlefield for long and also put what he perceived to be the best interests of his people first. Besides, his ability to enrich himself was admired by his followers, and the exterior signs of his advancement merely proved to the Meo the high regard in which he was held by the Laotian leadership and the United States.

At the beginning of 1953, Vang Pao was part of a hopelessly inadequate force of French and Laotian troops facing an invading army of Vietnamese, which was not only numerically superior but better armed and organized. The Royal Lao Army numbered no more than ten thousand men, while there were less than three thousand French troops in the country, many of whom were not combat personnel. Pitted against them was an army almost the size of the Japanese forces that invaded Burma in 1942. Four infantry divisions of the Vietnamese People's Army crossed into Laos, each ten thousand strong and equipped with heavy mortars and recoilless cannon. Each division was also supported by fifteen thousand civilian porters carrying ammunition and supplies. In addition, there were three thousand Pathet Lao troops. And this formidable force was personally led by the brilliant Vietnamese general Vo Nguyen Giap.

The general's plan of attack was the blueprint for all subsequent invasions of Laos. One division advanced in a wide arc over the top of Indochina in order to strike against the royal capital of Luang Prabang; the main force, consisting of two divisions, moved to conquer the central Plain of Jars, thus directly threatening Vientiane; the remaining division penetrated deeply into central Laos and attempted to reach the Mekong.

The French and Laotians were badly mauled, but by fighting fierce rearguard actions—sometimes defending outposts to the last man—they slowed down the Communist advance sufficiently to allow a vast airlift of reinforcements and supplies onto the Plain of Jars. The plain was held and the provincial capital of Xieng Khouang recaptured from the Communists. Bitter fighting in the Laotian panhandle similarly succeeded in blunting the Communist thrust there. But the royal capital was still in danger, and on April 23, 1953, Gen. Raoul Salan, the commander in chief of all French forces in Indochina, personally visited Luang Prabang to inform the king of Laos, Sisavang Vong, that the city could not be held and would have to be evacuated. The king, at that time the oldest reigning monarch in the world and descended from an almost unbroken line since the fourteenth century, refused to go. "The Vietnamese did not succeed in taking Luang Prabang when they attacked us in 1479. Neither will they succeed this time."[10]

French Foreign Legion battalions scrambled to build fortifications around the royal capital, helped by the Lao, but they were bewildered when one day their allies simply disappeared at the height of the danger. The French sector commander questioned the city's governor and was told that there was no need for fortification, as the fabled Blind Bonze, an old monk renowned for his predictions, had announced that the Vietnamese would not take the city. "So we are preparing a festivity to thank Buddha for having saved our city once more from invasion."[11]

The Blind Bonze was detailed and precise in his prognostications. He stated that the Vietminh forces of the 304th Division and of Regiment 98 would be halted and retreat northward. This proved to be the case. Six days later, after going into a trance, the bonze predicted there were no Communist troops on the road to Vientiane—a fact confirmed by French intelligence a few days later.

As rationalists, the French decided to investigate the Blind Bonze, one Pho Satheu, who never left the pagoda in which he lived. His uncannily accurate predictions were duly verified by scholars, down to the smallest details. Indeed, so accurate were the bonze's announcements that intelligence officers felt he must have connections with the Communists. This theory collapsed when he was able to tell an anthropologist, in front of witnesses, about a military countermove as it was being planned several miles away in French military headquarters.

The same anthropologist reported that the Blind Bonze had also successfully predicted—"merely for fun"—the winning number in Thailand's national lottery. In the face of such evidence one can only wonder at the folly of academics when the anthropologist in question ignored a direct warning from the Blind Bonze himself not to take a certain plane trip. The plane crashed, killing all occupants.[12]

Perhaps nothing illustrates the gap between the later American approach to things and that of the Lao than the Blind Bonze, a holy man whose reputation was such that no one in Laos would dream of questioning his authority in a time of crisis. One can imagine the hoots of derision from analysts at CIA HQ, or the hard men in the Pentagon, had some luckless American intelligence agent been foolish enough to forward a report based on the soothsaying of the Blind Bonze, however accurate the sage's predictions.[13]

The courageous decision of the king to remain in his capital forced the French into the defense of northern Laos, a political decision which had far-reaching military consequences. France signed a treaty of friendship and association with the royal government on October 22, 1953, in which France promised to come to Laos's aid if attacked. On November 20, 1953, Gen. Henri Navarre, the new French commander, sent a telegram to his government: "I have decided on a thrust upon Dien Bien Phu, whose reoccupation will cover the approach to Luang Prabang, which, without it, would be in grave danger within a few weeks."[14]

Dien Bien Phu was to be the battle that marked the end of the French in Indochina. Lt. Vang Pao was leading a force of *maquisards* marching to relieve the garrison when the fortress fell after a hellish fifty-six-day siege. Too late to be of help, Vang Pao's men stayed behind enemy lines to pick up the very few escapees from the bloody battle. (Out of an original force of sixteen thousand men, while most marched eastward only seventy-eight escaped through the jungle to Laos, and only nineteen of them were Europeans.) Meo villagers helped some to find rafts to navigate the rivers and provided armed escorts and guides.[15] Most histories ignore the fact that the French were finally defeated in Indochina defending Laos once more from an invasion by the Communist Vietnamese.

The settlement in Geneva in 1954 resulted in the loss of all Vietnam north of the 17th parallel to the Communist government of Ho Chi Minh. The intention, to keep Laos as an independent and neutral buffer between Communist China and pro-western Siam, soon proved a failure. The repeated invasions of Laos' northern provinces by Communist Vietminh proved politically beneficial to the enemy when two provinces, Phong-Saly and Sam Neua, were put under the administration of Vietminh-backed Laotian rebels who had proclaimed themselves Pathet Lao—the "Lao State" (although no Pathet Lao representatives were present at the conference, and a Vietminh general signed the ceasefire with the French on their behalf). Attempts by Prince Souvanna Phouma to build national unity had given the Communist Pathet Lao—never more than a front for the Vietnamese Communists who had sponsored them since 1949—undue political influence.[16]

The Meo were cruelly rewarded for their loyalty to the French. Even after the fall of Dien Bien Phu, and as the Geneva conference was underway, the French continued to field their *maquis* units against the better judgment of their officers on the spot. "I hesitated to throw the *maquis* against the North Vietnamese," Trinquier said, "because I knew the war was lost."

In an attempt to save them he organized the scattered *maquisards* into three regiments so they could be inspected by the commission of armistice and their numbers included in the negotiations, but the French negotiators in Geneva chose to ignore their existence as an unnecessary complication. "Everybody wanted to sign the agreement—they didn't want to lose time on those 'details,'" Trinquier said.

Although the first Indochina war ended on July 21, 1954, after the fall of Dien Bien Phu, the French continued to supply the *maquisards* with parachuted ammo and supplies until July 27. A Vietnamese division that was sent against them was destroyed, but at the end of the battle the Meo had no ammunition. Trinquier appealed to his American CIA advisers for help, but was refused. "So, as the people had no ammunition, they were defeated."

With the French out of the picture, the United States now took on the backing of the Laotian economy. U.S. policy toward Laos since the original agreement of 1954 had exacerbated an already difficult situation: a large amount of money had been thrown at the problem, which resulted in bloating the army to a force fifty thousand strong—the only army in the world completely paid for by the United States—and creating a new class of corrupt and opportunistic officers. Instead of containing Communist strength, U.S. efforts—costing $300 million, which came to $150 a head, or twice the national per capita income—actually helped the Pathet Lao extend their control over the country and forced many neutralists into the Communist camp. In a deliberate policy aimed at wrecking attempts to create a nonaligned regime, the CIA backed Phoui Sananikone, an anticommunist, prowestern politician, to replace neutralist Prince Souvanna Phouma. The new prime minister was in turn replaced by Gen. Phoumi Nosavan when the army occupied the principal buildings in the capital. (The replacement of Phoui by Phoumi led George Ball to remark that it "could have been a significant event or a typographical error.")[17]

Direct U.S. military involvement, albeit clandestine, grew incrementally. The State Department set up a disguised military mission in Vientiane in 1959 called the Program Evaluation Office (PEO), where members wore civilian clothes and were described as "technicians." In reality they were infantry officers, led by a distinguished U.S. Army general, whose task was no less than forming and training a serviceable army completely staffed and officered by Lao.

In April 1960 a rigged election, masterminded by the CIA, legitimized Phoumi Nosavan, whom the agency saw as an anticommunist military strongman. The military strongman proved something of a disappointment, however, when he refused to go to the capital for his swearing-in, fearful he would meet with a violent death as predicted by a soothsayer.

It was during this period that the CIA remembered the *maquisards*. A CIA officer made contact with Vang Pao, now a major in the Royal Lao Army, and agreed to support him. "I got notice on Christmas day to send 1,000 weapons up to Vang Pao, in Laos," said Brig. Gen. Harry "Heinie" Aderholt, then a USAF major whose responsibility was to support CIA operations throughout the Far East.[18] "I'll be frank—I didn't even know where Laos was and I was one of their planners." The weapons, including hand grenades, 40mm mortars, and all the equipment needed to supply a thousand men, were stored at the secret U.S. base of Tahkli in Thailand and then flown up to Padong—Vang Pao's HQ before the founding of Long Tieng—by C-46.

Aderholt's next task was to open a series of landing strips—Lima Sites—throughout the country, and find a plane that could land in them. He would fly over Laos together with Vang Pao and a CIA officer and drop a message to a village asking them to clear ground. "And if it looked all right we landed on it. There were strips that were just unbelievable—one off the PDJ was just four hundred and fifty feet long, while the thermals were so bad on another we called Agony that a landing could only be attempted in the early morning or late afternoon when they had died down."[19]

During this period the covert infantrymen of the PEO were replaced by four hundred clandestine Special Forces personnel from Okinawa, called White Star Mobile Training Teams. The White Star teams were particularly effective, it was noted, when working in conjunction with Gen. Vang Pao's Meo.

The problem of feeding and caring medically for noncombatant Meo, which had so taxed the French, was handed over to Pop Buell, the Indiana farmer, who had come to Laos with International Voluntary Services, a Bible-belt version of the Peace Corps. But Buell was effective because he was able to draw upon the resources of the CIA's Air America, rather than IVS.

At the same time that the Americans were increasing their military presence in Laos, the Soviet Union was also increasing its support of the Pathet Lao. Foreign meddling, especially the heavy-handed machinations of the United States, angered a young, idealistic army officer, Capt. Kong Le, who led his parachute battalion in an unexpected and successful coup on August 8, 1960. The "military strongman's" soldiers had broken and run when sent against him (perhaps intimidated by the young captain's reputation that he had personally vanquished the bad *phi* that ranged over the PDJ at night, and also that one of his officers had seen Nquoc, the legendary monster of the Mekong that appears in times of crisis and on this occasion had prophesied a Kong Le victory). The captain seized power in the capital and turned the government over once more to Prime Minister Souvanna Phouma, who again attempted to create a neutralist government representing all political factions. But the plan failed, and Laos was plunged into a three-way civil war between rightists, neutralists, and the Communist Pathet Lao. A political situation of the utmost danger had developed. The superpowers backed opposing factions, and suddenly the United States found itself in a head-on confrontation with the Soviet Union.[20]

Throughout all this the country had not changed much. The only modern thing about the place seemed to be the war. There was only a single stoplight in the capital (a second would not be installed until 1970), and there were only 470 miles of paved roads throughout the country. Legal exports never exceeded an annual three million dollars (although illegal opium transactions swelled the coffers). The population probably amounted to no more than three million, although statistics were vague, as befitted such a dreamy place. It was absurd, but this sleepy backwater kingdom had become a theater of the cold war, and was about to become the setting for a possible nuclear conflict between the superpowers.

President Eisenhower had drawn a bleak picture of the situation in Laos when he briefed young President-elect Kennedy on the world's hotspots.[21] Laos was the worst. Ike became emotional as he told

Kennedy that the country was the key to Southeast Asia. If Laos fell the United States would have to write off the whole area. Years earlier he had outlined what had become known as the domino theory—"You have a row of dominoes set up, you knock over the first one, and what will happen to the last one is that it will go over very quickly"—and now he was saying that Laos was the first domino and it was about to go.[22] It was imperative that Laos should be defended— with the United States going it alone if necessary.

It is difficult to remember today that in the spring of 1961 the world's attention focused upon Laos. (Vietnam was of only minor interest—the *New York Times Index* for the year has twenty-six columns on Laos, only eight on Vietnam.) The trouble in Laos struck the new Kennedy administration as a serious crisis in the guise of a farce—a "Kung Fu movie" is how George Ball described it.[23] At the first meeting on the crisis, Defense Secretary Robert McNamara inadvertently exposed his unrealistic view of the situation when he suggested arming a half-dozen AT-6s (old World War II fighters) with bombs and sending them against the Communists; the joint chiefs, on the other hand, said it would take 250,000 U.S. servicemen to control events in the distant jungle kingdom. The young president found himself hoist on the petard of his inaugural rhetoric—"to pay any price, bear any burden . . . to assure the survival and success of liberty"—which he was now obliged to honor.

As the situation deteriorated, Kennedy put the U.S. Marines in Okinawa on alert for possible intervention and sent five hundred Marines with helicopters to Udorn, Thailand, close to the banks of the Mekong. A Soviet airlift of arms and ammunition to the Pathet Lao, meanwhile, became the highest-priority supply operation since the Russian Revolution.[24]

The president appeared on television to explain his actions. Unable to bring himself to say that America was on the brink of a world war for a place called "Louse," Kennedy pronounced it "Lay-os" throughout the broadcast. He reminded his audience that Laos had been given its independence and guaranteed its freedom and neutrality by international agreement in 1954. The Communist military advances in that country had the external support of a Soviet airlift and heavy weapons and combat specialists from North Vietnam. "It is this new dimension of externally supported warfare that creates the present grave problem," Kennedy said.

"I want to make it clear to the American people and to all of the world that all we want in Laos is peace and not war, a truly neutral government and not a cold war pawn, a settlement concluded at the conference table and not on the battlefield."

But peace could come only if armed attacks by the Communists stopped. "If these attacks do not stop, those who support a truly neutral Laos will have to consider their response."

Nobody watching had any doubts what that response would be. It was a direct warning that unless the Communists backed off there would be war.[25]

The dangerous game of brinkmanship continued. The joint chiefs warned that U.S. intervention might result in an all-out Communist response—a North Vietnamese invasion of Laos backed by limitless Russian arms, and the ultimate possibility of war with China. Faced with such a risk, America had to choose between all or nothing. It was either back down now, or prepare to make a massive commitment of manpower, air cover, and possibly even nuclear weapons.

The last two years of the Eisenhower era had been taken up with fighting rearguard actions when the United States found itself on the defensive everywhere in foreign affairs. The State Department's policy concerning Southeast Asia was to contain the thrust of Chinese Communist hegemony into Indochina, and beyond to Indonesia. Confrontation had been considered inevitable.

And now this confrontation was about to take place in tiny, insignificant Laos. Younger diplomats like William H. Sullivan—destined to become ambassador to Laos—had other ideas. "I thought it was a pretty lousy place to make a confrontation."[26]

President Kennedy had already asked for ideas from people in the State Department about how to meet the problems ahead of him. Tom Corcoran, a retiring, donnish man, was on the Laos desk at the time, and he developed a retiring, donnish alternative to superpower confrontation. Dubbed the "Red, White, and Blue Solution," Corcoran's idea was to divide Laos into spheres of influence. The Americans and the Soviets would pull out, leaving the North Vietnamese (Red) a shade of influence on their border, the Thais (Blue) a shade of influence on their border, and the Lao (White), under Prime Minister Souvanna Phouma, the main part of the country. This colorful arrangement—which merged into a very muddy gray indeed—was to be codified in a declaration of international neutrality, under the king.

It was Sullivan who put the Red, White, and Blue Solution on paper—together with some ideas on relations with China—and caught the young president's attention. Away from the TV screen, Kennedy dropped the rhetoric about liberty and expressed the opinion that Laos was not a country "worthy of engaging the attention of great powers" and that the previous policy of attempting to turn it into an anticommunist bastion was ridiculous.[27] He believed neutralization to be the correct policy, but American prestige was now on the line, not to mention his own.

There could be no backing down, but there was a way out, and the Red, White, and Blue Solution, which offered something for everybody, seemed to be it. Krushchev finally accepted a third-power proposal for negotiations over Laos. The Red, White, and Blue Solution became the basis for protracted negotiations in Geneva during 1961 and early 1962. Besides, Krushchev could afford to wait. "Why take risks over Laos?" he said to Llewellyn Thompson, U.S. ambassador to Moscow. "It will fall into our laps like a ripe apple."[28]

The superpowers had approached the very edge, looked into the abyss, and drawn back.

The new king of Laos, Savang Vatthana, did his best to stay above and beyond politics. (All factions revered him, while ministers, officials, and governors of his kingdom took a long and solemn oath of loyalty, swearing on pain of the most awful retribution "not to stir up plots with unbelievers or foreign enemies . . . not to seek to kill the representatives of the government by means of spells.") He was a high-minded, serious man who had been educated at the Ecole de Science Politique in Paris and had both read and traveled widely. He saw himself in a tragic mold. At the funeral of his father he had remarked to Prince Sihanouk of Cambodia, in an accurate prophecy, "Alas, I am doomed to be the last king of Laos."[29]

The Americans interpreted his pessimism as the superstitious fatalism of an oriental potentate, and characterized him as indecisive and a "hand-wringer." They were not encouraged by the royal choice of automobile (a 1959 Edsel) and were suspicious of his obsession with Marcel Proust (he quoted frequently from A la recherche du temps perdu). They were embarrassed on several occasions when he wept openly in front of visitors, heartbroken by what he saw as the inevitable "demise of an ancient kingdom."[30]

But mostly the king was disregarded by the power brokers who jetted in and out of his country. They saw him as no more than an anachronistic if charming and exotic personality, to be paid the usual formal and ceremonial courtesies. In fact, his view of the Big Picture was crystal-clear.

On the eve of the Geneva Conference in 1961, when fourteen nations gathered to decide the future of his tiny kingdom, he addressed a message to his people: "Our country is the most peaceful in the world. . . . At no time has there ever arisen in the minds of the Lao people the idea of coveting another's wealth, of quarreling with their neighbors, much less of fighting them. And yet, during the past twenty years, our country has known neither peace nor security. . . . enemies of all sorts have tried to cross our frontiers, to destroy our people and to destroy our religion and our nation's aura of peace and concord.

"Foreign countries do not care either about our interests or peace; they are concerned only with their own interests."[31]

The negotiations over the future of Laos moved slowly. In Geneva the principal nations involved—the United States, the USSR, China, North Vietnam, and Laos—nitpicked their way through wads of fine print, week after week, for fifteen months. The negotiations were tedious in the extreme until even Soviet Foreign Minister Andrei Gromyko—no stranger to boredom—grumbled, "One cannot sit indefinitely on the shores of Lake Geneva, counting swans."[32]

The man in charge of the American mission in Geneva was Averell Harriman, a very experienced, wise, and tough diplomat who had been ambassador to the USSR at the end of World War II. He could be heartlessly straightforward and did not suffer fools gladly, and men whose heads he had bitten off for putting forward bad ideas dubbed him "the Crocodile." His instructions on Laos were simply that a military solution was impossible, and that he was to find a political solution.

On his arrival in Geneva he found what he considered to be a topheavy mission with more than a hundred people in it (the Chinese contingent was even larger, consisting of two hundred deadpan bureaucrats). It quickly became apparent that William Sullivan, a relatively junior officer only thirty-eight years old, was the brightest of the bunch, and Harriman immediately offered him the job of personal deputy. Sullivan was obliged to point out that there were numerous officers his senior. Harriman promptly reduced the mission by half and sent home all the officers senior to Sullivan, who thereupon became his deputy.

While the talks dragged on, the Chinese and North Vietnamese managed to pull off two small agreements, independent of the negotiations in Geneva, which were to give the Communists a strategic military advantage throughout the coming war. On a visit to Peking in April 1961, Prime Minister Souvanna Phouma agreed that the

Chinese might proceed with road construction plans linking Yunnan province with Phong-Saly and Nam Tha (the provinces' first roads). This gave China a legal right to put construction teams onto Laotian sovereign territory, where they were to remain for more than a decade, mushrooming into a force of twenty thousand combat engineers protected by formidable batteries of antiaircraft guns.

A similar agreement was also made by the Lao government with the North Vietnamese in 1962, allowing them to construct all-weather roads over the Annamite Mountains. By the end of the year the North Vietnamese had completed work on four roads: one over the northern passage from the Dien Bien Phu valley; one to Sam Neua, the Pathet Lao HQ; two others came out of the mountain passes on the Vietnamese border into the Laotian panhandle, one from the pass at Nape to Kam Keut, and another from the Mu Gia pass to Nhommarath. At the same time, Route 7, linking the Plain of Jars to the Vietnamese seaport of Vinh, was also reconstructed to take heavy-duty traffic.

Later, beginning in September 1968, the Chinese began an even more ambitious project, pushing their road construction south from the border, and then splitting in two directions—one to link up with a North Vietnamese road built from the Dien Bien Phu valley, and the other toward Pak Beng on the Mekong, only nineteen miles from the Thai border.[33]

In his memoirs Henry Kissinger describes this road construction as one of "China's strangest projects during the Vietnam war" and as something that "mystified" the Americans. There was nothing mysterious about it. Military men understood that the road was being used to funnel into the country North Vietnamese troops and supplies that had traveled from Vietnam across southern China. Eventually, when the road was completed, it would allow the Chinese to move troops rapidly across Laos to the Thai border, should the need ever arise. (Later, in 1974, Zhou Enlai further enlightened Henry Kissinger in regard to the long-term nature of Chinese strategic designs. With the Americans removed from Indochina, the Chinese worried once more about the expansionist ambitions of their former Vietnamese ally to dominate the whole of Indochina. The road from China into Laos, on the flank of their ally turned adversary, could now be used to contain this expansion.)[34]

Kennedy and Krushchev had agreed that Laos should not become an issue between the superpowers and that both of them should use their influence to make the country truly neutral. Both had difficult and unruly allies, and sporadic fighting continued within Laos throughout the months of negotiation, adding to their complexity. Krushchev suggested locking the two foreign ministers in a room until they found a solution.

An agreement was finally signed on July 23, 1962. The essence of the various accords, veiled behind complicated legalistic wording, was that Laos should be genuinely neutral. It was endorsed by Prime Minister Souvanna Phouma, whose first act as head of a provisional government of national union was to announce that Laos would "not recognize the protection of any alliance or military coalition." An International Control Commission was to supervise the cease-fire and ensure that all foreign troops were withdrawn within seventy-five days. All the signatories to the agreement promised they would "not use the territory of the Kingdom of Laos for interference in the internal affairs of other countries," which denied the North Vietnamese the use of the Ho Chi Minh Trail.

American forces had already been reduced during the negotiations, but the remaining U.S. military personnel were meticulously counted out of the country by the International Control Commission. In all they totaled 666.

It was a number of extraordinary ill omen. The fatalistic and highly superstitious Laotians would have trembled had they known the evil significance medieval occultists gave the number. A number of uncertain meaning, the ancient mystics often matched it with the Antichrist. According to St. John: "Let him that hath understanding count the number of the beast: for it is the number of a man: and his number is six hundred threescore and six."[35] St. John supposedly chose the number because it fell just short of the holy number seven in every particular, while straining at every point to reach it—an analogy the negotiators at Geneva would have appreciated.

Averell Harriman, when asked, in the face of evidence that large numbers of North Vietnamese troops remained in the country, how things were going, replied: "Just about as unsatisfactorily as we expected." He described the settlement as "a good bad deal."[36]

The International Control Commission, which was not permitted to visit Pathet Lao territory, was incapable of checking how many North Vietnamese troops had left the country. Only forty were counted passing through the single checkpoint the ICC was allowed to observe, while it was estimated that ten thousand remained.

It became clear that the United States had underestimated the enormous ambitions of the Lao Dong, the North Vietnamese Communist Party, which saw the Geneva Accords as nothing more than a tactical ploy. A measure of the agreement's failure can be taken by the enthusiasm with which it was received by the North Vietnamese, who hailed the Accords as a "success" and a "victory."[37] Far from reducing the number of troops in Laos, the North Vietnamese continued to build up and strengthen their forces while enlarging the Ho Chi Minh Trail—activities they pursued in secret.

In the southern panhandle of Laos two divisions of their crack regular troops manned the Trail, guarding and improving its skein of paths and roads, while countless thousands of soldiers and tons of supplies flowed to bolster the burgeoning war in South Vietnam. In the north of Laos the Vietnamese fielded their regular troops on a rotational basis, according to the season, as well as providing permanent cadre for the Pathet Lao army. Despite repeated complaints and accusations by Prime Minister Souvanna Phouma, the North Vietnamese simply denied everything: they had no troops in Laos, or in South Vietnam, they stated repeatedly, and the Ho Chi Minh Trail did not exist.

The United States now had to find a way to counter these North Vietnamese moves without provoking confrontation with the Soviet Union or China. President Kennedy reacted to the situation by fielding a deniable, clandestine force of a paramilitary nature, mostly run by the CIA, with strict instructions that all the actual fighting should be done by indigenous troops.

This *L'Armee Clandestine* had grown rapidly to number nine thousand men by the summer of 1961. Nine CIA specialists were assigned to it, nine Green Berets and ninety-nine Thai special-service types from the CIA-trained and oddly titled Police Aerial Resupply Unit (PARU).[38] The buildup of the Meo army was further intensified after the Geneva Accords when it became clear they would be needed to battle the North Vietnamese without the support of U.S. ground forces. By 1963 it was up to a strength of thirty thousand, mostly local defense units, but ten thousand were formed into Special Guerrilla Units (SGUs). Together the SGUs formed a battalion made up of three line companies and an HQ unit, armed with bazookas and mortars, and later 75mm and 105mm howitzers which moved from hilltop to hilltop by helicopters. In order to induce the CIA congressional subcommittees to approve funding to enable this army to grow further, the Agency indulged in some creative bookwork to reorganize Gen. Vang Pao's forces. "The problem was, how do you indicate to Congress that you have more than a hundred teams when you actually have only one fourth that number?" said Langley desk

Gen. Vang Pao, who first saw combat with the French at the age of thirteen, led the CIA-trained and -financed Meo guerrillas throughout the war until the end. *(Private collection of David Kouba)*

War bled the Meo nation of its me[n] until only children remained to fill th[e] ranks. A child holds a white phosph[o]rous marking rocket before it is loade[d] on a Raven O-1 Bird Dog. *(Private c[ol]lection of Michael Cavanaugh)*

Prince Mangkhra Phouma, the son of the prime minister, poses with a Meo soldier on the Plain of Jars in 1969. The boy had been singled out for distinction for his high number of enemy "kills." *(Private collection of William Keeler)*

Many of the Meo boy soldiers were s[o] young they were scarcely bigger tha[n] their weapons. *(Private collection o[f] Chad Swedberg)*

Two Meo "tots" on the ramp at Long Tieng help load white phosphorous "Willy Pete" marking rockets. *(Private collection of Harold Mesaris)*

The enemy, so young they looked like girls. One had written on the band inside his helmet, "Born in Vietnam—Die in Laos." *(Private collection of Craig Morrison)*

Long Tieng, the most secret spot on earth. "Spook Heaven," as the CIA base for Military Region II was known, was the base for Gen. Vang Pao and his Meo guerrillas. *(Kouba collection)*

The Mexican Banditos. The Ravens and their support troops posed for this photograph after a visiting Air Force general described them as "a ragged bunch of Mexican bandits." *(Mesaris collection)*

The ramp at Long Tieng with
-28 Meo fighters in the fore-
round and "titty" karst in the
ackground. (*Mesaris collec-
on*)

he O-1 Bird Dog, the Ravens'
ar chariot—"The most for-
idable weapon known to
an." (*Swedberg collection*)

ike Byers with Backseater in
ont of an O-1. (*Private collec-
on of Michael Byers*)

"Weird" Harold Mesaris gives Floyd, one of a pair of CIA pet Himalayan black bears, a beer—his favorite tipple. (*Mesaris collection*)

The "CAS" guys—the CIA men who r the secret war—standing here on t Plain of Jars, dressed as if for a round golf. (*Morrison collection*)

Tony Poe, the legendary CIA paramilitary operative, photographed as a young Marine. Poe helped get the Dalai Lama out of Tibet and fought in numerous clandestine operations. He was known to have paid a bonus for enemy ears and was rumored to keep the heads of particular enemies pickled in formaldehyde.

The CIA operations shack at Long Tie command center of the secret war in M II. (*Archives of the Edgar Allan Poe Lit ary Society*)

The golden gun—a .45 revolver—and its hand-tooled holster. (*Cavanaugh collection*)

Chuck Engle and "spook" relax against a bomb between missions. (*Mesaris collection*)

The Raven bar, tastefully decorated with parachutes. A favorite hang-out of Air America pilots and Ravens—the bears lived in a cage just outside. (*CAPLS Archives*)

The presentation by Mike Cavanaugh of Ross Perot's golden .45 to Gen. Vang Pao. From left: U Va Lee "The Indian," Mike Cavanaugh, Gen. Vang Pao, Burr Smith "Mr. Clean." (*Cavanaugh collection*)

Lee Lu, the Meo fighter pilot with five thousand combat missions, regarded by his American peers as one of the very best. (*Cavanaugh collection*)

The funeral of Lee Lu. Gen. Vang Pao walks in front of the coffin while his comrades-in-arms gather around. (*Cavanaugh collection*)

officer Ralph McGehee. "The answer was simple: the couple of dozen teams were divided, on paper only, into platoons of only a few individuals each, and instantly there were the necessary number of teams." Similarly, Langley put a lot of effort into picking the right name for its forces: "Hunter-Killer Teams" was rejected because it made them sound like assassins, while "Home Defense Teams" was considered too passive. The name finally adopted was "Mobile Strike Forces."[39]

As no U.S. military planes were allowed to be based inside the country, the CIA's proprietary commercial airline, Air America, played an essential role with its helicopters, transports, and specialized STOL airplanes. Paramilitary specialists seconded to the CIA were introduced into the country to help train and organize the Royal Lao Army and the Meo guerrilla units in the north of Laos. The Air Commandos set up a secret base across the Mekong in Nakhon Phanom, Thailand.

Every clandestine maneuver the United States made to match the North Vietnamese was done after consultation with Souvanna Phouma and with his permission. In turn, Souvanna demanded that his complicity in such arrangements be kept secret, lest his position in the country become untenable. However, under international law the United States was permitted to act against the North Vietnamese even without the permission of the Laotian government. The Hague Conference of 1907, which modified many of the rules of war, declared, "A neutral country has the obligation not to allow its territory to be used by a belligerent. If the neutral country is unwilling or unable to prevent this, the other belligerent has the right to take appropriate counteraction."[40]

The mechanisms for this secret war were mostly set up under Ambassador Leonard Unger, the first U.S. ambassador appointed to the country after the agreement. Unger was also responsible for giving Prime Minister Souvanna Phouma renewed confidence in U.S. intentions in the area. Although Souvanna Phouma would later be criticized by the Communists as an American lackey, he was a genuine patriot who tirelessly sought a middle course for Laos throughout his career. He had vigorously opposed previous U.S. policy aimed at confrontation in Laos and had expressed strong anti-American sentiments in the process.

But after Geneva, the intention of the United States was to prevent Laos from becoming a primary theater of warfare, and to do only what was necessary to prevent the Vietnamese from overrunning the country. Only a small portion of the paramilitary operation was actually in Laos itself, with all support housed in Thailand under a secret agreement.

At the same time the decision had been made by 1962 to fight the Lao Dong on its own terms in South Vietnam. Once the North Vietnamese had been stopped there, it was reasoned, they would ease back into their own country, have no further use for the Trail, and make no more encroachments on Laotian territory. The framework of the 1962 agreements would then be reconstituted.

The flaw in this premise was that everything rested upon the Americans winning in South Vietnam—and winning outright, quickly. The holding operation in Laos would buy time while the North Vietnamese were sent packing. A year, maybe two, was all that it was expected to take. Nobody could foresee that this small, deniable, clandestine arrangement would mushroom into a massive military commitment, an ever-escalating policy of devastating bombing, and a ten-year secret war.

The Americans in Geneva might have misjudged North Vietnamese ambitions, but not their warlike intentions. Sullivan had accompanied Harriman to a Geneva hotel during negotiations to meet North Vietnam's foreign minister, Ung Van Khiem—"a small stocky man who dressed in bulky Soviet suits with the sleeves so long they covered his chubby hands when he stood" was Sullivan's first impression.

It was not a successful meeting. Ung rejected every attempt at negotiation, denied any North Vietnamese complicity in the war in the south, and refused to acknowledge the thousands of troops fighting there. Sullivan's assessment of Ung's posture was that he was "brutally, arrogantly negative" and he judged the man himself an "insulting little thug."

Only at the very end of the meeting did Harriman's patience finally give way to display his contained anger. Towering over the diminutive Ung, he told him he was in for a long, tough war—a remark, of course, which cut both ways.

Negotiations were similarly rebuffed when Sullivan traveled with Prince Souvanna Phouma to the Plain of Jars to meet with the leader of the Communist Pathet Lao, who, in the Laotian Alice-in-Wonderland nature of things, happened to be the prime minister's half brother, Prince Souphanouvong, "an irritable, testy little character," according to Sullivan. (Most Laotians firmly believed that the brothers, as members of the royal family, had magical, intermediary powers with the unseen world, a belief which enhanced both men's influence with their followers.)

In Laos, the Pathet Lao faction "was nothing more than a handful of leftists who acted as a front for the Lao Dong party of North Vietnam," and Souphanouvong mirrored the stubborn bellicosity of his patrons. The meeting degenerated into fractious argument until Prince Souvanna Phouma stomped out of the room, leaving his half brother and Sullivan in an eye-to-eye confrontation. "Souphanouvong's North Vietnamese bodyguard came in, and he had a little submachine gun which he pointed at my head and took the safety catch off. Souphanouvong let him stay in that position for five minutes while we continued our harangue before he waved him off. That was the kind of gamesmanship he played."

These experiences left Sullivan with no illusions about Communist designs on Laos, although at the same time he was skeptical about U.S. policy concerning Vietnam. These views were strengthened to the point of cynicism when he took part in a war game in Washington, D.C., organized by the joint chiefs of staff in the spring of 1963. It was to prove uncannily prophetic.

The game was designed to explore what would happen if the United States got involved in a war in Vietnam. In the game, America became the Blue Team and North Vietnam the Red Team. Sullivan was military head of the Red Team (General Giap), drawing on the knowledge and advice of a Marine Corps general, members from all sections of the military, intelligence officers, and civilians from the relevant government organizations. The Red Team played according to the rules of guerrilla warfare, accepting heavy casualties and exploiting all the weaknesses that could be found in the traditional military doctrines of the United States and the vulnerabilities of an open, democratic country.

The game was played out deep in the "Strangelove" bunker of the National Military Command Center and took a week, representing a decade in real time. By the end of 1972 in game time it was all over. The Red Team was everywhere on the map of Indochina. The North Vietnamese forces controlled the countryside in South Vietnam, had overrun Laos, and had a free run in Cambodia. Despite inflicting severe casualties on the enemy, who had withstood massive bombing and 500,000 American troops, the United States was no closer to victory. It had spent huge amounts of money on the war and borne the brunt of hostile world opinion and student rebellion, while its own Congress was on the brink of revolt.

One conclusion of the game which was bitterly resented by high-ranking officers in the Air Force was that massive bombing seemed to promise little result. Gen. Curtis LeMay, chief of staff of the Air Force, became emotional at a critique session at the end of the game and charged that the Rand Corporation, which had drawn up the rules and acted as referee, had been biased against the Air Force—a particularly weak argument as the Rand Corporation was founded by the Air Force, which has always been its largest client.

LeMay believed in bombing, and was convinced that the Air Force would be able to interdict Vietnamese supplies, destroy its military installations, and shatter the morale of its population. "My solution to the problem would be to tell them frankly that they've got to draw in their horns and stop their aggression, or we're going to bomb them back into the stone age."[41]

As a result of LeMay's objections, a second game was organized, broader in scope than the first and with five teams this time (to bring in Russia, China, and South Vietnam). The United States fared a little better, but not much. Similar reservations about the effectiveness of bombing were voiced and the conclusion was the same.

One of the Air Force's gripes about the way the war game had been scored by the Rand Corporation was that Red Team hit-and-run tactics against installations within South Vietnam itself had been allowed to succeed. This was unrealistic scoring, the Air Force argued, and objected strongly when a war game operation by guerrillas to infiltrate and blow up a large number of U.S. aircraft at Bien Hoa airfield in a game-time date of 1964 was allowed.

Sullivan was to have cause to remember this particular argument. In November 1964 he was returning to Washington, after a stint in Vietnam, to be sworn in as ambassador to Laos. He looked out of the window of his airplane and saw black smoke billowing up from the airport below. It was Bien Hoa. A successful Vietcong guerrilla raid had destroyed fuel, ammunition, and U.S. aircraft. And this time it was not a game.

As the crisis in Laos seemingly dissolved, so the problems of Vietnam came to the fore. For the next ten years, Vietnam would dominate all of U.S. military and diplomatic activity, and the world's attention. Laos would be mostly forgotten, relegated once more to the background by more pressing American interests and considerations. "The Forgotten War" was how Prime Minister Souvanna Phouma described it. Or, as Secretary of State Dean Rusk inelegantly remarked: "After 1963 Laos was only the wart on the hog."[42]

William H. Sullivan arrived as ambassador to Laos in late 1964. An exceptionally bright and gifted diplomat, he was, at the age of forty-two, the youngest ambassador in the U.S. Foreign Service. His long dealings with the problems of Laos made him an ideal choice, and his realistic, hardheaded, pragmatic approach to the job combined an overview of the Big Picture with a detailed working knowledge of the reality of the war.

Sullivan came from an Irish-American background and had graduated from Brown University *summa cum laude*. Even as a student, with World War II looming before him, he believed that America's destiny was not to dominate the world, "but rather to live with and cope with other people, other cultures, and other powers . . . alien to our values and occasionally anathema to our ideals."[43] This was certainly an enlightened view from a young man about to go to war.

He enlisted in the Navy in 1942 and saw action on destroyers in the North Sea, against German submarines in the Mediterranean, in the Normandy invasion, and in the South Pacific. On the assault against Okinawa he witnessed a macabre mass suicide of Japanese troops when rank upon rank of defeated soldiers threw themselves to their deaths over the edge of a cliff onto jagged rocks 150 feet below. The incident was an object lesson in the fanatical motivation that could be instilled in men.

Sullivan had also experienced the strange psychological twists the mind can take in combat, and how it can brutalize the ordinary man into a callous form of behavior unimaginable in peacetime. A mine-sweeper that had taken a hit by a kamikaze pilot came alongside the ship Sullivan was on. Her skipper had suspended the martyred body of the Japanese pilot, who had been thrown from his plane when he hit, from the top yardarm of the ship's mast as a war trophy. The skipper was bewildered when a fellow officer began to shake with disgust and anger at the sight. "The reactions of young men at war due to the vagrant brutalities of combat are always impossible to predict," Sullivan concluded.[44]

Firsthand experience of war made him sympathetic to soldiers, and also shaped his philosophy when he went on to join the Foreign Service in 1947. America had emerged as the most powerful nation on earth, but Sullivan supported policy which sought a world order balanced on a number of cooperating centers of power, recognizing that much of American postwar paramountcy was artificial, because of the enormous destruction suffered by other nations. "We didn't see the world in sharp contrasting shades of black and white, but rather in the murky shades of gray that color most human endeavors."[45]

Ten years in various posts around the world confirmed this view, and in 1958 he returned to Washington, D.C., to spend three years in the Department of State dealing with Southeast Asia. He learned to operate despite the bureaucracy. "I prefer to get things done by a direct route of decision. The bureaucratic mentality is to put it all down on paper and push it through the maze of in and out boxes." He also consolidated friendships on Capitol Hill which would later prove invaluable. He was then assigned to Geneva to participate in the international conference on Laos.

It was Sullivan's conviction that big-unit U.S. military had to be kept out of the country. "The kind of war I undertook was strictly defensive and essentially of a guerrilla nature. Because of its unorthodox structure, Washington gave me a free hand to run it as best I could without interference."

To Gen. William C. Westmoreland, who had hoped to head a Southeast Asia Command, instead of just U.S. forces in Vietnam, the autonomy of Sullivan—and, to a lesser extent, of the U.S. ambassador to Thailand—was irksome. When the three men visited Udorn air base together and airmen swarmed around the general to take photographs, Sullivan remarked that Westmoreland seemed to have numbers of devoted followers. "Why would they want a picture of a general," Westmoreland retorted, "when they can snap two field marshals?"[46]

The nickname stuck, and indeed Sullivan was field marshal of Laos. "As experience accumulated and as the months and years went by, I eventually carried in my head, just short of my subconscious, a working knowledge of our deployment, the terrain, the roads and the trails, the enemy dispositions, and our aircraft availability. Many a night I was wakened from a sound sleep by a telephone call, and sitting on the edge of the bed, had to decide whether to order the evacuation of an outpost under attack, to hold on, to reinforce, to call for air support, or to mount a diversionary action to relieve the pressure on the front. It was a far cry from the normal pursuit of the striped-pants set."[47]

It was also very different from what was expected of the mainstream military man. There was no place in Laos for the sort of officer who accepted his year's tour in "Vietnam" with reluctance. The sort of soldier needed was an individual who could think for himself in a highly unconventional theater of operations. That meant men with special-operations backgrounds.

Sullivan had a high regard for this type. "To be a commando in special operations you have first of all to be a volunteer; secondly, you have to be prepared to take extraordinary risks, to function outside normal chains of command, and also to be able to make individual decisions of life and death immediately. It takes a special breed."

The proponents of strategic bombing and the captains of the big battalions needed to be kept at a distance. Specifically, this meant ensuring that Gen. William Momyer, head of the 7th Air Force, and Gen. William Westmoreland, commander of MACV, concentrated only on Vietnam. (It was reported of Sullivan that he saw his role as "keeping Westy's paws off Laos.")[48] Westmoreland bridled over the restrictions Sullivan forced him to observe in Laos and renamed the Ho Chi Minh Trail "Sullivan's Freeway."[49] Sullivan intended to rely on small, volunteer, commando-style units.

Lessons learned from the Washington war games had convinced Sullivan of the limited effectiveness of jet bombers in a guerrilla war. "A high-performance jet flying at eight hundred knots and carrying bombs as its ordnance was not the most effective instrument to use against truck convoys that were moving at a snail's pace down the muddy Ho Chi Minh Trail under triple-canopy tree cover. They could not linger long enough to identify their targets, and they could not aim accurately enough to destroy them. What we needed was something that was slow-moving, could see a target, and could zero in on it and stay with it until it had destroyed it with Gatling guns or cannon."

This flew directly in the face of current Air Force doctrine and the view of General Momyer, who wanted an all-jet Air Force and was committed to employing state-of-the-art aircraft in Vietnam. There had been an acrimonious interagency debate over whether propeller or jet planes should be used in Vietnam, with the Air Force arguing that jets were better for close air support than slower, prop-driven aircraft. This was nonsense, and the Air Force knew it was nonsense, but did not want to end up after what was expected to be a short, guerrilla war with an inventory of prop planes. In the long run the Air Force would need jets to match the Russians, so it fought for their use in the Vietnam War.[50]

Sullivan had different ideas for Laos, and set about cobbling together a force of so-called obsolete propeller aircraft suited for the war there. His earlier job in Washington had given him easy access to Robert McNamara, whom he persuaded to assign a number of A-26s (a World War II light bomber), a clutch of A-1 Skyraiders (an old propeller-driven Navy plane), and some modified T-28 Navy training planes from Pensacola, Florida. The units already in existence with experience with this type of airplane and special warfare operations were the Air Commandos from Hurlburt Field, Florida—some of whom had seconding arrangements with the CIA. "The gang that tumbled into Nakhon Phanom was a pretty wild bunch," Sullivan remembers fondly.

This odd mixture of men and machinery grew to become an entire wing, officially designated as the 56th Air Commando Wing; unofficially, this motley outfit was called Sullivan's Air Force.[51]

In the spring of 1964, Col. Roger Trinquier, who had retired from the French Army after a stint in Algeria, was approached by the United States to return to Laos to run the clandestine Meo army. He met in Paris with Stephen Enke, assistant to the president, but his earlier disillusionment made him refuse the offer. "When we created our *maquisards*," he wrote later, "we were absolutely sincere. We were certain that France—our France—would never abandon them, that we would fight with them and for them, against communism and for their liberty. The bonds of friendship we had forged appeared indissoluble. But the complete confidence they had invested in us we then betrayed when we abandoned them. . . . It would be impossible to return to face the Meo without feeling a profound sense of guilt, and why not say the word, shame. I am certain that, whatever the result of the war, they will be newly abandoned."[52] But at the time this bleak prediction was dismissed as little more than the bitter view of a defeated French colonialist.

The Meo were crucial to the U.S. effort in Laos. They could be relied upon because they were paid in cash directly by the CIA, which meant they received money regularly without the skimming operation in which the Royal Lao Army officers indulged, and, most important, they were capable of forcing the sort of war on the North Vietnamese that they in turn were pursuing so successfully in South Vietnam.

Every year at the beginning of the dry season the historic North Vietnamese 316th Division[53] marched across Route 7 to the west and attacked the Meo outposts. The Meo fell back, ambushing and harassing the advancing army as they did so, leaving behind friendly civilian populations in the villages, among whom were spies able to pass on accurate information on enemy numbers and movements.

The Lao strategy was to wait until the enemy forces were stretched out on a long line of communication, with their forces scattered in small units. The most vulnerable of these would be attacked with helicopter-borne Meo troops, supported by propeller-driven fighters. Then, when the rains started, large blocking forces would be flown by helicopter to the east of Route 7 to cut off the 316th as it withdrew to Vietnam. The Meo ambushed them time and time again, with U.S. air support, killing hundreds at each encounter.

It was a seesaw war, with both sides winning a seasonal upper hand but never making any permanent territorial gains. Although Hanoi was prevented from making any lasting conquest, it was able to send fresh troops to battle each year, while the Meo were being constantly bled. In an attempt to restore the balance, the Americans resorted to ever-increasing air power.

To the men who ran the air war from the hideous concrete bunker in Vientiane, the Big Picture was simply an enormous map of Indochina on the wall of their operations room. The building they worked in, a separate structure which stood apart from the embassy itself, had no windows.

"Embassy people—what a bunch they were!" Raven Mike Cavanaugh said. "Hundreds of people, big compound, restaurants—a big operation. Bureaucrats. Their whole existence was spent in this sleepy old colonial town, a neutral, protectorate zone. The difference between what was going on there and a few miles away was pretty devastating. None of them ever got killed or saw anybody die. They never even heard the bombs dropping."

The air war had developed from small beginnings. When the North Vietnamese had refused to leave the country in 1962, Prince Souvanna Phouma had asked the United States for aircraft and supplies for the Royal Lao Air Force, and a number of old T-28 fighter-bombers were delivered. The problem remained that there were not enough Lao pilots to fly them effectively in combat.

The gap was filled with a program code-named Class A, which involved American pilots flying T-28 fighters on combat missions out of Udorn, Thailand—just forty-five miles across the border from Vientiane. It was a small, highly classified operation involving a half-dozen pilots from the CIA airline Air America. "When you came out of the barracks you had your gloves on so nobody could see the color of your skin and question your nationality, and you had to wear your helmet with a dark glass visor down so nobody could see who you were and maybe identify you later," one pilot said. "You crawled into an unmarked T-28 and launched."

The political consequences of an American being shot down in an unmarked combat fighter were incalculable. Hence the Waterpump program, aimed at training Lao and Thai pilots to fly and maintain the T-28. It opened for business at Udorn in April 1964, with forty-one personnel from the Special Air Warfare Center (later renamed the Special Operations Force), along with four aircraft.

Waterpump was part of a larger program code-named Project 404, of which the Ravens were an integral element. This eventually supported air operations centers (AOCs) in each of the five military regions in Laos, where Air Commandos in the black, consisting of a commander, line chief, communications specialist, and doctor or medic, were attached to a native fighter squadron. It also provided Air Force and CIA personnel in various capacities to help support friendly troops in battle, including forward air guides. Project 404 also provided an adviser to the Royal Lao Air Force's AC-47 gunship program. The death or capture of such a man carried enormous political risk, and from early 1965 Waterpump began training English-speaking Lao and Meo to replace them.[54] Laotian ground forces were trained and equipped through another secret American group called the Requirements Organization, operating out of Thailand and run by the CIA using U.S. AID as cover.[55]

In the spring of 1964, Pathet Lao and North Vietnamese forces launched attacks against Neutralist forces on the Plain of Jars, prompting their commander, Gen. (previously Capt.) Kong Le to warn the Royal Lao Government that without air support the situation was hopeless, mostly because the troops of the Royal Lao Army had fled. (Neutralist, in the military sense, refers to the soldiers who followed Kong Le, who sought to remove foreign influence and foreigners from the country. Earlier circumstances had forced him into an alliance with the Communist Pathet Lao, but he broke with them when he came to understand they were serving their Vietnamese masters in the way that the Royal Lao Army was serving the United States. Later his troops fought against the Communists—but just to complicate things, a splinter group of leftist Neutralists fought with the Communists.)

In the United Nations, the United States charged the Pathet Lao with "an outright attempt to destroy by violence what the whole structure of the Geneva Accords was intended to preserve." There was ample evidence to back the claim. Navy and Air Force reconnaissance planes had come back with photos showing the Plain of Jars bristling with newly installed antiaircraft guns—sixteen sites in all, on or around the plain, housing guns capable of firing 150 rounds a minute, effective to a ceiling of fifteen thousand feet.[56]

Ambassador Leonard Unger, nearing the end of his term in 1964, obtained approval from the Johnson administration to release the fuses on previously delivered U.S. bombs, for use by the Royal Lao Air Force.[57] Prince Souvanna Phouma also authorized the use of U.S. fighters to accompany the unarmed reconnaissance jets over Laotian territory, and these missions became code-named Yankee Team.

A Navy Yankee Team plane was lost only days later, and two Air America helicopters were hit when they attempted to make a recovery three hours after the plane went down. They flew into a flak trap (a tactic the enemy were to employ for the next decade: the downed pilot was allowed to survive to call for help while enemy gunners lay in wait for the arrival of vulnerable helicopters).

The two Air America helicopters abandoned their rescue effort when two crew members were critically wounded in the heavy fire. The downed pilot was captured. A second U.S. plane was shot down the following day over the same area, except this time Air America managed to snatch the pilot out of the jungle the very next morning.[58]

In retaliation, President Johnson ordered a squadron of U.S. jets to attack a Communist antiaircraft installation at Xieng Khouang on the Plain of Jars. News of the downed planes was not officially announced but was learned by the U.S. media through the New China News Agency in Peking, loosing a howl of outrage from the press. "What in heaven's name does the United States think it is doing by trying to keep these air strikes secret?" the *Washington Post* asked in an angry editorial.[59] News reports of the U.S. air operations gained wide circulation for the first time, and one, a UPI story by journalist Arthur Dommen, "in effect blew the lid on the entire Yankee Team operation in Laos."[60]

Questions were beginning to be asked, both on Capitol Hill and in the press, but with the beginning of the extensive bombing of North Vietnam in late 1964, events in Laos were overshadowed and the public's attention distracted. They would not be answered for a further five years, when William Sullivan—who had then left Laos after serving from 1964 to mid-1969 to become deputy assistant secretary of state for the Far East—faced an interrogatory closed hearing before a Senate subcommittee. He explained that U.S. activities in Laos had been kept secret because Prime Minister Souvanna Phouma had requested it—the North Vietnamese brazenly violated his country's neutrality, covering their activities with barefaced lies, but in the circumstances the prime minister could not openly admit to support from the United States without sabotaging his own genuine efforts at obtaining neutrality.

The U.S. government never acknowledged more than "armed reconnaissance" flights in northern Laos until March 1970, and the term itself is a misleading euphemism. Translated from military jargon, "armed reconnaissance" means an attack sortie in search of targets of opportunity.

A major step toward the escalation of the air war was made in early December 1964, when the National Security Council approved a bombing program to complement Yankee Team reconnaissance missions in northern and central Laos. Code-named Barrel Roll, the program introduced twice-weekly missions of four aircraft each carrying bombs, but no napalm. There were to be no public statements about these bombing raids unless a plane was lost, in which case the United States government would "continue to insist that we were merely escorting reconnaissance flights as requested by the Laotian government."[61]

The next logical step in the escalation of the air war in Laos was to divide it into two. Barrel Roll would concentrate on flying combat support for the Royal Laotian Army and Meo forces ranged against the Pathet Lao and North Vietnamese in the north of the country, while a new program—given the code name Steel Tiger—was introduced to organize air strikes against the Ho Chi Minh Trail in the southern Laotian panhandle.

Over the course of the years, as the Ho Chi Minh Trail grew, Steel Tiger was to become very big business indeed, and itself split amoebalike into two. Extra Air Force reserves were put into a new program, Tiger Hound, concentrating on segments of the Trail closest to South Vietnam. Action against the Trail became a war unto itself, with its own FACs flying out of South Vietnam and Thailand. But air support of battles inside Laos remained the exclusive preserve of the Ravens.

* * *

Above all else, Laos was a CIA war. At first this was considered praiseworthy—a minimum of Americans were spending much less money than the big-spending U.S. military in Vietnam next door, and with more effect. "I personally feel that although the way the operation has been run is unorthodox, unprecedented, in many ways I think it is something of which we can be proud as Americans," was the way U. Alexis Johnson, former under secretary of state, put it when testifying before a Senate committee. "It has involved virtually no American casualties. What we are getting for our money is, to use the old phrase, very cost-effective."[62]

The parent organization itself—the CIA—was rather smug about Laos and boasted about its success there. After all, the Agency employed only 16,500 people—with a further 11,300 involved in clandestine services and backup—compared to the Pentagon's two and a half million. In October 1967, Senator Stuart Symington personally invited CIA station chief Ted Shackley, whose houseguest he had been on a trip to Laos, to testify before the Armed Services Committee. At the end of it the senator praised the Laotian program as a suitable way to fight a war—the CIA in Laos was spending in a year what the U.S. Army was spending in a day in Vietnam, Symington said. (Later, he was to reverse his view and express "surprise, shock and anger" over the CIA's secret war, even though he had been thoroughly briefed on Vang Pao's Meo army since September 1966, and had also personally witnessed bombers leaving Udorn on missions to Laos.)[63]

Critics of the CIA saw things differently. The president had, in effect, fielded his own secret army in Laos, complete with tens of thousands of mercenary foot soldiers, Special Forces commandos with sterile (non-attributable) weapons, and sheep-dipped fighter pilots commanding massive air support. After the disclosures of CIA bungling at the Bay of Pigs invasion of Cuba, along with the CIA role in various assassination plots, the idea of the same agency running a decent-sized war as a covert operation was cause for alarm. It was the liberal's nightmare—the notorious CIA pursuing secret, conspiratorial policies at gunpoint, a rogue elephant gone on a frenzied rampage.

These same critics would have been surprised to learn that people at the very top of the Agency tended to agree. Richard Helms, director of the Agency between 1966 and 1973, disliked large paramilitary operations such as Laos for the very practical reason that they were virtually impossible to keep secret. Leaked information regarding one covert operation threatened all of the Agency's operational assets—proprietary airlines, funding procedures, identity of agents, etc.—and brought it before the public eye. Exposure brought notoriety, played into the hands of the Agency's enemies, and led to the imposition of external oversight mechanisms and numerous legal restraints, all of which hampered its ability to pursue its main function—the collection and analysis of intelligence.[64]

Helms's successor, William Colby, director of the Agency from 1973 to 1976, held similar views. As onetime head of the CIA's Far Eastern division he had been intimately involved with affairs in Laos from early on, concluding, "A large-scale paramilitary operation does not fit the secret budget and policy procedures of CIA."[65] If the American government wanted to fight a war it ought to use the military—the CIA's directors resented being saddled with large-scale military commitments which the president dared not undertake openly.

Covert operations in general have always been an area of intense debate within the Agency, and those in Laos caused an eruption. The CIA played a central role in the three-year running battle, between 1958 and 1961, over whom the United States should back in the country. Not only did the CIA and the State Department support different people and favor opposing policies (fueling its critics' charge that the Agency had slipped its moorings and was pursuing its own policies), but there was a bitter division within the Agency itself. The CIA station chief in Vientiane at the time, Henry Heckscher—who had refused to tell the U.S. ambassador to Laos about some of the Agency's activities within the country—terminated one angry exchange of cables, "Is headquarters still in friendly hands?"[66]

In fact, the sins of the CIA in Laos should be largely attributed to presidents who often used it without fully informing the State Department what they were doing. The unsatisfactory situation of warring government agencies—and renegade factions battling within each—was resolved by President Kennedy's "Country Team" directive of May 1961. This placed all agencies operating within a foreign country under the direct supervision of the U.S. ambassador—especially relevant in Laos, where it allowed Ambassador Unger to take control of the CIA.

The signing of the Geneva Accords in 1962 resulted in the president's decision to use the CIA to fight a clandestine war within the country, and also necessitated that a structure be set up to enable it to do so. While the ambassador remained all-powerful, officially the CIA was just one of several equal agencies. In reality it was more equal than others. The CIA funded all the irregular forces in Laos, which gave it direct control over those forces; it controlled Air America and Continental Air Services; it also exercised operational control over both Army attaché's and air attaché's offices. "For God's sake, don't buck the CIA," air attaché Col. Paul Pettigrew told his replacement, Col. Robert Tyrrell, "or you'll find yourself floating facedown on that Mekong River."[67]

Almost from the very beginning there was a division between the CIA paramilitary types in the field—the "cowboys"—and the analysts and officers back in the embassy. Douglas Blaufarb, the CIA station chief in Vientiane between 1963 and 1966—during which time the mechanisms of the secret war were put in place—was decidedly *not* a cowboy. A graduate of Harvard and the Columbia Journalism School, Blaufarb was a mainstream 1930s-vintage liberal who had gone to war with conviction against the Nazis. He was also prepared to fight covertly what he saw to be the Communist threat to traditional liberal American values (although he was not an anticommunist ideologue, and worked to protect friends from the witch-hunting Senator McCarthy).[68]

Blaufarb's considerable knowledge of counterinsurgency was learned from books rather than the battlefield. He became intimately concerned with the Meo resistance, which he saw as an underground *maquis* similar to that in France in World War II.[69] However, despite Blaufarb's scholarly leanings he displayed, along with other CIA operatives, a complete lack of interest in earlier French efforts to organize the Meo into an underground fighting force. (The CIA continues to take credit for discovering Vang Pao and arming the Meo—both of which the French had done before them in the early 1950s.) "For better or worse, history for its own sake does not play any part in the lives of active operations officers in the CIA, and I never thought to delve into events of the years before I became involved," Blaufarb said.[70] Neither, apparently, did anyone else— with the result that the CIA was forever reinventing the wheel in Laos.

But a very different type of CIA man came to dominate the war in Laos. The secret nature of the conflict demanded a logistic chain outside the country, and this was established in Thailand, where "volunteers" were also recruited and trained alongside Lao in special jungle commando camps. The CIA "logistics" office in Thailand— 4802 Joint Liaison Detachment—operated out of a large compound at

Udorn Air Force Base. This was headed by Pat Landry, a large, tough former Cincinnati police captain who strutted about Patton-style, flicking his boots with a riding crop. CIA station chiefs in Vientiane and Bangkok came and went, but Pat Landry stayed on and on.

The exact division of duties between Udorn and Vientiane is difficult to evaluate, but Landry's power grew as the war progressed. It was a power exaggerated by secrecy. Landry and his agents in the field behaved like warlords in their own private fiefdoms. Landry was said to run a personality cult: a man's face had to fit, and the sort of face he favored was that of a former Green Beret or Special Forces soldier, preferably with a good line in right-wing, anticommunist rhetoric. When the CIA attempted to put a man in above Landry at Udorn he used his connections with the Thai prime minister to have the appointment quashed.

Two Air Force officers also stationed at Udorn who worked in the "black" with the CIA were Martin "Quietly" Kaufman, who handled the extraordinarily complex task of negotiating contracts between the CIA proprietary airline Air America and the U.S. government, and Richard V. Secord, a brilliant clandestine operative who handled the operational and logistical side of the U.S. Air Force's involvement in the secret war in Laos. Secord, known among his West Point classmates as "The Fat Man," had previously been awarded the Distinguished Flying Cross for a rescue mission in the Congo and had also flown two hundred secret combat missions in fighters in South Vietnam before his arrival in Thailand in 1966. He became known as "The Buddha" among the secret warriors, because he was perceived as inscrutable, the fount of great secret powers, and round.

"Heinie" Aderholt, the Air Commando commander at Nakhon Phanom, had brought Secord into the war to run a number of clandestine operations—including secret C-130 missions into Laos using unmarked Air Force planes at night, and at least one unconventional attack on the enemy which involved dropping a planeload of Calgonite dishwasher detergent on the Ho Chi Minh Trail to make it too slippery for the Communists to travel. Secord did not personally endear himself to his commander, but good work earned his respect. "I thought he was arrogant," Aderholt said. "He acted like a general when he was a captain. But he was the best goddam officer I ever had. The smartest man in the whole show."

The most famous of the CIA's Laotian warlords is Anthony Posepny—the legendary Tony Poe, also known as Bill Gibbs, Upin, and an assortment of operational aliases. Poe is an ex-Marine—said to have been at Iwo Jima in World War II—with a history of leading CIA secret armies all over the Far East: in 1956 he helped train Tibetan Khamba tribesmen and engineered the escape of the Dalai Lama; in 1958 he was one of two paramilitary agents sent in to help avert the defeat of a rebel uprising against Sukarno in Indonesia; in 1960 he trained Nationalist Chinese paramilitary units bound for mainland China.

Poe likes to describe himself as a "Bohemian Scot," and is one of those red-blooded American crusaders who have spent very little time at home in their beloved United States. As a Marine recruit Poe looked like a young Marlon Brando (and in late middle age has grown to resemble the mad figure of Colonel Kurtz, whom Brando plays in *Apocalypse Now*—except instead of slothful, maudlin introspection, Poe exhibits furious activity coupled with absolute certainty). Stories of his courage are legion—he once carried a wounded soldier a dozen miles on his back, even though he was wounded himself. He has been badly wounded half a dozen times, and one hand is a claw, maimed when a jungle booby trap went off, killing a friend. War is never far away from Tony Poe, and even when traveling in peaceful places he always carries a boxer's mouthpiece in case of bar fights.

People who knew and fought with him said that in their opinion perpetual jungle warfare had turned him into a heavy drinker and brutalized him. Somewhere along the way, CIA colleagues say, Tony Poe went "bamboo." One explained: "You can't put a man in the jungle to fight an endless war where he has to live with natives in a primitive environment, and the only entertainment is to drink a couple of bottles of Scotch a day, and not expect him to go a little mad."

In Laos, Tony Poe began life as Vang Pao's case officer, but seems to have fallen out with the general by 1965, when he complained that there were too many "round eyes" (Americans) at Long Tieng—and also that the general was corrupt. It was always a moot point whether Vang Pao was run by the CIA or vice versa, and it is probable that the general resented Poe's strong, domineering personality.

(In a later run-in with Long Tieng base chief Tom Clines, Vang Pao ruthlessly demonstrated who was in charge. Six prisoners had been brought in by the Meo, and Clines demanded that his men interrogate them. Vang Pao nodded to an aide, who immediately had the men taken outside and shot. The CIA man took the point. "What I meant to say, general, is that I would *appreciate* it if you would *allow* us to interrogate prisoners, *please*.")

Poe moved to northwest Laos, where he ran all western operations, including cross-border forays into Burma and China. Northwest Laos is populated by a diverse mixture of tribal minorities, and Poe learned to speak several dialects and married a Yau princess. The war was complicated locally because of the annual cross-border opium caravans of the Burmese Shans, and the relentless construction of a road by the Communist Chinese (allowed by an agreement with the Laotian government before the Geneva Accords). The road, which would eventually stretch 250 miles from Dien Bien Phu to the Mekong, was, in effect, an extension of the Chinese border cutting off fifteen thousand square miles of northern Laos. It was protected by antiaircraft guns and thousands of Chinese troops, and was ordered off limits to all U.S. personnel to avoid provoking the Chinese. Tony Poe was kept on a very short lead and given almost no support by the embassy. His reports of North Vietnamese troops coming into the country from across the Chinese border and using the new road were pointedly ignored. Unofficially, Poe was given support by the Air Commandos, who used Thai pilots flying T-28s to attack the road and North Vietnamese troops, while Poe talked Air America pilots into loading their planes with large rocks with which to bomb the enemy, and dropping primed hand grenades in mayonnaise jars onto them (a dangerous technique which involved pulling the pin of a grenade, and then placing it in a jar to keep the lever down—when the jar broke the grenade exploded).

He offered his native troops a one-dollar bonus for a set of Communist ears, and they deposited their ghastly trophies in a plastic bag specially kept for the purpose. "They used to hang on strings on the porch of Tony's house like chitlings," said Charlie Jones, an Air Commando Butterfly FAC—the precursors of the Ravens. Irritated by the embassy's open skepticism over his claims of a large enemy body count (U.S. officials in Vientiane questioned the very existence of North Vietnamese regulars in Poe's section of Laos), he stapled a bloody batch of freshly sliced ears to his next report.

But Poe finally canceled the scheme when he landed on a remote strip and saw a small boy without any ears. "What happened to your ears?" Poe growled.

"My father took them to get money from the Americans," the boy replied matter-of-factly.[71]

He was also rumored to preserve the heads of particular enemies in jars of formaldehyde, dropping one into the village of a hostile village chief who had shot at his plane. "If you do everything according to the orders, you'd be in a straitjacket. You have to break the monotony sometimes."[72]

In 1968 Poe sustained a stomach wound when leading a group of his men into battle, in contravention of the most stringent embassy orders that CIA case officers were not allowed to take part in combat. He was immediately thrown out of the country by Ambassador Sullivan—but seems to have been protected by Pat Landry, for he resurfaced in Thailand, where he ran a Special Forces training camp. The Thai commandoes he trained adored him. "Mr. Poe was very nice and polite," one said, "and a *very* good dancer."[73]

In the interregnum between Sullivan's departure from Laos and Godley's arrival, Tony Poe slipped back into the country, where he continued to work until at least the early 1970s. His notoriety is an embarrassment to many Americans who worked in Laos. ("You ought not to quote him so much," Ambassador Godley said, referring to the author's previous book, *Air America*. "Tony was an exception.")

Exception or not, Tony Poe fought in the secret war in Laos for a decade. One of the Ravens was with Poe when he returned to the United States for a CIA retirement presentation ceremony. "They sort of said, 'You did a wonderful job, now go back to Thailand and never bother us again,'" Karl Polifka said. "I drove him out to the National Airport afterward, accompanied by some Agency people who seemed to want to make sure he got on the plane, and it was as if they couldn't get him out of D.C. fast enough."

The majority of the paramilitary types in Laos displayed none of Poe's gaudier excesses, although many of them proved to be equally gifted as leaders of native troops. There is no doubt that most of them were exceptionally brave and committed men—contrary to popular opinion, CIA paramilitary case officers are not cold-blooded and cynical killers, but often moral and idealistic. Many developed a passionate attachment to the Meo and their cause, and they suffered agonies of guilt and self-recrimination when U.S. policy dictated that the CIA move on and abandon them.

There was clearly an enormous disparity between the college-educated CIA analysts in the embassy and the paramilitary types, who were often the equivalent of a Special Forces sergeant. There seemed to be no provision made to bridge the gap. It was as if an army were forced to go into battle with only staff officers and sergeants, without a body of competent officers of all ranks between them. In Laos it was all sergeants and generals.

One exception was a CIA colonel with a military background, who had commanded a parachute division in World War II, advised the division commander in the war against the Greek Communists, and been a senior adviser to a corps-sized division against guerrillas in Korea (and was later chief of the CIA overflight program). The colonel saw the scope of the problem when he first arrived in Laos and inspected machine-gun pits set up by a CIA case officer in a Thai position. "They were just pointing out into space," the colonel said. "I told him he had to get angles of fire—very basic stuff. That he didn't want his machine gunners to see what's coming at them because they'll get frightened and fire in one direction instead of putting out bands of fire. He was a good sergeant but just didn't know his stuff.

"People were used beyond their capacity in Laos. One, who could have handled anything up through a company grade, was put in as senior adviser to a corps-sized group of twenty thousand men." When the colonel made the criticism at a meeting at the embassy he was embarrassed to find people looking at him as if he were a West Point snob. In the field the sergeants ran the show.

Policy tended to be improvised. "I think it was day-to-day," a senior CIA man said. "Policy was something we discovered as we went along and it became policy. We were just trying to protect what we had to allow the government to continue."

But one policy pursued relentlessly by the CIA was secrecy. In Laos it had become a way of life. The press were naturally considered a danger, but so was any outsider—even from the military. John Clark Pratt, an Air Force historian, arrived in Udorn with the necessary security clearances to allow him to go up to Long Tieng and interview Gen. Vang Pao for a classified Air Force study he was working on. The CIA at Udorn demanded an additional handwriting test—"to make sure you are who you say you are"—which involved sending a sample by mail to Washington.

After a considerable delay, which gave ample time for the Udorn spooks to warn their counterparts in the Secret City of the impending arrival of an Air Force snoop, Pratt was allowed to go up to Long Tieng. He was met from the plane by a CIA man, who told him he needed a fingerprint check. While this was being verified, Pratt was incarcerated incommunicado in one of the back rooms of the CIA hootch. He assumed it to be the library: four bookshelves were packed with rows of dog-eared paperbacks, all of which fitted into the spy, action-adventure, shoot-em-up genre—James Bond, John Le Carré, John McDonald, Louis Lamour, etc. (Life did not so much imitate art, in the world of the spooks, as pulp fiction.) After four hours the CIA man returned to say that verification had come through, but unfortunately Gen. Vang Pao was no longer on the base. Pratt returned to Udorn empty-handed.

Tom Shera, a Raven who returned to Laos to work in the air attaché's office, explained, "The CAS guys didn't even want the other agencies to know what was going on. In 1970 the general officers on the Air Staff of the USAF had no idea that there were that many Air Force people in Laos. And when they found out, the vice chief of the Air Force personally came over to get a briefing, because nobody at the Pentagon knew what was going on." (The Air Force tried to exact its revenge on the CIA by encouraging the Ravens to give them intelligence first, "so we can be one up on the spooks at the Country Team meetings.")

The difference between the U.S. approaches to the wars in Vietnam and in Laos can best be understood by taking a close look at the personalities and careers of the individuals who ran the CIA in the country. Ted Shackley—previously the boss of the CIA's Miami station set up by President Kennedy after the Bay of Pigs—took over as station chief from Blaufarb in July 1966 and remained until August 1968. An ambitious technocrat, Shackley was known inside the Agency as a ruthless, hard-driving, no-nonsense boss with a penchant for filling key jobs with personal friends. Tall, thin, and exceptionally pale, he was the type of man some of the case officers who worked under him found "weird." He was considered "cold" by colleagues, a man who kept people at arm's length, but who was also fair. There were those who judged him "brilliant"—although others felt his computerlike rhetoric and convoluted reasoning seemed more profound than it was.

Shackley was a hard-line anticommunist who could be shrill to the point of fanaticism in his dire warnings: "Make no mistake. We—all of us—*are* locked in a struggle for survival," he wrote in his book *The Third Option*, in which he argues the case for covert operations as a necessary choice of weapon from a limited arsenal. "At one end there is the give-and-take through the normal channels of negotiation and diplomacy; at the other lies the unthinkable: war. But there is yet one more. Experts in revolutionary warfare and paramilitary operations call it the third option."[74] This is a standard argument often heard from the CIA's clandestine operatives—that the Agency offers a tool of middle resort, somewhere between diplomatic protest and military intervention. But in Laos the definitions of "covert operation" and "war" differed by no more than semantic nuance.

Laos was the place where Shackley could put his counterinsurgency theories into practice. He understood that the Meo "were quick to recognize that one does not eat rhetoric and propaganda."[75] The CIA's nation-building formula established pig-breeding centers, fish farms, kilns to make bricks, schools and vocational training, and co-operative retail stores that were particularly successful. U.S. AID was funding around two hundred hospitals, serving more than 150,000 patients a month, and was also training hundreds of new medics each year.

But there was another side to Shackley's theory. When he went on from Laos to become station chief in Saigon—a very important job at the time—he had something of a mixed reputation. A group of Special Forces officers asked their CIA liaison officer what they should do with a Vietnamese double agent and were told to kill him. After all, the CIA officer said, the CIA's station chief in Saigon, Ted Shackley, "had been responsible for 250 political killings in Laos and one more wouldn't make any difference."[76]

In Saigon Shackley encouraged personnel to "recruit, recruit, recruit—that is bribe, inveigle, and hire anyone and everyone to work for us as agents," CIA analyst Frank Snepp said. The station's spy roster swelled accordingly and was soon sending five hundred reports a month back to Washington.[77]

Shackley took over Western Hemisphere Division in 1972, the CIA's Clandestine Services' Latin American arm. His first act was to cancel most of the division's operations and fire those agents he feared Philip Agee might have either named to Cuban and Soviet intelligence agents in 1971, or who might be named in Agee's upcoming exposé on the CIA (*Inside the Company*). But when the book appeared few of those fired were mentioned.[78]

Shackley later returned to the Far East as head of the CIA's East Asia Division, where he reaped the dubious harvest of his earlier recruitment drive. In 1974, as the Agency scrambled to clarify Hanoi's cease-fire strategy, it was reported that over a hundred of Shackley's Vietcong "agents" were no more than enterprising fabricators, "intelligence" entrepreneurs making money from selling unreliable information cobbled together from newspaper clippings and gossip.[79]

(The clandestine world is a strange and, in the end, small place. After a premature retirement in the mid-seventies, Shackley has reportedly resurfaced in West Berlin, named as the go-between for the Iranian arms dealer, Ghorbanifar, and the White House, in the

Iran-Contra scandal. Other secret war people have also been named, notably Richard Secord and Tom Clines, Long Tieng base chief. Together the three men had formed a highly publicized Unholy Trinity.

By 1981 Secord had risen in the Pentagon to become the deputy assistant secretary of defense, a job which involved formulating U.S. defense policy concerning almost forty countries; Shackley was considered by many to be a possible future director of the CIA; Clines, who had practically grown up in the CIA, where he started life in the mail room in 1949, had left the Agency to set up a private company to sell arms to Egypt following the Camp David accords.

Secord returned to Washington in 1978, after a stint in Iran advising the Shah on the best way to spend the billions of dollars he had budgeted for his Air Force. Together with Shackley and Clines he often spent the weekends at the palatial country estate of Ed Wilson, an ex-CIA agent to whom Clines had once acted as case officer, now turned international arms dealer. The men had all known each other since the war in Laos—where, on one occasion, Wilson had delivered a load of electronic beepers to Shackley, which were eventually placed in Pathet Lao units by infiltrating Meo enabling the CIA to monitor Pathet Lao movements and call in air strikes on them.

But Wilson was an agent who had got out of control and had, in effect, turned terrorist. One of his money-making enterprises involved funneling arms to Libya's terrorist dictator, Col. Muammar el-Quaddafi. Wilson fled after an investigation into his activities, and is now serving a 52-year prison sentence for illegally selling arms to Libya. During his trial he claimed that both Secord and Shackley were silent partners in a company that was accused in 1982 of bilking the federal government of $8 million. The men denied the charge, but Secord was suspended from duty while he came under investigation by a federal grand jury for conspiring with Wilson to defraud the government. Similarly, Shackley was effectively forced into early retirement because of his relationship with Wilson. Although not indicted, and reinstated in his job, Secord left the Air Force in 1983 and went into partnership with Albert Hakim, who he met during his time in Iran, to become the president of Stanford Technology Corporation—a company which Wilson had once represented as a salesman.

Then in October 1986 Eugene Hasenfus, a one-time cargo kicker with Air America in Laos, was shot down on a clandestine supply mission to the Contras in Nicaragua. Telephone records of calls from the safe house occupied by the crew in El Salvador revealed that frequent calls were made to Secord's home and office at Stanford Technology—which was linked in turn to Lt. Col. Oliver North's private-aid network. And so the secret warriors of the Laotian War became linked to Iranscam, where money from arms deals made with the Ayatollah were funneled to the Contras in Nicaragua.)[80]

Lawrence Devlin took over as CIA station chief in Vientiane in August 1968 and held the position until December 1970. He was seen by his colleagues as sincere, pleasant, and relatively easygoing after his predecessor. "Larry was an idealist," one CIA man said. "Pretty much the knight on the white charger."

Idealism apart, Devlin also has a murky covert past. He had previously served with Ambassador Godley as station chief in the Congo during a period of intense CIA activity. John Stockwell, a former CIA man, described Devlin as the famous *éminence grise* of the Congo program, where he shuffled new governments like cards. One colleague said Devlin was "one of the CIA's historic great 'operators' " who had "dealt with younger case officers and agents like an Irish-American politician, giving out patronage and coming down hard on any who stood in his way."[81]

The trouble in the Congo arose when Nationalist leader Patrice Lumumba received direct aid from the Soviets in his newly independent country, which had immediately sunk into chaos and bloodshed. Allen Dulles, then head of the CIA, saw Lumumba as "a Castro—or worse." The United States favored Joseph-Désiré Mobutu, who seized power in a coup. Lumumba sought refuge with the United Nations force in the country, which put him under protective custody.

It was reported that "easygoing" Devlin received a cable from Dulles himself which said that "High quarters . . . sought Lumumba's removal an urgent and prime objective." Used to reading between the lines, the station chief interpreted the cable as a strong indication that the president of the United States wanted Lumumba killed. "We wish to give you every possible support in eliminating Lumumba from any possibility of resuming governmental position." An "Eyes Only" channel was set up between CIA HQ and Léopoldville, and the sum of $100,000 was authorized for the assassination.

A CIA "science adviser" personally delivered two assassination kits to Devlin in Léopoldville. They consisted of rubber gloves, gauze masks, hypodermic needles, and a lethal biological agent. This was potent stuff. A cocktail concocted by the Army's biological warfare corps, it was designed to cause in its victim tularemia (rabbit fever), brucellosis (undulant fever), tuberculosis, anthrax, smallpox, and—just to make sure—Venezuelan equine encephalitis (sleeping sickness).[82]

The CIA hired two professional killers to carry out the planned assassination, neither of whom was American or knew of the other's existence, and each was given a kit. Devlin requested a case officer to supervise the assassination, which included a plan to put the biological agent on Lumumba's toothbrush.[83] Despite the elaborate planning, the poison was never administered, but Lumumba was beaten to death on January 17, 1961, by henchmen of Congolese politicians —who had close relationships with the CIA.[84]

Devlin was later called back to Washington to testify before the Church Committee, which concluded that although the CIA personnel had wanted to assassinate Lumumba, they had been beaten to it by others. Not everyone is convinced of the CIA's innocence, and Devlin is suspected of knowing more about it than his testimony revealed. One CIA man, for instance, told a colleague that he had driven all over Lubumbashi after curfew with Patrice Lumumba's body in the trunk "wondering what to do with it."[85] News of the death prompted the CIA base chief in Elisabethville to cable HQ: "Thanks for Patrice. If we had known he was coming, we would have baked a snake."[86]

Devlin became chief of Africa Division after his stint in Laos, and on his retirement in 1974 he accepted a four-year contract with a New York financier, based on his intimate friendship with Mobutu, who succeeded in becoming one of the world's richest men on the backs of an impoverished population.

Devlin's successor in Laos was Hugh Tovar, who served from October 1970 through 1972. He was sophisticated and intellectually oriented, an upright man and a good Catholic. "I have nothing but admiration for Hugh," a CIA colleague who worked with him said. "You could not ask for a better boss or a more considerate person."

It was Tovar who launched an all-out campaign against drug smuggling in Laos—with limited success. But despite his reputation as an intellectual, Tovar also had a swashbuckling clandestine background. He had dropped into Indochina by parachute as a young OSS lieutenant in World War II with the group ordered to make contact with Ho Chi Minh. Later he served as station chief during the ill-fated uprising against Sukarno in Indonesia.

Such were the men who ran the CIA's war in Laos, a very different breed from the generals who ran the war in Vietnam. Intelligence gathered in Laos by the CIA throughout the conflict was good—both from the native agents among the enemy and from electronic intercept programs (the backbone of which was the highly classified EC-47—Electronic Goon—consisting of the most sophisticated electronic equipment built into a compact unit and housed in the back of the ubiquitous C-47, the antiquated work horse of Air America). The military planning of the CIA was less impressive—little more than a series of reactions to enemy initiatives. And, as the roster of CIA chiefs demonstrates, the plans were made by covert "operators" rather than by soldiers.

But the oft-expressed fear of the time, that the CIA had slipped its moorings in Laos and that the war there would become a precedent for its future actions, must be judged unfounded in retrospect. The CIA was put into Laos by presidential directive, pursued the war according to the dictates of ambassadors, and duly withdrew when ordered to do so.

The seesaw pattern of the war in northern Laos continued year after year until, in the dry season of 1968–69, the North Vietnamese changed their tactics. For the first time their advance was characterized by a scorched-earth policy. Meo villages were razed to the ground as Communist soldiers passed through, denying the Americans their most valuable intelligence asset—the villagers themselves. The North Vietnamese calculated correctly that this time when they fell back in the rainy season they would be less vulnerable to ambush. The Americans responded with increased bombing.

The arrival of tens of thousands of refugees on the outskirts of Vientiane alerted the world's press to the real scope of the war in Laos. From now on the secrecy would boomerang on the Americans. The reports led to congressional critics accusing the U.S. military of indiscriminate saturation bombing. The Nixon administration responded that the refugees were fleeing the North Vietnamese and the strictures of life under the Communist Pathet Lao—rice and porterage taxes, forced labor, and so on. The Americans pointed out that the refugees fled into the arms of the Royal Lao Government, where they were cared for by U.S. AID, and not into Communist-controlled terrain, something Ambassador G. McMurtrie Godley—who replaced Sullivan—described as "voting with their feet." Press reports cited the impossibility of normal life under the rain of American bombs, and many of those opposed to the U.S. presence claimed that the bombing was the principal cause of the flood of refugees.[87] There were, of course, tens of thousands of Meo refugees as a result of the war *before* widespread American bombing.[88] The issue has never been satisfactorily settled in favor of either argument. One thing is clear: the combination of the two—harsher Communist military tactics and increased U.S. bombing—created a sea of refugees. And what these people were fleeing was the war.

Such was the Big Picture. It was something that eluded the Ravens as they flew into battle, a higher politics they were scarcely aware of and did not need to know. But unlike the war in Vietnam, which so many had come to see as a dubious military proposition, there was something simple and straightforward in Laos to fight for: the Ravens were there to help the Meo resist a traditional enemy who had invaded their country and threatened their survival. It was possible in Laos for the Ravens to believe they were the good guys, which was important if they were to sustain the will to combat through the worst moments of a nasty little war.

And by the end of 1968 there was another piece of the Big Picture which could not elude them—both sides had upped their stake in the conflict, and the Meo were taking a terrible beating.

PART III

PART III

6

AIR POWER

The Meo had failed to take the Rock, the sacred mountain of Phou Pha Thi, and now suffered one defeat after another. Everywhere they were pushed back. Gen. Vang Pao had lost face before his people. He felt the humiliation so strongly and his depression was so profound that his CIA advisers began to fear a complete psychological disintegration. The general wandered around Long Tieng blank-eyed and without purpose, unwashed and dressed like a tramp, a man at the very end of his tether.

At the beginning of 1969 the North Vietnamese fielded the entire 316th Division, previously deployed only in small detachments on a rotating basis.[1] Intelligence estimates reckoned that the combined North Vietnamese and Pathet Lao forces inside the country had increased from 51,000 to more than 110,000—the North Vietnamese contingent comprising an estimated 34,000 combat troops, 6,000 advisers, 18,000 support troops, and more than 13,000 engineers involved in road building.[2]

The enemy pushed into the foothills of the Plain of Jars, bringing armored vehicles and 175mm artillery pieces capable of shelling Long Tieng itself with their range of thirty kilometers. The enemy's scorched-earth policy denied the Meo and the Americans the invaluable asset of behind-the-lines intelligence, and there were indications that this time the North Vietnamese intended to make the most of their advantage and remain in the country during the monsoon season. The precarious seasonal swap of terrain and political control, which had been observed by both sides since the signing of the Accords seven years earlier, with neither combatant wishing to upset the balance for fear of inviting large-scale, superpower military intervention, was abandoned.[3] The gloves were off and a vicious no-quarter war was about to begin. And the battlefield was to be the Plain of Jars.

The Plaine de Jarres, as the French named it, is a beautiful plateau forty miles wide, lying at an altitude of more than three thousand feet, covered with grass and small hills, and spread over an area of approximately five hundred square miles. The Americans translated the French name into the Plain of Jars, which military men shortened to the PDJ, or just the J. The great stone jars which gave the plain its name are thought to be the funeral urns of another culture, although archaeologists cannot agree which one. They appear to be over two thousand years old, made from a gray stone found nowhere in the region, and artifacts found with the jars fail to relate them to any of the known civilizations of the area. Attempts by Air America pilots—driven by some atavistic vandal urge—to lift out one of the jars, using their most powerful helicopter, proved completely unsuccessful. (There was talk of taking a jar—weighing four thousand to six thousand pounds—to CIA HQ, Langley, Virginia, to act as the Tomb of the Unknown Case Officer, but the idea was rejected.) And extraordinarily, despite the hail of bombs unleashed upon the plain, no jar was ever damaged throughout the war.

The Meo were comparative newcomers to the area, but the plain was the geographic center of the small, once autonomous kingdom of Xieng Khouang. Before the war the temperate climate of the plain supported tea plantations and cattle grazing, and every year fairs took place at the provincial capital, where the Meo sold their mountain crop of opium to European smugglers. Walking on the plain could be magical: sunflowers grew to a height of eight feet, above which fluttered great clouds of butterflies of every variety.

Since the war, the plain had become of vital strategic importance to both sides. Several airfields were situated upon it, and a number of roads crossed it: most important, Route 7, running in an east-west direction and connecting the Vietnamese border to Route 13, the north-south road linking Luang Prabang to Vientiane. On the eastern edge of the plain, at the village of Ban Ban, it meets Route 6, which winds north to the Pathet Lao capital of Sam Neua and then continues into Vietnam. The Meo fought for the plain because it was the center of their ancient kingdom; the Laotian government fought to control the plain because any invading army from the north was bound to come across it; the Vietnamese wanted it both as a passage to the south and to protect the back door to their own country. Anyone seeking military control of northern Laos needed first to control the Plain of Jars, and as a result it became a battleground.

Only the Ravens, operating out of Long Tieng to the southwest of the plain, and the air power they could bring to bear stood in the way of the enemy. Individual, haphazard, and uncoordinated strikes were the extent of government resistance at this time, but the war in the north was such that the destruction of a half-dozen trucks or two or three tanks could tip the balance. In the beginning of January, Dick Shubert was putting in an air strike on the edge of the Plain of Jars when a chance combination of sun and shadow clearly outlined a freshly dug ditch. It gave away the position of an interconnected series of ditches and trenches which the North Vietnamese had laboriously worked upon until they reached the edge of the plain itself. The network had been dug to house the big ammo for the 175mm cannons and 120mm rockets, also being brought forward on tracked vehicles. Shubert directed a bombing strike onto the ditch, and the secondary explosions were massive. The stored ammo cooked off for a day and a night at the rate of eighty explosions a minute. A single Raven had temporarily blunted the entire thrust of the enemy.

The destruction of the enemy's ammunition cache on the edge of the Plain of Jars saved Long Tieng from direct attack. The enemy turned their attention to Site 36, Na Khang, which they surrounded. As the only TACAN (tactical air and navigation control system) in northeast Laos, since the loss of the Rock, it was high on the enemy's list of priorities.

The situation became chronic in the spring of 1969 when bad weather closed the whole of Laos to U.S. air. Only Papa Fox managed to get off the ground from Long Tieng, spinning up among mountains and cloud in a maneuver akin to Russian roulette. He flew below the weather to Site 36 and landed. Sitting on the ground in his O-1, he heard the commander of a firebase screaming over the radio that the enemy were upon him.

It was a small outpost just a few miles north of Na Khang, certain to be overrun without air support. The weather was so bad that the Lao T-28s based in Vientiane were inoperable. Papa Fox loaded his O-1 with high-explosive and Willy Pete (white phosphorous) rockets, commandeered a Backseater, and flew out to the firebase. Talking to the commander through the Backseater, he told him to position his troops behind a certain line and tell them to keep their heads down. He was going to attempt to drive off the attack on his own.

Once Papa Fox had spotted the firebase he had to pull up into the low clouds in order to gain sufficient altitude to enable him to dive and fire his rockets at the enemy. It was a tricky maneuver but seemed to work. Fifteen times he returned to Site 36 to reload with rockets and gas. On each run he dropped out of the clouds, flying directly over the heads of the friendlies into a hail of ground fire as he pounded the North Vietnamese with rockets. Finally the enemy broke and pulled back, dragging their wounded with them and leaving fifteen dead in the wire surrounding the base.[4]

The outpost was saved for the time being, but the enemy were everywhere, and in force. Their vulnerability lay in extended supply lines. The CIA now planned a counterattack intended to cut them off, split the advance guard from the forces in the rear, and push the entire force back to the north of Site 36. Code-named Nighty-Night, the operation was to stage out of Lima Site 108, the Neutralist HQ of Muong Soui, situated to the west of the Plain of Jars. The U.S. Army had a uniformed adviser on the site working with Kong Le's Neutralist forces—Joe Bush, a Ranger captain with the official title Assistant Military Attaché to the U.S. Embassy. The base also housed a large fixed artillery position manned by the Thai. In preparation for the attack, two large barrack-style tents were erected to house the fifty American radio operators, mechanics, and armorers who were flown in, and Air America planes began to ferry ammunition, and a large bomb dump was built up.

The plan was for the Neutralist troops to move out from Site 108 and, in a coordinated push with Vang Pao's guerrillas in the south, advance onto the Plain of Jars and force the North Vietnamese back. Air support would be provided exclusively by Lao, Meo, and Thai pilots flying T-28 fighters from the strip at Muong Soui itself, rather than staging out of Vientiane.

The Raven assigned to the mission was Fred Platt, who had arrived in Laos the previous month, and he found the program suited him so well that sometimes he thought he had died and gone to Valhalla. As a child, he had devoured the improbable aerial adventures of a fictional World War II ace in a series of books, *Red Randall's One-Man War,* and while other children crawled around in the dirt with stick guns, Platt flew over them in an imaginary plane. "Even as a small child I realized that the Air Force were a much cleaner lot." At the age of seventeen he met a Texas barnstormer who flew him from Austin to

Houston in an antiquated biplane with an open cockpit at ten dollars a trip. "I took a couple of rides with this guy and knew from then on I had to fly airplanes."

The moment the Downtowners clapped eyes on him they sensed trouble. His cowboy boots and Texas drawl immediately earned him the nickname Cowboy, duly logged in the embassy computer. He won no friends when he used a senior army officer's bed on his first night in Vientiane to romp with one of the local girls. An outraged embassy TWIX preceded his arrival at Long Tieng: "Reference Cowboy. Is not to RON [remain overnight] in Vientiane under any circumstances. If duties require his presence in Vientiane he will arrive and depart during daylight hours."

Platt leaned naturally toward the unconventional paramilitary CIA men rather than his own Air Force hierarchy, and he adored the cloak-and-dagger aspect of the operation. After his first classified briefing from Burr Smith—Mr. Clean—he asked for poison capsules. "I'm not going to be taken alive, and I'd like to use my bullets to shoot at them. What do you have?" He was given a belt buckle which concealed a knife and had a small wheel at its center which was a compass. The needle, which could be unscrewed, was smeared with a quick-acting shellfish toxin which the CIA had spent three million dollars to develop.

It was also as well that Platt had arrived in Laos with three new airplanes, for he would need them. He exhibited an uncanny propensity for crashing. Between engine failures, emergency landings, and being shot down, he would crash a total of eleven airplanes—a dubious achievement that is an uncontested Raven record, and possibly an Indochina one.

The planes he did not crash were brought back with a large number of bullet holes and sometimes had great gashes gouged out of the fuselage by exploding flak. It seemed to the mechanics, as they went through reel after reel of typhoon tape, that he came back from every mission with an excessive number of bullet holes. After a month they started calling him Magnet Ass, and the name replaced Cowboy in the embassy computer.

On Fred Platt's very first crash he was accompanied by Joe Bush, the U.S. Army attaché. Neither U.S. air nor the Lao T-28s were able to fly because of bad weather, so the two men had gone out onto the Plain of Jars in an O-1, hauling along their own homemade ordnance—fifty-pound 155mm howitzer shells wrapped around with primer cord and fuse igniters, which Bush dropped by hand as an airburst weapon. The crash was unspectacular by Platt's standards; he brought the plane down in friendly territory and the two men were able to walk to safety without incident.

It occurred to both of them, however, that with Operation Nighty-Night about to be launched, and the necessity of Platt flying in and out of the base in battle, a spare plane might be needed. The Thai artillery battalion owned an O-1 Bird Dog, ostensibly for use as a FAC plane, but it was never used and the commander was happy to hand it over to Platt for one hundred dollars.

A word with Stan Wilson the following day resulted in a Filipino Air America mechanic flying up from Vientiane to overhaul the plane, on the understanding he would be flown from the base at the end of the day. "I don't stay up-country at night," the mechanic insisted.

Platt promised to fly him back if he would stay, and waited in Joe Bush's house for the man to finish his work. Bush cooked steaks for the assembled group: a black American sergeant, the CIA "Customer"—as Air America referred to its employer—who lived in the house next door, and a Royal Lao Army colonel. It was dark by the time the man knocked on the door and was ready to be flown back to Long Tieng.

A night landing at Alternate was against all the rules and always an unpleasant experience, but Platt flew in over the jeep lights marking the end of the runway and landed safely. Nighty-Night was to be launched the next day and Platt needed to be in the air at first light. He left a message with the radio operator to call him at 4:00 the following morning.

The wake-up call came earlier than expected. The radio operator burst into Platt's room at 2:00 A.M.: "Muong Soui is under attack."

Platt took off in the dark and headed for Site 108. A frenzied babble of conflicting reports came over the radio and it was difficult to glean any hard information. Sappers had infiltrated the camp, that much was certain, and it seemed Joe Bush had been wounded.

At the first report of the attack, Cricket had diverted A-1 Skyraiders to drop flares over the base in an attempt to mark the retreating sappers. Meanwhile, Air America flew in and out to evacuate the American personnel. Now Platt worked air on the base perimeter in the artificial light of the flares.

As dawn broke he landed on the runway at Muong Soui. North Vietnamese sappers had come onto the base in the early hours of the morning and sabotaged the massive bomb dump. The black sergeant had been shot and left for dead, but despite a heavy loss of blood, he had hauled himself to safety. The Customer, who had returned to the neighboring house, had rolled off his bed and pulled the mattress over him. In the dark the sappers had entered the building, but quickly moved on, thinking the man had run out.

Joe Bush had been asleep when the first rockets hit the far end of his house. He burst out of the front door firing his Swedish-K submachine gun, and ran around to the rear. Two sappers were trying to break in through the back door, and Bush killed them with a grenade. A fierce firefight ensued, in which he wounded two more sappers, before running across to the house where the Customer lived. There, on the steps to the front door, he ran straight into AK-47 fire, which cut him in half.

The Neutralist troops had fled, without either sounding the alarm or firing their weapons, the moment they had seen sappers laying gasoline-filled bottles with burning wicks at the base of their guard towers. The American personnel in their tents, under strict orders not to engage in combat, had sat tight waiting for Air America.

Platt watched the bomb dump burn from the landing strip. He walked across to Joe Bush's house and entered the burned-out building. The whole of one end had been destroyed, and Platt picked his way through the rubble to look at the radio operator's room, where he was to have spent the night on a cot. It had been demolished by a direct hit from the first of the B-40 rockets. The sappers had known exactly where to strike. Their intelligence had been so accurate it seemed obvious that only a traitor inside the camp itself could have supplied the information. Platt felt in his bones that the culprit was the Lao Army colonel with whom he had dined the previous night.

He flew out of Muong Soui in the late morning with murder in his heart. The Pathet Lao were broadcasting the names over the radio of Bush, the black sergeant, and himself—clearly a boast of the Americans killed in the sapper attack. And further evidence that the enemy had detailed information from the inside.

Platt and Bush had homed in on the Communist radio station before and knew it to be somewhere on the plain. They had never been able to locate it, as the station always went off the air before being pinpointed. But this time the moment Platt picked up the frequency he used his radio direction finder. When he had the needle steady he could actually make out the antenna itself less than half a mile in front of him.

According to the Rules of Engagement, it was off limits. The embassy based its rules on old French maps, where every dot represented a village or structure of some kind. The radio station was such a dot, and therefore unable to be targeted. Platt buzzed it and saw a 37mm in a camouflaged hut. He decided to ignore the rules and called Cricket for air.

"Coming your way."

Within minutes two F-4 Phantoms were on station. Despite intense ground fire from antiaircraft guns, they went ahead and destroyed the radio station and its gun position. It was some small satisfaction on a bad day.

Operation Nighty-Night was called off. The reaction of the Neutralists to enemy attack illustrated once again to the Americans the abysmal performance of Laotian troops in battle (and the Neutralists were considered marginally *better* than the soldiers of the Royal Lao Army). The absolute futility of basing any ambitious military operations on them was driven home. Only the Meo forces could be relied upon, and even they were being cut to ribbons in the face of the North Vietnamese onslaught.

Gen. Vang Pao was dispirited by the news from the battlefront and seemed to have lost the will to victory. He spoke endlessly of defeat and threatened his CIA advisers that he would pull all of his troops out of northeast Laos and concentrate them in the northwest, where he would make a defensive stand. Nothing the CIA could say seemed to change his mind.

Pop Buell, the Indiana farmer who ran the AID mission in Sam Thong, was persuaded to talk to him. One night Pop visited the general and the two men sat together on logs before an open fire drinking *lau lao*. The old man drew a deep breath and plunged into some straight talk.

"It's time somebody shook you up. You're like a little boy sulking because he's lost a game. If you could look at yourself right now, you'd see what I mean. Your face looks weak. You're dressed like a bum, worse than me even. You've let your people down. Now you're letting your whole army down. Who do you suppose is running the army while you sit around feeling sorry for yourself? Nobody, that's who. And nobody will, until you crawl out of your tent and start acting like a man again."

Instead of being angered, the general was moved almost to tears. "What can I do?" he said brokenly. "Tell me. What can I do?"

Pop Buell told him to clean himself up, put on a fresh uniform, and get back in the field. No one else would have dared speak so bluntly. Vang Pao was silent. He drank another glass of *lau lao* and then rose. Formally and without warmth, he bade Pop a stiff good night, leaving the old man to wonder about the effect of his words.

The general was on the strip at dawn, washed, shaved, and wearing battle fatigues. By the time he returned to the base at nightfall he had visited eighteen Meo villages and military camps by helicopter. But in his conversation with Pop over dinner he remained deeply pessimistic. "Last night you told me what I had to hear. Now we must face the future. I think we will mostly have bad times. Many people will die."

It would be difficult not only to go forward, but even to hold what they had. "Someday, probably soon, the Americans will leave Laos, no matter what happens," the general said. He needed to act quickly.[5]

The abortion of Operation Nighty-Night allowed the enemy to continue to strengthen their position on the Plain of Jars. All of the most northerly friendly positions were now behind enemy lines. Na Khang, in particular, came under terrible pressure. Ravens flew continuously to support holding actions where beleaguered outposts on remote mountaintops fought to beat off enemy attacks. Even with Gen. Vang Pao back in form, it would be some time before it was possible to launch a new offensive.

There was a limit to how many dead and wounded the Meo could sustain, and Vang Pao intimated it had already been reached. The Meo's tired force of children and old men, who received a maximum of three months' training, were no match for the North Vietnamese soldiers, trained for a year and rotated annually.

The general began to make demands on the Americans. If the United States expected the Meo to continue the fight, he wanted a massive increase in air support in return. He also wanted the Rules of Engagement relaxed to allow Ravens to use U.S. air to bomb the enemy who had moved into the towns and villages of the Plain of Jars, which they had turned into strongholds. And he wanted his Meo pilots based at Long Tieng, under his personal command, instead of at Vientiane, where they were under the nominal control of the Royal Lao Air Force.

It was the first of many requests for increased airpower over Laos, and while the Americans had little choice but to comply, the escalation made the policymakers nervous. They continued to issue misleading statements to the press designed to conceal the extent of U.S. military activity in the country. A story filed by United Press International early in 1969, and carried in many newspapers throughout the world, reported that Prime Minister Souvanna Phouma had admitted U.S. planes were bombing North Vietnamese troop concentrations and infiltration routes in Laos. The American embassy quickly pointed out that the prime minister had actually said "our" planes—meaning the aircraft of the Royal Lao Air Force, not the United States.

A telegram fired off by CINCPAC—Commander in Chief, Pacific Command—to the air attaché's office in Vientiane reaffirmed official Defense Department policy: "The preferable response to questions about air operations in Laos is NO COMMENT. If pressed you are authorized to state, 'At the request of the Royal Laotian Government, the United States has since 1964 been conducting reconnaissance flights over Laos escorted by armed aircraft. By agreement with the Laos government, the escort fighter aircraft may return fire if fired upon.' "[6]

In fact, U.S. fighter-bombers flew attack missions inside Laos as a daily routine. A set of Phantom F-4s arrived on station on the rim of the Plain of Jars—three days after the CINCPAC telegram to the air attaché's office—to hit a target marked by Papa Fox.

The Raven watched the first fighter enter its run and saw the bombs drop, but just as the Phantom was beginning to pull off it started to come apart. It was incomprehensible. There had been no ground fire, or even reports of antiaircraft guns capable of taking a jet out of the sky at 3,500 feet, but the plane had turned into a ball of smoke.

Inside the cockpit of the F-4, Mike Heenan, the copilot, had got on the stick the moment he sensed something was wrong. He heard the pilot grunt, as if he were also fighting to get the aircraft under control. They were diving fast, but an aerodynamic nose rise made it seem as if the plane might be recovering. Not until they were very low did it become apparent that the F-4 was going to dive straight into the ground.

At the same moment that Heenan went for the handles to eject he heard the pilot cry, "Get out, Mike—get out!" In the split second between hearing his colleague call to him and being blown out of the plane, Heenan accepted his death. "I knew I was going to die. It was a very warm feeling—it surprised me how comfortable it was—how easy it was to accept."

Heenan blacked out on ejection, and when he came around he was hanging from his parachute, which had caught in a tree. He had smashed through its branches and slammed into the trunk and was bleeding profusely. A small, sharp branch stuck through one of his hands like a dagger, and his helmet had been ripped off, laying bare a part of his skull, but he felt no pain. He hung helplessly from the tree, badly confused and in shock, while around him everything seemed deathly quiet. "I could not believe I was alive!"

A moment of panic followed. He fired his flares and began to shout for help into the hand-held survival radio. Papa Fox, identified over the air as Raven 44, came up on the radio and told the downed pilot to keep calm—and to get to the ground. Heenan unbuckled himself from the parachute and allowed himself to fall, hitting the ground hard at an awkward angle and spraining his ankle so badly he thought he had broken it.

He felt swallowed by the silence. The chute was draped over the tree like a tent, a beacon that stood out in a plain mostly made up of bushes and dotted with only a few tall trees. He began to crawl through the elephant grass away from the chute, but looked back to see that he was leaving a clear trail not only of crushed grass, but of blood as well. He began to worry excessively that the smell of blood would attract tigers. He felt terribly thirsty and searched for his water bottle, but it had fallen from the pocket of his flight suit on ejection. Most of all he was scared.

Papa Fox came back on the radio. According to all the training manuals, a pilot was supposed to keep his composure, reserve his flares, and observe correct radio procedures. Papa Fox knew the reality was different, and remembered that the first thing he had done when shot down was to run wildly into the forest.

He explained patiently that a fully fledged search-and-rescue (SAR) operation was going to take time to mount, but they would have him out soon enough. He urged Heenan to move in a northeasterly direction to a better pickup spot. "I had no clue which way northeast was," Heenan said. "I had a compass in the top left-hand pocket of my survival vest, but I had forgotten it was there. Rather than call me a dumb shit, Raven 44 flew over to show me the direction." He scrambled three hundred yards to the northeast and backed into a bush, painstakingly covering himself with foliage.

There were Jolly Greens—HH-3E super rescue helicopters—on

alert only twenty-two miles from where the Phantom had disintegrated, which meant Heenan could have been picked up within ten minutes of the crash. But cumbersome Air Force procedures dictated that the choppers could not take off until A-1 Skyraiders had been scrambled from Nakhon Phanom, in Thailand, and successfully suppressed all ground fire in the area. When the A-1s did arrive, one almost flew straight into Papa Fox, missing him by less than a hundred feet.

It had been quiet for the first forty-five minutes that Heenan was on the ground. There were no enemy in the near vicinity and he heard no ground fire, but by the time the A-1s arrived the North Vietnamese had spotted the chute in the tree. A few scattered shots began to be fired, slowly building to a crescendo of automatic-weapons fire. From his position on the ground the most visible thing to Heenan was Raven 44, endlessly crisscrossing the sky above him, checking to see if it was safe for the Jolly Green to land.

Although Heenan could not see the enemy, he heard them yelling to one another—something which scared him much more than the shooting. He was armed with a .38 Combat Masterpiece revolver, but with only one hand in use he was forced to alternate between holding the weapon and the radio. Backed into the bush, he remained frozen, afraid to move lest the rustling leaves attracted attention. The sound of enemy voices came from behind him. "The worst fear of all was that I could not see death approaching me."

The enemy were closing in, firing at the airplanes above them as they moved. The Jolly Green came in low to attempt a pickup. Heenan realized he had been blacking out intermittently through loss of blood when, without hearing the chopper's approach, he saw it was right beside him. A crew member was sitting with the rear ramp down, firing both mini-guns. "He was putting out a sheet of flame six feet long. It was really beautiful."

But the Jolly Green had not seen him, and when the chopper began to take heavy ground fire it moved off. The Skyraiders made a pass and laid down smoke to give the Jolly Green cover for a second rescue attempt, but the drop had been misjudged and the smoke was put directly on top of Heenan, screening him from sight. The rescue mission was rapidly degenerating into a shambles.

Heenan had now been on the ground for almost two hours, and continuous bleeding meant he was beginning to black out for longer and longer periods of time. Unable to see anything through the smoke, and with enemy fire coming closer by the moment as they tightened the circle around him, he began to wonder if the recovery had been abandoned. He called Papa Fox: "How long do you think it's going to be?"

"Be good," Papa Fox told him. "We're coming to get you, don't you worry about it."

In fact, Papa Fox was running out of patience himself with the way things were being run. According to the regulations he was obliged to give up control of the SAR the moment the lead Skyraider arrived on station, but the operation had degenerated into a frenzied muddle. If something was not done, Heenan would be dead within half an hour. Relying on force of personality over rank or regulations, Papa Fox resumed command of the rescue.

He called the Jolly Green on the radio. "Get on my ass, I'll take you down there—let's get the son of a bitch." Cranking down the flaps of the O-1 and flying as slowly as possible without stalling, he led the chopper through the smoke to where Heenan was hidden. The Jolly Green hovered over the bush, while a crew member lowered himself on a hoist.

Heenan scrambled toward him, and together they were winched up into the helicopter. The moment Heenan was on the hoist he felt his rescuer give him a powerful hug and was deeply affected. At that moment a strong human embrace was exactly what he needed, although in reality the airman was merely clasping him tight while he aimed an M-16 at the enemy who had come running from the cover of nearby bushes. The airman fired two full clips of ammo before the men were pulled into the chopper.

Later the Jolly Green crew visited Heenan in the hospital at Udorn, and he thanked them for saving his life. Papa Fox arrived with a bunch of grapes—most of which he had absentmindedly eaten—and Heenan thanked him for his extraordinary patience. He knew that Raven 44 had put himself "at grave personal risk" coming in low to lead the Jolly Green through the weeds to pick him up. He knew that if Raven 44 had not been unorthodox and taken over the mission, he would never have been picked up. Papa Fox shrugged, somewhat embarrassed, and gave Heenan the remains of the grapes.[7]

Fred Platt's unilateral decision to change the Rules of Engagement, by hitting the off-limits enemy radio station, sent a frisson of alarm throughout the embassy. The assistant air attaché, Gus Sonnenberg, flew up to Alternate to find out what was going on. He spoke to Burr Smith, of the CIA, and questioned the Ravens. Platt shrugged: "I'm hitting enemy targets."

Gen. Vang Pao took Platt's part: "He kill many enemy." The general used the presence of the Downtowner to reiterate his argument for a wider use of U.S. air. With Long Tieng at risk, the whole of Laos was at risk. Maybe it was time to change the rules.

The embassy took the point. It called the CIA and the Head Raven down to Vientiane to discuss possible reinterpretation, and relaxation, of the Rules of Engagement. In the meantime, in the midst of all the talk, Na Khang fell on March 1, 1969.

It had been a particularly brutal encounter. Two battalions of the 174th and three battalions of the 148th regiments had been launched by the North Vietnamese in the offensive, while an all-out effort to save the site through air power had been staged as a countermeasure. So many U.S. aircraft were diverted to the scene that Ravens were unable to handle them properly, and American fighter pilots stationed at Udorn paid a high price in men and machinery.

Maj. Mark Berent, on his second combat tour in Southeast Asia, wrote home to a friend: "We've lost so many here it no longer seems real. . . . if our birds aren't smacking into 2–3,000-foot karst ridges suddenly rising from nowhere they are stitched end to end by 23mm, 37mm, or 57mm. . . . Naturally I'm forbidden by all sorts of silly directives to mention exactly where I fly, but the astute reader of *Time, Newsweek* or the *New York Times* or any of scores of publications can obviously pronounce the four-letter word. It's such a ridiculously piddly effort at such a high cost it borders on criminal negligence."[8]

The enemy hid in small groups in the jungle, which swallowed the massive amounts of ordnance being dropped. AC-47 gunships poured fire into the jungle hour after hour, but did not stop the North Vietnamese in their attack.

At first it seemed to the troops at Site 36 that they were surrounded on three sides, and that the enemy had left the traditional opening for retreat. It was the Laotian way of war: when a battle had gone on long enough to decide its outcome, the losing side was allowed to withdraw with honor. When the battle at Na Khang reached its height the enemy crashed over the lines and the defending troops began to withdraw. But this time the North Vietnamese had also changed the rules. Instead of partially encircling the position, the enemy had surrounded it in a keyhole pattern. As the Meo poured from the fortified site and descended into the valley, they found themselves surrounded by two battalions who cut them down in a relentless crossfire. They were slaughtered without the possibility of surrender.[9]

It was during this period of defeat in the spring of 1969 that Sullivan relinquished his role as ambassador and returned to Washington. He shared Vang Pao's pessimistic view of the future, and reported that with the Meo forces depleted the next dry season was likely to bring the Communists major successes.[10] What had been conceived as a "holding operation" in 1962, intended to buy time for a year or two while the North Vietnamese were dealt with, now became questionable, Sullivan thought. "Certainly, by the time I got back to Washington and again got in charge of the Vietnam business and got a picture of what was going on there, I came to the conclusion that this was not a winnable proposition."

But the fall of Na Khang had driven home Vang Pao's argument. It was a waste of time to bomb the enemy hidden in the vastness of the jungle, while self-imposed restrictions forbade any attack on them in towns that they had turned into fortified camps with antiaircraft guns and tanks. Either Gen. Vang Pao was to be allowed to hammer the enemy wherever he could be found, or the war was over.

The embassy responded that from now on the Ravens could hit any targets on the Plain of Jars if fired upon, and that enemy-held positions—including areas that might be shown on the map as villages or towns—would be considered for targeting. The ten-mile buffer zone along the border with North Vietnam was kept, while civilians remained strictly taboo.

Gen. Vang Pao was encouraged, with the help of his CIA advisers, to launch a counteroffensive code-named Rain Dance.

The air attaché's office set about lobbying for increased sorties of U.S. fighter-bombers, and beefing up the Raven program to handle them. A new position was created to help smooth out supply and maintenance problems, filled by a lieutenant colonel. The Ravens were wary of this and greeted the arrival of *Mister* Mel Hart with skepticism.

Hart had twenty-six years of experience in the service and had worked his way up through the ranks. He had previously run the secret USAF Prairie Fire helicopter missions into Laos, so he knew the war. His new job was to oversee the site commanders, improve the safety program, and streamline the delivery of supplies and fuel, ammo, and rockets. He rotated around the various bases, ensuring the enlarged program ran smoothly.

"There was no question of the quality of the work the Ravens were doing," Mel Hart said. "I had seen too many examples of people interfering with a successful operation, so I made no effort to interfere with the way the job was being done. They had enough trouble as it was without having some jerk from HQ laying additional rules on them. I made very few demands on site commanders. I couldn't care less about the length of their hair." This was the sort of senior officer the Ravens could live with (although there was some annoyance that the new colonel drank his beer over ice—he drank a lot of beer so there was never any ice).

After the fall of Na Khang, Hart accompanied the air attaché, Col. Robert Tyrrell, to a sortie allocation conference for the 7/13th Air Forces in Saigon attended by officers from every branch of the air war. The object of the conference was to make sure the available air power went where it was most needed. Vietnam was the priority, but at this point in the war there was such an enormous amount of air available there was plenty for everyone. As the meeting progressed and the various fighter squadrons were assigned their sorties, it became clear that even after everyone had been given exactly what he wanted, there was going to be an enormous surplus.

The air attaché turned to Hart and asked in a stage whisper that could be heard throughout the hall, "What do you think we can handle?"

"We can take everything they don't use."

Gen. Vang Pao's small war was about to be given *one and a half times* the number of air sorties allocated to the whole of Vietnam.

The number of Ravens in Laos doubled over the coming months to deal with the massive escalation of the bombing. Don Service, a major, was sent up to replace Dick Shubert as Head Raven at Alternate, at the same time as a fresh batch of FACs, including John Bach, Karl Polifka, Danny Berry, and Mike Cavanaugh, arrived. An extension to the Raven hootch had to be built to provide new bedrooms.

Service flew out over the Plain of Jars to the outskirts of Xieng Khouang. The enemy had moved into the town in force, together with artillery pieces, ammunition, and supplies. Gen. Vang Pao, together with Burr Smith and a guerrilla unit, had been choppered out to the side of the hill overlooking the town.

The airstrip of Xieng Khouang was on the plain, but the town itself—the provincial capital—was some distance away to the southeast in a narrow, mountainous valley. Service was joined by Lee Lue, flying solo in his T-28. It was a dull day, with little activity, so the two pilots decided to liven things up and entertain the idle Meo troops with a display of marksmanship. Lee Lue rolled in and fired a rocket into the hillside. Service followed suit, attempting to place a rocket as near as possible to the one fired by the Meo pilot. It was an amusing way to pass the time on a slow combat day.

The Meo moved their position to within four hundred meters of Xieng Khouang itself, and the following day John Bach flew directly over the town, from east to west at an altitude of 2,500 feet. Inexperienced himself, he was accompanied by a Backseater who had been checked out only the previous day. Suddenly the sky exploded around them. Antiaircraft gunners had been waiting patiently, and now opened up in concert. A round of 37mm hit the cockpit and a further shell blew off the wing, and as the plane spun to earth it continued to be buffeted all the way down by multiple ZPU and 12.7mm guns.[11]

Two of the 37mm guns then depressed their muzzles and began to fire upon the Meo forces on the ground. Gen. Vang Pao, trained by the French, insisted upon strutting up and down in front of his troops to show his courage, until his CIA aides pulled him to the ground, where they held him for most of the afternoon, much to his disgust.

Ravens from all over the area raced to the scene. Don Service was the first to arrive, with Karl Polifka a minute behind him. "It was a real zoo," Polifka said. "I was glad Don had beaten me to it by a minute because the roar of the 37s was so loud it was actually deafening in the cockpit. They had been there all the time but just hadn't opened up before. I saw Don's O-1 disappear in tracer so that you couldn't see the plane. It happened time after time, but he would somehow emerge without taking a hit. It was really kind of scary."

The cloud ceiling was down to fifteen hundred feet, while the murky brown haze of the burning season rose to ten thousand feet above it—conditions which made it almost impossible to put in fighters accurately. Service called Cricket for air and was given Thuds (F-105s) out of Tahkli. He told the pilots the weather was so bad that all he could do was give them a bearing off the TACAN at Alternate, after which they would have to let down blind on time and distance. "You'll break out of cloud at fifteen hundred feet and the target is going to be right in front of you—and the moment you break out of the clouds they are going to be shooting at you. I can guarantee that. And you can't use bombs, only your cannon. But there won't be any mountains in the way."

It takes great faith and extraordinary courage for a pilot to fly time and distance in thick haze, drop out of the clouds to below fifteen hundred feet onto a target of antiaircraft guns already primed and firing. In addition, the Thuds could only use their guns to destroy the target.

They rolled out of the clouds firing their 20mm cannons, and a furious duel followed. There were two 37mm positions, at least two ZPU 14.5mm, and numerous 12.7mm, and the gunners on the ground never quit. As one crew was killed, another manned the guns, pushing the dead aside until some of the positions were piled around with the corpses of three successive teams. But the Thuds came in again and again in a series of blazing, strafing passes and finally silenced the positions. In an active and long career Don Service had never seen anything like it.[12]

Service himself flew through clouds of flak for forty minutes, as he directed numerous strikes onto the guns. He was relieved by other Ravens who worked fighters for a further three hours, until Vang Pao and his troops could be evacuated.

A two-day air campaign against Xieng Khouang followed. The recent death of a colleague sharpened the Ravens' desire to carry the war finally to the enemy. "We were really mad," Don Service said. "We completely annihilated the area around Xieng Khouang." In the town some fifteen hundred buildings were flattened, and as many as two thousand more all over the Plain of Jars. The towns of Lhat Houang, Ban Ban, and Khang Khay (the town itself was some distance from the Chinese mission of the same name) were wiped from the map. By the end of the year there would not be a building left standing.

Gen. Vang Pao's troops stormed into the smoking ruins of Xieng Khouang and seized a vast cache of enemy arms and supplies. Several of the surviving antiaircraft guns were taken back to Long Tieng, where they were cleaned up and proudly displayed as war trophies outside the general's house.

Don Service flew into the nearby strip in an Air America Caribou. He was accompanied by the flight surgeon, who walked over to a cave entrance and discovered an entire hospital complex hidden inside. The sophistication of its medical equipment, including X-ray, far exceeded his expectations. The capture of the hospital, with its equipment and drug supplies, was to prove an even more significant haul than the tons of ammunition and military hardware. Unknown to the friendlies, they had destroyed the enemy's medical base.[13]

Gen. Vang Pao had now experienced something of the awesome effects of air power. The enemy had been mercilessly punished and blasted with bombs and pushed from the Plain of Jars. He began to believe that with this new tool at his disposal he had a chance of winning at last. What he did not fully understand was that although the enemy could be pushed back with bombs temporarily, it took men to go in and hold the ground. Unless the Meo could successfully defend the ground they took, the enemy would always return. Air power, unsupported by adequate battlefield forces, was the military equivalent of means without end.

Even the Ravens began to question the general's bottomless belief in air power. "The *audacity* of Vang Pao at this time," Service said. "He expected air support in all weather and expected us to come in and annihilate anything that was in his way if he ran into resistance. It was ridiculous. Every day I would go back to where I had just dropped bombs and there would be somebody there. It was not the way to do it."

The enormous effort began to seem futile, as if the Meo were chained to a treadmill of war they could never leave. They had died in their thousands, and the Ravens had died beside them, not in an attempt to win a war, but as a consequence of faulty diplomatic agreements. The new levels of intensity of the North Vietnamese attacks and the massive escalation of the U.S. bombing in response were making even such committed people as the Ravens question the fundamental policy behind it all.

"It was hand to mouth, day to day," Service said. "Winning the war was a preposterous concept. We were just holding the line. Which was ridiculous to begin with—you don't win a football game by saying we are not going to let them get over the fifty-yard line. You have to score to win. It began to puzzle me. What are we here for?"

Pop Buell had witnessed the effects of the bombing with similar misgivings. It had created a new flood of refugees who would have to be cared for, and he thought his friend the general had become captive to a strategy which was an illusion. "We say we help them fight their wars," he told a friend at this time, "we use them only to fight our wars—wars we start."[14]

* * *

The new level of bombing and the devastation left in its wake led to some serious soul-searching among certain of the Ravens. They were warriors, in daily combat, but did not accept the war blindly. Most of them enjoyed the clandestine nature of the program—it appealed to their romantic natures—but there were also those who felt instinctively it was somehow un-American.

The Raven whose conscience was most disturbed by the nature of the war was Gerry Greven, a Californian, who had grown up in a liberal environment in Palo Alto. Handsome, unconventional, bright and witty, he flew into battle shirtless, with wide bell-bottom jeans flapping around his legs. As a FAC he was a tiger, graded by his peers as a first-rate and courageous pilot, but his conscience was burdened.

"I grew up naive and idealistic in suburbia—the war was a dose of reality. Suddenly you were given the ability to pick and choose what to destroy—dictate what village got hit and who died. VP's view was, 'If it's not us—destroy it!' It was an awesome responsibility, and one which in the end came down to each of us individually."

Greven was disturbed by two things—the brutality of the war in Vietnam, and the secrecy of the war in Laos. He agonized over both on a regular basis, putting himself through mental torture almost every evening. As a history major, he felt the United States was involved in the war in Vietnam for the wrong reasons, and possibly even on the wrong side. As a FAC in Vietnam he had carried out the recon on the first secret B-52 raid on Cambodia, and when he complained that the bombers had struck across the border he was told his maps were wrong. He had also been ordered to drop napalm on fields flanked by huts, outside of a provincial capital in Vietnam. He had refused and been threatened with court-martial.

Another thing that preyed on Greven's mind was the routine targeting of Vietcong hospitals. Army intelligence had provided the coordinates of suspected Vietcong hospitals three or possibly six times, to Greven's knowledge. The way the NVA operated meant that there was no separation between corps HQ, ammo dumps, and hospitals. The hospitals were camouflaged and were not marked with red crosses or flags. One of the certain ways for a FAC to spot an enemy concentration was to watch where troops dragged their wounded. Greven rejected this rationale, and thought it was simply wrong.[15]

"I've hit a few," Mike Byers admitted in conversation with Greven. "I don't see a hell of a lot of difference between a wounded soldier and a healthy one."

"It's against the Geneva Convention," Greven said.

"No shit. So's skinning people, and you know the enemy have done that," Byers argued. "The Geneva Convention specifically prohibits shotguns, and nobody observes that. There is no humane way to conduct a war. If you're going to have a war—which is a pretty stupid way to resolve your problems—kill them as quick as you can and get it done. But yeah, I blew up a hospital. So you're a wounded Communist—now you're a dead Communist. What do you mean it's *wrong?* The whole goddam thing is wrong."

"America's going to have a guilty conscience about the Vietnam war for a long time," Greven said.

One thing everybody agreed upon was fighting for the Meo. "In Vietnam I would rather have been on the side of Ho Chi Minh whipping up on LBJ," Mike Byers said. "Morally it would have felt better. But I have no doubts I'm on the right side here in Laos."

"This is more like a real war," Greven agreed, "not the guerrilla activity of Vietnam. Also the people here are so wonderfully warm, so nice and innocent—I've got a real affection for them I never had for the Vietnamese."

There was more agreement on the secret nature of the war. Greven felt that the American people should be told the truth. "The bad guys know about it. How come the American people don't?"

"I agree one hundred percent," Byers said. "I could sell this war to the American people—we're on the right side. Our politicians are so stupid they won't even tell people the truth. The truth is we're doing good for folks. Here we are, a small group of American volunteers fighting side by side with a bunch of oppressed hill tribesmen who have the gall to take on the might of the North Vietnamese Army. I'd have every grandma in the world sending me her life savings to buy ammo.

"We're on the right side—let's blow the buggers up, but don't let's lie to the people who are really in charge of the decisions—the people of the United States. Let's tell them what we are doing. And if they don't want us to do it, then we'll quit. But let's not lie."

"If you're going to tell the American public, then you might as well go home," Craig Morrison said. "It's just going to turn into another Vietnam, and they're not going to let you win the war—especially with the growth of the antiwar movement.

"I guess it's a question of what your duties are. I think that when you live in a country like America you owe something. And the country is not going to be right all the time—any more than we are—but you still owe something."

But the feelings men go through in war are confusing and contradictory. Greven and Morrison returned from an afternoon mission when they had destroyed seventeen trucks between them in an hour and a half. As they flew home they could see great plumes of smoke billowing up from the burning vehicles. Both men were elated. "Son of a bitch, that's the way to do it!"

"Yeah, we've earned a beer."

Greven also had no qualms in bombing any site or village which shot at him, but flying along the Ban Ban valley Greven spotted piles of rice. It was usual to burn rice or kill water buffalo in enemy territory to deny the troops the food. Crouched beside one pile was an old farmer. He did not attempt to hide, but seemed to be kneeling beside his crop challenging anyone who intended to destroy it to kill him. It was a foolhardy, almost suicidal, act of courage. Greven had the rice pile in his sights and was about to fire a high-explosive rocket into it when he saw the man. He pulled off and flew home. Somehow the image of the old farmer kneeling beside his meager crop, more than all the smoke and noise of bombing, made Greven hate war very much.

Returning from a full day's flying to cook the evening meal was beginning to tax even Papa Fox's reservoir of energy. The men had to prepare their own breakfast and lunch as it was, while numerous requests to the embassy for a cook had produced no results. Papa Fox decided to find one and steal him.

He flew down to the base at Nakhon Phanom in Thailand with the intention of testing the delights of the chow hall, and if it passed muster, stealing the Air Commandos' cook. He enjoyed his meal, although there was definite room for improvement, and asked to see whoever it was who ran the canteen. Papa Fox's presence—grubby, casual clothes, unkempt ginger beard, hair sticking out all over the place—had attracted some attention in the mess hall. Certain of the diners had noticed the 9mm sidearm he wore, and by the time the message reached the kitchen it took the form that a contract killer was in the hall with his sidearm laid out on the table, threatening to shoot the cook. S. Sgt. Manuel Espinosa came out of the kitchen with some reluctance. "Is everything okay?"

"Yeah, okay," Papa Fox said, picking his teeth. "How about a little adventure?"

Papa Fox explained about the secret program up in the combat zone, and the Ravens' need for a cook. There were not many of them, so it would not be too much work. Espinosa was intrigued. Actually, he told Papa Fox, he was bored by life in Nakhon Phanom, and he could do with a change, but he doubted whether the authorities would agree to a transfer.

"Pack your bag," Papa Fox said. "I'm transferring you." In less than an hour Staff Sergeant Espinosa was in the back of an O-1 flying up to Long Tieng.

The authorities displayed some consternation over the kidnapping of the Air Commandos' cook. The Air Force pondered its options: court-martial of Rinehart for abducting the sergeant; court-martial of the sergeant for going AWOL; court-martial of both for all of the above or a host of minor infringements in between. But common sense prevailed. The Raven program was growing, and it did need a cook. Espinosa was allowed to stay.

His role in the Raven kitchen was that of permanent *sous-chef*, for he did not embrace the high culinary standards of Papa Fox. ("He didn't know shit about cooking.") The limit of Espy's—as he became known—expertise seemed to be eggs, but he became more accomplished cooking alongside Papa Fox each night, and developed a way with pork chops.

Papa Fox was approaching the end of his tour. He had already experienced a feeling of burnout, and had spent the final month down in Pakse, the country club. When the other Ravens asked him what the war was like down there he told them, "You fly from ten to twelve and from one to three. You don't fight on Saturdays or Sundays. Targets have to be approved by the enemy."

He had used his newfound leisure time to advantage. At an embassy party in Vientiane he had met Nancy, the daughter of a director of U.S. AID. Romance blossomed and, to the amazement of the Ravens, Papa Fox announced wedding plans. The marriage was the secret war's social occasion of the month. Invitations were sent out—"war permitting"—to the extraordinary assortment of men who had become friends and acquaintances. Even members of the Pathet Lao delegation in Vientiane were invited. Gen. Vang Pao sent his regrets—he wished Papa Fox and his bride every good fortune, but he would be unable to attend the wedding as he could not get away from the war.

* * *

Lima Site 32 on the mountain of Phou Nok Kok to the north of the Plain of Jars lived in a state of perpetual siege. The position was strategically important because it overlooked the Ban Ban river valley, which ran east-west into North Vietnam, and operations could be run from it down across Route 7 and onto the northwest of the plain. To the enemy the site represented the linchpin of the plain, and offered control of the road out of Ban Ban.

It was defended by a force of five hundred Meo who lived on the mountain with their families. The troops were commanded by Black Lion, the code name of Will Green, a black CIA paramilitary officer who had become a legend throughout Laos. He was a tall, wiry, quiet-spoken man who might have been a college professor, and he had earned the respect and admiration of everyone who came in contact with him. He was a former Special Forces counterinsurgency expert, a professional soldier, and an inspirational leader. He ran a tight operation and his sites looked like state parks, unlike many of the Lao or Thai army outposts, which were littered with spent ammunition and trash.

The CIA told Black Lion in late April that a high-ranking defector had come across the lines to them with details of an imminent attack on Site 32. The soldier was the operations officer of the North Vietnamese regiment ordered by Hanoi to take the site at any cost. He had defected because he had been looking forward to going back to the North for a period of well-earned leave after two years of combat in South Vietnam, but he had been sent directly to Laos instead. The soldier brought hand-drawn, large-scale maps that showed the enemy knew every detail of the site. He told the CIA that the attack was to be mounted by two battalions of North Vietnamese and one of Pathet Lao soldiers. The orders included strict instructions not to allow any avenue of escape—the same no-quarter tactic deployed against the defenders of Na Khang.

In a detailed debriefing the defector drew sketches and maps marking the planned axis of attack, the position the North Vietnamese artillery would assume, where their ammo was stored, and the location of individual foxholes. He listed the types of weapons each battalion had available, and even gave the times the enemy changed guard.

In preparation for the coming attack Air America began to fly Caribou aircraft in and out of the site to evacuate the women and children of the defenders. Black Lion sent out patrols to check the accuracy of the defector's information. They reported back that a large force of the enemy was exactly positioned in the places indicated. Black Lion's men strengthened the site's fortifications, but even with such detailed knowledge of enemy plans the only hope of survival was air power.

The North Vietnamese must have been aware of the defection of a senior officer, but went ahead and launched their attack according to plan. Black Lion sent out Meo patrols to make contact with them. Once the enemy were located, the friendly patrol immediately radioed its position to a Raven, who gave them ten minutes to leave the area before directing fighters onto the coordinates. Enemy artillery positions, accurately marked by the defector, were worked after dark by U.S. AC-47 gunships flying out of Nakhon Phanom.

The enemy kept up their attack day after day, and throughout the night, for more than a week. One night they managed to penetrate the site's barbed-wire perimeter. The Meo were reluctant at first to take them on in hand-to-hand combat, fearful of regular North Vietnamese troops. But when it became clear the invading soldiers were Pathet Lao they moved upon them. Unable to use guns in the confined area for fear of hitting each other, the Meo hacked the enemy to death with machetes. The next morning Ravens flying low over the site's airstrip saw the bodies of a large number of dead stacked beside the perimeter like cordwood.

Despite strict orders to take Site 32 at any cost, the enemy had sustained such high casualties they were unable to maintain the attack. Tactical air power had saved a strategically important base and repulsed a massive enemy attack, while the Meo had suffered fewer casualties than usual. Once again Gen. Vang Pao saw the strength of air power without understanding its limits.

The course of the war in 1969 was increasingly dictated by the weather as the monsoon season came in, and there would be whole days of inaction followed by frantic periods of activity. Fred Platt made the most of one fine morning by putting in nine sorties of T-28s flown by Thais ("Friendly Third World Power"). He was in the U-17, accompanied by an eighteen-year-old Meo who was new to the job. The last of the Thai T-28s had completed their run and a set of Thuds (F-105s) had just arrived when the cockpit of Platt's plane was rocked by a round of 14.5mm antiaircraft fire.

The shell shattered the leg of the Meo, seated beside him. Platt tried to apply a tourniquet to stem the bleeding, but it was hopeless. The man's leg was hanging in tatters with the badly splintered bone clearly showing through. He was also losing blood at such a rate he could not possibly survive the brief flight back to base. He thrashed and flailed beside Platt, making control of the airplane difficult.

Platt made a drastic decision. He pulled out the large Bowie knife he always carried in a sheath strapped to his leg (the blade of which was fashioned from one of the original rails on the first Houston-to-Galveston railroad) and began to work quickly. Piloting the plane with his feet, he used one arm to hold the Meo down in the seat while he sawed through the bone of the man's leg with the other.

Throughout the crude amputation blood was being pumped onto the cockpit floor, until it was awash. The Meo's eyes had rolled to the back of his head, and he continued to flail his arms in panic until he passed out. Platt threw the tourniquet onto the leg above the cut and squeezed off the blood supply as well as he could. He then flew as quickly as possible to the hospital at Sam Thong, unloaded his passenger, and returned to the target area.

(The Meo survived. He was not unhappy with his fate. The amputation of his leg meant he would no longer be called upon to fly or fight in the war, the Meo version of a million-dollar wound.)

The enemy always made their boldest moves on days when U.S. air was unavailable because of bad weather, and it was on such a day that word came through to the Ravens that a hilltop position was being overrun by a force of North Vietnamese. U.S. air was out of the question, and even the T-28s were unable to launch, but it was thought that if a Raven could get through to the area he might be able to direct the T-28s of the Laotian Air Force out of Vientiane.

Platt flew to the sight accompanied by a hysterical Backseater. "Very bad—many enemy—weather too bad. We no fly." It was a horrible flight, and then while snaking down the valleys below the hundred-foot weather ceiling he received the news over the radio that the T-28s were unable to take off.

There seemed nothing to do but return to base. Back at Alternate, Platt settled into a game of combat bridge (a form of contract modified by Raven rules) and prepared to write the day off, until a message came through from Vang Pao. The hilltop position was under heavy attack and going down. "Please help. Need Raven. Need Raven now."

The Ravens discussed the dilemma. It was only a matter of time before the Meo at the site were massacred unless they had close air support, but there were no fighters available in the whole of Laos. Someone came up with the madcap plan of flying up there in formation and using the O-1 Bird Dogs as attack planes. Platt, who had flown to the site and therefore knew the route, was chosen to lead the formation.

Dick Shubert, Jerry Hare, Paul Merrick, Scotty Shinn, and Bob Passman (a new Raven on his first day in Long Tieng) all volunteered to go along. Three Ravens would act as pilots, the others as armed Backseaters. Helped by their armorers, the men worked to replace their marking rockets with high explosive and T-275s, the deadly antipersonnel flechettes. They loaded cases of grenades, grenade launchers, machine guns, and boxes of ammo, and took off in a three-ship formation and flew up to the site along the valley floors, grazing the sides of mountains.

It also promised to be tight work on station. Men at the besieged site had lit a flaming arrow to indicate the direction of the enemy, who were already on the outer perimeter of the camp. By flying in low along the bottom of the valley the Ravens were able to come up behind the hill position and climb over it to attack the enemy. They buzzed around the site like a swarm of flies, firing M-79 grenade launchers, tossing fragmentation grenades out of windows, and strafing with machine guns. The unexpected arrival of the Ravens and the surprise tactics broke the attack, and the enemy began to retreat in a shambles. The Meo came out of their defensive positions and pursued them as they ran. By the time the battle was over, sixty North Vietnamese dead were accounted for.

The mission was reported in full to the Country Team—the senior officials—meeting at the embassy the following morning. The air attaché's office was horrified. The Downtowners did not see the action—undertaken in terrible conditions by men using their initiative, to save a friendly position from certain massacre—as courageous. All they understood was that yet another gross violation of the Romeos had been committed by the Ravens, instigated by that unruly and uncontrollable cowboy Fred "Magnet Ass" Platt. The pilots had taken off in below-minimum weather conditions in non-IFR (Instrument Flight Rules) airplanes and flown in an illegal formation, had used reconnaissance aircraft as attack planes, and had expended ordnance of an unauthorized kind. It was time to kick Platt out of the country.

The CIA passed on details of the meeting to their HQ at Alternate, which informed Gen. Vang Pao of the embassy's reaction. The general remarked dryly that perhaps U.S. policy had changed—the Americans no longer even intended to hold the line, but actively sought to lose the war.

Vang Pao recommended Platt for the Air Force Cross. As a man who recognized raw courage when he saw it, he was profoundly grateful on behalf of his men. Several nights later he held a *baci* in honor of the action, with the commander of the hilltop position sitting on one side and Platt on the other. (The *baci* is the Laotian ceremony to celebrate the arrival or departure of friends, the birth of a child, or anything of social significance. There is feasting and drinking, and the person in whose honor it is held has strings tied around his wrist by the other participants, as a gesture of goodwill.) The general presented the Raven with a Meo musket, horn accouterments for powder, flint, and shot, and a monkey-skin rain cover for the flash pan. "They no give you but they not take away. I give you from all my people."

When Karl Polifka, in his capacity as Raven decorations officer, later heard about the mission he wanted to recommend the entire group for a medal. "Shit, let's write that up for a Silver Star. That's pretty heavy stuff, driving off a North Vietnamese attack in lousy weather and terrible ground fire, in airplanes that can be blown out of the sky with a rifle bullet."

The recommendation was rejected out of hand by the director of operations at the air attaché's office, Vientiane. Polifka, who had only recently arrived in Laos, shook his head in disbelief. "In South Vietnam guys were awarded the DFC for falling out of their bunks to the sound of rifle fire."

Not only was the recommendation rejected, but court-martial proceedings against the participants were still being considered, although Vang Pao's open support for Fred Platt had presented the air attaché's office with a dilemma. Was Platt to be treated as a hero or a heretic?

The CIA also stuck up for the pilots, threatening to take the matter further up the Air Force chain of command. The air attaché's office backed down. Two of the pilots were awarded the Silver Star, while the Ravens who flew in the backseats received DFCs. Platt was awarded nothing. The only remark on his bravery by the air attaché's office was "He's lucky we dropped the court-martial."

But somebody in the embassy had learned a lesson from the Raven tactic. If Ravens using three O-1s could beat off an attack when all other air was unavailable, what might they be able to achieve if they were allowed to FAC out of T-28s? It was well understood that all FACs were frustrated fighter pilots at heart, and were capable of getting into enough scrapes in the O-1 without giving them fighters.

The fear was that the introduction of T-28s might mean the end of the Ravens as a FAC program and the creation of an unruly squadron of Yankee Air Pirates. But again, the CIA and Gen. Vang Pao backed the Ravens, and it was decided to check some of them out in the fighter. (Earlier Raven FACs who had flown the T-28 had done so in direct violation of the rules.)

The first Raven chosen to present himself at Udorn to fly a T-28 up to Long Tieng was Mike Cavanaugh, a volatile and emotional man whom even the Ravens considered wild. He had grown up in Oakland, California, where he lived next door to the number three man in the Hell's Angels, and rode with the motorbike outlaws at the age of fifteen, to the dismay of his parents and teachers at high school. Cavanaugh liked to describe himself as a "Rejectionist": "A guy who takes nothing at face value, acts independently, and has a lot of disregard for authority."

Unaware of these views, the air attaché's office sent him down to Udorn to check out in the T-28. The fighters were the property of the Air Commando Waterpump program—set up to train native pilots—and the man in charge of their maintenance was Lt. Col. George Vogel. He kept his airplanes as immaculately as his uniforms, and on the wall behind his desk hung the threat "If the Props Do Not Rotate the Personnel Will."

The colonel explained with military precision that the plane had to be flown within strict time limits and brought back to Udorn in twenty-eight days for its one-hundred-hour phase inspection. He circled the date on a calendar behind his desk when the plane had to be returned, and emphasized that the one hundred hours of flying time should be spread evenly over the coming four-week period. "I understand," Cavanaugh said. "Or it turns into a pumpkin."

He returned to Udorn with the plane out of time ten days later. The colonel could not believe his eyes, especially when he saw the appalling condition in which the plane had been returned. Meo observers had vomited repeatedly in the backseat, a shell had blown a hole in the cockpit, and the wings were haphazardly patched with typhoon tape to cover a variety of bullet holes.

"You son of a bitch, who do you think you are?" the colonel exploded. "I'm going to put that airplane in the back of the dock for three weeks and I'm not going to touch it, because that's when it's scheduled."

Cavanaugh stayed overnight in Udorn and returned to the Waterpump flight line very early the next morning. The only people on duty were two Thai mechanics. "I'm here to get my airplane," he told them, nodding toward a gleaming T-28. "I'm taking this one right here—the one with the rockets on it."

Cavanaugh flew the plane up to Long Tieng, where it was used in nonstop combat for four days. The silence from Udorn was deafening. Every night when he returned to base he expected some terrible retribution to be exacted, but he heard nothing. There was a simple explanation—no one had missed it.

Only on the morning of the fourth day the T-28 was discovered missing. A hectic search ensued. There was a ramp check at Udorn, followed by radio inquiries to all the places T-28s were usually kept: Korat, Ubon, Savannakhet, Pakse, and Luang Prabang. On the morning of the fifth day an inquiry, of what seemed to be a routine nature, was sent through to the Raven radio operator. He met Cavanaugh as he returned to the strip in the T-28 at the end of the day. The plane had lost its earlier gleam: It had six holes in the wing, one of the guns had burned up, the canopy had been hit and was off its rollers, and the cowl flaps were not working properly. "They're looking for airplane number 479."

"I cannot tell a lie," Cavanaugh said. "Tell them I have the plane."

The following morning Cavanaugh returned the plane and presented himself to the colonel. "Do you have another one ready for me? I use them like Kleenex."

Before the colonel could explode again, Cavanaugh launched into an enthusiastic spiel on behalf of the Raven program. It was all very nice to restrict the use of a T-28 to one hundred hours a month in a training outfit like Waterpump, but there was a lot of war up at Alternate. The restrictions weren't realistic. Ravens flew ten-hour combat days, and the bullet holes they picked up were put there by the enemy. Cavanaugh was lyrical about the war in the north, about fighting alongside the Meo, who were so brave and had paid such a high price already. He had a lunatic charm and a zest for the fray that was infectious.

Colonel Vogel was not an Air Commando for nothing. "Okay, goddammit, I am going to back you up. I know you're fighting a war up there. I am going to give you an airplane. Just let me know what's going on and I will help you out."

From then on Vogel became one of the Ravens' staunchest supporters, and they came to refer to him as Uncle George. He was judged to be a "tough, fair, stand-up guy," which in Raven parlance meant he was prepared to break every rule in the Air Force book to help men in combat.

* * *

In a world without women, or any of the emotional comforts of family life, some of the Ravens lavished affection on pets. (Cavanaugh even took an interest in the country's extraordinary bug population: "In the latrine were some of the strangest insects that have ever been seen by anyone. Their variety amazed me. They were really strange.") Ravens tended to pick up the occasional stray running loose around the village, until there was a collection of dogs and civet cats attached to the hootch.

Fred Platt favored the exotic. The local children first brought him the cub of a Himalayan black bear—the same breed as the CIA bears. He was black, about a foot tall, and had a white V-marking on his chest, which made him look as if he were wearing a college crew-neck sweater. Platt named him Ho Chi Bear. He used to take the bear flying with him on occasion, an experience the animal seemed to enjoy more than many of the Backseaters.

Platt's attachment to Ho Chi Bear was known among the Ravens, so when he went away on leave and the bear escaped and was killed by local dogs, nobody wanted to give him the bad news. When he asked one of the mechanics where Ho Chi was, the man looked crestfallen. "The bear is dead."

Local children who had heard the news of Ho Chi Bear's death brought a fierce tiger cub to the hootch. Platt adopted him and put the cat in a cage next to the kitchen. Efforts to tame him, so that he too could fly in combat, proved futile. Platt was attacked again and again, and scratched from head to foot. "I figured any animal who wanted his freedom that much didn't deserve to be in a cage. I took him in a jeep out into the jungle and let him go."

The children next brought in the "Critter." This was a strange beast that looked like a cross between a sloth and an armadillo. It was a foot long, covered in armor plating, and had a long tail and pointed nose. It seemed able to hang from anything and was very affectionate. A deal was struck. Platt handed over a fistful of *kip*, chocolate bars, and several cans of Coca-Cola. "For twenty-five cents I had a prehistoric beast nobody had ever seen in his life. The Critter wrapped himself around my arm with his tail in his mouth and I would walk around with him hanging on to me. I don't know if that dumb an animal can feel affection, but it seemed like I was Daddy. Nuzzled my ear with his little wet nose."

Clamped to Platt's right arm, Critter bravely weathered the most fierce firefights, impervious to both airsickness and antiaircraft fire.

At the Raven hootch he was fed leftovers and enjoyed the occasional sip of beer in the evening. "A fat little critter," Fred Platt said, not without pride. Then, after a particularly hard day when the Ravens were unwinding over a round of martinis, one of the drinks was knocked over onto the coffee table. The Critter waddled across to it, took three laps and began to shake from head to tail. Critter rolled onto his back, his legs kicked in the air, and he was dead. "Stiffer than anything you ever saw."

Absurd as the circumstances were, Platt was inconsolable over his pet's death. "I was heartbroken. I lived with death all the time, saw it all day long, but the death of Critter was more shocking and moving to me than the death of a strange human I didn't know. Critter was my friend. I was horribly upset. I didn't know what to do about it."

He realized he had never known to which species Critter belonged. An empty gallon jar of mayonnaise was filled with vodka, gin, and white rum and Critter was lowered gently into it. A picture was taken and sent to the Smithsonian Institution in Washington, D.C., with an accompanying note asking for information. Baffled, the Smithsonian staff replied that they had never seen a creature to match the photograph. Someone suggested asking the French, who had spent a long time in Laos. Platt sent a photo and letter to the subbureau of natural history at the Sorbonne. French scholarship was also seemingly dumbfounded by the photograph of the strange creature floating in the mayonnaise jar, for there was no reply. (The Ravens, Francophobes to a man, all agreed that was about what you could expect from the Frogs.)

"I began to believe that I would become famous and have a whole species of Critter named after me—Critter Laotian Plattotian." The mystery of the Critter remained unsolved, until Platt went into the Vientiane post office to buy a complete set of postage stamps for a collector friend in Houston. One of the sets was of indigenous Laotian animals, and among them was Critter: *Panis auritas*.[16]

The monsoon of 1969 broke in June, but the enemy did not go home. The weather was so bad it was impossible to fly, while the North Vietnamese were hampered on the ground by deep mud. "The opposition were reading dirty Vietnamese books in their foxholes and we were sitting in Long Tieng going nuts," Mike Byers said.

He had arrived on a day of gray fog and wet green karst and was taken out in pelting rain on an area checkout. "Jesus Christ, I couldn't see anything," he remembered. Taking off out of Alternate was unnerving enough, with the mountains spiraling around and almost seeming to move in the shifting rain, and advice given on the checkout did little to bolster confidence: "If you get absolutely lost and you know you are going to die, ask for help from Air America. Those old cats have been flying around these mountains since Shep was a pup and they'll take you home."

On his second day Byers flew out alone. The weather was impossible, but he took comfort in the thought that the enemy probably could not see through the rain clouds to shoot. The rain grew steadily worse, and Byers turned around, intending to head back to Long Tieng. He wandered aimlessly, unable to see through the driving rain, and brought the aircraft down low in an attempt to get a bearing from the ground.

He began to worry that he would soon run out of gas and looked around for landing strips. Below him was a site scarcely larger than a chopper pad, but a Continental Porter was taking off from it. Byers got on the common frequency and asked, in as cool a manner as he could summon, "Say, you wouldn't happen to be going to Long Tieng, would you?"

"I'm going there now." The Porter was piloted by Al Adolph, a Continental veteran who knew Laos blindfolded.

"Slow down a bit, I'd like to slip in behind you." And Byers flew back to Long Tieng.

Weather was a deadly enemy in Laos. During the five months of the monsoon season—which lasted approximately from June through October—a disoriented pilot would often be forced to drop low into a canyon to wait for a hole in the clouds, or to search for a certain rock formation or even a familiar tree, in order to find his way home. There were only minimal navigational aids throughout the country, and the O-1 carried no radar. Conditions were made worse by the altitude, high winds, and quirky air currents around mountaintops, some of which were strong enough to uproot oaks.

It was not enemy fire that was the greatest danger in the monsoon season, but the constant risk of plowing into the side of a mountain—the sudden impact with a "rock-filled cloud." It was a finely balanced argument whether Ravens faced the most risk in the dry or monsoon season: in the dry season the enemy was on the move and FACs had to contend with the murk of a thousand fires lit by slash-and-burn farmers; during the monsoon there were terrible rainstorms, thick clouds, and appalling runway conditions.

The war was pursued on isolated days of good weather during the monsoon. Gen. Vang Pao had launched diversionary attacks on Routes 6 and 7 in an attempt to force the enemy to withdraw from Routes 4 and 5 to the south and east of Muong Soui. Enormous additional U.S. air support had been planned, but bad weather interfered with the bombing of 150 targets and the Special Guerrilla Units met with stiff resistance from fresh enemy forces sent across from Sam Neua.[17] Despite the weather, the Ravens occasionally managed to get through to direct U.S. air in support of beleaguered outposts, but with the guerrillas bogged down it was essential the Neutralist troops move out of their HQ at Muong Soui and engage the enemy. (There were three types of Neutralists in Laos: those who fought for the government, described as Rightist Neutralists; those who fought for the Communists, who called themselves Patriotic Neutralists; and a small band who did their best never to fight at all, also called Neutralists. To make matters even more complicated, the three factions had changed allegiances over the years, depending on the political situation. However, the main body of Neutralists was fighting alongside government troops and Meo at this time.)

Karl Polifka flew into the base for a briefing on the coming operation from the Neutralist commander. He was an immaculate figure dressed in starched fatigues, and he gave a Leavenworth Command and Staff School–style briefing on an acetate-covered map. Polifka was impressed by the textbook planning, but a brief conversation with the U.S. Army adviser dampened his initial enthusiasm. The Neutralists were so reluctant to face the North Vietnamese that the U.S. adviser was obliged to resort to shaming the troops into moving a mere eight kilometers to the east of Muong Soui. The commander, significantly, remained at the base.

The Neutralists reached a horseshoe-shaped ridge and dug in. They held the center of the U of the shoe, while the North Vietnamese advanced along both prongs, using a force of battalion strength. It was all the U.S. Army advisers could do to keep their men in position, but they adamantly refused to advance. It was hoped that a large U.S. air attack might dislodge the enemy and encourage the Neutralists to move in on them.

Polifka put in the first sorties, and then waited for the troops to advance. They sat tight. He flew back to Muong Soui and talked to the commander. "I am going to put in a lot of air in the next hour. When I give you the word, your people had better charge. We can't take ground for you." He flew back to the ridge and directed strike upon strike of fighter-bombers, and before an hour and a half was over thirty-eight tons of bombs had been dropped on the enemy. The prongs of the ridge along which they had been advancing were denuded of vegetation, and a great many North Vietnamese had been killed. However, a good number survived by retreating into tunnels and foxholes.

The Neutralists continued to sit tight. Polifka ranted over the radio that the infantry now had to move to clear the enemy from the ridge—repeatedly stressing that air could not take ground—but still the troops did not move. Disgusted, Polifka returned to Muong Soui, where he told the commander that all of his U.S. Air Force support was cut off.

The commander resorted to imploring Vang Pao to send in his Meo T-28s or all would be lost. The town of Muong Soui was the gateway from the Plain of Jars to the major road connecting the royal capital of Luang Prabang with Vientiane. Its fall would imperil Long Tieng.

Gen. Vang Pao directed Lee Lue to lead the eight T-28s at his disposal in full support of the Neutralists. During the next five days they flew continuous bombing missions against the enemy. At the end of this infernal bombardment, after the smoke had blown away and the surviving troops emerged from their foxholes, the Neutralists retreated.

In the meantime Polifka had been flying farther north to help relieve Meo guerrilla units cut off by the enemy in positions close to the Pathet Lao HQ of Sam Neua. He flew twenty feet off the ground for thirty minutes, directing F-4s onto an enemy company by rocking the wings of his plane in an exaggerated manner. His work saved one squad of Meo and a large number of undefended civilians, but at the end of it Polifka was completely out of gas.[18] Unable to reach Alternate, he decided to make a detour down to Muong Soui. The place was eerie. There was no one on the airfield, and the town itself seemed unnaturally quiet. Polifka tipped over numerous empty drums, unscrewed their tops, and managed to milk a couple of gallons into an oil can, the bare minimum needed to get him back to Long Tieng.

Back at Alternate he radioed Vientiane asking why no gas was available at Muong Soui. The air attaché's office replied that as the town was in immediate danger of being overrun by the enemy, gasoline shipments had been cut off three days earlier, once Lee Lue and his pilots had completed their bombing campaign. No one had thought to notify the Ravens.

Sporadic fighting continued around Muong Soui, but it was not until ten days later that the North Vietnamese launched a major offensive. Their orders were the same as those issued in the case of Na Khang—the town had to be taken at any cost.

On paper, the Neutralists were in good shape. Intelligence reports indicated they outnumbered the North Vietnamese three to one. There were four thousand infantry defending the town, strengthened by a three-hundred-man Thai artillery battalion. Unlimited air would become available to stave off a full-scale attack. By all classical military standards, the enemy needed a reverse ratio to succeed.

At dawn on June 24, the North Vietnamese launched a tank-led attack. It was the first time they had used their Soviet PT-76 tanks as offensive weapons, rather than as mobile artillery pieces. Air strikes directed by Ravens destroyed three and damaged more, but failed to stop them. The enemy pressed on and captured three 155mm and five 105mm guns, and parts of the nearby dirt strip, Lima Site 108.

At the same time the enemy moved on Muong Soui itself and tightened the noose around each of the far-flung Meo hilltop positions. The only lifeline left to the friendlies was from the sky, and Air America planes droned through curtains of cloud and rain to drop rice, ammunition, and the occasional pig. Mike Cavanaugh battled through the weather to keep the enemy pinned down and prevent them from launching direct frontal attacks on the positions.

"How's it going today?" he would ask cheerfully over the radio as he flew over some besieged hilltop.

"Not so good," a Meo would reply mournfully.

"How about some TAC air?"

"Please."

Scar, in the backseat, talked endlessly on the radio to all the forward air guides operating from different mountaintop positions, trying to assess who needed air support most. The enemy were everywhere. "We have en-em-ee to the south, en-em-ee to the north," Scar reported. "We have en-em-ee to the east, en-em-ee to the west. Man-ee, man-ee en-em-ee."

"Shit, can't you be a little more specific?" Cavanaugh asked. "Where's the best place to put some bombs?"

"Anywhere."

The entire Meo resistance was in danger of collapse, and Cavanaugh worked as hard as possible to help the troops hold on. It was often difficult to convey the urgency of the situation to U.S. fighter pilots fresh out of comfortable quarters in Thailand or South Vietnam. For them the *real* war was in North Vietnam, and they had a tendency to see Laos as little more than a place to dump bombs when a mission could not make it through.

Cavanaugh always worked hard to sell his small war to the pilots who came on station. The moment he heard the distinctive heavy breathing over the radio—the sound made by jet pilots inhaling oxygen through their face masks—he began his rapid patter, sounding more like a tobacco auctioneer from the deep south than a forward air controller.

"Gentlemen, I want you to be as interested in this war as I am. I have a terrific target for you today. I know it's not North Vietnam and it is not Hanoi, but we have an exciting war going on down here. You don't read about it in *Stars and Stripes*, but it's one hell of a war. Some of my troops are in trouble—enemy in the open. . . . Here we go, boys—*my people need your bombs!*"

On the day after the fall of Muong Soui, Cavanaugh had worked ten flights of fighters on a target close to the border of North Vietnam. Halfway through directing the last flight, Cricket came on the radio. "Raven 48, can you take some more fighters?"

"Negative that. I only have enough fuel to get home."

"Get home?" There was a pause. "Raven 48—we got word that Long Tieng is socked in."

"You've got to be shitting me!"

Cricket had been working Cavanaugh nonstop because he was the only Raven in the area, and had failed to calculate that he was weathered out of his home base. He was left over enemy territory with half an hour of gas and nowhere to go. Cavanaugh forgot about the enemy and directed his venom at the crew of the orbiting command center. He turned the O-1 around and immediately headed back in the direction of the Plain of Jars. Long Tieng was his only chance. "I *will* get in," he told Moonface, his terrified Backseater. "The Big Weatherman is going to let me make it."

Cricket gave him details of the dismal weather front. There were buildups of cloud from ground level to a height of forty thousand feet with no sign of lifting. Before Cavanaugh reached the front he could see the weather, and the plane began to be rocked by squalls of rain and high winds, while bolts of lightning assured worse thunderstorms ahead. The lightning lit up a solid black wall stretching across the horizon from east to west and rising from the ground into a limitless sky.

Cavanaugh flew directly into the storm, attempting to penetrate it with the feeble power of the Bird Dog, but his plane was batted about by its great force and thrown back. It was impossible to fly under the weather or to climb over or around it. The only alternative, the airstrip at Luang Prabang, was more than an hour away and there was not enough gas for the journey. He was left with the unappealing options of crash-landing on the Plain of Jars, now fully controlled by the enemy, or attempting a landing at Muong Soui, where they held the southern end of the strip.

He called Cricket, asking for a search-and-rescue operation to be launched. "I'm going down. Probably the PDJ. And if I live through this I'm going to get every one of you bastards on that 130 and break your coffee cups—and after that I'll murder every goddam one of you. *If* I live. But before you go, I'd like some SAR, *please*."

Jerry Hare, another Raven beaten back by the weather and heading for Luang Prabang, came up on the radio and asked if he could help. "Jerry, I am hurting," Cavanaugh said. "I'm out of gas and going to try making it into Muong Soui."

"They have some gas hidden there," Jerry Hare said. "Down on the east side of the runway."

It was some small comfort, although Cavanaugh still had to face the North Vietnamese sitting on the south end of the runway with their guns in place. It was getting dark and Cricket had been replaced by Alley Cat, the nighttime airborne command post. Cavanaugh called them on a hunch. "I want Zorro 50," he said.

If there was one pilot Cavanaugh had faith in to get him out of a hole it was Dale Brink, who flew a Skyraider out of Nakhon Phanom under the call sign Zorro 50. Alley Cat said they would see what they could do, and passed on the information that the Army attaché had confirmed that there were two fifty-five-gallon drums of gasoline in a bunker close to the strip. By the time Dale Brink came on station, accompanied by another A-1 flown by Rich Rose, Cavanaugh was ready to attempt a landing.

He lined the O-1 up for an approach, with both Skyraiders directly behind him, but the moment he neared the strip the North Vietnamese began firing. The empty left gas tank of the plane was riddled with bullet holes, but through sheer luck neither burned nor exploded. Cavanaugh immediately pulled off, while the A-1s strafed the field and took out a gun site on a small hill on the northwest side of the runway with five-hundred-pound bombs.

As the Skyraiders continued to bomb the buildings where the gunfire was coming from, Cavanaugh brought the plane in and shut down right in the middle of the airfield. He had entered into a state he had experienced several times before when he became possessed by a complete calm that he described to himself as a "combat daze." It was not a condition shared by Moonface, who was sobbing in terror and had defecated in his pants.

Rain was lashing diagonally across the dark airfield as Cavanaugh ran to the side of the runway where he had spotted drums of gasoline. He moved from one to another, tipping them over wildly, but they were all empty. Off to the side was a yellow handpump the Ravens used for refueling. Moonface dragged it back to the plane, while Cavanaugh moved farther afield in search of the hidden cache of gas.

He found it at the far end of the runway, almost a thousand feet away in a bunker behind a rickety door, the most precious and beautiful barrels of gas he had ever seen. In a feat of strength which he could never have undertaken in normal circumstances, he rolled one of the barrels up the grass incline onto the runway and back to the plane. The enemy were so close that troops on the south side of the airfield were shooting across the left wingtip of the O-1. He could hear the clatter from fragments of exploding mortar shells as they rained onto the empty gas barrels at the side of the runway. Only the constant strafing runs of the Skyraiders kept the enemy pinned down.

"No, no, no, we die," Moonface chanted miserably.

"We are not going to die. We can make it."

They now had gas and a pump, but no means of opening the drum. Cavanaugh took out his .38 and began hammering the top of the drum with the butt of the gun. Inspired, he broke off the wooden pieces of the gun butt and discovered that the stripped metal handle exactly fitted the wedged cap of the barrel. He unscrewed the top, climbed onto the left wing of the plane, and put the nozzle of the gas hose into the tank, while Moonface manned the pump. Bullets whistled about them as Cavanaugh yelled at the Meo to work faster. He pumped for a minute at such a rate Cavanaugh could not see his arms move. "Enough?"

"No, not enough—more. *Pump, pump.*"

The storm had now moved directly over them. It was so dark, and the rain was falling so heavily, it was almost impossible to see. When he figured there was enough gas in the tank to get them out, Cavanaugh jumped down from the wing scarcely able to believe they were still alive. He climbed back into the cockpit to find that a bullet had hit the battery, and acid was bubbling up from it and pouring down the side. "I had no electrics whatsoever. The most deadest feeling I ever had was sitting in that airplane. It looked quiet, it sounded quiet. As I hit the start switch, I thought, 'Nothing is going to happen.'"

The A-1s had never given up on him, despite having lost all contact, and continued to bomb and strafe the southern end of the airfield. A fragmentation bomb exploded, momentarily lighting up the runway, and Cavanaugh tried to fix in his mind the point in the darkness where he needed to aim the plane on takeoff. He cranked the start switch, sick with dread, but it fired immediately. He had an engine at least—but no windows, no radio, and no lights.

He let the throttle out fully, released the brakes, and kept imagining the spot in the darkness that the bomb had illuminated as the end of the runway. He waited until the engine sounded right for takeoff and roared into the dark, lifting into the storm. Once airborne he headed in the direction of Luang Prabang. The weather that had almost killed him now shielded him from enemy fire.

Cavanaugh had never been to Luang Prabang before and had difficulty finding it. Even when he was over the town he had no idea what the airfield would be like, and there were no landing lights to guide him. Don Moody, the commander of the air operations center at Luang Prabang, had already shepherded in two Ravens unable to make it back to Long Tieng, and when he heard the drone of an O-1 overhead he drove out to the end of the runway in a jeep and parked with the lights on. Cavanaugh came staggering in over the dim light thrown by the twin beams.

It was a rough landing. Having escaped an overrun enemy airfield, he now nearly smacked up his aircraft on a cement strip in friendly territory. When the plane came to a stop he sat slumped in the cockpit, trembling from the cold in soaked clothes, and utterly exhausted.

The Ravens, who had been drinking beer for several hours, drove out to the plane to collect him. They lifted him out of the cockpit and helped him into the jeep. One of them remarked on the ripe smell emanating from Moonface. "Had a little accident," Cavanaugh explained. "We both had a little accident. I'd be dead if I'd been alone."[19]

Back at the hootch, Cavanaugh took a drink and fell into a deep sleep. The Skyraider pilots had seen him land but had missed his takeoff, and had subsequently listed him as MIA. Nobody at Luang Prabang was in the mood to make a radio report, so he kept the status overnight. The next morning the message was sent out: "Raven 48 at our location."

The reply was immediate: Raven 48 should get airborne ASAP and get back in the war. He was needed at Alternate.

The initial thrust of the North Vietnamese attack had exhausted itself. The fighting had died down and remained sporadic for three days (the period in which Cavanaugh had landed at Muong Soui). But the Neutralists were in complete disarray. The tanks had terrified them and they had failed to repulse the weaker force. The Thai artillerymen, aware that their infantry support could not be relied upon, also began to abandon their positions.

The Americans began to evacuate the dispirited and routed troops by air. A helicopter task force twenty-three strong—made up of thirteen Air Force and ten Air America craft—was assembled at Long Tieng, and on the afternoon of June 27 the evacuation began. It took only two hours to lift out the 350 men of the Thai unit, after which the evacuation of the remaining Neutralist troops, still huddled in a defensive position on the northern end of the runway, got underway. Time after time the helicopter crews flew back to enemy-controlled territory, at minimum speed and altitudes in terrible weather, and staggered out overloaded with their human cargo. One of the Air Force CH-3s was shot down, but the crew and passengers held off the enemy with rifles and grenades until an Air America H-34 flew in to rescue them. The entire Neutralist force, including two hundred families who lived in the town, was carried back to Long Tieng.[20]

The downed chopper was later destroyed by an air strike, and Ravens directed numerous sorties against abandoned supplies, guns, trucks, and ammo (the final tally included nineteen 105mm artillery pieces and eighty-four trucks). "We got great BDA"—bomb damage assessment—"out of Muong Soui," Karl Polifka said. "Unfortunately it was all our own stuff."

The loss of Muong Soui was a blow felt by the Royal Lao Government in Vientiane. An outnumbered, outgunned enemy with no air power of its own, fighting in the worst conditions, had overrun the strategic Plain of Jars. Once again morale plunged. Only Gen. Vang Pao and his men stood between the enemy and the capital itself.

Keeping faith with air power, the general again took the offensive on July 1. The enemy at Muong Soui were pounded by U.S. air, directed by Ravens, and the Meo T-28s. Lee Lue excelled even his extravagant standards, flying as many as ten combat missions a day.

Crouched in their foxholes, the enemy offered little resistance until Meo guerrilla units and a thousand Neutralist troops reached the town itself. Appalling weather hampered air operations, so that on July 8 only six sorties could be flown. Neutralist troops failed to move as planned, and the government advance slowed to a standstill.

Lee Lue continued to fly support. The enemy were so close that a mission never lasted more than thirty minutes, and it sometimes seemed as if he were always on the ramp at Long Tieng loading bombs. At the end of a ten-hour day Lee Lue would land in his fighter, taxi to the ramp, and shut down. A small group of Meo always gathered around the plane, while the fighter pilot sat slumped in the cockpit, paralyzed with fatigue. One of the Meo would climb up on the wing and begin to massage his neck and shoulders. Others would gently lift him out of the cockpit and help him down to the ground, where they walked him around to revive the circulation in his cramped legs.

The Americans who witnessed this ceremony each evening— conducted with all the dignity of a religious ritual—found it an intensely moving sight. The tenderness and care with which Lee Lue was treated and the enormous respect he received from the entire Meo nation could not fail to impress. He had become a symbol of Meo resistance, a mythical figure of untold value and power, and one of the central props of his people's morale.

The legend of Lee Lue had spread throughout the American fighter squadrons of Southeast Asia, and while his political significance was not always understood, the stories of his reckless heroics went the rounds. Here was this little guy from some mountain village, who had been a teacher before the CIA taught him to fly at the advanced age of twenty-seven, flying the hell out of a junk propeller airplane and receiving the unqualified admiration of American fighter pilots in the latest jets. An American who had flown one hundred missions over North Vietnam earned the awe of the O club and wore a special patch on his flight suit. Lee Lue was flying an average of 120 combat missions a month—month after month after month without respite. It was estimated he had flown more than five thousand combat missions, all of them over enemy territory, and a great many of them only a few feet off the ground.

As one group of Ravens was replaced by another, they all learned to love Lee Lue and marveled at his absolute fearlessness and total disregard of the law of averages. He was living proof of the credo secretly held by every Raven—it always happened to the other guy.

Older heads worried about Lee Lue. His symbolic value, over and beyond his prowess as a fighter pilot, carried such importance that the thought of his death sent a chill through the policymakers at the embassy. The CIA suggested to Vang Pao that he use his single greatest war asset more sparingly.

The wing commander of the Air Commandos, Col. Heinie Aderholt, suggested taking Lee Lue out of the combat zone altogether. He wanted him assigned to Waterpump, at Udorn, where he could teach and inspire new Meo pilots. There was a move in Vientiane by the prime minister's son, Prince Mangkhra Phouma, to have the pilot declared a national hero. But Gen. Vang Pao said he could not spare him, and besides, Lee Lue did not want to go.

Vang Pao shared the pilot's innate fatalism and sense of invincibility, and pushed him even harder, committing him to more and more missions in support of his men. Even when Lee Lue was physically sick—and the Meo were wracked by malaria, hepatitis, amoebic dysentery, and a variety of exotic tropical illnesses on a more or less permanent basis—he always managed to stagger to his plane.

"They'll never get me," he said, grinning broadly. "Never get me. I'm too good."

The Ravens laughed and tended to agree, although it took extreme insensitivity for a fellow pilot not to register the toll that fatigue was taking. But maybe, the Ravens argued, there really were guys who were just beyond the reach of death's envelope—perhaps every once in a while Buddha smiled upon a fighter pilot and kept a protective eye on him.

And then it happened. "The blackest of black days yesterday," Burr Smith wrote to his wife, Mary Jane, on July 12. "Lee Lue, the last and the best of the Meo pilots—and incidentally the bravest human being I have ever known—was shot down and killed before my eyes. VP was with me and he broke down immediately in sadness and despair. Lee Lue was his cousin, but in the Meo custom was also his son (and my brother). The plane passed over our heads, on fire, and crashed a few hundred yards from our position."

Only two days earlier Burr Smith had chided the pilot for flying too low—on one pass he was so close to the ground that when he dropped his bombs they failed to explode. On the day he was shot down he had been bombing and strafing the enemy at Muong Soui, flying low as usual, and was pulling off a run in his habitual slow and casual manner when a 12.7mm antiaircraft gun opened up and raked the plane down one side. Burr Smith, who had been in contact with him over the radio, screamed that his plane was on fire and Lee Lue should bail out, but there was no answer.

The plane flew a few hundred yards and crashed into the ground in a ball of fire. As it exploded the Vietnamese gunners fired red victory rockets from their positions, celebrating the death of one of their most feared enemies. There was never any mistaking Lee Lue's style of flying, and the gunners always worked extra hard to hit him.

Gen. Vang Pao headed immediately for his waiting helicopter, and together with Burr Smith flew back to Long Tieng, sobbing openly as he chanted the Meo song of the dead. "It was heartbreaking," Burr Smith wrote. "We were all crying like babies—rather odd when you think of the hundreds of Meos killed here every year. Now he is gone forever, who was such a good and faithful comrade.

"Of course he was doomed from the first day he stepped into an airplane—he was extravagantly courageous, and took terrible chances each time he flew against the enemy. Times without number he flew close support missions, alone, when no other aircraft would face the weather—time after time he was the deciding factor in battles with the enemy.

"The other members of his flight are in near shock—each blaming the other side for not covering his attack. But in reality nobody could cover Lee Lue—he was a loner from the day he was born, and never waited for his wingman to be in position when he had a target. He was not afraid—I feel certain he died with a smile on his face. He knew he would get it eventually, and he died as he lived—courageously. I feel terrible—his death has brought home most forcefully the great sadness of this war.

"Tomorrow I will write of different subjects, but today I can think of nothing but my friend and comrade-in-arms who is gone forever. I mourn with all the Meo—and especially my heart goes out to his family and to VP—both of whom have lost their greatest strength."

A three-day funeral began in honor of the memory of one of the Meo's most valued sons. The grief of the Meo nation was awful to see, and all of the Americans who lived and fought with them were deeply moved. Battle-hardened CIA paramilitary men wept openly. The Ravens mourned the dead pilot more than if he had been one of their own. Gen. Vang Pao's face became purple and bloated with grief. No one flew combat, and the Meo were too stunned to fight.

Burr Smith took a helicopter out to the crash site the morning after Lee Lue's death in search of his remains. The plane had exploded and been scattered over a large area, and the pilot's body with it. Only a few fragments of his helmet and several pieces of bloody cloth could be found. These were carried back to Long Tieng like holy relics, where they were placed in an elaborate coffin.

The enemy, as exhilarated by the death as the Meo were crushed, launched a new offensive against the troops surrounding Muong Soui. Taking advantage of the lull in air support and the total dejection of the government forces, they easily overran them, inflicting heavy casualties.

The burial of Lee Lue took on the proportions of a state funeral. The ceremony was a mixture of the Buddhist and animist religions to which the Meo subscribed, although it was the Meo's custom to bury their dead. Every important general officer in the Royal Lao Army attended, and for many of them it was their first visit to the fabled secret city of Long Tieng. Their presence was something of a diplomatic coup for air attaché Col. Bob Tyrrell, who had worked hard to ensure the attendance of the important Lao military figures. Their presence acknowledged a public acceptance of Gen. Vang Pao and the Meo, and showed a respect long overdue.

The general presented a somber, dignified presence at the funeral. A large crowd marched to the graveyard to pay homage to Lee Lue. A photograph of the pilot, hung about with colorful paper streamers and flowers from his family, was laid upon a pillow resting on the ornate carved coffin. The Meo folded their hands in prayer, holding three sticks of burning incense between their fingers, then marched on their knees to the coffin, where they placed their offering in a vase and prayed. One after another, those closest to Lee Lue paid their respects, and then the Ravens followed suit. "I considered him my brother," Mike Cavanaugh said. "Lee Lue was one of only two people I have shed tears over in my Air Force career," Karl Polifka said.

Colonel Tyrrell stepped forward and pinned the American DFC on the pillow, and read aloud a simple speech. The Lao generals, bemedaled like the heroes of a Chinese opera, also made appropriate speeches about a shared loss and solidarity in the face of a common enemy. It was yet another irony of the war that it took the death of one of the Meo's greatest warriors to bring the armchair generals of the Royal Lao Army to the front.

7

ABOUT-FACE

It was on the first day of Lee Lue's funeral in July 1969, when Communist advances reached new levels of success, and morale had not only crumbled among the Meo but in the capital of Vientiane itself, that the new American ambassador, George McMurtrie Godley III, arrived in Laos. An array of disturbing problems faced him with no ready solutions to hand.

At the same time, in Paris, Prince Souvanna Phouma charged that there were sixty thousand Vietnamese waging war in his country, and admitted that he had authorized U.S. bombing raids on the Ho Chi Minh Trail.

As a diplomat Godley was something of a peculiarity, one of a handful of the State Department's paramilitary ambassadors who had experience working hand in glove with the CIA. Godley had cut his teeth in the Congo in the mid-1960s, first as deputy chief of mission and later as ambassador, where he had controlled a clandestine air force flown by Cuban mercenaries and commanded a covert army. He had played a critical role in crushing the Stanleyville uprising and building up President Joseph Mobutu as a pro-American military strongman.

The relationship had turned sour when Godley refused the president the use of the CIA mercenary air force to napalm the Stanleyville native quarters, a vast area of bamboo huts that would have burned like tinder. "There was no question that it would have killed thousands, if not tens of thousands, of women and kids," Godley said. "So I grounded his air force."[1]

In retaliation, Mobutu ordered Godley to leave the country before he was declared *persona non grata*. (The ambassador often appeared at informal parties in Vientiane wearing a garish African shirt, with facing portraits of Mobutu emblazoned across its left and right panels. He joked that the president had made up thousands of pairs of trousers, with the beaming portrait of Godley sewn into the seat, which had been distributed free throughout the Congo.)

Godley had become closely acquainted with the operation in Laos when he visited Vientiane as the head of a State Department team on a two-month inspection tour of the embassy. "I was very much impressed with the show that Bill Sullivan was running and the work that the Country Team was doing. I thought very highly not only of the government's objectives but also of the way in which we were trying to achieve them." He returned to Washington to spend a year as deputy assistant secretary of state for Far Eastern affairs before becoming the ambassador to Laos in July 1969.

Godley was a hawk, although his military expertise was limited. He had volunteered for the U.S. Marine Corps at the end of World War II and had served briefly as a private. He joked that when the Japs heard Mac Godley was coming they gave up—but the North Vietnamese proved to be made of sterner stuff.

The Americans were resigned to an extremely pessimistic view of their military options in Laos by this time. At the beginning of August 1969, plans and policy officers of the joint staff had already come to the conclusion that only political considerations could prevent the Communists from eventually overrunning most of Laos. A gloomy State-Defense-CIA paper was sent to President Nixon. The only bright spot in the report was the observation that the enemy had difficulty reacting to surprise behind-the-lines assaults launched by Meo guerrilla units operating from helicopters and supported by fixed-wing airlift.[2]

The advent of the Nixon administration, at the beginning of the year, had brought with it a change in military strategy that had altered the nature of the war in Vietnam and upped the stakes in Laos and Cambodia. Under Johnson, military strategy was composed of a mix of three ideas: gradual escalation, highly restricted operations, and acceptance of sanctuaries. It was also stated policy that the United States did not intend to threaten the existence of the North Vietnamese regime. The goals of this strategy were to negotiate for an independent South Vietnam, while keeping China and the USSR out of the war.

Nixon favored massive and quick military action, increased bombing of the north itself, and cross-border operations into the sanctuaries. Declared policy was ominously silent as to what might happen if North Vietnam persisted. At the same time, to avoid the risk of bringing China and the USSR into the war, the president pursued a policy of détente attractive to them both. Secret peace negotiations with North Vietnam, meanwhile, were opened in 1969 by Dr. Henry Kissinger.

The war was escalating, but at the same time America began withdrawing troops, which meant strengthening the army of South Vietnam to the point where they would be able to take over the war—a policy called Vietnamization. Firepower lost by the dwindling U.S. forces was to be replaced by an ever-increasing rate of bombing.

In Laos, where there were not enough human resources to replace the Meo, Thailand was encouraged to send more "volunteers." And still more bombing was scheduled. (Before 1969 a total of 454,998 tons of bombs had been dropped on Laos—from now on more than that would be dropped each year.)[3]

Although since the departure of Ambassador Sullivan the Rules of Engagement had been relaxed to allow wider bombing of inhabited areas on the Plain of Jars, they were not abandoned completely, as critics have charged. But the increased bombing sorties, combined with the successes of Communist troops, led to a growing sea of refugees and an inevitable rise in civilian casualties—each time the war forced a move 10 percent of the refugees died. (These consequences of escalated bombing were immediately blamed on the new ambassador, who came to be called "Bomber" Godley by some journalists and disaffected members of his staff. Significantly, the massive increase in bombing sorties was allocated to Laos during the interregnum when Ambassador Sullivan had returned to the United States and before Ambassador Godley arrived.)

"Never in the history of warfare has a military element been more shackled in its operation than was the USAF in Laos," Godley stated. "The rules of engagement were voluminous, complex, and precise. It could not engage enemy ground forces unless requested by the Lao government and approved by the embassy. It could not bomb within one hundred yards of an inhabited dwelling, nor could it endanger inhabited villages. The types of ordnance it could use had to be approved, *etc., etc., etc.*

"If there was the least deviation from existing rules in target selection, this had to be approved by the embassy . . . reviewed

. . . occasionally disapproved or modified. . . . We were repeatedly charged with indiscriminate bombing of civilians. Nothing could have been further from the truth. Errors no doubt occurred, but I am convinced they were not willful. In every case when we heard of an alleged mistake, the Air Force investigated it as thoroughly as possible and, in some cases, meted out severe disciplinary action."[4]

Inevitably, the gap between embassy policy and battlefield reality was a large one. It was impossible to monitor the rules and control the placing of every bomb in Laos, although this was the intention under Godley, as it had been under Sullivan. The embassy had no right to monitor or control where the Lao or Meo T-28s put their bombs. And all the Laotian regional military commanders had the right and the ability to attack where they wished.

But throughout all the interviews conducted with Ravens, Air Commandos, and Air Force fighter-pilots—who in individual instances openly admitted to hitting civilians by mistake, or bombing wats (Buddhist temples) they knew to contain guns, or even field hospitals known to shelter enemy troops and caches of ammunition— no one ever conceded that civilians were deliberately targeted (unlike the French who, in Laos during the first Indochina war, regularly razed troublesome villages and dropped napalm as a matter of routine).[5] Civilian casualties were a consequence of the overreliance on air power, not a deliberate tactic or matter of policy.[6]

But the war was becoming enormously unpopular at home and Godley's hawklike utterances, and apparent relish for the job, alienated many journalists and the more skeptical members of his staff.

On the first day of Lee Lue's funeral it seemed as if his death had broken Gen. Vang Pao. Yet somehow, as the elaborate mourning and drinking stretched out over the days, he seemed to draw on some hidden reserve of superhuman resilience. Perhaps he had been strengthened by the show of solidarity of the Laotian high command who had come to Long Tieng to pay their respects (and who had left greatly impressed by the Meo operation); perhaps, mulling over the possibilities of combining surprise tactics with air power, he foresaw new opportunities; perhaps he wished to avenge the great warrior of the Meo nation. Whatever the reasons, by the beginning of August 1969, Gen. Vang Pao had resolved once more to go on the offensive.

At this stage in the war, defeatism had reached a very high level of strategic thinking, and the last thing the Americans expected from Gen. Vang Pao was victory. Even the optimists dared not hope for more than the Meo doggedly holding on at Long Tieng, but the general knew that the enemy were overextended by their victories, and their lines of communication were stretched—factors that had been intensified by an unrelieved period of terrible weather.

Gen. Vang Pao planned to turn this to his advantage in Operation About-Face. Flown in by Air America choppers, and supported by Ravens and T-28s operating out of four Lima Sites in enemy-held territory, Meo and Thai guerrilla units led by the general would disrupt supply lines in the rear, particularly Route 7 leading back into North Vietnam. At the same time, Royal Lao Government forces, supported by massive U.S. air, would reestablish their presence on the southern fringe of the Plain of Jars and press forward. But in order to launch this ambitious offensive, with all of the necessary air support, a break in the weather was needed.

Stuck in the hootch at Alternate, the Ravens looked out on the relentless rain. The mountains surrounding them were hidden from view by dark clouds, and all the meteorological predictions for the future were dire. They had been told by the CIA that the weather was likely to remain bad for the next three months. But Operation About-Face was planned to kick off on August 15, only days away.

As the day approached, the weather grew worse. Gen. Vang Pao remained supremely confident: "Buddha tells me the weather will be good." It seemed as if the general, in his eagerness to hit back at the enemy, had become a victim of wish fulfillment and self-delusion. In the meantime the CIA and the air attaché's office dickered with the 7/13th Air Force about the amount of air to be allocated to the offensive. The Barrel Roll sortie rate had already fallen to half its daily quota because of the weather.

As the morning of August 15 dawned, Karl Polifka went to the window of his room and looked outside. It was clear as a bell. There was a chill in the air and a few scudding clouds fringed with gray, but otherwise it was a bright, sunny day and the sky was a brilliant blue. Polifka shook his head, scarcely able to believe the change so accurately predicted by Gen. Vang Pao. "This guy's got a connection to somebody."

The weather was to remain good enough for uninterrupted air operations for the next eight weeks, a seasonal freak. Using aircraft like artillery, a force of six thousand Lao troops and Meo guerrillas moved against the enemy. Tactical air sorties totaled 150 a day, enabling the government troops to take the hills, although the battles were bloody.[7]

Time and again it seemed as if Vang Pao was in the lap of the gods. Shortly after the launch of the operation he climbed into a helicopter, turned around in the cockpit, and announced, "Buddha tells me not to take this helicopter." He got out and took another. The first Huey took off and exploded in midair because its gas tank had been sabotaged with a grenade.

There were numerous instances of combat extrasensory perception that the Ravens experienced and accepted, but could not explain. It was as if a man grew so immersed in the details and realities of the battlefield, by flying so many hours each day, that he began to respond to its dangers subliminally, making critical decisions based on the experience of a hundred missions. "I certainly felt a lot of it on that tour," Polifka said. "Numerous times I would be flying along and, I swear to God, I could hear the clank of the gears on a traversing 37—which is quite impossible. But something would make me brake right or left—and I would turn off and the shells would explode in the path of where I would have been. There is no normal explanation for it."

Operation About-Face was launched from Site 204, on the southern edge of the Plain of Jars—where the passes came out of Long Tieng—and from Site 15, on its western edge. Two mountains were attacked—one on the northwest edge of the plain, called Phou Khean, and the other on the southeast, called Phou Tham. They were tough, fierce operations with many casualties on both sides, but after two weeks the mountains were in the hands of the friendlies.

At the same time, troops from Site 32—Boun Long—moved down in an attempt to choke off Route 7, where it came out of Ban Ban, and also take the 7/71 road junction. A small mountain just south of 7/71 was still held by North Vietnamese troops even after bombing had denuded it of all vegetation. The operation called for repeated ground assaults. Somehow, the enemy still managed to man machine guns and beat back each attack, but were finally overrun in a brutal fight.

Once the mountains on the ridge of the plain were taken the troops moved onto the plain itself, and the Ravens began to operate out of three strips—one to the south of the plain, one in the middle (Hotel Lima), and the Xieng Khouang strip—landing on the grass, where Air America refueled from drums of gas flown in by helicopter. (Most of the strips were pockmarked with bombs where the USAF had attempted to destroy them when in the enemy's hands—a wasted effort, as the enemy had no planes.) The native T-28 pilots excelled themselves, except they suffered from an unusual problem that led to a number of aborted takeoffs: eager to supplement their poor diets, the pilots were overloading their aircraft by stuffing the small baggage compartment with meat from water buffalo slaughtered in combat.

It was at Hotel Lima that the Ravens got their first glimpse of their new ambassador. A chopper landed and Godley jumped out—wearing jungle boots and khaki cutoffs, sporting a three-day growth of beard, and carrying a submachine gun. It was the first time a senior Downtowner had ever been seen at a forward strip in the combat zone, and the word soon spread among the Ravens that the new ambassador was okay. It was a habit Godley had brought with him from the Congo, where he made a point of "eyeballing" the situation for himself, convinced it was impossible to get a feel for events by sitting behind a desk and reading reports. There were risks in going to the front, but the ambassador was prepared. "I always carried a snub-nosed .38 in my belt—I had no intention of being captured by the enemy."

As About-Face continued, massive air support, delivered at a time of year when the enemy was usually invulnerable and combined with the new tactics, proved a brilliant success. The enemy were prized from their mountain fastnesses and driven from the plain itself. The offensive moved so quickly that the North Vietnamese seemed to be taken completely by surprise.

The Chinese evacuated their mission at Khang Khay in such great haste the CIA were able to fill a C-123 transport with captured documents found abandoned in their HQ. The Chinese were worried that their military advisers might be captured by the Meo—a fate that befell one colonel. To the consternation of the CIA, who were keen to interrogate the Chinese officer, his throat was cut by Meo troops before they could reach him.

Meanwhile, Meo guerrillas, dropped in by helicopter behind enemy lines, were also meeting with surprising success. Troops from Site 32 set up positions on the west side of Route 7, while Black Lion led a guerrilla unit to take the heavily fortified hilltop position on Phou Nok Kok overlooking the road where it came out of the Ban Ban valley. Another CIA Special Forces adviser had previously spent a month trying to capture the position. Black Lion took only a single day to pep up his men and storm the mountain, working in close cooperation with Raven-directed T-28 fighters and Phantom F-4s carrying two-thousand-pound bombs. As the last bombs fell on the position, Will Green led his men in a run up the mountain slope. They took the position and held it for ninety days against an average of two ground assaults a day.

With Route 7 cut off, the North Vietnamese were forced to haul supplies overland or abandon them. Enemy supply lines were cut and large amounts of supplies captured. Although pockets of cut-off North Vietnamese troops remained operational, the Plain of Jars became relatively safe, and Ravens enjoyed the occasional free hour driving around in a captured Russian truck, taking photographs of each other posing beside the stone funeral jars.

It seemed that a winning formula had at last been arrived at. Massive air, used on a less restrictive basis and followed up by aggressive ground assaults, was doing the trick. The Ravens flew so much they became punchy (the low man for the month of September flew 156 hours—the high man notched up 210). From the beginning of the operation they had two hundred Barrel Roll sorties allocated to them daily, with each U.S. plane carrying twelve bombs. In addition there was the T-28 capability—an approximate total of 350 sorties a day. It was a great many bombs if every one was to be made to count.

The Ravens alone could not control all of the fighters, which led to the utilization of the Fast FACs. Fast FACs came out of Thailand, flying high-speed jets at a great height. They did not know the territory and could neither remain over the target long enough nor fly low enough for pinpoint accuracy. The result was a number of indiscriminate bombings that later were to have far-reaching political consequences. Friendly troops had pushed so far forward so fast that an imaginary line had been drawn from east to west across the middle of the plain, and it was stipulated that no U.S. air independent of Raven control should be put in south of it. It was a line every Raven carried in his head, but Fast FACs were not so finely tuned.

Early one morning one of them spotted a helicopter pad and tents out in the open. Assuming the camp to be North Vietnamese, they attacked, and the result was the death of twenty friendly troops. (Polifka ran into the pilot after the war at Eglin Air Force Base. "*Absolutely* no regrets at all. Didn't give a shit. Just Asians are Asians, and they are all enemy." He was sickened and infuriated to learn that certain of the Fast FACs purposely saved ammunition so they could strafe villages for fun on the way home.) In other incidents over a three-week period at the end of August into September, three hundred friendly troops were lost to errors made by Fast FACs. A village was hit and 250 women and children were killed. The Ravens could make mistakes too, but they were infrequent and never of this magnitude.

The 7th Air Force had also decreed that Fast FACs should hit the caves on the north side of the Ban Ban valley daily with Bullpups—

air-to-ground guided missiles—despite Raven and intelligence reports that the enemy had long since abandoned them. "We began to get our first realization that the U.S. Air Force was not the most professional organization in the world," Polifka said.

Once again there were furious confrontations between the men branded as Yankee Air Pirates and the Blue Suiters of the 7th Air Force. And once again it was an argument over control. The Air Force tended to feel used in Laos, never fully in command of its own assets. The air attaché's office issued a whole new slew of rules which led to an emotional and somewhat drunken argument at the Raven hootch when a Downtowner came up to explain them. "We told him flat to get screwed," Polifka said. "We were going to drop bombs where we damn well pleased to support our people, and that's what our job was."

"Your job is to do what the Air Force tells you to do," the Downtowner argued. "And you work for the Air Force."

"The Air Force pays us, and that's all they do." The Ravens listed their priorities: Gen. Vang Pao, the CIA, the ambassador—with the Air Force running a poor fourth. The Ravens trusted the men they went into battle with, and these were the CIA paramilitary people, not the Downtowners at the air attaché's office. Every night, during major operations, several of the Ravens spent as much as two hours going over CIA intelligence. It could be very good and very specific, down to the status and intentions of every North Vietnamese regiment in the country.

"Christ, it was a CIA war, CIA-led and CIA-financed," Polifka said. "Our role was to support it. There were Air Force generals who forgot that. There would be generals with three months' experience in Southeast Asia who wanted to sit down at a table with four or five Agency guys with a total of one hundred years in Southeast Asia, and they would try to tell them about the war. It was pathetic."

"The Air Force certainly didn't have the faintest idea what they were doing with air power there," Byers said, "and they would have been insulted if you said that air was a very mobile artillery, which is exactly what it is."

When Gen. George Brown of the Air Force visited Long Tieng he asked CIA man Tom Clines how many Americans were in town. "With the Air Force and us, I guess about twenty-five."

"Jesus Christ, if the U.S. military was here there would be a hundred thousand people. But I'm not sure I like lieutenants and captains running their own war."

Clines cocked his head to one side, took a draw on his cigar, and smiled broadly. "Well, George, that's really too bad—they're the only people we've seen from the Air Force who know what the fuck they're doing."

But the flagrant mistakes of Fast FACs made the Ravens' case for them, and the Air Force was once more severely limited in its area and type of operation in Laos. Barrel Roll was broken down in geographic sectors, known as Raven boxes, which only the Ravens could work. The Fast FACs were left with route interdiction north and east of Ban Ban, diminishing the potential for damage to friendly troops and population.

The number of Ravens was growing—although there were never more than twenty-two at any one time—and the CIA and the air attaché's office had reorganized them into more effective units. Valuable lessons were being learned during the course of About-Face. But the greatest lesson of all—the correct use of air power in Laos—was to be ignored.

A CIA case study reported more than 7,500 tons of booty captured. Rows of captured Russian tanks, which the enemy had abandoned after locking their turrets, were lined up on the plain. Beside them were whole batteries of 85mm guns, trucks with their tanks full of gasoline, and cases of Soviet sniper rifles still in their original Cosmoline.

The sudden, unexpected flight of the enemy posed some teasing questions. Why had the enemy not sabotaged the tanks, trucks, and supplies as they retreated? In the case of the captured artillery, the guns had been firing only shortly before the position was taken and boxes of Chinese hand grenades were found nearby. Ambassador Godley pondered the morale of such troops, "troops who couldn't even take the time to drop a hand grenade down the barrel of any of the guns."[8]

Curiosities among the captured equipment included a range of musical instruments—the prize of which was an accordion looking like something out of a German polka band; a 1956 Chevrolet station wagon with Oklahoma license plates, found at Arrowhead Lake; a cave full of freshly laundered Red Chinese uniforms and boxes of Maxa Chinese toothpaste. Mike Byers, who discovered the cave while out on a ground patrol with Burr Smith and a platoon of Meo guerrillas, threw half a dozen tubes into his pack. "I thought, if nothing else, I'm going to brush my teeth for the rest of this tour on

Chairman Mao." When he used it for the first time he felt he had discovered the underlying reason for enemy intransigence. "No wonder they're so mean, having to brush their teeth with this stuff every morning." The toothpaste had the consistency of valve-grinding compound, but was useful for polishing out scratches on helmet visors.

To celebrate the stunning victories of About-Face, Gen. Vang Pao threw a large party on the roof of his house. There was unlimited beer, *lau lao*, and White Horse whisky, and excellent food for a change. "I don't know where he got the abalone from," Byers said, "but it was outstanding." Village children formed a band and played on the captured instruments, which added to the familiar accordion-like wheezing of the *khene*, the stone-age gourd pipes of Laos. The Ravens also contributed musically. "Raven 47," Vang Pao said, "*un chanson, s'il vous plaît.*" Byers stood up and sang an approximation of Josh White's "Nobody Knows You When You're Down and Out." The gathering responded to this American cultural gem with polite applause.

It was good to be celebrating victory again after such a long period of defeat, and Meo morale soared. It was the first time they had taken and controlled the PDJ since 1964.[9] Gen. Vang Pao pursued the success of About-Face with follow-up operations and continued to push the enemy back. Operation West Wind concentrated on the area to the west of the plain, toward the Vietnamese border, while Operation North Wind hit at enemy concentrations to the north of the royal capital of Luang Prabang, toward the Chinese border.

The 316th Division of the NVA had been badly mauled. Operation West Wind was launched to destroy the supplies being prepositioned on Route 7, inside the buffer zone on the border with Vietnam, for the 312th Division as it came into Laos to relieve exhausted comrades. The new Vietnamese soldiers, unused to conditions in Laos, were ripped apart. They had been taught that they could shoot down F-4s with rifles—true, if they were low enough—and continually gave away their positions by blazing away at jets flying overhead at twelve thousand feet. Casualties were terrible. In the first two months they were in Laos, three battalions disappeared off the face of the earth and were never heard of again, while in another case only three survivors of a five-hundred-man battalion managed to struggle back to their regimental command post.[10]

Toward the middle of October 1969, the joint chiefs at the Pentagon announced that the buffer zone, previously ten miles wide, would be pushed back five miles. Gen. Vang Pao held a briefing where he told Ravens that everything within the new five-mile band counted as enemy and could be attacked. For three days the Air Force provided an extra eighty sorties a day, and the enemy were caught off-guard. "It was fantastic," Polifka said. "I have never seen so many secondary explosions. Every time you dropped a bomb, something would go off. I had one Thud roll in on a fifty-two-structure complex, drop four five-hundred-pounders, and fifty-two buildings disappeared in a blinding flash at least fifteen hundred feet in diameter. It almost blew me out of the air. The whole thing was gone in ten seconds. The Thud's wingman was halfway down the chute and had to abort the run because there was nothing left . . . just the outlines of fifty-two foundations where the hootches had been. The fireball was like an atom bomb. It just disappeared. I thought I had dreamed the whole thing."

The HQ of the Communist Neutralists—the so-called Patriotic Neutralists led by Col. Deuan Sunnalath—now came inside the target area, no longer protected by the buffer zone. The camp had always been clearly marked on maps by the CIA, but had been strictly off-limits. Mike Byers had longed to bomb it. "In a World War II context, not being allowed to get him would not have made any sense. Here is Hitler in his HQ, and you can fly over it every day but you can't bomb it."

On October 13, a clear and beautiful day, Byers took a T-28 loaded with Willy Pete rockets and flew up to Deuan's HQ, arriving at 6:00 in the morning. A flag flapped on a pole outside the staff tent, and no one on the ground seemed perturbed at the sight of the fighter. Two sets of F-4s arrived on station, but Byers could not use them as they only carried napalm, the use of which was restricted against structures. While Byers waited for more fighters to arrive he took the T-28 on a pass over the HQ and fired one of his rockets, setting off a large secondary explosion. He must have hit a cache of rocket motors, for they whirled into the air like giant fireworks. A second set of F-4s arrived and successfully bombed and strafed the HQ, which burned and blew for twenty-four hours. By the time Byers returned to base, Deuan's HQ no longer existed. CIA intercepts later confirmed that the entire Communist Neutralist staff had been killed, except for Deuan himself, who had been in Vietnam.

It was during this period that U.S. air in Laos finally peaked. It had already been increased 100 percent in June, and was again being increased significantly. The Laotian air war now involved up to three hundred fighter-bomber sorties a day—a rate equal to that flown at the height of the air campaign against North Vietnam.[11] Ravens were directing an average of 120 sorties a day, and on some occasions there were only three of them available to do so. Each Raven had to manage forty sorties, flying as many as six combat missions a day, and often returning to base in just over an hour because they had fired all their marking rockets. "It was like taxi cabs in Times Square, with fighters coming in from every direction," Polifka said. "And when you are working from five minutes after takeoff until five minutes before landing, you get damned tired."

It was an irony that U.S. air activity over Laos was reaching its peak at the very moment the "secret" nature of the war was being disclosed. Ambassador Sullivan, together with air attaché Robert Tyrrell, had been summoned before a Senate committee back in Washington to give an account of the war in Laos at a closed hearing. The hearing, which lasted for three days, often took the form of an interrogation. The substance of the hearing would remain classified for several months, but Sen. J. William Fulbright stated in an interview on October 28 that U.S. involvement in Laos was a "major operation" run by the CIA and approved by the past three administrations.

One of the results of the hearing before the Senate was that a bevy of high-ranking Air Force officers started to take an interest in the war in Laos and began to arrive at Long Tieng. Visitors included the head of the 7th Air Force, Gen. George Brown, and the head of the 7/13th Air Force, Gen. Robert L. Petit. The Air Force, as ever, was anxious to exert more control over the "major operation" so many of their assets were being used in.

It seemed to the Ravens that while the Air Force had given them so many more sorties to handle, it was somehow trying to trick them into breaking the Romeos. Napalm was not allowed to be used against structures, yet endless flights of Phantoms arrived on station carrying nothing else. They would be followed by RF-4 reconnaissance planes, which made passes after every Air Force strike to photograph the results.

In the vanguard of their first sustained tactical success, Ravens became blatant in their disregard for the rules. Polifka talked F-4 pilots reluctant to go against the rules into making a strike. "Look, nobody's going to know if you drop nape. You have got to go on the ground and see if nape is dropped. I don't think 7th Air Force is going to do that." Byers simply logged false coordinates, recording the genuine ones for himself in parentheses. "I did it a lot."

And then two weeks after West Wind had been launched, reports began to come in that the targets hit behind the buffer zone were not all enemy, although Ravens who flew in the vicinity saw only large amounts of prepositioned enemy supplies and found the absolute lack of visible civilian population eerie. The Meo advance had been so rapid they had outrun their own intelligence, and the area Vang Pao had designated as a free-fire zone contained large pockets of friend-lies.[12] At a CIA staff meeting Byers asked the general about it.

"Ooooh, very bad," Vang Pao said, wincing.

A terrible miscalculation had been made, and the general knew it. "I think we made a horrible mistake there," Byers said, "the only one that happened while I was there."

By December 1969, the North Vietnamese had built up their forces. The new troops in the 312th Division had become rapidly experienced by necessity and began to put intense pressure on the forward, mountaintop positions. Black Lion's fastness of Phou Nok Kok seemed to take the worst beating of all.

The enemy pounded the hill with half a dozen large 85mm mortars and had placed two 37mm antiaircraft guns on a mountaintop level with the position and only a kilometer away. Black Lion's troops were shot at all day, every day. It seemed to the A-1 pilots who flew up from Nakhon Phanom to help out that the whole mountaintop was on fire. "It was a fantastic sight," Maj. Al Preyss, one of the pilots, said, "where you could almost have said it was pretty if you weren't aware of the havoc it was bringing and the destruction. . . . It must take just a fraction of a second for that 37mm to fire its seven-round clip, and they have a beautiful red tracer to them." The guns were putting the shells directly onto Black Lion's position. It must have taken some sort of fantastic courage, Preyss thought, to stay there day after day.

It was growing dark, visibility was about two miles, and the presence of antiaircraft guns meant the A-1 pilots could not operate with their lights on, so were unable to see one another. But despite the poor conditions the pilots felt Black Lion was in such trouble they would try to help somehow. "You could just hear in his voice the pressure of the moment," Preyss said. "He was really being hammered. . . . He was literally pleading for us to come over there."

The Skyraiders flew over to the hilltop with their load of napalm, CBU-14 (small packaged hand grenades), and bombs. They attacked the guns, using the burning nape on the ground as a reference, and were shot at continuously. "We kept expending ordnance," Preyss said, "and Black Lion kept calling us to drop more, drop more, expend everything, and we told him we were doing our best and how tough our situation was. And he just kept pleading, and I really mean *pleading!*"

The A-1s stayed on station for over an hour before climbing back into the clouds, having dropped all of their ordnance. Black Lion continued to plead for help. They still had 20mm ammunition for their guns and decided to drop flares through the clouds, then ask Black Lion if he could see where the guns were in relation to them.

"So he gave us directions and we rolled in from about ten thousand feet," Preyss said, "pointed straight at the ground, and fired our 20mm and actually pulled off going through the clouds. . . . It lit up inside of the cloud like a Christmas tree and the flashes were so bright that I had to put my head down in the cockpit and fly instruments on the pull-up."[13]

Black Lion's position had survived another day, but could not last.

Gen. Vang Pao gave a tremendous *baci* the night before Karl Polifka, Bob Dunbar, and Al Daines left Laos. Just before the festivities began, Mike Byers returned to the hootch to find a young man dressed in Air Force tans and wearing 1505s (the Air Force's tropical uniform) with second lieutenant's bars, accompanied by an older, stocky man in a sports jacket—possibly the only one in Long Tieng. Byers eyed the Air Force officer with suspicion. If uniformed REMFs were going to be regular visitors to the secret base he figured it was time to move on.

Unaware that the short man in the sports jacket was none other than General Petit of the 7/13th Air Force, and the officer his aide, Byers merely grunted at the two strangers and poured himself a large drink on his way to his room, where he changed before going on to the *baci*.

The party proved to be a wild and emotional occasion. The general was losing three good men and he knew it, and toasts in White Horse and *lau lao* followed one upon another in rapid succession. When it came time for Vang Pao to toast the departing Ravens he produced a bottle of exquisite old French cognac—although the level of intoxication was such they would have equally enjoyed a beaker of rubbing alcohol. By the time the American contingent staggered from the house, with strings tied from their wrists to their elbows, everyone—except Daines, a teetotal Mormon—was extremely drunk. The CIA men returned to their bar to carry on with the party, and it was there that an unfortunate incident occurred, related with relish ever after throughout the Indochina theater.

General Petit, still dressed in civilian clothes, stood at the bar, accompanied by the aide in his starched summer uniform. The young aide was anxious to please, and attempted to engage those around him in conversation. A CIA paramilitary officer, called Igor, took a deep, instinctive dislike to him. The young aide compounded the situation by breaking one of the cardinal rules of the Other Theater— never ask a CAS guy a direct question. The lieutenant thought he was making innocent conversation when he introduced himself and asked Igor who he was and what he did. Igor growled into his drink.

He was a large man, with a reputation for having a short temper, and he became violent when drunk. Without saying a word, Igor grabbed the young aide by the scruff of the neck and thrust him through the bar's large plate-glass window onto the top of the bear cage. Floyd, who had been drinking heavily along with the group, seemed to sense that the human sprawled above him was an unwanted interloper. He began to make savage swipes with his claws through the bars, while the aide's dancing feet beat a tattoo on the bars of the cage, a performance much enjoyed by the assembled partygoers.

General Petit was assaulted in a friendly manner by Stan Wilson, who was the worse for wear after a week's binge in which he had failed to take a shower. "How the fuck are you?" Clean Stanley asked cheerfully, as he applied a hammerlock to the general. "You stupid old son of a bitch." As more and more drink was consumed, things continued their rowdy, downhill course. At 3:00 in the morning Dunbar decided to get back to the Raven hootch by walking across the roofs. Drunken CIA men threw darts at him through the bar's broken window as he tottered along his way. He tried to clamber into the room shared by Terry "Moose" Carroll and Mike Byers, who fought him off with a board.

Byers had gone to bed early, and relatively sober, in order to take a T-28 on the dawn patrol. He rose at 5:30, took a shower and shaved, and was drinking a cup of coffee in front of the map that covered one wall of the hootch when General Petit entered. Byers used the map as a meditation aid to help him concentrate his thoughts on the coming day. He hardly looked up at the stranger.

He was still unaware of "the little dude's" identity, vaguely imagining him to be a new CIA case officer. General Petit looked about him with scarcely concealed disgust. Manuel Espinosa had gone home, leaving the Ravens without a cook once again, and the hootch had degenerated into bachelor squalor.

"Good morning, young man," the general said stiffly. "And what are you going to do today?"

Byers nodded toward the map. "Right up here on Route 7 there's sixteen—maybe eighteen—trucks and I'm going up there to blow them up."

"Have you got any photos of them?"

"Oh boy, I wish I could get that. I can't get a thing off a goddam Air Force recce. They can't take a picture for sour owl shit. But I know they're there and we'll blow them up." Byers winked. "You bet."

The stranger in the sports jacket did not seem to like the course the conversation had taken. "I don't think they are there," he said in a voice that was stern and commanding. "I think you drop those bombs anywhere."

"You're right," Byers said, picking up his gear to go out and fly. "I just drop them and those dumb motherfuckers drive underneath them."

It was not until he returned at midday that he learned how much he had angered the general in command of the 7/13th Air Force. The general's morning had been as disturbing as his night, and he had been infuriated by one final incident before he left Long Tieng in disgust. In the corner of the operations shack was a body bag containing the remains of an F-105 pilot, which had been brought in by a CIA case officer. No one seemed to give it a second thought as they went about their business, and the callous indifference shown to a fellow Air Force officer killed in combat made the general's blood run cold.

"What is that?" he asked a Raven, indicating the body bag.

"Some Thud jock one of the CAS guys bagged and brought back—sitting over there till we can get him on a flight to Udorn for positive ID."

"I *meant* what is it doing dumped in a corner like that?"

The Raven looked over toward the body bag as if he were inspecting it, and there was a long pause while he pondered the question. "Not a whole goddam lot."

General Petit returned to Udorn with a nightmare version of the Air Force operation up at Long Tieng. The Ravens were undisciplined, ill-dressed, and insubordinate, lived like animals in filthy quarters, and spent their time in drunken native revels. His aide had been brutalized by drink-crazed CIA men who had jammed him into a cage with two savage drunken bears. The general himself had been similarly insulted by a filthy, drunken CIA mechanic. Worst of all, they displayed a monstrous lack of respect for fellow Air Force officers killed in combat. He could only assume that the excellent bomb damage assessment the Ravens always seemed to report was manufactured and, in reality, nothing more than gross exaggeration: "The Raven FACs at Long Tieng are nothing but a ragged band of Mexican bandits."

The Ravens rather liked that. Joe Bauer, a newly arrived intelligence officer, sent off for posters of Zapata and Pancho Villa, which were stuck up on the walls of the hootch. With Christmas only days away the Ravens posed for a group photograph, variously hung about with bandoliers of T-28 ammo, marking rockets, and Meo muskets. One or two clamped knives between their teeth. They signed it and sent it down to Udorn as the Raven Christmas card: "With love to General Petit—from the Mexican *banditos*."

If the Ravens were becoming a little ragged and brutalized, both physically and psychologically, it might have been the unspoken, subconscious stress brought on by a sustained period of combat without a mortality. It could not last, and secretly each of the Ravens eyed one another and wondered who would be next.

When Craig Morrison first arrived in Laos he felt he had achieved his life's dream. He came from a family of fliers, where even his mother had a pilot's license, and passed the years of his adolescence, before he was old enough to fly, jumping freight cars and riding them across country, a disreputable hobby which horrified his upper middle class family. After graduating from Sewanee, the prestigious university of the South—modeled on Oxford—he felt life could begin. "I had three goals—chase fast women, drive fast cars, and fly fast airplanes." The T-28 was not fast, but it was a fighter.

As the months went by, and Ravens seemed to survive against all the odds, he grew increasingly uneasy. Three Phantoms and an F-105 had already been shot down during December, but the Ravens had escaped. Bill Kozma had nearly been nailed by a couple of antiaircraft guns on December 17, and Morrison had the same experience the following day. "All the shit that was happening to us, and for three months nobody had been killed. We were taking bunches of hits— how often can you get an airplane shot up and take it home? It seemed like we were living charmed lives."

Every day the Ravens came back with their aircraft peppered with bullet holes. Sometimes a plane would have taken as many as fifty separate hits, and still have survived without anything sensitive being touched. It was a run of extraordinary luck that would inevitably have to end.

"I felt it was getting tense," Morrison said. "The weather was dogshit and we were losing the PDJ and were really on the retreat. When you're moving forward you feel you've got the momentum behind you, but when you're backing up . . . I just felt it couldn't go on much longer before somebody busted his ass. I just couldn't believe it hadn't happened already."

It was a period of particularly bad weather, when the procedure for leaving Long Tieng was to take off blind into the clouds, fly for fifteen seconds, push the nose of the O-1 over, and turn hard left to avoid a nine-thousand-foot mountain. With a little luck, a Raven found himself lined up to fly onto the Plain of Jars. There was an opening in the mountains, shaped like a saddle, which led onto the plain, and if a pilot could see between the cloud base and the mountain he could make it out.

The presence of a single T-28 on days of really bad weather would often deter the enemy, who used its cover to move troops and mount assaults without fear of air attack. Five days before Christmas 1969, Morrison took a T-28 out of Long Tieng on a day thick with cloud, and flew toward the North Vietnamese border, where a friendly outpost was being attacked by the enemy. The weather was so bad that Skyraiders were unable to get into the valley, and the North Vietnamese were able to press their attack with impunity. Morrison was able to work a set of A-1s, trapped above the clouds, by popping up beside them and then leading them down and onto the target.

It worked well, and the Skyraiders had been able to clear the enemy off a mountaintop and relieve the pressure on the friendly position. Morrison climbed back into the clouds to rendezvous with a second set of fighters and lead them down onto the target. He rolled in and fired a rocket, and was pulling off to the right when an antiaircraft gun on a nearby hill opened up. The gunners had held their fire during his first pass and had waited patiently until they were offered the belly of the T-28 as a target. They had calculated the pilot would pull to the right and opened fire before Morrison had actually begun the maneuver. Once committed to the roll there was nothing he could do but fly directly into the gunfire. "I flew right through the tracers and had it been night I could have read a newspaper by the flashes around the cockpit."

Morrison gritted his teeth and waited for the plane to disintegrate. Somehow, he emerged from the tunnel of flak, but a shell had entered the engine and exploded, bending but not breaking a push rod and blowing the head off one of the cylinders. Miraculously, the piston continued to move inside the cylinder, and as Morrison pulled off the engine was still running.

Oil flew over the canopy, and with the power pulled back the T-28 did not have enough RPM to fly. The plane dropped lower and lower, into an area so filled with enemy that Morrison despaired of surviving even if he was able to bail out. "I was pretty tense when I got to the point of adding power. I wasn't sure if the engine was going to come apart."

He added power and the plane picked up a little speed, just enough to struggle back toward Long Tieng. The Skyraiders stayed on his wing, and it was comforting to see the monstrous old planes beside him. Halfway back to base he was called by Cricket, who wanted to know why Raven 49 was heading home when there was another set of fighters coming in. "A little engine trouble," Morrison replied.

He banged the damaged plane down onto the strip at Long Tieng, and when he came to a halt on the ramp a mechanic ran out and whistled admiringly through his teeth. "Sure messed up this plane." He put a finger on the bent push rod and it snapped.

On an impulse, Morrison collected his maps out of the cockpit of the T-28, walked across the ramp, and climbed into an idle O-1. Airborne again, he called Cricket. "Hi, it's me again—Raven 49. Give me those fighters, rendezvous same position over PDJ."

The weather had broken sufficiently to allow the Skyraiders to find their way into the valley, and Morrison put them in on the enemy. By the time he returned to base he had destroyed two guns, silenced an 82mm mortar position, set off a secondary explosion of ammo and fuel, and killed a score of enemy troops.

Back at the hootch that night he relaxed over a beer and worked on his correspondence law course. Together with Moose Carroll he pinned up plastic sheeting over the screened area of his bedroom— temperatures had fallen to forty degrees at night. Joe Bauer, the intelligence officer, wanted to know how he should write up the crippled T-28. "Battle damage?"

"Yeah," Morrison said. "I guess you could say that."[14]

The day's events were recorded in a half-page entry in his journal. "Got the shit shot out of my plane today and but for a small piece of steel would probably be a POW right now." The arbitrary nature of life and death was beginning to obsess him. "As a matter of prophecy, it won't be long before they get one of us—Smokey [Greene], Moose [Carroll], Koz [Bill Kozma], and myself have all had *very* close calls and the law of averages is bound to catch up."[15]

Just before Christmas, Craig Morrison landed at Wattay and was amazed to see a lime-green Boeing 707 parked at the end of the runway. Cut off by the war, he had never seen a commercial aircraft painted such a frivolous color. He asked who owned it, and was told, "Some wealthy Texas dude—he's brought over a load of POW wives and widows and a planeful of Christmas presents he wants to take up to Hanoi and give the POWs."

Craig Morrison shook his head. "Bullshit."

The "wealthy Texas dude" was H. Ross Perot, the Dallas billionaire. The embassy had organized a party for him and his entourage, and certain members of the Ravens were asked to attend. The intention was that they could give Perot a firsthand account of the war, and generally sympathize with the POW wives. The Ravens were unenthusiastic. Weeping women and a fat cat in a lime-green airplane full of Christmas presents did not add up to the sort of party the Ravens enjoyed. ("Ask not for whom the women weep," was the callous Raven quip at the time, "they weep for *you*.") Only a couple of Ravens showed up for the party, and beside the military demeanor and severe crewcut of Ross Perot they looked like hippies. But as they listened to the man they warmed to him.

They learned that Perot had been asked by Henry Kissinger to persuade the North Vietnamese to change their harsh treatment of the POWs, and he was using his own money to work to that end. "It had been estimated that Vietnamization would take three years," Perot said. "The intelligence community had predicted that half the prisoners would die of brutality and neglect during the period. The Christmas trip and all of the other activities were staged to embarrass the Vietnamese in the eyes of the world to the point where they would change the treatment of the prisoners."[16]

As the Ravens listened to the passionate ideas put forward by Perot, and enjoyed his undiplomatic remarks expressing his low opinion of Defense and State Department employees in both Vientiane and Saigon, they were won over. Here was a man who was spending his own money to cut through all the red tape and bureaucracy to help captured Americans, who often seemed to have been forgotten.

"How much money does this guy have?" one of the Ravens asked.

Critter—Fred Platt's prehistoric pet. *(Platt collection)*

Chad Swedberg and Princess Hamburger— the photo is inscribed by Swedberg, "Town fool and friend." *(Swedberg collection)*

Lloyd Duncan with the fighter pilots of the Royal Lao Air Force in the panhandle. *(Kricker collection)*

Hal Mischler beside an OV-10 he flew as a FAC over the Ho Chi Minh Trail just before leaving for Laos. *(Whitcomb collection)*

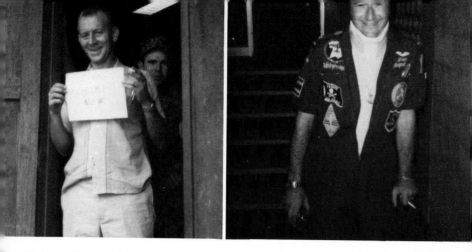

om Palmer during the siege of Long
ïeng in 1970, holding up a sign with
he Backseaters' favorite phrase written
n it—"We go home now." (*Morrison
ollection*)

Fred Platt, in neck brace and party
suit, after the war. (*Personal collection
of Fred Platt*)

im Hix and his Backseater Phanti
•eside an O-1 he "dead-sticked" into a
ice paddy after the engine quit. Phanti
arries a captured Russian AK-47; Hix
arries a Car-15 and a 9mm automatic.
Private collection of Jim Hix)

Craig Morrison and Scar (*right*) with
captured Chinese rifle. (*Morrison collection*)

Larry "Pepsi" Ratts with his squeeze
box, and wearing his Volga boatman's
hat, outside of the Raven hootch in
Pakse. (*Kricker collection*)

Ambassador Godley (in his Joseph Mobutu shirt from his days in the Congo), Frank Kricker with his newly awarded Silver Star, and an informal Robert Seamans, secretary of the Air Force. (*Private collection of Frank Kricker*)

Ambassador William Sullivan.

Grant Uhls wearing holster and .45 beside a T-28. (*Swedberg collection*)

The perils of making a mistake at Long Tieng—a T-28 is arrested by the vertical speed brake. *(EAPLS Archives)*

Chuck Engle, who was awarded the Air Force Cross, checks the fuel level on an O-1. *(EAPLS Archives)*

Chad Swedberg and Frank Birk in front of an O-1. *(Swedberg collection)*

Bob Foster at Long Tieng in the haze of the opium "burn" season. *(Private collection of Bob Foster)*

Republic F-105 "Thunderchief," nicknamed the Thud. *(USAF photo)*

Air Force CH-3 helicopter used in Jolly Green Giant search-and-rescue operations. *(USAF photo)*

An A-1 Skyraider, flown by the Air Commandos out of the secret Nakhon Phanom air base across the Mekong in Thailand. *(Mesaris collection)*

A Raven using a T-28 as a FAC plane. Note the marking rockets under the wing and grease-pencil, bomb-damage-assessment notes covering the cockpit. *(Mesaris collection)*

Gen. Vang Pao with a group of Meo on the Plain of Jars. Burr Smith, a CIA case officer, strides beside him in dark glasses, while Mike Byers is to his right carrying detcord. (*Byers collection*)

A squad from one of Gen. Vang Pao's Special Guerrilla Units waits to board an Air America UH-1 Huey to fly into battle. (*Private collection of Darrel Whitcomb*)

Weird" Harold Mesaris, a self-portrait.
Mesaris collection)

Lor Lu, the Raven orphan, carrying a
Meo musket and wearing a combat
fatigue hat. *(Mesaris collection)*

raig Morrison in Pleiku, Vietnam,
efore volunteering for the Steve
anyon Program. *(Morrison collection)*

Scar, the "Number One" Backseater, for
whom war satisfied some dark sense of
fun. *(Morrison collection)*

"*Billions*."

"Maybe the U.S. should put the whole damn war out to contract to him—we can clean up and go home."

Christmas itself was a festive affair. Patrick Mahoney had developed an informal relationship with several Pan Am operatives by scrounging equipment for their quarters in Saigon and Cam Ranh Bay they were unable to get themselves. Through them he sent the word back to San Francisco that he was looking for fresh turkeys (rolled turkeys were not acceptable). He began to receive phone calls from Pan Am people all over the States—who knew him by his code name, Clipper Patrick—with offers of turkeys. One place would have a couple, another four or five, and so on, until Mahoney was overwhelmed with turkeys. A large shipment was rerouted to Gen. Vang Pao at Long Tieng, after being flown directly from the United States by Pan Am. The general presented Mahoney with three of the captured Soviet sniper rifles as a token of appreciation.[17]

All the general's family, his senior officers, and the Americans at Alternate sat down to lashings of roast turkey. Floyd and his wife, the CIA bears, enjoyed a turkey to themselves. The Meo seemed bewildered by the soft, flaky meat that melted in the mouth, but enjoyed the gravy very much, pouring it over rice.

Spirits were high during the Christmas of 1969 at Long Tieng. A sustained period of victory had been enjoyed for the first time, and despite the setbacks of the past couple of months, it had been a good year. The Meo had regained their confidence, and Gen. Vang Pao was his old self.

PART IV

PART IV

8

THE WAR TURNS

> . . . I am in blood
> Stepp'd in so far, that, should I wade no more,
> Returning were as tedious as go o'er.
> —William Shakespeare,
> *Macbeth*

And then the enemy came smashing back. The new Communist offensive had been launched in December 1969, when the North Vietnamese Army moved in fresh troops and road construction teams, taking full advantage of a lull in air sorties over the Plain of Jars as the USAF switched its attention to the Ho Chi Minh Trail.[1]

The enemy snatched back the plain piecemeal, moving so fast they recaptured some of their own tanks and artillery pieces lost in About-Face. It was now the North Vietnamese's turn to wonder why their adversaries had not spiked guns or sabotaged tanks. By the beginning of the new year, 1970, thousands of civilians in encircled positions immediately northwest of the plain were threatened, and a massive evacuation began.

In less than two weeks, Air America, reinforced by ten Air Force choppers, lifted out four thousand refugees together with their livestock and possessions and moved them to Muong Soui.[2] Intelligence reports stated that the North Vietnamese were pouring men and supplies through Laos and Cambodia and down the Trail into South Vietnam. Antiaircraft guns in Laos had tripled in number in little over a year.[3]

Fred Platt flew out to the east of Xieng Khouang on January 11, accompanied by a new Backseater. The weather was bad, so he decided to try working glory holes (isolated openings in an overcast sky where a Raven could rendezvous with fighters and lead them down through the cloud and onto a target). He spiraled up and down through the cloud breaks but had no luck finding targets.

He radioed Cricket and said he was going to try some armed recce along Route 7. The Backseater was new to the job, and Platt attempted to show him the ropes. Along the road he found a stock of oil drums that had been brought in during the night and were still uncamouflaged. Instead of calling in fighters, Platt rolled in on them himself and fired a Willy Pete rocket directly into the fuel cache.

As he made the pass he heard the unmistakable sound of a 12.7mm antiaircraft gun open up, then saw green tracers arcing toward him. One shell hit the elevator surface, which did no great damage, but a second went between the accessory case and the engine block. The plane began to spew oil and caught on fire.

"Raven 47," Platt called in to Cricket, "I've just taken a hit on Route 7. I'm going to point it toward Alternate, but the engine's running rough. Try to get a fix on me—get a location. I'm going to keep broadcasting until the radio goes dead."

Oil from the burning engine left a trail of thick black smoke, and flames began to lick around the outside of the cockpit. "Heavy fire, black smoke—shutting down the engine now," Platt radioed Cricket. He punched off the rockets, which made the plane lighter and allowed him to gain altitude. He maintained a steady glide until a limestone ridgeline loomed up directly ahead of him. "If you've got a tracking beam on me," Platt said to Cricket, "I'm going to try for an Alaskan bush landing on the karst."

This was an extremely tricky maneuver—the same one that had killed Bing Ballou. The technique is to bring the plane in low until it is barely above the ground, and point it in the direction of an uphill slope; the pilot slows it down almost to a stall, and then at the last moment yanks up the nose, forcing it to stall. The idea is to make the plane slide back on its tail and hit the ground the instant before gravity takes over and the heavy nose plummets.

Platt dropped the flaps to a quarter and dived toward the vertical karst, tensing himself for the landing. An updraft suddenly picked the plane up, giving it enough airspeed to lift over the ridgeline. Behind the karst was a wide valley with rows of rice paddies, punctuated every two hundred yards by dikes, while at the far end stood an abandoned earth stronghold.

As he dropped to a height of three feet above the ground he saw that part of what he had taken to be a dike was in fact a two-lane highway. It was forty feet wide, sunk between two banks twenty feet deep, and overlain with camouflage. He lifted the plane to fifteen feet, pointed its nose toward the first bank, which lay directly across his path, and pulled on the stick. The tail dropped onto the highway; he hit the far bank with the underbelly of the airplane just beneath the engine cowling, and he felt the wings ripping from the fuselage.

As crash landings went, he was doing well, except that when the plane hit the ground his shoulder harness snapped. He flew forward and hit his face on the crossbar of the cockpit, and his knees smashed into the instrument panel. He had also lost his back pressure on the stick when the harness broke, so that the plane retained too much airspeed. As it bounced the propeller dug into the ground, making the plane flip over onto its back.

Platt and his Backseater hung upside down in the crashed aircraft. The cockpit roof was a bed of broken Plexiglas, but he had no choice but to reach down and release his seat belt. Platt fell heavily onto the splintered plastic, kicked open the door, and rolled out of the plane. The Backseater remained hanging, unharmed but dazed. Platt shook him. "Come on, come on—bye-bye."

The man remained where he was. Platt reached for his seat buckle and released it. The Backseater fell on his head and was momentarily stunned. As he came around he began to moan, and then to pray. In the distance Platt heard noises, and saw enemy troops coming over the hill half a kilometer away.

He grabbed his map case, an M-79 grenade launcher and a bandolier of shells, and a Swedish-K submachine gun and a shoulder bag full of ammo. Looking toward the earth stronghold, he saw a high bank and decided that it would be the ideal place to make a stand while they waited for help. He began to run toward it, shouting to the Backseater to follow him, but the man stood rooted to the spot, too shocked to move. Platt went back, grabbed the Meo and threw him over his shoulder, and ran through the paddy fields.

He wondered, as he ran, whether the onetime defenders of the abandoned stronghold had ever mined its surroundings, and he dimly expected to be blown into the air at any moment, but he reached it without mishap. He stopped at the edge of the bank and propelled the Backseater over the side and then jumped over himself. Both men squatted in its shelter while Platt tried to get someone on the radio. Meanwhile, the enemy had reached the crashed plane and gathered around it. They had not seen Platt's dash for cover, but now they spread out to find and capture the downed pilot.

Tom Harris was working glory holes out toward Site 46, about twenty miles from where Platt had been hit, when he heard the initial call for help. He followed the trail of black smoke left in the wake of the O-1 and flew into the valley searching for the wreck. The enemy troops dropped down at the sight of the plane, but as Harris pulled off they began to move up the road again. Platt fired M-79 grenades at them, using the long-range launcher on maximum elevation in order not to give away his position, and was careful to conserve ammunition.

The Jolly Greens had launched from Long Tieng, but had been ordered to stand by, hovering over the base, while a full-scale search-and-rescue operation was organized. In the meantime, Dave Anckle-berg, the pilot of an Air America chopper, had heard the Mayday call over the company frequency. Together with his crew chief, he kicked off the cargo he had been loading and headed toward the crash site.

Platt had been on the ground only half an hour when he heard the rotors of the Air America chopper in the valley. It came in over the bank and settled down ten feet behind the stronghold. The two men ran toward it, and Platt grabbed his companion by the seat of the pants and gave him a one-armed boost into the chopper. He then threw all his gear in and reached up for something to grab to pull himself on board. Inadvertently, he grabbed the side door's release latch. The door of the H-34 spun off and landed in the paddy. The crew chief signaled him to abandon it, and as enemy soldiers ran down the road toward them, he hauled Platt aboard. The chopper lifted off and they flew back toward Alternate.

The crew chief asked Platt if he was hurt. "No, I feel great." Grateful to be alive, he began to shower the pilot with profuse thanks and removed the kilo gold bar he kept strapped to the calf of his left leg (partially worn as a counterbalance for the large Bowie knife strapped to his right leg). He offered it to Anckleberg in appreciation for saving his life. The pilot shook his head and waved the gold ingot away. "No sweat, Raven."

The Ravens were on the ramp to meet the chopper as it came in to land. Platt asked for a T-28 to be made ready and grabbed the Backseater. "Hey, we go back—we get gun." The Meo looked at him blankly and quietly walked away. (He resigned from the Backseater corps after this single experience, and returned to being a lieutenant of infantry.) "I want to go back and get that damn gun," Platt insisted.

"Don't you think I ought to fix that nose first?" asked Clyde Elliot, who had also come down to the ramp to meet the chopper. Platt put his hand up to his nose. It had been badly broken and was skewed off to one side of his face. "I'm not going to let you go," the doctor said. "You're in shock."

Platt was helped back to the hootch. His knees were beginning to hurt, but the pain receded after a couple of stiff shots of whisky. He was aware that his neck had become stiff, and his back was stiffening too, but drinking seemed to help. The postmortem on his crash turned into a party, and Platt drank a bottle of Scotch before he staggered to bed. "Fuck it—I'll go get the gun tomorrow."

The following morning he awoke and felt nothing. His knees no longer hurt and his back and neck were not stiff. But when he tried to get out of bed he could not move. It was then that he first realized he was paralyzed from the neck down.

Fred Platt needed to be flown to the Air Force hospital at Udorn as a matter of the greatest urgency. He stubbornly refused to be taken on a Jolly Green, arguing that if they were reluctant to pick him up in combat he could manage without their services now. He was folded into the back of an O-1 and Mike Byers flew him across the border into Thailand.

By the time they arrived Platt could move his hands, although he was still unable to feel anything. He watched his toes wiggle and his fingers curl as if they belonged to someone else. At Udorn, Byers taxied the plane to a waiting ambulance on the Air America ramp. Platt was strapped to a board and taken to the hospital, where he was put in a neck brace and subjected to a series of X-rays. Both the hospital's radiologist and the orthopedic surgeon were on weekend leave, so it was left to the staff doctor to inspect the X-rays and prescribe treatment. This involved strapping Platt to an angle board while an elaborate web of weights and pulleys stretched his limbs. Every two hours the weights were taken off, and he was strapped into a circular trundle bed and moved around. The treatment continued for two days, and although he was still able to move his fingers and toes, he felt nothing and remained paralyzed.

The orthopedic surgeon returned from Bangkok and examined the X-rays. They showed a spinal concussion and seven separate hairline fractures. "This man's neck is broken and he has a fractured spine," the doctor announced. "You're just pulling it apart with these weights."

When he spoke of Platt to the other doctors, he did so in the third person, as if the patient did not exist or were stone-deaf. It was a procedure with which Platt was to grow familiar during his treatment in military hospitals. The weights were removed and he was placed in a trundle bed. The doctor remarked to his colleagues that he was amazed the patient had lived so long—twenty-four hours was surprising, seventy-two hours little short of extraordinary.

"How bad is it?" Platt asked.

"With therapy you may regain the use of your hands," the doctor replied, addressing him personally for the first time. "You'll never walk again."

Platt was silent for a moment as the full meaning of the doctor's words sank in. Then he recovered something of his old spirit. "Bullshit."

He was wheeled into the office of the hospital commander, where he spoke over the phone to his brother, Dr. Melvin Platt, a surgeon at Massachusetts General in Boston. Then his brother spoke with the Udorn doctor. "Looks bad, Fred," he said bluntly. "But with therapy you're going to make it. I'll get them to ship you back here."

"Don't tell the folks."

Platt determined he was going to walk out of the hospital or die there, and listening to the gloomy predictions of doctors and staff around him, he concluded the odds were on the latter. He began to give away his guns, the only personal things in Laos he had to give—his 9mm pistol, his Swedish-K submachine gun, his folding-stock AK-47. He told Burr Smith, who had come down to visit, that he wanted Scar to have his M-79 grenade launcher.

At first Platt made light of his crash, turning it into a good yarn for Mr. Clean. "If ever they hold the hundred-meter dash for people with broken backs, handicapped by a hundred-pound Lao over one shoulder and a hundred pounds of ammo over the other, I know there is not any human being who will ever beat the record I set."

Burr Smith smiled. There was a moment's silence, and then Platt began to speak in earnest. "I can't go home all gimped up like this. My mother could accept the fact I'm dead—but I can't go home looking like this. I can't handle it—it's not the way I want to do it." He lowered his voice. "If I can't walk out of this place, come kill me."

Burr Smith looked away.

Therapy was slow and very painful. Platt was lifted from the trundle bed while nurses and staff manipulated his arms and legs. It made him stiff and sore, but he began to regain some feeling and felt certain he would be able to walk if only he was allowed to try. The hospital staff looked skeptical, but put him into separate back and neck braces and also strapped braces onto both legs.

Encased in this framework of metal supports, he was awkwardly lifted to his feet. Willing himself to walk, he concentrated all of his energy into taking the first step. He felt one leg inch forward, and then the walls dissolved around him as he fell headlong onto his face.

As Communist military pressure continued to build on the Plain of Jars in early 1970, the war-weary Meo proved no match for it. The success of Operation About-Face had proved ephemeral. The Meo guerrillas were formidable as helicopter-transported shock troops in small battalions, but it was beyond their ability to face a highly trained enemy of division strength.[4] They could take ground in lightning attacks but had difficulty keeping it, and when the NVA fielded tanks against the airstrip at Xieng Khouang the youthful Meo panicked. Terrified at the sight of the advancing tanks, they fled—closely followed by the town's garrison of fifteen hundred men.[5]

But it was imperative to delay the enemy advance. If it was not stopped it would be the first time the NVA would be in striking distance of Long Tieng at the time of the year when the weather favored them. It was clear that the Meo alone, even with increased sorties of Raven-directed U.S. air, would not be able to check the advance. Impotent in the face of enemy attack, the U.S. military now debated whether to unleash the B-52 on the Plain of Jars.

B-52s had never been used in northern Laos before, although they had bombed the Ho Chi Minh Trail in the southern panhandle since 1965. CINCPAC—Commander in Chief Pacific Command—had proposed its use in the north seven months earlier, when Communist forces had threatened the royal capital of Luang Prabang, but only now did Washington consider the issue in earnest.

The B-52 Stratofortress was the backbone of the Strategic Air Command, the bomber built to deliver nuclear weapons. The Air Force had hurriedly trained crews in the delivery of conventional weapons, and since June 1965 it had been used in Indochina on a daily basis. Its white belly—so painted to deflect the glare of a nuclear explosion—had been painted over, and the bomb bay had first been adapted to carry more than fifty 750-pound iron bombs, while later models carried more than a hundred 500-pound bombs. The B-52 could neither be seen nor heard from the ground, and released its bomb load at forty thousand feet, at which height the bombardier had to allow for the curvature of the earth in targeting calculations. A sortie usually consisted of a cell of three B-52s, and the damage inflicted was awesome.

The Ravens were asked their opinion regarding the potential use of the bomber in the war in Laos. An Air Force officer gathered a group of them together and questioned them in particular on the pros and cons of using the B-52 on the Plain of Jars. Their answer was surprising—unanimous condemnation of such a move. Sitting in on the meeting was Craig Morrison, and he noticed that just as his colleagues were about to applaud the use of extra firepower against the enemy they all seemed to have immediate second thoughts. "You could see them about to mouth the words, 'Sure! Great—pile it on the bastards,' and then the thought changed." Not a single Raven polled favored the use of the B-52, either on the Plain of Jars specifically, or the Trail, or anywhere else in Laos.

"We said forget it. It won't work," Morrison said. "B-52s are great—they blow up lots of territory. But that's not our problem. On downtown Hanoi it would be pretty devastating—but up in northern Laos it was the wrong weapon. Overkill. We needed more T-28s and A-1s carrying the right ordnance at the right time. And even if you kill the enemy, without troops to hold the territory you're just spinning your wheels. You'll be playing your last trump card, and the enemy will find out it's no good. You'd be better served holding on to the trump as a threat." The Ravens rejected the use of the B-52 in northern Laos on practical, military grounds and were merely expressing in their own words an accepted military axiom: the precision of any lethal weapon system's use can never be made equal to its destructive power.

In addition, the ambassador was convinced it would prove to be a political mistake. "I was certainly opposed to the use of the B-52," Godley said. "It was just another escalation. I just felt that if we could hold our own without using them, why use them?

"The B-52 was portrayed as the answer to everything, which is rubbish. It's all a lot of luck, let's face it. An air raid is just as good as your targeting. If you happened to have troops in the open or dumps, it's damned effective. On the other hand if your targeting is no good you are just cutting grass."

Back in July 1969, when Godley had just arrived to take up his position as ambassador to Laos, he had given a briefing on the military situation in the country to President Nixon and Henry Kissinger, who were passing through Bangkok, Thailand. During the briefing Godley made the unfortunate remark "Some idiots want to use the B-52 in northern Laos," an idea he contemptuously dismissed. Afterward, he was taken aside by Kissinger. One of the "idiots," Kissinger said, was the president of the United States. Another, of course, was Kissinger.

Both the military advice of the Ravens, on the edge of the war, and the political advice of the ambassador, who actually ran the war, were studiously ignored in Washington, where the debate over the bomber's use boiled down to a power struggle between Defense Secretary Melvin Laird and the Pentagon on the one hand, and Henry Kissinger, head of the National Security Council, and the White House, on the other.

"A stately bureaucratic minuet" is how Kissinger describes the high-level wrangling over the decision to use the B-52 on the Plain of Jars.[6] In his memoirs, Kissinger writes that the request was generated by Ambassador Godley on January 23, asking that the B-52 strikes be used against a concentration of four thousand Vietnamese troops massed on the plain. In fact, Godley was instructed by Washington to ask for B-52 strikes. Armed with the request, Kissinger set about polling those in the chain of command in Washington on the wisdom of such a move.

Secretary of State William Rogers stated flatly that he was against the use of B-52s in northern Laos. According to Kissinger, Mel Laird told him privately that he favored using B-52s against the target, but did not want it discussed at an interagency forum for fear of leaks. He wanted it approved through the same channels as the secret strikes in Cambodia, so that the Pentagon would go on the record as opposing the strike, despite Laird's personal view. (Both Rogers and Laird had previously opposed the use of the B-52 in secret raids on Cambodia, even after Nixon and Kissinger had decided to launch such an attack.)

Kissinger had met his match with Laird, described by colleagues as a wily bureaucrat with highly developed political instincts, a truly formidable adversary in any Washington power struggle.[7] Miffed at the defense secretary's nimble evasion, Kissinger writes, "The president would take the heat for the decision."[8] Not Kissinger.

His account of conversations with Laird glosses over a much more heated disagreement over the issue. The joint chiefs had already expressed the wish to withdraw B-52s not currently required in Southeast Asia, but the request was refused by the White House on the grounds that they should remain in the theater for "contingency purposes." Later, the Pentagon suggested a more flexible use of sorties, geared to enemy activity—a piece of military common sense the men fighting the war in Vietnam had always asked for. Kissinger refused, insisting that the number of tactical air strikes and B-52 sorties that had already been approved for the next financial year be flown regardless of the military situation. "Anyone that addresses the problem starting with a set number of sorties doesn't understand the problem and isn't qualified to discuss it," Melvin Laird responded angrily.[9]

But Kissinger knew what Laird did not, that the "contingency" was already mooted—an invasion of Cambodia. Even so, the faith the White House put in the B-52 strategic bomber flew directly in the face of the evidence. Reports specifically commissioned on the subject emphasized the military ineffectiveness of the B-52: it had failed to interdict supplies and troops on the Trail and failed completely on the bombing of base camps, while the number of enemy soldiers killed in strikes was a question for debate. Tactical air used to support ground troops—exactly the business the Ravens were involved in—was, on the other hand, much more effective.

Lacking support for his plan to use the B-52 on the Plain of Jars, Kissinger then asked Gen. Earle Wheeler, chairman of the joint chiefs, whether the target could be attacked with tactical aircraft rather than B-52s. ("For some reason, tactical air strikes seemed to provoke less of an outcry than B-52s," Kissinger mused vaguely.[10] Good reason, actually. Tactical aircraft can be controlled and diverted onto a target by FACs, are more accurate, and can be called off at the last minute if necessary. The chances of civilian casualties are greatly reduced by using tactical air. A B-52 strike is planned days in advance and its bombs are released at such an altitude that they are considered to be accurate if they land within a hundred meters of the target. Perhaps the American public, and worldwide opinion, instinctively understood this, for to those opposed to the war the B-52 bomber had become the symbol of remote, cold-blooded killing, the modern American way of war at its most unacceptable.)

Wheeler told Kissinger that the enemy on the Plain of Jars *were* being attacked by tactical aircraft (they had, of course, been bombed by tactical aircraft for the last six years), but this was proving ineffective, and in the circumstances he favored the use of the B-52. Kissinger went back to Laird and attempted to persuade him that a concentration of four thousand North Vietnamese troops presented a target worthy of a B-52 strike. Laird replied—perhaps ironically—that, indeed, the massing of so many troops presented the best target since he had become secretary of defense, but stressed they would soon disperse.

But there was no such target. Kissinger was quoting an inaccurate press report in an attempt to win Laird around, rather than the intelligence reports of the CIA, DIA, and Air Force—to which he had instant access. These put the real figure at four hundred. The mistaken press report was the result of a misunderstanding when a military briefing officer told news agency reporters that four thousand enemy soldiers were involved in the offensive on the plain. This was taken to mean that an enemy force four thousand strong was attacking a command post on an airfield. It is inconceivable that the NVA would have risked concentrating four thousand men in open country.

The upshot of Kissinger's various conversations over using the B-52 on the Plain of Jars was that he had no consensus whatsoever, and that he had received direct advice against it. It is disingenuous of Kissinger to suggest that the world's most powerful men in the world's most powerful nation would exert their collective energy over a single classified B-52 strike. The "stately bureaucratic minuet" was a game. Larger issues were at stake.

The White House felt that Vietnamization was proceeding too slowly and that the South Vietnamese Army would not be able to bridge the gap left by the continual U.S. troop withdrawals. Air power was to bridge that gap, adding yet another political dimension to a bomber that was already employed for organizational purposes and interagency rivalry. The B-52 was to become one of the cornerstones of U.S. policy in Indochina, buying time for both Vietnamization and the Nixon Doctrine. Like Gen. Vang Pao, the White House put inordinate faith in air power without fully understanding it. (The Air Force histories for this period are entitled "The Administration Emphasizes Air Power" [1969] and "The Role of Air Power Grows" [1970].)

The precedence given to the political rather than the military use of the B-52 worried Defense Secretary Melvin Laird, who felt that the White House accepted uncritically every claim the Air Force or the joint chiefs made for air power, and that Nixon and Kissinger had no clear idea of what it could or could not do. He even asked an aide to produce a briefing, "to begin educating Dr. Kissinger."

"It's a very big job," Col. Robert Pursley, his military assistant, remarked. "The president and Dr. Kissinger both believe everything 7th Air Force has told them."[11]

The other issue at stake was who had power in Washington, D.C. Kissinger was involved in arm wrestling with the Pentagon, State Department, and joint chiefs. The winner was whoever had their way with the president.

After a month of bureaucratic infighting, Kissinger went to President Nixon with his request for a B-52 strike on the Plain of Jars. He told the president that the long-feared North Vietnamese offensive had finally broken and that Prime Minister Souvanna Phouma had made a formal request for B-52 strikes (an idea generated and suggested to the Laotian prime minister by the U.S. embassy in Washington). "I recommended that the president authorize B-52 strikes if the enemy advanced beyond Muong Soui, the farthest point of communist penetration before the government offensive of the previous summer. The President agreed."

Ambassador Godley was told of the decision to use the B-52 by Henry Kissinger, who said he was speaking on behalf of the president. In face of such authority Godley only voiced "mild objections." The clandestine B-52 bombing of Laos was code-named Good Look— the same name that was used for the secret bombing of neighboring Cambodia. "We began using B-52s on a very highly classified basis," Godley said. "We never admitted using them."

As a prelude to the February raid it was decided to evacuate all civilians from the southern rim of the plain and move them further south. It was the war's most dramatic helicopter evacuation, when Air America and Continental Air Services aircraft lifted out more than thirteen thousand refugees from Lat Sen airfield. Pilots kept their engines running at the hot and dusty locations while the refugees boarded the transport aircraft to be flown to Vientiane.[12] American reporters and photographers witnessed the exodus of the impoverished people, and accounts were published in the press.

The president had authorized the raid if and when the enemy advanced beyond Muong Soui. "The Communists were beyond Muong Soui within twenty-four hours," Kissinger records in his memoirs. "An attack with three B-52s was launched on the evening of February 17–18."[13]

But the enemy had not taken Muong Soui by this date, as documents declassified since the publication of Kissinger's memoirs show.[14] The B-52 strike went in anyway. And the raid was not confined to a cell of three bombers, as stated by Kissinger. Thirty-six sorties of B-52s dropped a total of 1,078 tons of bombs, according to official USAF accounts.[15] No one in the know in Laos thought that even such a massive raid would stop the enemy, and it didn't— although the Air Force expressed satisfaction on the bomb damage assessment, which reported many secondary explosions and numerous casualties. (Also the precedent had been set, and from now on the B-52 would be used in thousands of sorties over northern Laos before the end of the year.)

Burr Smith was out on the plain with a hand-held movie camera to film the strike. It fell considerably closer to him than planned, which suggests it was off target, and parts of the film—now buried in some archive in CIA HQ, Langley, Virginia—are very shaky due to rapid rearward crawfishing.[16] CIA radio intercepts reported the enemy complaining of deafness after the raid, but it failed to stop them.

Impressive though the raid was, it neither bolstered Meo courage sufficiently to make them hold fast nor broke the enemy's will. The B-52 failed to put a dent in the enemy's offensive, and they moved on to take Muong Soui unopposed by ground forces late in the afternoon of February 24. At the first glimpse of the approaching enemy the town's meager 120-man defending force abandoned their positions and fled.

The bombs of the B-52 had been absorbed by Laos without protest as simply more of the same, but they would find their mark in Washington, D.C.

A mixture of superhuman will and Texan cussedness enabled Fred Platt to take a few steps across his hospital room. The staff, who were perpetually picking him up from the floor, considered him a difficult patient. Slowly, he reached the point where he could cross the room from the bed to the door, tottering precariously in leg braces. Within two weeks he could take the same journey without the leg braces, using crutches. It was a painful and heartbreaking business, but he achieved what the medical profession had declared to be impossible.

Platt was the only person on his floor hospitalized by combat injuries. One patient had broken a leg playing softball, another's foot had turned septic after stepping on a nail, while two others were incapacitated with virulent cases of gonorrhea. Surprisingly little sympathy was extended to the single patient who not only had been wounded, but had also emerged from the brutalizing, psychologically warping business of war. The staff's patience was tried by a man who loudly declared he had little faith in their recipes for recovery and was intent on curing himself despite medical advice. Worst of all, Fred Platt did not do what he was told. One evening, as dinner was being served along the corridor, he was pointedly ignored.

"Where's my supper?"

"If you insist on getting out of bed," the nurse replied primly, "the ambulatory patients go to the dining hall and get their own meals."

"Fine," Platt said, containing his anger. "Thank you."

Dressed in his hospital gown, he stumbled on his crutches to the front of the building, where he flagged down a passing jeep. The driver dropped him off at the O club. His entrance was dramatic, and word of his arrival spread through the club: "Old Magnet Ass is out of the hospital."

He was propped up against a table and whisky was poured down him. The fighter pilots gathered around and an impromptu party began, until it was interrupted by a commotion at the front door of the club. Platt had been reported by the hospital authorities as AWOL, and the air police had arrived to pick him up.

An uproar of booing and hissing broke out, while fighter pilots formed a phalanx to block off the sky cops. A young captain walked over to General Petit, commander of the 7/13th Air Force, who happened to be in the club. "The club officer wants you to know the air police are here, sir. There's an officer AWOL from the hospital and they have a report he's here in the club. They've come to arrest him and take him back."

The general still harbored strong reservations concerning the Ravens, but they did not extend to disciplining a man shot down in the combat zone who left the hospital for a drink with comrades-in-arms. He told the captain to inform the air police that they needed the presence of both the squadron and the base commanders to effect an arrest in the O club. While the sky cops spoke into their walkie-talkie radios, Platt slipped out the back door, where the general's staff car was available to drive him back to the hospital.

He hobbled back to his room, where he was greeted in icy triumph by the nurse. "They arrested you, didn't they? That will teach you to run away."

"You told me to go eat—I'm just through eating dinner," Platt said, reeking of whisky. "Nobody arrested me. I got a lift back from the general."

A letter was sent by the hospital commander to the air attaché's office, Vientiane, reporting the incident. Platt was duly sent a formal reprimand, which stated that his lack of officer qualities reflected badly on the program as a whole. Enclosed with the reprimand was the paperwork on his third Purple Heart.

Doc Elliot came down from Long Tieng. "The treatment you're getting here is horrible," he pronounced. "I'm going to move you out."

A hospital room was set up in the Charoen Hotel, where Elliot oversaw Platt's treatment. "I trusted him and he did a hell of a good job on me. Everything hurt, but I was beginning to get feeling back. I could move my hand. I would be standing holding a pencil and it would fall out of my hand and I would never know that it was gone. I would fall down and never know that my legs weren't there anymore. It was a question of opening up new circuits and learning how to walk and move my arms again."

A large part of the therapy was provided by the professional masseuses from the local bathhouse. They came in relays and worked around the clock, gently massaging the feeling back into Platt's body.

Soon he was strong enough to get around to the various Udorn bars. He ran into Dave Anckleberg, the Air America pilot who had picked him up, and tried again to give him the gold bar. Embarrassed, Anckleberg again turned it down. It became a game whenever the two men met. Platt ordered a thousand-dollar bill through the bank and went to the Air America Club and offered it to the chopper pilot. "I owe it to you for saving my life, and if you don't take it I'm going to burn it."

Anckleberg laughed, thinking the bill was funny money. But a thousand-dollar bill attracted attention among the mercenaries of Air America, and a crowd gathered. Platt pulled out a cigar, lit it with the bill, and then let the burning money drop to the floor. Everyone began to stamp on it—"It was like an African stop-the-rain dance." Anckleberg never did receive the money, although no one admitted retrieving the bill.

Platt now believed he was well enough to fly, even though he was still encased in neck and back braces. The idea was firmly rejected by the embassy, which gave him a date for shipping out. It really did look as if the war was finally over for him, so he decided to throw a party.

Two representatives from every fighter squadron in Vietnam and the Other Theater were sent invitations, as well as every colonel on the base at Udorn, the Thai generals, and all the flotsam and jetsam of the secret war. The Charoen Hotel was rented for the night, together with two bands. There was Thai food, free drink, ten rooms for the overtired, twenty-five prepaid hookers and another twenty-five freelance. Platt had his tailor, the Sikh Amarjit, whose shop was opposite the base's main gate, make him a tuxedo out of camouflage material—destined to become the high-fashion garment of the war. He stood in the door, immaculate in his combat tuxedo despite the neck and back braces, leaning on a pair of canes, cigar clamped between his teeth. Amarjit stood beside him, handing out business cards (he received 250 orders for combat tuxedos in the following week). Had the Vietnamese had the ability to launch a sapper attack on the Charoen

Hotel on the night of Fred Platt's party, the USAF would have been fighter-pilot impoverished for a generation. It seemed that every fighter jock from the war was present, together with an extraordinary ragbag of spies and mercenaries. "The most bodacious party God and man have ever known," Platt declared afterward.

It distressed Platt that the Air America chopper crews had never been given any recognition for their bravery in picking up downed pilots in Laos, something they were not obliged to do. One evening, sitting in the colonels' section of the O club with Gus Sonnenberg—now operations officer for the 7/13th Air Force—he brought the subject up. He would like to see someone like Dave Anckleberg get the Presidential Medal of Freedom, he said, not just for himself but for all the Air America guys. "It's something we ought to do."

Sonnenberg replied that with Air America's connections—owned lock, stock, and barrel by the CIA—nobody was likely to be given anything. The less publicity the better.

"Forget that they have their share of thieves, crooks, and outlaws," Platt insisted. "When it comes down to conscious acts of bravery they deserve the big medal. When a Raven's down, there isn't one of them who wouldn't fly into the most horrendous fire to pick up a guy."

Sonnenberg said that when he got back to the office he would work on it, find out what the requirements were and what was needed for a submission, but that the spooks were sure to squash it. He finished his drink and left.

Unfortunately, a Jolly Green colonel, sitting at a nearby table with two lieutenant colonels, had heard the conversation, and it rubbed him the wrong way. He began to speak in a loud voice for the benefit of Platt, who was dressed in civilian clothes and did not have the regulation crewcut. "Goddam Air America pilots—run around with all them goddam long-haired hippies. We go through all this fire, our buddies get shot down, and all we get is regulation Air Force pay. Here they're trying to give Medals of Freedom from the president to these mercenaries who get fifty thousand dollars every time they pick somebody up."

Platt thought the lieutenant colonels looked like the dogs seen in the back of Fords with spring-loaded nodding heads, they wagged their heads in agreement so hard. He began some loud musing of his own. "There are a lot of people who get to be full colonels in the Air Force who are so full of shit that you can smell them all the way across a barroom. They go around spreading rumors and lies about Air America getting fifty thousand dollars a rescue, when in fact they don't get a dime. In the case of the guys who picked me up they lost a day's pay. While the Jolly Greens were hovering over Long Tieng in those goddam armored battleships of theirs, an unarmed H-34 kicks off its cargo and goes out there and picks up a man in the middle of the jungle. Not because he's got five hundred other people involved suppressing fire, but because he's got the balls to go and do it."

The colonel sprang from his seat, maddened with rage. He moved to Platt at the bar and stood in front of him yelling so hard his face turned purple. Platt turned back to his drink. "Fuck you, colonel. You're so full of shit you don't know what you're talking about."

The colonel lost all control and swung a wild right. Platt blocked the punch, hauled himself onto the bar stool, and kicked the colonel in the chin. He fell to the floor, and Platt went with him. It had happened so quickly that the lieutenant colonels had sat rooted to the spot. Now they jumped from their seats and rushed over. Platt pulled himself to his feet, grabbed his canes, and hobbled to the door.

The next morning everybody on the base at Udorn wanted Fred Platt. At the squadron office an airman regarded him with awe. "Everybody's looking for you. They want a piece of your ass."

"How big a piece do they want?"

The airman looked at him appraisingly. "More than you've got."

"That's all I need, one more report."

"Did you really hit the colonel?"

"Yeah, I did."

"Goddam."

At the 432nd Central Base Personnel Office, Platt was told that a large awards and decorations file waiting to go through had been held back, and a court-martial was being considered. "If they court-martial me I'll scream holy hell and demand a civilian trial. I'm goddam *Mister* Platt. Take the gongs but keep your hands off my ass."

Platt had already been awarded a Silver Star, three Purple Hearts, and the DFC, and had been recommended for a whole collection of other medals, which were now variously downgraded or dropped. Even so, he received forty-eight decorations from his time in Laos. On his way out of the country he met a new Raven on his way up to Long Tieng. Platt showed him the three Purple Hearts. "Jesus," the newcomer exclaimed. "What have I volunteered for?"

It was a question all sorts of people were about to ask. The secret war in Laos was about to go public. Although the B-52 bombing followed the same secret reporting procedures as those in effect for the clandestine bombing of Cambodia, news of the strike was leaked to the meager press corps in Vientiane, and a report was carried in the *New York Times* the very next day.[17]

Laos, which had been largely ignored by the press corps, suddenly became a hot political issue. The B-52 strike for which Kissinger fought so hard had proved to be not only militarily ineffective but also an enormous political blunder. "One B-52 strike was enough to trigger the domestic outcry," Kissinger writes in his memoirs, seeming both surprised and angry that this should be the case.[18] The antiwar activists in Washington had been given exactly what they needed.

In an attempt to counter criticism, the administration replied, truthfully, that it was helping the Laotian government resist North Vietnamese aggression. But the secrecy was now to boomerang, and the explanation was not enough. The report of the raid in the *New York Times*, followed up a week later with stories of "armed Americans in civilian clothing" in Laos, loosed a fusillade of criticism, and senators stood in line to denounce the U.S. action.[19]

Dr. Kissinger attempted to explain. He seems to have accepted as reality the diplomatic version of events in Laos, repeated for so many years in Washington, by both Democrats and Republicans through three administrations. "No American administration could possibly desire a war in a country like Laos," Kissinger said. "It would not make sense to expand the conflict into Laos, except for the minimum required for our own protection, when we were busy withdrawing troops from South Vietnam."[20]

There was no war in Laos, Kissinger seemed to be saying, and from this preposterous premise it was easy to make the logical conclusion that no American had been killed in it—something the president very much wanted to believe. The uneasy equilibrium which the United States had always accepted, Kissinger went on, had been disturbed in January when the NVA fielded an extra thirteen thousand troops in Laos on their push through the Plain of Jars.

This threatened Prime Minister Souvanna Phouma and U.S. relations with him, Kissinger writes. "If he abandoned his acquiescence in the bombing of the Ho Chi Minh Trail, Hanoi's logistical problem would be greatly eased, exposing us in South Vietnam to growing peril." This was what the Americans had always believed, although the North Vietnamese had proved themselves capable of surmounting any interdiction effort the United States could stage. "Worse," Kissinger continues, "if the North Vietnamese troops reached the

Mekong, the war would lose its point for Thailand. Bangkok would then be under pressure along the hundreds of miles of the river dividing a plain without any other obstacles. We would almost certainly be denied use of the Thai airbases essential for our B-52 and tactical air operations in Vietnam."[21]

These views, at the very least, were controversial. Various Vietnam experts in the State Department insisted that the North Vietnamese January offensive in Laos was nothing new—designed as always to put Vang Pao's troops and the Royal Lao Army on the defensive, and keep the Trail open. But even if the NVA intended to battle through to the banks of the Mekong, common sense would suggest that the war for the Thais, faced with their deadly enemy on a long river border impossible to defend, might not "lose its point" but become of the utmost importance. (Faced with that reality today, Thailand receives massive military aid from the United States.)

But even if Kissinger's grasp of military realities in Laos was weak—a single B-52 strike was supposed to succeed where a million tons of bombs and eight years of continuous war had failed—it is hard to understand why he had not foreseen the political consequences of such an action. It was the one act which brought the flimsy card house of "secrecy" in Laos tumbling down.

Kissinger's recommendation had proved to be a political blunder. He now recognized the need for some formal statement of administration policy and intentions in Laos, and it was agreed that the president himself should make it. "Why I agreed to a procedure that would put the White House in the direct line of fire on every factual dispute—whether it was bureaucratic inexperience or simply exhaustion with endless attempt to pass the buck—is impossible to determine at this late date."[22] Out of context the ambiguity is ironic— Kissinger did not mean to suggest he was exhausted by his own attempts to pass the buck.

A public statement was prepared by his office, the draft of which Kissinger had taken charge of himself, and was delivered by President Nixon to the nation on March 6. While no doubt he would not have made the secret war in Laos public except for the intense political pressure he was under to do so, Nixon went much further than either Johnson or Kennedy in telling the American people what was going on in Laos.

Unfortunately, this tentative step toward disclosing the larger truth about Laos was overshadowed by the details of the statement, which

included a number of half-truths and one clear misstatement—
information that was fed directly to an unsuspecting president by Dr.
Henry Kissinger.

The press listened to the statement and looked for the story. Nixon
had stated that there were fifty thousand North Vietnamese soldiers
in Laos, while more than thirteen thousand additional combat troops
had been fielded in recent months. The press added the two figures
together (some newspapers even rounding the figure out to 70,000).
Unfortunately, the night before the presidential address, Jerry Doolittle, a USIS official in the press attaché's office in the embassy in
Vientiane, announced at a press briefing that there were only forty
thousand troops in the country. Difficult as it was to make an accurate
estimate, the discrepancy was ludicrous.

"We had to ask guidance from Washington, and they came back
saying they had good, solid intelligence," Doolittle said. "What they
had done was add up every conceivable estimate." Doolittle wondered why, if Washington information was so accurate, it was not
being made available to the men whose job it was to fight the war.[23]

Worse than the conflicting reports on the numbers was the bald
statement "No American stationed in Laos has ever been killed in
ground combat operations."[24]

Kissinger goes to considerable lengths in his memoirs to explain
how this happened. He claims that Nixon intimated to him that the
best way to prove that no Americans were involved in ground combat
in Laos was to emphasize that none had been killed in such activities.
"No one cares about B-52 strikes in Laos. But people worry about our
boys there."[25] People clearly did care about B-52 strikes in Laos, and
Nixon knew they cared, but this is what Kissinger claims he said. He
now went about giving the president what he wanted.

Winston Lord, Kissinger's special assistant, reported that there had
been some casualties among American reconnaissance teams—code-
named Prairie Fire—on special operations over the border. Kissinger
chose to ignore these, "since these activities were clearly related to
the war in Vietnam and had nothing to do with battles in northern
Laos." Careful wording, it was thought, would be able to change
reality. "We thought we could sustain a sentence to the effect that 'No
American stationed in Laos has ever been killed in ground combat
operations.' "[26]

The special-operations people did not count because they "were
not stationed in Laos"; the CIA contract people did not count because
they were secret; the Ravens did not count because "technically" they

were stationed in Thailand; Air Commandos and Air Force ground personnel were also classified Top Secret; Air America and Continental Air Services did not count because they posed as civilians. Even so, when the draft statement went over to the Pentagon it was returned with the line referring to no American combat deaths struck through *twice*. Kissinger allowed the statement to stand.

Two days after the president's address, the *Los Angeles Times* carried an account of Capt. Joe Bush's death in the firefight at Muong Soui airfield the previous year. Nixon was now caught in a blatant lie. "Nixon was furious at what he considered to be a failure of my vaunted staff," Kissinger writes, shifting the blame to those who worked for him.

Kissinger now set about absolving himself from blame. "Making a flat statement of fact on matters extending over nearly a decade is a certain sign of inexperience. One can never be sure what facts are stacked away in the recesses of the bureaucracy that will suddenly appear. I soon was to be given a lesson in the perils of being too categorical."[27]

Kissinger was irritated by the major controversy which blew up over the statement, as if it were an unwarranted fuss "produced in part by the agencies' being less than meticulous about supplying my staff with all the details (since they would not be taking the heat), in part by an honest bureaucratic bungle."[28] Again, neither would Kissinger take the heat—President Nixon received the full blast of press criticism over the Laotian statement. Not a single paper tied Kissinger to the deception, a reflection on the masterful way he managed the Washington press corps.

Kissinger was irritated further when the Pentagon told the partial truth. "The bureaucracy suddenly began leaking to the press what it had not been able to bring itself to inform the president—that some very few Americans stationed in Laos, civilians and military personnel *not* in combat, had in fact been killed by random fire over the previous nine years."

The White House was "forced to acknowledge" on March 8 that it now had information from the Defense Department that six civilians and one army captain, "who was not engaged in combat operations," had been killed in Laos since the beginning of 1969. "An average of four Americans had been killed in Laos in each of the preceding years." These figures, too, were nonsense. Two hundred Americans had been killed in Laos, with another two hundred missing or taken prisoner. These figures had been put on the record by Ambassador

Sullivan in the classified hearing the previous year. (Sullivan, as deputy assistant secretary of state, was subjected to an FBI wiretap until February 10, 1971.)[29]

"Subsequent inquiry into who was responsible for the errors produced the unstartling conclusion that it was a result of a series of misunderstandings and a failure of communication," Kissinger writes. One reason the conclusion was so unstartling was that the postmortem was conducted by Kissinger's own man and "close personal friend," his special assistant, the luckless Winston Lord.

This was not good enough for Defense Secretary Laird, who forced Kissinger to take responsibility for his blithe dismissal of Pentagon statistics on combat deaths in Laos. A letter of half-apology was wrung from him, a copy of which was sent to the president. Kissinger accepted responsibility and explained the gaffe over combat deaths thus: "I was under the misapprehension that this was a result of Prairie Fire and therefore adjusted the statement to take account of that."[30]

It was as well that the Ravens never saw the *New York Times* at Long Tieng and knew nothing of Washington's high-level machinations. Their reaction to the president's national security adviser, Henry Kissinger, referring to their colleagues killed in combat as "facts stacked away in the recesses of the bureaucracy" or to the bloody and brutal war they fought as "random fire" might have been mutinous. Perhaps they would have questioned the sacrifices they were making, and been angered into making public disclosures. But they were too busy fighting a rearguard action, and vainly attempting to prevent the Meo from being chopped to pieces, in the land where there was no war and Americans never died.

9

LONG TIENG BESIEGED

We were expelled from paradise, but paradise was not destroyed. In a sense our expulsion from paradise was a stroke of luck, for had we not been expelled, paradise would have had to be destroyed.

—Franz Kafka,
"Paradise"

It was as if all the efforts of 1969 were in vain and its victories had not happened. Nothing seemed to slow the enemy's advance. Numerous interdiction sorties were directed by Ravens along Route 7 in an attempt to cut off enemy supply lines; the road was seeded at night with antipersonnel mines to delay its repair; gunships of every description—AC-47, AC-119, and AC-130—flew night attack missions against enemy trucks. Worse still, the enemy were now finally in position to threaten Long Tieng itself.

Gen. Vang Pao deployed his troops defensively along a string of hilltop positions in the vanguard of the base, and the crescent they formed around the southwest corner of the Plain of Jars became known as the Vang Pao Line. But despite everything, the enemy managed to circle to the rear of the line undetected, and troops were spotted only two miles away from the secret city itself.

The airstrip at Sam Thong came under heavy attack in the early morning of March 18. The Meo took to the hills—some 42,000 abandoning their homes—while the Americans, and the wounded from the hospital, were flown south. The North Vietnamese stormed into the town in their wake, burning down the American bungalows which had housed the HQ of U.S. AID and refugee relief. Sam Thong had fallen.

In Vientiane, Pop Buell, clothes rumpled and eyes red from lack of sleep, was interviewed by the press. He wondered pessimistically how much longer Vang Pao and his Meo could keep up the fight. Pop Buell had witnessed the punishment they had endured during the previous years, and felt that maybe they could last a couple more—but eventually they would be forced to make some accommodation with the North Vietnamese. He buried his leathery face in his hands and mumbled, "It's all been running and dying, just running and dying."[1]

The thick haze and smoke of the burning season screened the enemy from air attack as they moved onto Skyline Ridge above Long Tieng. The troops on the Vang Pao Line had dissolved, leaving no one to defend the secret city. Panic broke out in the town. The fall of Long Tieng itself seemed inevitable and only hours away. "Everybody woke up in the morning and thought, 'We better get the hell out of here,' " Craig Morrison said.

Among the first to leave were eighty bedridden Meo patients from Long Tieng hospital, evacuated in an Air America C-123. Villagers laden with belongings trudged to the ramp to board Air America planes, which were landing or taking off at the rate of one every two minutes. "They would come down to the end of the runway and turn around and lower the ramp and all of these refugees would run into the airplane. They'd just fill it up and off they'd go, and another would come in." Vang Pao's own family were flown down to Vientiane. Many refugees, fearful that the enemy would destroy the airfield before they could get out, began to walk south. Air America dropped hundred-pound bags of rice to them from the air.

It was a heart-rending spectacle—thousands of Meo villagers with their children and whatever possessions they could carry, forced out of their homes by the war. For some of them it would be the fourth such exodus.

"The most pitiful sight I have ever seen were the refugees," Morrison later wrote in his journal.[2] "It made tears come to my eyes to see the little boys and girls about five or six years old carrying packs on their backs looking so goddamned helpless—and mothers with crying babies—old men and wounded soldiers all looking for a way out."

Morrison was soon to go home, but the plight of the Meo moved him deeply on this day and made him want to stay. "It was awful. They were such nice people. I didn't care so much about the defeat—'By golly, they took our flag'—as what was going to happen to the Meo. It made me want to stay. Just give me an airplane and some bombs and I'll blow the shit out of these bastards all day and all night. Forever. Until they just went away. Go back to North Vietnam, kill your own people if you want to, go fight the Chinese if you want, but leave these people alone."

CIA men began to bring armfuls of classified documents—secret intelligence reports and battle plans—from the operations room, dumping them in empty gas cans and setting them on fire. Ravens were encouraged to burn personal letters in case they fell into enemy hands (the North Vietnamese built up dossiers on U.S. pilots whenever they could, using personal data during interrogation if they were captured).

Inside the operations room itself, CIA men, certain the NVA would soon take the town, hung up Red Chinese Air Force recruitment posters, suitably amended to read "Fuck Communism" and "Shove It up Your Ass, Ho Chi Minh." Tom Palmer wrote the Backseaters' favorite slogan on a piece of paper and stuck it on the hootch door— "We Go Home Now." A large quantity of frozen shrimp was discovered in the general clean-up, which the Ravens feasted on throughout a North Vietnamese mortar attack.

And throughout everything the Ravens continued to put in air strikes to hold back the enemy. While the population fled and an air armada moved everything out, still more planes brought in reinforcements. Three hundred crewcut Thai troops, loaded with full field gear, steel helmets and wearing uniforms without insignia, stepped smartly from unmarked transport aircraft. They appeared, marching in military parade formation through the mist, in sharp contrast to the bedraggled, exhausted, long-haired Meo guerrillas scattered through the town. Another five hundred Laotian irregulars were airlifted in from other military regions, including one battalion that had marched all night to reach the boarding strip. Once in Long Tieng they were repositioned to hill and defensive positions by Air America and Air Force helicopters.

It was decided that the only Americans who would stay overnight would be one CIA man, the air operations center commander, and two Ravens. An enemy attack was considered imminent, and expected the following morning. The Ravens would be needed to direct air at first light. Brian Wages and "Weird" Harold Mesaris were picked to stay (Mesaris, a large man with red hair and a large red walrus mustache, had been dubbed "Weird" by one of the maintenance men, and the name stuck—not to be confused with "Weird" Neil Hansen of Air America. The Meo were convinced that all redheads were possessed of the devil, but believed Mesaris could work bad magic on the enemy.) The CIA were still burning documents when the Ravens went to bed, exhausted after a twelve-hour combat day. They slept fitfully, eaten alive by mosquitoes, only to be awakened at 2:00 A.M. The enemy were about to attack, they were told, and they might have to shoot it out on the ground.

They stayed awake for the remainder of the chill early hours of the morning, watching an endless procession of people with flashlights and burning torches climb the hillside behind them. As it grew light they discovered that everybody in front of them had moved back in preparation for the coming attack, and they alone formed the frontal defense unit.

The other Ravens had flown down to Vientiane and were scattered throughout the town in whatever lodgings they could find. Late in the night, Bob Foster, the Head Raven, received a call from the Company. Long Tieng was being hit hard and the Ravens would be needed at first light to begin putting in air strikes. His dilemma was how to contact the dispersed Ravens.

Foster jumped in a jeep and spent the night driving around, tracking down Ravens. He left signed notes on each of their pillows: "Be at the flight line at 4:00 in the morning."

Sure enough, almost all of the Ravens reported for duty at dawn. Those who failed to show up had never received a note. Foster had been accompanied the previous night by Maj. John Clark Pratt, an Air Force historian who had been sent up to Laos the previous year to record the events of About-Face, and who had since made the secret war his specialty. He was astounded at the Ravens' turnout. "I can't believe an operation where you can't call the guys on the phone, you can't get them on the radio, you leave a note on their pillow and they come." (He was impressed to the point that it sowed the seed for what was later to become a controversial novel.)[3]

The Ravens launched at first light and directed T-28s and U.S. air onto the enemy all day. But although the North Vietnamese continued to shell the town and had launched sapper attacks during the night, they made no effort to assault it directly. (In one of the sapper infiltrations, where a team had attempted to set up a mortar inside the town's perimeter, the bodies of seven Vietnamese female troops were discovered.)[4]

John Clark Pratt flew into Long Tieng on March 21. "Prior to landing, all we could see in the Long Tieng valley were murky mountain peaks obscured by the haze and occasionally blotted out by thick columns of brown smoke from ground fires. Often, black burnt particles, some as large as pieces of carbon paper, flew by the aircraft. Visibility was about one mile or less with the air-to-air visibility effectively zero. Aircraft appeared from all sides."[5]

Heavy rain fell on March 23, clearing away the cloud cover and improving visibility. Air strikes now found their targets and disrupted Communist resupply movements from the Plain of Jars to the battle-front.

The Ravens continued to live down in Vientiane—in new quarters nicknamed Silver City—but flew up to Long Tieng, which they used to stage out of. They called the daily flight there and back, in which they snaked along a river valley, the "commute."

Hank Allen, an exceptional pilot with eyes like a hawk, took off with Dick Elzinga in the front seat of his O-1. Allen was "short," soon to return home after a tour in which he had notched up four hundred combat missions, and he planned to return directly to the States and marry his fiancée within a fortnight. Elzinga had only just arrived in Laos, and it was his first trip up to the secret city. Allen intended to use the "commute" as a checkout ride. It was a cloudy day. He took off and reported over the radio to Cricket that the O-1 was airborne. It was the last thing ever heard from them. Neither of the pilots, nor the plane, was ever seen again.[6]

They had disappeared. Each of the Ravens spent at least two hours, on top of their usual day's flying, searching for the wreckage. No Mayday call had been heard, nor had a beeper signal been picked up from the survival radio, and no clue to the airplane's whereabouts was discovered. The disappearance was a complete mystery.

Weird Harold Mesaris was appointed the missing pilots' summary court officer, with the responsibility of collecting their personal belongings and writing to the next of kin. Mesaris wrote a suitable note of condolence to Hank Allen's father, the only surviving parent.

"Somehow between Vientiane and Bangkok they managed to lose Hank's things. We're not talking about much, but it would have meant a lot to his pa to get them back. We lost his son, now we lost his personal effects. I had to write another letter telling his father he wasn't going to get anything. It made me feel terrible."

Later, Mesaris received three letters written to Hank by his fiancée. Even though she had already been notified of his death, she could not accept it and wrote in the absolute conviction that he was alive. Mesaris found the love letters sent to a dead man unbearably moving.

The enemy never did take Long Tieng, despite an eleven-day assault and bombardment by mortars, artillery, and 122mm rockets. Everyone, from the Ravens through the CIA to Henry Kissinger, speculated on the reasons. (Henry Kissinger felt it was the introduction of the Thai troops that had tipped the balance, a decision he had pushed in the face of almost unanimous opposition in Washington. The Thais had always been in Laos, of course, but on a limited basis, and they had previously been deniable "volunteers." The Thai battalions that arrived in Long Tieng were the first regulars used in Laos in a policy—linked with B-52 bombing—intended to bridge the gap left by the depopulated Meo. The Thai presence in Laos would grow to a strength of seventeen thousand before the end of the war.) The Ravens felt the enemy did not want to "dig in" a position like Long Tieng because they would have been vulnerable to air attack—a point they were to prove in the coming months at Sam Thong. Gen. Vang Pao claimed that an enemy of greatly superior numbers had suffered a disastrous defeat, and that but for the help of the Ravens and U.S. air, "an NVA general would now be living in my house."

The battle to retake Sam Thong now got underway. The enemy were pounded by air and ground artillery, and Meo units moved out in the afternoon of March 24 to clear them from the ridge. They beat off an enemy counterattack, and after the 7th Air Force managed to launch 185 sorties the enemy finally withdrew two days later.

By the end of the month, Gen. Vang Pao had retaken Sam Thong. Morrison wrote in his journal: "A bad six days, these last have been. A tally of 3 T-28s, 2 O-1s and 1 U-17 with two dead or presumed so (Hank and Dick) and one hurt rather badly. But we've retaken Sam Thong—is it worth the cost I wonder?"[7]

The misstatements included in the presidential pronouncement on Laos were spice to the media. There had never been a great deal of interest in Laos before, except as a charming, exotic sidetrip to be tagged onto a stint in Vietnam. Suddenly the world's press corps was attracted to the country.

In Sullivan's time the press had been mostly sympathetic to American goals and were surprisingly compliant to the ambassador's request that they observe discretion in their reporting of the "secret" war. The Soviet Union was sensitive to publicity given to American activities in the country, he explained, and it could sabotage the agreement between them. "It's one of the few areas of agreement we have with them."[8]

The political situation in Laos was complex, and the press corps had to operate without the benefit of helicopters laid on for them by the military, so most visiting journalists settled for a "color" piece and a visit to Madame Lulu's oral sex parlor.

"I did not consider the press a problem," Sullivan said. "They were always pleading to be allowed to go up to Long Tieng and all these exotic places where they knew things to be going on, but of course we would jolly them along and not let them go."[9]

In the war next door in Vietnam a fluctuating press corps of around five hundred men and women covered the story, while in Laos there were rarely more than half a dozen visiting journalists, and only one permanent American correspondent. (There was also a Frenchman from Agence France Presse, whose reports went largely ignored by monoglot foreign editors in America—press reports of life under the Pathet Lao and the bombing had appeared in the French press in mid-1968, but had been ignored in the United States.)[10] The news agencies were covered by stringers: a Chinese who worked for UPI, and a native Lao who wrote for Associated Press. Both had wives and children in the country, which obliged them not rock the boat.

The single American had ended up in Laos by accident. T. D. Allman had applied to the *Bangkok Post* for a job and was sent to Laos on the sole qualification of being able to speak French. He was paid seventy-five dollars a month—an adequate amount in Vientiane at the time, and a fortune after the forty dollars he had received as a member of the Peace Corps in Nepal. Laos, where Allman had an entire war to himself and a secret one at that, was a young reporter's dream.

He had arrived in July 1968, and while no one from the outside world read his reports in the *Bangkok Post*, other journalists did. Allman was a clever young man and wrote well, and before long he was the stringer for Time-Life, the *New York Times*, and the *Washington Post*, various Australian newspapers and magazines, and the *Far Eastern Economic Review*. "Nobody had ever really told the story and I started writing it. I was the right person in the right place at the right time. I was sitting there and every word I wrote was published everywhere in the world."[11]

Unlike previous journalists, who were sympathetic to the American position and complied with the embassy's requests for restraint, Allman was opposed to the war. "I wound up being a war correspondent because I didn't want to get drafted."

By 1970 the embassy had turned into a sieve full of disaffected foreign service officers ready and willing to leak. There had been plenty of press reports over the years on the war, but none of substance. The success of Operation About-Face in 1969 had attracted outside press interest and raised questions about the extent of U.S. involvement in the country, but it was extraordinary that the "secret" war had remained secret for as long as it had.

It was Allman who followed up rumors of the B-52 raid on the Plain of Jars and reported the sea of refugees supposedly created by the raids, and both stories were published in the *New York Times*. (Agence France Presse had carried the first report of the B-52 raid, in a low-key, unsensational story. Again, this was not picked up in the States.) Allman had gone to his own sources inside the U.S. embassy and had the story wrapped up in twelve hours.

The official spokesman, Jerry Doolittle, explained the new policy to the journalist. "Pssst, got a big secret for you." He spread his arms to underline the irony. "We fight a wider war with fewer troops—*we can't lose*."

It was Allman who had been at the embassy briefing which had announced forty thousand enemy troops the night before the president announced a much higher figure. (When Allman went back to the embassy the following day for an explanation he was told, "The president must have access to information we don't have.") It was Allman who had filed stories of Americans killed in Laos. "It wasn't difficult to get the stories. I spoke French and a little Lao. The Lao are very nice people. You would ask them what a building was and they would say, 'Oh, that's where the CIA work—they direct the bombing of the PDJ from there.'"

Reporters who had been told for years that only "armed reconnaissance" was being conducted in Laos—and who had failed to understand the true meaning of the military euphemism—now began to see for themselves the extent of U.S. bombing in the country. They were appalled. "The continuous hell of bombing compelled them to live in caves," an English reporter wrote about life on the Plain of Jars. "Anything that moved was hit . . . by 1969 the bombing became so heavy that they had to abandon their villages. . . . As one villager put it, 'the bombs fell like a man sowing seed.'" Journalists who interviewed refugees from the plain were given a horrific picture of life under the bombing. Other writers contrasted the breathtaking natural beauty of the plain against the destruction wrought by the bombing. "Xieng Khouang was mostly rubble . . . and Khang Khay was a shell of houses."[12]

The press now discovered Laos with a vengeance, and a swarm of 150 of them flew up from Saigon. They were taken to Pakse in the panhandle, but clamored to go to the north; they were flown up to Luang Prabang, but soon grew bored with the temples. In an effort to placate them, they were taken to Sam Thong to see the 200-bed hospital and schools of the civic action program, which would at least allow them a Plain of Jars dateline. Pop Buell, the local celebrity, was wheeled out, but things seemed disappointingly peaceful. It was all something of an anticlimax. They wanted the war.

Among the correspondents was T. D. Allman, who was accompanying John Saar, *Life* bureau chief from Saigon, and Max Coffait, from Agence France Presse. The three men found the trip exceedingly dull. "I'm so bored I wish I'd never got out of bed," Allman complained. Coffait nodded toward a track which climbed into the mountains—it was the road to Long Tieng, the secret city.

No press man had ever visited the base, and Coffait suggested they try to walk to it. What did they have to lose? The men, festooned with cameras, began to walk toward the road, trying to look casual, as if going for a stroll, and expecting to be stopped at any moment. They reached the end of the valley and began to trudge up the hill. No voices shouted from behind them, and there were no running feet. As they crested the hill they could see Long Tieng a long way off below them. Allman knew from the first glimpse of the place that he was on to a big story. "There it was—this gigantic, secret base. It wasn't New York—but it was the busiest American base I had seen anywhere."

A jeep came along the road, driven by a native soldier. They flagged it down and were given a lift into the town (they must have looked much like CIA men to the soldier). The first thing they saw in Long Tieng was a sign in English on a barber shop, "Welcome." They walked around the town and runway area for forty-five minutes, attempting to talk to Americans. But they did not need to speak to anyone to get their story. Here was a base bristling with antennae and Americans, Thai troops (who were not supposed even to be in Laos), and numerous war planes. From the journalists' viewpoint it was ample proof that Americans were actively involved in violating the Geneva Accords.

A portly, casually dressed American walked up to the journalists. He seemed amused by their presence. Allman knew he was CIA and took his photograph.

"You're T. D. Allman, aren't you?" the CIA man asked good-naturedly.

"Of course I am! What's your name?"

"You know I can't tell you that." He took the cameras. "We'll give them back to you after we've exposed the film." He also confiscated

Coffait's notebook. He then told them an embassy official would fly up from Vientiane to escort them back.

The journalists settled down to wait, enjoying themselves in what they knew to be the greatest caper any reporter had ever pulled in Laos. "We were in no way mistreated," Allman said. "Treated perfectly courteously. It was fun."

But Gen. Vang Pao had heard of the journalists' intrusion into his secret world and was not amused. Foreign reporters had gate-crashed the base, and according to his CIA advisers, no one could stop them from leaving and publishing their stories, which, without doubt, would have far-reaching political consequences. He was furious.

In the general's eyes, the journalists were no more than spies, and he wanted them dealt with as spies. He gave the order to have them killed. The idea was to set the journalists up in a jeep and blast them, and to attribute their deaths to enemy action. It would have been easy enough to stage. The general waved his hand toward the mountains. "Many, many enemy."

His CIA advisers drew deep breaths. They had seen the general summarily execute prisoners, directly against their wishes, just to demonstrate who was in charge. To provoke him when angry could be disastrous. They spoke quietly, trying to change his mind, arguing that to kill the men would make enemies of the entire press corps, who would remain in Laos to cause even more trouble. The citizens of three countries—America, France, and Britain—were involved, and their deaths would invoke an outcry. Much as they sympathized with the general's feelings, killing foreign journalists was more trouble than it was worth.

Perhaps the general accepted the political arguments put forward, or perhaps he thought it was yet another example of the half-cocked American way of doing things. Journalists had infiltrated his secret compound, uninvited and unwanted, and the CIA met them with smiles and arranged for a plane to take them home, where they would expose Long Tieng to the world. But he let them live, and they boarded an Air America plane to fly back to Vientiane—the 160-kilometer ride back to Vientiane cost $450, which the journalists complained about bitterly (they might have thought it cheap had they realized the fate which almost befell them).

The story the journalists filed in 1970 blew the cover on Long Tieng and the secret war for good. The Ravens had been seen in their O-1s and were described: "There were several O-1E reconnaissance planes, flown by U.S. pilots and used to mark targets for American jet bombers we heard roaring overhead. . . . Farther down the runway were three Jolly Green helicopters . . . living proof that the U.S. bombs Laos. . . . their American crews wore US Air Force flight uniforms. . . . We calculated an American aircraft landed or took off each minute. U.S. helicopters were stacked in a holding pattern above the valley, waiting to land. Long Tieng, with 40,000 people, is one of Laos' largest settlements, but because its existence is supposed to be a secret it appears on few maps. . . . There are more radio antennae in Long Tieng than trees. . . . Most . . . sprout from CIA houses which are easily recognized by the air conditioners protruding from windowless buildings."[13]

The secret war was out in the open, and one of the consequences of almost a decade of secrecy would be an almost permanent bad press from now on. Embassy attempts to balance the picture with press releases on enemy activity were not believed and were mostly ignored. It was the inevitable price of secrecy disclosed. The press, once so indulgent, now became a scourge. It began to seem that Laos, forgotten and ignored for so long, was now to be featured regularly on the front pages of the world's newspapers. But a coup against Sihanouk in Cambodia (another country the press had mostly ignored throughout the war), followed by a U.S. invasion, shifted interest to the sideshow war there. Laos, it seemed, was never able to capture the world's imagination for long.

Adding gasoline to the flames of controversy over Laos back in Washington, the wily antiwar senators who had held the hearings on Laos in which Sullivan, Tyrrell, and two Army attachés had given evidence the previous October now released a large part of the transcript to the press, timing the release to do the administration the maximum amount of damage, while at the same time attracting the maximum amount of publicity. Newspapers ran the story under front-page banner headlines—even the military's own *Stars and Stripes:* "U.S. War Role in Laos Disclosed for First Time."[14]

The release of 90 percent of the 421-page transcript came after a five-month dispute between the Senate subcommittee, which wanted to release it all, and the executive branch of the government, which originally wanted nothing released. The remaining 10 percent was censored by the State and Defense Departments. This included lists of personnel killed in Laos, answers to questions about Thai troops operating inside the country, and the testimony of CIA director Richard Helms.

It was finally admitted officially that two hundred Americans had been killed in Laos, with another two hundred missing or taken prisoner—contradicting not only Kissinger's assertions that no Americans had been killed in the country, but also a later White House statement that fewer than fifty Americans had lost their lives.

Details of Project 404 and the Requirements Organization were given, and the ambassador's role was described as that of "military proconsul." Although the senators had received detailed, classified briefings on the war in Laos since the mid-1960s they expressed very quotable shock and outrage in the public prints. "I have never seen a country engage in so many devious undertakings as this," Sen. William Fulbright said, referring only to U.S. transgressions and choosing to ignore the mirrored deception of the North Vietnamese. Sen. Stuart Symington stated: "The point we are trying to bring out is not only that the American people have no knowledge at all that this is true and neither does the Congress—and neither does this committee nor the Senate Armed Services Committee."

In fact, Symington had been in Laos several times and had accompanied Sullivan on a visit to Udorn in 1966 during the bombing halt against North Vietnam, and been briefed on the 378 strikes going into Laos that day. The knowledge made his "apprehension about Laos worsen," an apprehension, however, he was able to accommodate over the years. On later visits to Laos he stayed as a house guest of Ted Shackley, CIA station chief in Vientiane at the time.

The senator's antics were thought despicable by Sullivan. "Senator Symington decided that in order to be reelected he had to convert from being a hawk to a dove. This was the cheapest cheap shot he could take. Congressmen and senators were given classified briefings all the time I was in Laos, and before when Leonard Unger was there. They were certainly told about the bombing. Symington was a regular visitor to Laos. It was less than forthright statesmanship. He needed a dovish plank in order to run again, and he had been so much tarred as a hawk he was able to issue this to say that we had deceived him. Knowing full well he had not been deceived.

"Ironically, at an earlier date I had been invited back to an executive session of the Senate Foreign Relations Committee by Symington, after he had been in Laos, because he was using Laos then as an example of how we could fight the war more cheaply than they were doing it in Vietnam. I tried to get that classified executive session transcript on the record, and Fulbright blocked it. He wanted the support of Symington, so he said the earlier hearings were informal, executive sessions which he controlled, and they couldn't be put on the record. It's the games people play on Capitol Hill."

As a follow-up to the disclosures from the hearings, Godley was brought back to Washington and put on the witness stand for an eight-hour grilling. "As I sat there I felt a dagger was between my shoulder blades. That if I made one false move . . . Symington is the epitome of the most despicable type of politician. A former secretary of the Air Force, who was on this special committee and had all the information necessary, getting up there and pontificating, 'Nobody tells me anything.'

"I cannot get the text of those hearings. It is still classified. And strangely enough I can't even get a classified version—the Freedom of Information Act notwithstanding. They say it's a technical problem—they don't have the copies."[15] One more ploy in the games people play on Capitol Hill.

Fred Platt's threat to demand a civilian trial had stopped all court-martial proceedings in their tracks. He had no legal right, but the last thing the Air Force wanted, as the attention of Washington and the world's press swung momentarily onto Laos, was a loquacious, opinionated Texan, who happened to be a highly decorated officer, on trial for misconduct in the secret war in which he had been badly wounded.

In one of the more pragmatic moves by the Air Force staff in the Vietnam War, they decided to reverse themselves and make Platt a war hero instead. Back in the States, Platt was awarded his three Purple Hearts, Silver Star, three DFCs, and twenty air medals in a public ceremony, which ABC, CBS, and NBC television covered but never aired. On the very same day the Kent State killings occurred—weekend soldiers from the Ohio National Guard opened fire on fellow Americans and shot dead unarmed students on the campus of their university. The invasion of Cambodia had triggered massive antiwar sentiment and civil disorder in the United States and had eclipsed the disclosures about Laos. War heroes were not much in demand on prime-time TV by mid-1970, although the press might have been more interested in Fred Platt's little ceremony had they known all those decorations were for acts in an ever-escalating secret war.

Back in Laos, the Ravens continued to fly twelve-hour combat days. Ravens arrived in Laos, flew their tours, and went home. Many of the pilots were so exceptional it sometimes seemed impossible that they could be replaced, and yet somehow another extraordinary individual always seemed to materialize. Chuck Engle was one of the finest natural pilots ever to join the program, even judged by the rigorous standards of the Ravens, and enjoyed barrel-rolling the O-1—an extremely difficult and dangerous aeronautical stunt. He had been brought up on an Indian reservation and had the dark complexion of a Cherokee. Just before graduating pilot school he received the news that his father had committed suicide. It disturbed him deeply and he often spoke of it to fellow Ravens, until one or two of them wondered if Chuck Engle didn't have something of a death wish himself.

His idea of fun could be breathtaking. He liked to meet up with Skyraiders on their own level at twelve thousand feet, buzzing them as they came on station by dropping down out of the clouds. At a contact point on the Plain of Jars one set of A-1s impatiently asked for a mark, having been startled when Engle jumped them.

"Wait a minute," Engle said. He pulled the nose of his O-1 up into a stall and plummeted earthward in an endless spin. Down and down, around and around, he fell, until at fifteen hundred feet he recovered control, took the plane out of the spin, pushed the nose over, and fired a rocket accurately at the target. The wild maneuver was carried out as a smooth, fluid series of coordinated actions, and the A-1 jocks watched the show in awe.

Engle also held the Raven O-1 altitude record. The Bird Dog became temperamental over heights of ten thousand feet, and extremely difficult to control, but it was Engle's goal to take it to twenty thousand feet. To nurse the O-1 to any height at all demands the patience to overcome repeated stalling—which can result in the plane falling thousands of feet—and great pilot skills and stamina. Engle climbed for what seemed like eternity, on the edge of a perpetual stall, and suffered intense cold and almost passed out from lack of oxygen, while the small, underpowered engine of the O-1 strained to its limit. Eventually, at 19,720 feet, Engle gave in and let back down.[16] One way or another Chuck Engle established very early in his tour that he was a Raven who would leave his mark.

In late June the NVA and Pathet Lao opened an uncharacteristic offensive in the north. Sometimes FACs in OV-10s, with the call sign Nail, came over from Vietnam to lend a hand, with varying results. One Nail, bored by a slow day out on the Plain of Jars, hooked up with an RF-4 recon bird, and the two pilots began taking pictures of each other. It was a day of poor weather, with banks of dark cloud broken up by sunny patches, and somewhere among the clouds the two pilots lost sight of each other and collided. The pilot of the OV-10 bailed out, while the RF-4, which was less badly damaged, limped home.

One Raven picked up a weak transmission in which the Nail said he was all right and under cover, while another sighted the discarded parachute on the southern rim of the plain. Chuck Engle was the first Raven to arrive in the area and dropped to twenty-five feet to make a series of passes in an attempt to pinpoint the pilot's location. Engle found him in a clump of trees to the north of his abandoned parachute.

Automatic gunfire, located only twenty-five meters to the north of the survivor, raked Engle's plane. Heedless of his own safety, Engle attacked the enemy position with Willy Pete rockets, simultaneously giving instructions to the Skyraiders stacked overhead to obliterate the area north of his mark.

As the fighters struck and strafed the enemy position, the Nail radioed nervously to say that the ordnance was dropping awfully close to him, and that there was heavy ground fire directed at all aircraft. An Air America H-34 flew in to attempt a pickup, but a hail of gunfire forced it to pull off and return battle-damaged to base. The Skyraiders saturated the area with strafe, allowing a second Air America helicopter to attempt a pickup. As it hovered directly above the Nail an automatic weapons position only forty meters away opened fire. The pilot screamed into the radio he had taken a serious hit in the fuel tank, and he began to break away.

Engle dived his O-1 between the enemy and the chopper, giving the Air America pilot time to escape. An AK-47 round entered the Bird Dog in the root of the left wing, spun through the cockpit over Engle's head, and severed a fuel line feeding from the auxiliary tank. Gasoline began to stream down the left side of the aircraft, both outside the fuselage and inside the cockpit, and drenched Engle.

The enemy had now moved so close to the Nail that Engle dared not leave despite the condition of his aircraft. Gasoline continued to spray over him, so he shut off the radios to reduce the risk of fire, directing the fighters over his hand-held survival radio. He also armed a rocket on the right wing, away from the flowing gasoline, and fired it accurately at the target. He circled the Nail until he could clear the fighters in to strafe the area, and only when the enemy gunfire was silenced and he was certain the downed pilot was no longer in immediate danger did he tell anyone of the serious hit he had taken.

He nursed the O-1 back toward Long Tieng, but just as he was on final approach, the engine quit. It took all of Engle's exceptional piloting skills to glide the powerless plane over the karst peaks at the end of the runway and dead-stick it onto the strip. Safely back on the ground, he jumped out of the useless O-1 and immediately ran to another. He climbed in, his clothes still soaked and reeking of gasoline, and flew back.

Again he dropped to treetop level and continued to mark troop concentrations, as well as a 12.7mm machine gun which opened fire on him from a hilltop. Only when the area was saturated with CBU and a wall of smoke from burning Willy Pete rockets was laid down did the Jolly Greens manage to go in and pick up the downed pilot.

Engle returned to the hootch, changed out of his gasoline-soaked clothing, and took a shower. He sat down to dinner after an exceptional day's work—he had risked his life in a display of extraordinary courage on three separate occasions in a single afternoon. It was to earn him an Air Force Cross—an award he was never to receive.[17]

Volunteer Ravens presented a problem opposite that facing most military commanders—they needed to be held back, not egged on. It was the Head Raven's job to spot the signs of combat exhaustion among his men before it killed them. Bob Foster, who was twenty years older than most of the Ravens, had a sharp eye for all the obvious signs.

"People cracked, but not in the manner you would think," Foster said. "It wasn't someone who suddenly couldn't fly anymore or refused to get out of bed one morning. They simply started to make mistakes. Didn't change the fuel tank. Didn't think about it until they were damned near in the ground. How could an experienced combat pilot do such a dumb thing? I looked for mistakes, and then made them take a rest or moved them south." (Some Death Wish cases were easy to spot. One new Raven arrived on station dressed entirely in black—black cowboy hat, black shirt and jeans, and black boots. He told Bob Foster that his reason for volunteering for the program was that Laos seemed to be a good place to die. Foster sent him home.)

One of the Ravens he felt needed to be watched was Jim Cross. Just before Foster went on leave he ordered Cross to stay out of the combat zone and restricted his flying to checking out new pilots.

Cross moved down to Vientiane and busied himself buying stereo gear and bamboo furniture to ship back to the States.

One of the newcomers Cross was supposed to check out was Dave Reese, an amiable young man distinguished by a scar across his nose. Cross had been instructed to check out the new Raven in the Vientiane area and then fly on up to Alternate. On the way Cross thought he would take Reese out onto the Plain of Jars, as they were flying in the long-range U-17, and keep on going until they reached the Ban Ban valley.

Mark Diebolt was out on the Plain of Jars in a T-28 when he heard Cross's Mayday distress signal. Unknown to the pilot, the NVA had moved a mobile 37mm antiaircraft gun into the Ban Ban valley—always a potential flak trap because of the number of guns positioned there—and the U-17 had taken three hits. One shell had blown a massive hole in the wing. "I've got full trim—everything's jettisoned," Cross said over the radio. Moments later he made his final transmission: "I can't hold it—it's going down."

The plane had lost all power, glided into some trees, and exploded. Diebolt flew over the wreckage and saw the great gaping hole in the right wing made by the shell. It had been yet another of those deadly Old Head–FNG checkout rides, where the combination of overconfidence and inexperience had proved fatal.

Foster had still been on leave in Singapore when the crash occurred, and the loss of the men grieved him. It was another mistake, and one which he had foreseen and tried to prevent.

John Fuller was the next Raven to be shot down. Again, Diebolt heard the Mayday call and caught up with the damaged T-28 halfway across the Plain of Jars. Fuller was cruising at three thousand feet, trailing smoke, and so much flame was curling over the right wing that it was cooking off the .50 caliber ammunition. He was close enough to see that there was no hope the pilot might nurse the fighter back into Alternate. "Punch out!" he yelled into the radio. "Get out of that thing!"

The later T-28s were fitted with ejection seats known as the Yankee Extraction System. (This was not technically an ejection seat at all, because the pilot was literally extracted from the plane when a rocket attached to the seat shot into the air, pulling the pilot after it. The nasty thing about the T-28 was that when the canopy was pulled back it exposed a metal bar across the front. Anyone trying to go out with the canopy open was certain to be cut in half. So for ejection purposes the pilot was punched through the canopy. A pilot about to bail out pulled the detcord which was supposed to blow most of the Plexiglas out of the canopy, clamped his helmet visor down and hoped things would not be too painful.)

Diebolt saw the rocket of the Yankee seat shoot through the canopy of Fuller's T-28, but there was no pilot attached to it. Somehow the rocket had become detached from the seat, leaving the pilot behind. The shattered open canopy now became a furnace, sucking the fire in from the wing. It shot across Fuller's legs and moved up his crotch to his head. He should have opened the canopy at this stage, but the axiom of always keeping it closed to bail out had been drummed into him too often to disregard. He used his bare fist to smash the remaining jagged Plexiglas.

The plane had already gone into a spiral and fallen to less than a thousand feet when Fuller, who was now badly burned, crawled through the canopy and jumped clear. He hit one knee on the rudder as he fell, which spun him into a position that delayed the opening of the parachute. He found himself falling upside down and much too fast as he yanked repeatedly at the cord. It seemed only seconds after the parachute finally opened that he swung into the side of a mountain and broke his back. But he was alive.

He had fallen directly into the center of enemy-occupied territory, and his survival depended on a rapid pickup. Within ten minutes an Air America chopper was on the ground, and the crew pulled Fuller aboard. Enemy troops were so close that the helicopter took hits from small-arms fire as it lifted off.

Back on the ground in Vientiane the doctor gave Fuller shots to relieve the pain and calm him down. Bob Foster was out at the airport to meet the chopper as it came in, and the young Raven stared up at him from his stretcher. "Mr. Foster, I have died three times today. Once out on the PDJ when they first hit me, then when the parachute didn't work, then when I hit the mountain. What else happened to me?"[18]

Diebolt landed his T-28 directly behind the Air America chopper. "Doc, how is he?"

"Burns. A broken back."

"Get him in the hospital, get him the fuck out of here—I gotta go fly," Diebolt said, and walked back to his plane.

Bob Foster now thought he saw all the signs of combat exhaustion in Mark Diebolt. He had lost his sense of fear, become reckless, and complained endlessly of boredom. Although he showed little emotion outwardly, the death of four young Ravens in quick succession had left the more experienced thirty-seven-year-old Diebolt feeling somehow responsible.

Madame Lulu also seemed to sense the danger surrounding him. The two were good friends, partly because Diebolt was old enough to share her nostalgia over the Edith Piaf records she played endlessly. When the ruined old madame had been ill, Diebolt had tended bar and tucked her up in bed with aspirins, hot milk, and whisky. He went to the *Rendezvous des Amis* just after the second set of Ravens had been killed. "I am very sorry," Lulu said simply before Diebolt had even opened his mouth.

"About what?"

"The death of the two Ravens."

"How do you know about that, Lulu?"

"Everybody knows."

"You're not supposed to know that."

Lulu shrugged. She handed Diebolt the figure of Buddha, his hands over his eyes, on a gold chain. "It will save you from harm."

"Lulu, I thought you were a Catholic," Diebolt said, smiling, taking the Buddha and hanging it around his neck.

"I have lived in this country a long time."

The next day Diebolt went out to the Plain of Jars together with Jeff Thompson. Both men were flying O-1s and searched for the 37mm antiaircraft guns the NVA had moved onto the road near Xieng Khouang. They circled the area at seven thousand feet, scouring the ground with binoculars, while Weird Harold Mesaris flew high-speed passes over the area in a T-28. "The idea was that they would shoot at me and give away the position," Mesaris said, "because they were so well camouflaged we couldn't find them."

Mesaris traversed the whole area, crisscrossing it at low level, but the NVA gunners maintained fire discipline and resisted the temptation to shoot. (A T-28 flying low and fast was a difficult target.) Frustrated at not being shot at, Mesaris headed farther north to support a mountain site under attack.

Deibolt stayed on and was circling, with his feet on the rudder and peering through binoculars, when the 37mm opened up on him. He took a round through the bottom of the engine cowl. It exited right in front of the windshield, leaving a gaping hole two and a half inches wide with the metal around it peeled back. It had also knocked one of the magnetos as it passed through the plane, but the shell failed to detonate.

Mesaris heard Diebolt talking to Cricket on the radio, and could tell from the shaky quality in the voice that he was in trouble. "The *only* time I ever heard that man shaken about anything."

Diebolt staggered back to Long Tieng in his wrecked O-1 and banged it onto the runway. That night he went to the *Rendezvous des Amis* and told Madame Lulu the story. He was convinced the gift of the Buddha had saved him. "I told you it would work," Lulu said, crossing herself.

Not content with fighting the enemy, Diebolt also did battle with the CIA and Air Force intelligence. At this stage in the war, after the outcry over Americans killed in combat in Laos, CIA case officers were flying into sites in the morning and leaving before dark. "The CIA guys were getting up at meetings saying that sites were secure, and I would say it was abandoned at four the previous day—right after they had flown home. How could they advise an army without having advisers out there at the critical times, the time when the witches came out—at night?"

Air Force intelligence coming from satellites and fast-moving reconnaissance birds gave a false picture of events. Diebolt wanted to take the few colonels and generals who visited Laos (he was convinced they only made the trip to buy cheap gold) out in the backseat of his O-1 to see what things were really like. "Let's go check it at first light when the dew is still on the grass. We'll see the footprints— where the elephants have walked, where the deer and bears have walked. You can't see that from a goddam satellite."

His outspokenness endeared him to neither group. One morning when he came down for breakfast he was met by Bob Foster. "Don't go to work today. They don't want you up there anymore."

Privately, Foster was relieved to have an excuse to remove Diebolt from danger. He was a man he both trusted and liked, and he largely sympathized with his views on both the CIA and Air Force intelligence, but he felt Diebolt needed a break from the war. "He gave me a plane and told me to take it any direction but north," Diebolt said.

The new CIA policy, ordering case officers back to base before dark, was very disturbing to the best of them. Black Lion now flew to and from his hillside positions as if working office hours. Life had never been so safe for Will Green, and he hated it. Every time he left his men to fly back to Long Tieng he felt he was abandoning them.

One evening, safely back at Alternate, he received a visit from an old friend, a CIA paramilitary case officer in charge of operations on the Bolovens Plateau in the panhandle. He had flown up especially to see Will Green, worried that his friend might learn of what he had to say through some hastily tapped-out embassy cable. But face to face with the man, he wished he were somewhere else, for he brought terrible news. Will Green's wife and child had been killed in an auto accident on the New Jersey Turnpike when their car had skidded off the road in bad weather and hit a telephone pole.

It was awful to see the tall, courageous man sag beneath the impact of the news. Black Lion returned briefly to the States to attend his wife and child's funeral, before returning once more to the war. He had nowhere else to go.

Undeterred by the reversals of the war, Gen. Vang Pao launched yet another offensive—Operation Leapfrog—on August 18, 1970. As the name suggests, helicopter-borne assault troops were the vital element in the attack, and five hundred guerrillas were flown to the rim of the Plain of Jars in Air America and Air Force choppers. Now that the friendly troops had seen the awesome power of the B-52 and other U.S. air, they often refused to move unless a suspected enemy position was first softened by multiple air raids. It was as if the purpose of air power were to bolster morale rather than hurt the enemy.

The quantities of U.S. air demanded by Vang Pao, and delivered in part by the Americans, became both ludicrous and grotesque at the same time. The general had become an early and zealous convert to air power, and his opinions were backed up by CIA advisers who were often no more versed in military doctrine than a competent sergeant. At the other extreme, the use of air had become the official policy of the U.S. government, a major plank of Vietnamization. Ambassador Godley put the realist's view: "We had nothing else."

But the Ravens, who were always in the forefront of the air war, had become extremely skeptical about air power's limits. The more they piled it on, the harder the enemy hit back.

"The Company kept telling VP that the Air Force owed him more missions," Bob Foster said. "We wanted less of everything. The problem was to get the right load of weapons to the right target. More missions meant dropping more bombs, and whether it did any good or not wasn't important."

The CIA argued that Vang Pao was a very unsophisticated man who had been promised a level of support by the Air Force which he simply was not getting. The general counted the airplanes, the CIA said, and he was disappointed. The Agency even went as far as trying to make Foster sign a legal contract to guarantee a certain number of missions and to deliver an agreed tonnage of ordnance. He refused, saying that he was unable to guarantee what they requested—and that he wouldn't do it even if he could. "The Company did not even care about body count, or targets destroyed—they just wanted mass."

Bob Foster had to fight to put a stop to the indiscriminate dropping of Dragonseed mines out of C-130s in the north. The Dragonseed was a tiny mine the size of a silver dollar, designed to deny an area to the enemy—it could blow the tire off a truck, or the foot off a soldier. It had been used extensively on the Trail, with mixed results (one Air Commando colonel used to back his staff car over the stuff to demonstrate how many duds it contained, while CIA intelligence reported the NVA throwing it at each other as a joke).[19] "In Laos there were too many nice smiling people running around who were not all combatants," Foster said. "I really felt you couldn't control something like that. You didn't know who was going to pass through a seeded area—people wouldn't know we had put it in there. If a guy is a combatant you should shoot him, but if he's not a combatant you shouldn't. Dragonseed was designed for maiming, not killing. I'm a soldier. I don't maim people."

Arguments over policy apart, the Ravens continued to work long days out on the Plain of Jars, supporting Vang Pao's new offensive. Chuck Engle and Craig Duehring often flew together, and while they were cruising along an often-used road Duehring noted his companion increase the jinking motion of his aircraft, and then heard him swear suddenly over the radio. "Taking a little ground fire?" Duehring asked facetiously.

"I've been hit!" Engle yelled. Small-arms fire from an AK-47 had peppered the aircraft. Engle had been flying with one window of the cockpit open, and a round had entered to the left of his head, shattering Plexiglas into his face, and the bullet had slowed down to the point where he actually saw it pass in front of his eyes. At the same moment he felt a sharp pain in his left ankle.

The two Ravens climbed and headed back toward Long Tieng, while Duehring put out a distress call to Air America and other FACs in the area. Engle described his wound: he was not in great pain, but his left leg was growing numb and he was losing a lot of blood. He did not have a tourniquet on hand, so Duehring suggested he retie his flying boot as tight as he could.

There was still thirty minutes' flying time to Long Tieng, and on the way Engle complained that the numbness in his leg was beginning to wear off and the pain was increasing. Duehring began a patter of combat small talk to prevent his colleague from losing consciousness.

"Craig, what was that poem you wrote the other day about Arrowhead Lake?" Engle asked.

Duehring had concocted a verse of doggerel a few days earlier expressing his feelings about the antiaircraft guns around Roadrunner Lake and Khang Khay, the Chinese Cultural Mission on the Plain of Jars, and had assailed fellow Ravens with it over the radio. He quickly recited it again.

"Arrowhead, Arrowhead, you're such a pretty lake,
I wish that all the guns by you were nothing but a fake.
I wish that all the rounds that go up into the sky,
Would fall back into your waters so all your fish would die."

There was silence over the air after Duehring finished the recitation. "Chuck, do you want me to recite it again?"

After a pause Engle's voice came over the radio. "No, please don't." He explained that when he had first heard the rhyme he did not have his tape recorder in the plane, but now he had captured its genuine awfulness on cassette. Moments later he began to complain of nausea.

Ten minutes out of Long Tieng an Air America Huey intercepted them and took over the job of escort. Duehring circled overhead while Engle made his approach. The pain in his ankle was now excruciating, and he was dizzy from lack of blood. As he touched down he felt the plane roll gently toward the right, and realized he had lost control and was about to run off the edge of the strip. Mustering his last ounce of strength and steeling himself against the pain, he mashed the bloody, useless limb against the left rudder pedal and pulled the mixture to idle/cutoff. The Bird Dog slewed around, ground-looping in a great arc, but when it came to a halt it was still on the runway.

The last thing Engle did before he was pulled from the plane was retrieve the bullet rolling around the floor of the cockpit. He was helped into a waiting Air America Volpar and flown immediately to hospital in Udorn, where the wound was found to be a clean one—the bullet had gone through the leg bone immediately above the ankle itself. Later, as he grew stronger, he enjoyed watching his Raven visitors turn green as he pulled the gauze from the hole. He asked that no notice of his injury be sent home to his family, and also that he be allowed to stay with the group until his leg had time to heal and he could return to fly. In the meantime he had Mr. Han, the owner of the Vientiane jewelry store Villay Phone, mount the bullet on a gold base and attach it to a solid gold necklace. He intended to wear it, hanging alongside his Buddha, when he returned to the war.

Gen. Vang Pao continued to push forward, his Special Guerrilla Units leading in helicopters, while Royal Lao Army and Neutralist troops followed in his wake in order to hold the ground already taken. There was a big push to retake Muong Soui, the Neutralist HQ, in what became a three-month operation. Again and again air power proved no substitute for intestinal fortitude on the part of the troops. "There was one mountain there that I swear we lowered fifty feet by bombing," Chad Swedberg said. "They had to have it because it overlooked the runway, and I can remember watching the friendlies storm it at last. Then one of the enemy, with his last dying breath, fired a shot and the whole Neutralist army turned tail and ran back down the mountain. So we lowered it a couple more feet and they went back."

Vang Pao kept on going, determined this time to reach the Pathet Lao HQ of Sam Neua. But his advisers, and the American embassy, had different ideas. Alarmed by the boomerang effect of the general's success in the previous year when the enemy came back so strongly, they wanted to keep him in check. Vang Pao ignored them and continued to push forward.

He was issued with an ultimatum by his own CIA advisers—the United States would not support him if he moved any farther. He called their bluff and crossed to the far side of the Ban Ban valley, where Route 7 came out of North Vietnam. The United States immediately cut off all U.S. air power, as well as Air America rice and ammo drops to his men. The Ravens, as demoralized as the general himself, began to ask themselves, "What are we doing here?"

They still flew every day, but with no air to direct they could not give the general much help. "We were up there doing acrobatics and stuff like that to keep the troops entertained," Jim Hix said. "For several days I went up there and did loops and rolls to keep morale up."

Vang Pao had no alternative but to fall back and begin a slow retreat.

The non-Meo friendly forces proved as unreliable as ever. In the middle of the night, the Ravens heard that Muong Soui, only recently retaken at great cost and now held by Neutralists, was under attack, including a frontal assault by tanks. The Neutralists made it sound as if they were engaged in one of the biggest battles of the war, but when the Ravens flew to the town at first light they discovered that the Neutralist forces had simply abandoned their HQ when they heard from the Pathet Lao that an attack was about to be launched. The Neutralists suffered no casualties and allowed the enemy to walk into Muong Soui unopposed.

The fall of Muong Soui meant the loss of the Plain of Jars, with scattered friendly outposts cut off to the north. The enemy now made a concerted effort to take Site 15, Ban Na, on the southwest corner of the plain—ten miles northeast of Long Tieng. Known as the Jungle's Mouth, it held a large Thai artillery position and was one of the plain's crucial "hold" points.

Air power, Thai reinforcements, the relentless stamina of Gen. Vang Pao and the Meo seemed to be all in vain. The balance of the seesaw war had tipped in favor of the North Vietnamese and would never again be righted.

10

VALENTINE

Chuck Engle returned to the war on crutches. Although he was hobbled by a wounded foot, the experience of being shot down had neither dimmed his enthusiasm for the war nor diminished his skill as a pilot. He had always been able to fly better than he could walk anyway. He soon abandoned the crutches and graduated to using a single cane, and his colleagues watched him limp briskly out to his O-1 with mixed feelings. No one doubted his ability or courage, but the Ravens sensed something dark inside of him, a force willing him toward increasingly hazardous combat missions. He had become reckless and displayed a blatant disregard for the laws of probability. Whenever the conversation turned to Chuck Engle, everyone agreed: death wish.

Many other pilots would have taken a bullet wound as a legitimate reason to return to the United States, but it was the last thing Chuck Engle wanted. How *could* he die? The bullet with his name on it had passed before his very eyes—he had cheated death itself—and now he wore the Golden BB around his neck at the end of a gold chain.

A personality in contrast to Engle was Park Bunker, a tall, reserved man who kept his distance. A senior captain in his early thirties with a receding hairline—and married, with two children—he was looked upon as ancient by his companions.

Despite his reserve on the ground, Bunker shared Engle's indifference to enemy fire and held the current record among his group for the most bullet holes in his O-1. Just before the new year he flew out to the northern edge of the Plain of Jars, near Roadrunner Lake, to verify a reported sighting of enemy tanks. Sure enough, he spotted the front of a tank protruding from a group of trees and dropped low for a better look. A rapid-fire 14.5mm antiaircraft gun—deadly to a height of 4,500 feet—opened up at close range and nailed the engine.

Bunker put out a Mayday call before managing to dead-stick the O-1 onto a flat area in the middle of a horseshoe formed by a bend in a small river. When Bunker climbed out of the cockpit he found himself in open country, empty of vegetation except for a single stunted tree. He lowered himself into the cover of a small gully choked with brush, one of hundreds scattered over the plain. Unknown to him, a large group of NVA soldiers were bivouacked along the bank of the distant treeline that followed the curve in the river. He was surrounded on three sides.

Four Ravens heard the distress call and headed toward the downed plane. Bunker said he was hiding in a gully by the side of the O-1 and was being shot at from three sides. Gunfire could be heard over the radio. It seemed to build and grow louder until Bunker announced he was going to make a run for it.

Willing their planes to fly faster, the Ravens raced toward the crash site, listening helplessly to their colleague's desperate transmissions. When Bunker next came on the radio, he was out of breath. "They're all shooting at me! I've been hit! I'm hit! I've been hit twice—God, I've been shot five times. I'm not going to make it. I'm as good as dead."

By the time the first Raven reached the crash site, enemy soldiers were swarming around the plane. There was no sign of Bunker's body. It was a point of honor among the Ravens either to declare a colleague dead—"negative objective"—or get him out. The thought of a live Raven in enemy hands was unbearable.

Chuck Engle braved the guns to take his plane down to almost ground level for a closer look. He roared across the lake, with his wheels almost dipping into the water, and then hopped over the treeline running along the riverbank. This maneuver left the guns the minimum amount of tracking time, but the moment he cleared the trees his plane disappeared in a cloud of tracer. "There's something under the tree all right," Engle screamed into the radio, "but I don't know what it is." He pulled the O-1 up and cut away from the gunfire. "And fuck it—I'm not going back in there."

Engle's plane was so badly shot up he had to return to Long Tieng. A Skyraider pilot volunteered to take a look, but was met with the same withering fire as he took his plane low. "There's a body underneath the tree," he yelled as he pulled off. "And it looks like it's wearing a survival vest—but the back is just a mass of blood."

The description certainly sounded like Bunker, who always flew to war in a chocolate-colored walking suit and a green survival vest, while most of the other Ravens draped theirs over their seats. The growing dark made it impossible to check, and when the Ravens returned the following morning the body had been removed.

Bunker was declared dead—no one wanted to give the Air Force the excuse to declare him MIA, the limbo status which would leave his wife and children hanging in uncertainty for seven long years. The timing of the crash (between Christmas and New Year), the fact that Bunker had only thirty days to run before the end of his tour, and that he was married with children, depressed everyone.

On the second day of the new year, 1971, Chuck Engle was flying over the Plain of Jars when he heard over the radio that a Fast FAC in a Phantom—call sign Tiger—had been shot down just east of the 7/71 Split, the spot where the main route coming onto the Plain of Jars from the east split in two. It was an area which could no longer be worked by Ravens in light aircraft because of the quantity of heavy antiaircraft guns that the enemy had moved into it—guns powerful enough to bring down a high-flying F-4. But Engle immediately headed toward the location of the downed aircraft, dropping below the thousand-foot overcast in order to conduct a methodical search for the missing crewmen.

After several sweeps over the road junction he saw the burning fighter below him. "Give me Voice or give me Beeper," he radioed, the standard call to a downed pilot. Within minutes he had made radio contact with two survivors, who told him that enemy patrols had already moved in toward them.

The first fighters on station were the Skyraiders, and although Engle brought them down below the overcast they were forced by the low ceiling to jettison their bombs along the road, but returned to strafe the area surrounding the survivors. Both Tigers reported that all three aircraft were taking heavy ground fire on each pass, but Engle continued to direct the fighters onto the smoke of his marking rockets to buy time while a search-and-rescue could be assembled.

More A-1s arrived, carrying CBU and strafe, and relieved their colleagues until one of the planes took a hit in the engine and was forced to break off and head for home. Two Phantoms, carrying "snakes and nape"—high drag bombs and napalm—arrived next.

They dropped their bombs on the road, unable to use them because of the proximity of enemy patrols to the survivors, and returned to use their napalm in close support. As they prepared to make their second pass the Tigers reported an enemy patrol moving directly toward them.

The problem of how to drop the napalm without hitting the Tigers was compounded by the steep hills rising on three sides of the survivors. The only possible route for attack was to fly directly over the Tigers, a course which demanded precision marking by the Raven and split-second timing for the drop by the fighters.

Engle took the O-1 down low and flew over the heads of the Tigers to fire a marking rocket at the foot of the hill in the direction from which the enemy were approaching. The Skyraiders followed on his tail, dropping their napalm to splash uphill until the end of the flame hit the smoke. It wiped out the enemy patrol and hit so close to the Tigers that a gob of burning nape splashed onto one's boots.

Engle continued to direct the fighters around the survivors, ringing them with burning napalm as a wall of protective fire. Only when he had fired all of his rockets and was low on fuel did he return to base. That night he heard that it had grown dark before the Tigers could be picked up.

In the Raven hootch the general opinion was that the Tigers were SOL—shit out of luck. Engle's courage and accurate marking had bought them time, but the enemy would move in even more anti-aircraft guns overnight and surround the area. Anyone returning the following morning was going to be eaten alive by flak.

In case the men were forced to spend another day and night on the ground, two "survival" kits were prepared. Each one contained an M-16, bandoliers and clips of ammunition, hand grenades, a lined field jacket, gloves, a radio, batteries, food, and water. They were wrapped in a blanket and held together by nylon fiber packing tape. The plan was for a CIA Pilatus Porter to pre-position itself at Lima 35, and if antiaircraft fire thwarted a successful SAR, the plane would make a high-speed, low-altitude pass over the survivors at dusk the following day and kick out the bundles.

But Engle was in his O-1 at 4:30 A.M. to fly onto the plain. The same cloud deck as the previous day covered the area around the 7/71 Split, and he dived beneath the overcast to make contact with the survivors. They had suffered badly from exposure during the night, and reported that the enemy were all around them and closing in.

Two Phantoms, loaded with napalm and CBU-24, checked in at first light. Engle brought them down beneath the clouds, where they would be forced to operate in an extremely cramped arena. He told them to run parallel to the road, three hundred meters apart, and to drop their ordnance the moment he fired his smoke rocket. Their explosives fell within five feet of the survivors.

Despite a barrage of antiaircraft fire from the guns, which had been moved in overnight as predicted, Engle brought another set of Phantoms down through the clouds and continued to lay an ever-widening circle of ordnance around the survivors, forcing the enemy back. When the Jolly Green went in to make the pickup it looked as if the Tigers were on a barren island surrounded by a black sea of scorched ground. Both men were snatched from the ground alive.[1]

Chuck Engle became the toast of fighter squadrons throughout Thailand, and his reputation reached its zenith. There was no question about Engle's courage, the Ravens agreed, but there were *limits*. The guy was crazy, people muttered, and there was more talk about his subconscious death wish. But Engle shrugged it all off, and swung the chain around his neck holding the bullet. It was simple—the enemy had taken their best shot and *missed*.

The next Raven to be shot from the sky was Jim Hix. In early February an enemy gun position in the Jungle's Mouth was shelling the Thai artillery outpost at Ban Na, a strategically important hilltop position ten miles northeast of Long Tieng. Hix, flying a T-28 and accompanied by Tom King in an O-1, had been directing numerous sets of fighters in support of the base. After he had completed eight passes holding to the same pattern, an extremely unwise and reckless thing to do, the enemy found his range.

Hix knew he was hit by the noise—inside the cockpit it sounded as if a giant spring in a clock had burst. A shell had pierced the propeller drum so that it was over-revving, and although he managed to get the runaway prop under control by reducing the manifold pressure, he was unable to see because the engine was spewing oil over the windshield.

Tom King attempted to steer him by giving directions over the radio, a procedure which was complicated by the T-28's rapidly pulling away from the slower Bird Dog. When he estimated that Hix was over friendly territory, King gave him the word to bail out.

With only fifteen minutes of gas left and smoke filling the cockpit, Hix was pleased to be leaving. He pulled the cord on the Yankee

Extraction System, the explosive detcord blew the Plexiglas out of the canopy, and the rocket fired, hauling him into space. It was only after the explosion that he realized he had left his visor open, and slivers of Plexiglas were blown down into his face, ripping the skin off the left side.

Once the parachute opened, Hix was able to peer around to find his bearings. He knew the area intimately—well enough to know that he was nowhere near friendly territory. At first he was scared, but this feeling changed almost instantly to fury. He was enraged at King's mistake and wanted to kill him. The idea actually made him reach for his .38, which he wore in a tie-down holster, but the gun had hit the side of the canopy rail as he punched out and had spun into space. The realization that he had no weapon with which to defend himself snapped his mood back from rage to terror.

He landed safely and immediately ran away from the parachute and crouched down among some bushes. Pilots were supposed to check their survival gear regularly, but young immortals like the Ravens rarely did so. Hix had been no exception, merely glancing at the battery level on his survival radios once a month. Both were useless, and his flares were duds too.

He set fire to a small bush to mark his position, blowing furiously at the meager flames for them to catch. The burning bush gave off a thin pillar of smoke, but it was enough to guide in Air America. It also marked his position for the enemy, and as the chopper wheeled to hover over the downed Raven it took ground fire. He was hauled into the cabin and landed in a heap as the bird banked steeply. "I kissed the floor of that helicopter."

After a brief stop at Long Tieng he was flown down to Vientiane, gulping whisky and talking endlessly as the adrenaline coursed through him. He was picked up at the airport by Chuck Engle and on the way into town insisted on stopping the jeep at a store to buy a Buddha. Engle was skeptical. "You're not supposed to *buy* one," he said. "You're supposed to be given one."

"What the hell—some protection is better than none."

After a shower and a change of clothes, Hix went out on the town in Vientiane. It was very good—quite extraordinary, really—to be alive, and he celebrated by drinking until dawn.

The gun that had nailed Jim Hix was a part of the main force of the NVA 312th Division, moving rapidly across the Plain of Jars. Its intention was to hit the Thai artillery position at Ban Na and then move on Long Tieng. Two heavy field pieces—thought to be an 85mm gun and a 122mm howitzer—began a night-long shelling of the position and inflicted heavy casualties.

Two days after Hix had been shot down, the Ravens were still out searching for the gun that had done the job. Grant Uhls flew up to the area around Ban Na, where he noticed an unusual amount of fresh truck activity. As he circled, a 12.7mm machine gun fired several bursts at his aircraft. He pulled off abruptly and began to climb, radioing the coordinates of the gun, together with several other likely looking antiaircraft locations, to three other Ravens flying into the area.

It was Jim Hix's first day in the air since he had been shot down, and he felt an extraordinary sensitivity and connection to the airplane he was flying. It was as if he could hear every turn of the propeller and each time the spark plugs fired. He had also been careful to stock up with fresh flares, and had checked the batteries of his survival radios more often than was necessary. He kept one eye perpetually cocked for the best spot on which to crash-land or to bail out over, should the need arise.

He flew up to the Plain of Jars alongside Chuck Engle, and they worked together around Muong Soui. Over the radio Hix displayed a brittle sense of bravado, and his conversation with Engle would have struck any of his colleagues as more than a little ironic. The two men boasted to each other how they had cheated death, and how ready they were for any eventuality. Both had to agree—they were damned good.

As they spoke they heard Grant Uhls report that he had taken fire, and immediately headed toward Ban Na. In the meantime, Uhls had flown away from the gun in a wide semicircle and then doubled back into the area from another direction.

As he scouted the area for the original gun that had fired at him, another more powerful machine gun—a ZPU-2—had opened up on him. Flying at three thousand feet, he was beyond the reach of the 12.7mm, but in comfortable range of the ZPU. He immediately broadcast a warning to the approaching Ravens and attempted to pull out of the range of the powerful weapon. His voice sounded as if he were taken completely by surprise that ground fire was actually threatening his plane. "Damn, I can't get away from it."

Then there was silence. Hix could see the aircraft in the distance trailing a thin spume of smoke, and he watched it make a large, slow circle. "Don't go so low," he yelled into the radio. There was no response. The plane began to circle in an ever-decreasing radius, and each circuit brought it closer to the ground. At the very end it seemed to veer, possibly the last attempt of a badly wounded pilot to save himself. Somehow the futile action disturbed Hix deeply.

As the plane crashed into the ground it was as if the horror were enacted before Hix's eyes in slow motion. The right wing folded over the fuselage, and he saw the aircraft splinter and disintegrate for a brief moment before it exploded into a fireball. As he watched, something in him snapped. "It was as if my system flipped over inside. It really screwed me up."

He sat in his O-1 and began to direct the Thai artillery from Ban Na onto the area he suspected the gun to be in, working in a daze like an automaton. Chuck Engle's voice came over the radio. "Why don't you guys get down there and help him out?"

"There's no way," Hix replied.

"Bullshit!" Engle took his plane down to ground level, and the enemy opened fire on him. He flew over the crash site and then pulled off. "Ain't no way anybody could live through that."

Hix called Cricket. "Negative objective," he said, giving the code that meant the pilot was dead and no SAR would be needed.[2] He flew back to Alternate and walked into the operations shack, where he sat saying nothing, his eyes filled with tears. He had been close friends with Grant Uhls at the Air Force Academy, and their time together in the Raven program had sealed that friendship. Finally, Hix stood up. "Screw it," he said, and slammed out of the shack.

He flew down to Vientiane, drove back to the Raven hootch, and got drunk. Two new Ravens, Jim Roper and Ernie Anderson—replacements for the dead—met Hix for the first time at dinner that night. It was a grim welcome. Hix, whose face was still a torn mess of bruises and scabs, had drunk so much he had moved into a tortured world of his own, and sat in a corner muttering to himself, "This is bullshit! Cannon fodder. Just a bunch of cannon fodder."

The new Ravens exchanged glances and rapidly swallowed a few drinks themselves.

Hix was still sleeping off his hangover late the following morning when he was awakened by the houseboy shaking him. A message had come over the phone that the Ravens in Long Tieng were under attack. The NVA had crossed the southern ridge and were shelling the airfield, the town, and the compound.

Earlier in the month, Gen. Vang Pao had announced, "We shall defend Long Tieng to the last man."[3] Now it looked as if the enemy would force him to keep his word.

Ban Na had been under nonstop, round-the-clock attack, and the Ravens had been busy directing ton upon ton of ordnance around the area of the camp. The enemy had pushed their way across the Plain of Jars and were on the ridges to the north of Long Tieng, where there were a series of firefights. Natives living in the area, including most of the population of Alternate, had been evacuated yet again. Altogether some fifty thousand Meo dependents had been moved into the already overcrowded Ban Son resettlement area south of Long Tieng. (By the middle of 1971, U.S. AID estimated, 150,000 hill tribe refugees, the majority of which were Meo, had been resettled.)[4]

There was always a complement of Ravens living at Long Tieng during this period, and the quality of life had been improved beyond measure by the acquisition of a pool table. They had become settled to the point of having pets again, the star of which was Princess Hamburger. The princess was the runt of the latest litter of pups belonging to Squirrely, a mongrel concupiscent as a rabbit and known among the Ravens as "the Queen of the Whores." "Hamburger" was the vogue word among the Ravens at the time to denote a swaggering, boastful John Wayne type. Fat Danny, an Air America mechanic blessed with the genius of the kasbah, had developed a strong sideline out of Squirrely's offspring, selling them as rare Meo temple dogs—at thirty dollars a clip—to gullible Air Force helicopter pilots who visited Long Tieng on evacuation flights. But no one believed Princess Hamburger, an oddly colored individual tending toward the ugly, was a rare temple dog. Fat Danny made a present of her to Chad Swedberg. The Princess's low whine in the face of enemy shelling acted as the hootch alarm system.

Oddjob, the original Raven orphan, was long gone—officially adopted by an Air Force mechanic and taken back to the States—but the Ravens still had a soft spot for the local children. A favorite was a cheerful little girl with a withered leg. A native shaman had begun imitating the American medical magic of seemingly curing all ills with a single injection—penicillin worked wonders among the Meo, who had built up no resistance to the drug. Usually the shaman's shots were harmless enough, consisting as they did of various colored liquids, but in the case of the little girl he had struck a main nerve and crippled her. An Air Force flight surgeon examined her at Udorn and determined that nothing could be done. One of the CIA men made a crutch for her, which he replaced as she grew taller. The Ravens saw her every day, dragging her useless limb behind her.

The NVA had slowly been closing in on Long Tieng, and the base had come under rocket attack on three successive nights. "After a while my reflexes became so attuned to the crackling of supersonic rockets flying overhead that I was able to roll out of bed and under it before I even woke up," Craig Duehring said.

None of the rockets hit the Raven hootch, but a number found their mark in the village and on the runway. Civilian and military casualties were treated in the local hospital. On a visit to the doctor, Duehring saw a portly Thai artillery captain lying on his back on a table. The entire side of his left cheek had been torn away by shrapnel. The gaping hole bared an uneven row of gold teeth set in a ghastly butcher-shop grin like that of an animal's skinned head. The Thai captain seemed quite comfortable, and Duehring was surprised at the almost complete absence of blood in the case of such a terrible wound.

The persistent enemy rocket attacks moved the American maintenance personnel to build a fortified bunker between the old wooden house that served as the Raven HQ and the more recently built two-story concrete-block building that housed the bedrooms. A half-decent bunker was constructed, using sandbags and pierced steel planking. It was intended to have only one entrance, with a zigzag turn in it, but it was left with an opening at each end when work was interrupted by enemy action.

A friendly 105mm field artillery piece, set up by the king's house south of the runway, kept up a steady fire at the rate of a shell a minute, day and night, to harass the enemy. The Ravens slept through its steady, explosive boom as if it were nothing more than the familiar loud tick of a large clock.

At 3:00 A.M. on the morning of February 14—St. Valentine's Day —an ominous silence fell on the valley when the big gun suddenly stopped firing. Craig Duehring, who slept soundly through rocket attacks and artillery fire, was awakened by the sudden change in the rhythm of the war, startled by the unnatural silence. There was an eerie moment of total calm, and then the boom of the 105 was replaced by a series of explosions, accompanied by small-arms and automatic-weapons fire.

Duehring looked out of the bedroom window and saw the flash of various explosions in the distance and pinpricks of flame from the muzzles of numerous weapons. He thought perhaps the friendlies were engaged in a skirmish with an enemy patrol that had infiltrated the valley.

He reached for his movie camera and began to film the flashes of fire in the dark. Suddenly he heard a yell from one of the other bedrooms: "Incoming!" He dropped to the floor. A large artillery round, probably from a DK 82mm recoilless rifle, hit the side of the building. Duehring grabbed his M-16 and pistol belt and ran from the room.

The first time Chad Swedberg knew about the attack was when an Army attaché and a couple of Ravens burst into his room and yanked his bed away from the window so they could look out of it. Swedberg was not unduly alarmed at the sound of gunfire, as firefights had raged on the ridgelines for several nights, and he had even slept soundly through the explosion of the shell hitting the hootch. Violently awakened from a deep sleep, he was further angered when he saw that a crate of grenades had been stashed under his bed without his knowledge, in preparation for an enemy attack.

The Army attaché began firing his M-16 out the window, a pointless exercise as the enemy artillery was more than a mile away, and dangerous, because the ammunition contained tracer and allowed the NVA to pinpoint the Raven position. Swedberg wished they would all go away so he could get back to sleep. "This is my goddam bedroom," he yelled. "Cut it out!"

It was only as more shells exploded around the compound that he fully understood the seriousness of the position. In the corridor a horde of people crammed themselves down the stairs and ran toward the newly constructed bunker. Swedberg was swept along with the crowd. Halfway down the stairs he remembered Princess Hamburger and tried to return, but he was pushed forward by the panicking, stampeding horde.

The last man out of the building, Air Commando Jim Rostermundt, saw the dog whimpering beneath a bed, scooped her up into his arms, and ran with her to the bunker. (Immensely grateful, Swedberg wrote him up for a DFC—never awarded—for "saving the life of an indigenous friendly under fire.")

As people crowded into the bunker, artillery rounds were coming in at the rate of one every six seconds. Various buildings in the compound were hit in the barrage, which was to continue for the next two hours until dawn. An NVA unit had worked its way around to the south of the base and launched an attack on the men firing the 105mm artillery piece. Taken by surprise, the friendlies were overcome after a brief fight. A member of the Thai artillery crew had the presence of mind to toss a thermite grenade down the gun's barrel. Had the enemy captured the gun intact and trained it on the compound containing the Americans, the battle would have been over.

But even without the big gun, by using the weapons they had brought in with them, the enemy were able to direct a fearsome barrage directly into the compound. By counting the muzzle flashes the men in the bunker calculated the number of guns firing at them—a mixture of six 60mm mortars and 82mm DK-82 recoilless rifles.

As shells continued to land in the compound it became clear that the NVA were after the Americans. Although armed to the teeth and accompanied by some tough Meo, the Ravens felt horribly unsure of themselves as front-line troops on the ground. "We were terrified," Craig Duehring said. "I recall very vividly the feeling of absolute panic and the almost uncontrollable urge to throw down my M-16 and run. I had nowhere to go, but I thought I was going to die. And I did not want to die."

Shep, one of the CIA men, was caught outside in a shell blast and pulled into the Company blockhouse with a badly cut leg. Burr Smith called the bunker, excitedly demanding to know where the doctor was.

"Is the doc here?" the radio operator asked.

"Yeah," came the reply, out of the dark.

The radio operator swung his flashlight toward the doctor, a short, squat man with gray hair. The Americans were used to seeing kindly Dr. Venedict Osetensky working in the hospital, but as the flashlight fell on him it lit a figure transformed: an M-16 lay across his legs, he wore a combat helmet, and a bandolier of ammo was strapped across his zippered flak vest. The doc had become a front-line grunt. "It's Shep, doc," the radio operator repeated as another enemy shell sent a shower of earth and stones across the steel-and-sand roof of the bunker. "He's been hit with shrapnel."

"So?" the doc asked. "What the hell am I supposed to do about it?" The sight of the doctor laden down with combat equipment and his laconic answer somehow combined to relieve the fear every man in the bunker felt, and they broke out in spontaneous laughter.

Crouched in their jerry-built bunker, the Americans soon realized they were "blind" and needed to set up an observation post in the Raven hootch. Several made a run for it back to the two-story barracks. The general feeling of the group was that an air strike should be directed onto the enemy position, an idea Chad Swedberg was against. He felt it too risky with the enemy so close—a short round might hit the Raven hootch or the town. A squabble of a nonmilitary nature ensued, there was some name-calling and macho posturing, and Swedberg felt himself pushed toward a decision that went against his better judgment. "There were some real hard feelings that night."

The Ravens set up watch in the doctor's corner room. It was somewhat larger than the others, although packed with medicine chests, and its two windows gave good visibility over the valley. Fat Albert, the Air Force intelligence officer, took up a defensive position in the latrine, pointing his M-16 through the window. The Ravens peered into the night across the concertina wire at the perimeter of the compound, beyond the village and toward the muzzle flashes of the enemy guns. The ground in front of them sloped gradually for half a mile to the bottom of a small valley. Beyond, the main valley, covered with trees, shrubs, and grass, climbed steeply for a thousand feet. It was on this hillside that the enemy were hidden, blocking the only reasonable escape route out.

The Company blockhouse, located at the end of the compound to the left, had a .30 caliber machine gun set up beside it, while a .50 caliber machine gun, capable of reaching the enemy, was set up in the corner of the Raven compound to the right.

Burr Smith was able to radio an SOS message to Alleycat—the nighttime airborne command post—which sent a Laotian AC-47 gunship. In spite of repeated directions, the gunship stood off and fired its entire load of ammunition into the mountainside more than two miles away from the target. Swedberg and Duehring watched the worthless exercise from the doc's bedroom window. Hurrying home to sell the empty brass shell casings, Duehring thought as he saw the gunship pull off. It then dawned on him, as reality for the first time, that nobody was going to make it out alive.

They heard a lone T-28, manned by a Meo pilot, start up on the ramp and take off into a black sky filled with invisible mountains. The pilot attempted to make a pass over the enemy, but his bombs missed the guns and the antiaircraft fire was so intense he was forced to retreat and fly south to recover.

The single O-1 that came under Laotian command—used by Gen. Vang Pao—also took off into the night. The Ravens learned it carried the general and Jerry Daniels, his CIA case officer. There was silence as the significance of this news sank in. In a quiet, matter-of-fact voice someone said, "That's it, then."

Dawn broke on a day murky with brown haze. The argument over calling in an air strike had been resolved when Chad Swedberg agreed to direct fighters at first light. He stood in the window of the doc's room, with Craig Duehring beside him, and talked to Cricket via his hand-held survival radio. Two Phantoms out of Udorn, ominously named Killer flight, would be on station within minutes. Lead carried CBU, while Two was loaded with wall-to-wall five-hundred-pound bombs. Both Ravens worried aloud that the fighters, flying into the brown haze in the half-light, would not be able to see a damned thing.

The moment Swedberg picked up Killer flight on his radio he began to describe the target on the hillside among the trees and said he was going to mark it using the .50 caliber machine gun, firing tracer. "Tracers are going into the hillside and ricocheting—do you see tracer?"

"Roger."

"Cleared in hot."

Lead made a pass but lost sight of the tracer halfway down the chute and pulled off. Suddenly, Duehring experienced a deep feeling of dread—something was wrong. "Chad, I don't trust them," he said. "Put Two south of the target about a kilometer and work him in. A big column of smoke would make a hell of a good marker."

Swedberg cleared in the second Phantom, which dropped its bombs and pulled off. They were wildly inaccurate, at least a kilometer off target. "Thank God we moved him out," Duehring said, "or it would have been down our throats."

It had grown lighter, but Swedberg realized the Phantoms were still hampered by poor visibility because of the haze. "If I had been smart I would have called off the air strike right then," he said, "but I wasn't smart."

The exploded bombs at least provided a pillar of smoke as a mark to direct the fighters from. Swedberg also reoriented Lead from the .50 caliber tracer, and repeated a visual description of the target. "You see the smoke—the village—where the tracer ricochets?"

"I see it. Am I cleared?"

"We don't see you," Swedberg said, "but if you see everything we're talking about you're cleared."

The F-4 went in, but instead of returning to make multiple passes the pilot took the lazy course and pickled off his entire load of six CBU canisters at once. Shep, his leg hastily bandaged, was outside with Burr Smith and a platoon of Meo guerrillas when the plane screamed over. Shep looked up and saw the CBU pods come off the aircraft, and then watched in horrified fascination as the clamshells flew apart and the bomblets were spewed out. He yelled to his companions and hit the ground. When he raised his head, after the CBU had passed beyond him, Burr Smith, himself, and a single Meo survived.[5]

The exploding CBU tore through the village like a hurricane. Huts, trees, and telephone poles disintegrated before the Ravens' eyes. "You're dropping on the friendlies!" Swedberg yelled into his radio. "You're dropping on the friendlies!"

A wall of destructive flame raced toward the Raven hootch. "You sorry-assed son of a bitch," Duehring shouted, and dived for the floor.

It was even worse than Swedberg feared. The pilot had misunderstood his instructions regarding the tracer and exactly reversed them—he had not dropped the deadly load where the tracers were ricocheting, but on the friendly machine gun itself.

Those in the hootch had hit the floor and were squirming on their bellies to get under the bed or behind some sort of cover. The CBU broke over the building, peeling back the roof. It set the operations shack on fire, along with the Company sleeping quarters, the Air America hostel, and the Raven dining room, blasting the pool table into fragments. The CIA bar took a direct hit and burned to the ground. But the wily bears survived the holocaust by pressing themselves against the rock wall at the rear of their cage, which was built out from a cave.

It was obvious that the F-4 had dropped CBU, and from a great enough height for it to have a large pattern. (Clamshell CBU explodes in a doughnut pattern, creating a circle of fire around a hollow. What looked to the Ravens like a solid wall of fire approaching them was actually a circle surrounding them—and the .50 caliber machine gun was directly in the center of it.)

With the building burning down around their ears, the Americans prepared to move back to the bunker, where a series of sporadic explosions made them think they were under renewed attack. It then dawned on them that the continuing explosions were their own ordnance. "Christ," somebody groaned, "some of that shit is time-delayed."

"Confirm CBU-24," Swedberg radioed Cricket.

"CBU-24 confirmed," Cricket responded. There was a pause. "Also CBU-49 mixed in there."

CBU-49 was a canister of time-delayed, baseball-sized bomblets that, according to the book, went off randomly over a thirty-minute period, each one blasting out 250 white-hot ball bearings. In reality they often continued to explode for as long as two hours, and now they were littered throughout the compound. The men dodged among them to reach the bunker and huddled inside. Although the structure had taken a direct hit during the raid, it was still standing. The building beside it continued to burn, and smoke began to fill the shelter. Outside the CBU bomblets continued to explode.

After an hour the Army attaché decided to make a run for one of the other buildings. It was a risk, and he knew it. He stepped outside of the bunker and one of the bomblets exploded directly in front of him. "Good God," thought Duehring, who was sitting just inside the entrance. "He's gone."

But the colonel stepped back into the bunker alive, drained of blood and shaking. When he could speak he explained he had seen the CBU lying intact at his feet the split second before it exploded. The rest was a roar of confusion. He found himself still standing and untouched after the blast, miraculously unharmed.

Directly after the Phantom raid the Meo T-28 fighters took off. They flew over their home town, burning furiously below them from ordnance dropped by Americans, and heard over the radio of their fellow Meo's casualties. Swedberg tried to talk to one of the pilots, but the man was crying so hard at what he saw from the cockpit of his plane that he was incoherent. Emotion ran very high among all of the Meo pilots, and a couple of them were so angry there was a moment when it seemed they might sweep over the American compound and strafe and bomb it in their fury. Things became so tense that rescue forces were put on alert in Udorn, in case it became necessary to save the Americans from their friends. It took Burr Smith, trusted and respected by the Meo, talking endlessly on the radio, to explain the mistake and implore the pilots to understand the anguish felt by everyone.

Once the time-delayed CBU had finally stopped exploding, after a period of almost two hours, the Long Tieng Ravens emerged from the bunker. By late morning things had returned to normal and the Ravens went down to the ramp to await the Meo pilots' return. They talked to them after they landed, and although they remained visibly upset, they nodded their understanding as the Ravens explained what had happened.

The first Raven in the air over Long Tieng, once the Phantoms had departed, was Chuck Engle. He flew up from Vientiane to direct wave after wave of fighters onto the enemy position, but the NVA had already pulled back, swallowed by the jungle.

The Ravens took the undamaged Bird Dogs, with American personnel in the backseat, and flew down to Vientiane. They gathered that night at Lan Xang #9, the Raven hootch, and discussed their various experiences during the day. It had been an eventful twenty-four hours. Swedberg still felt responsible for the short round. "I did a terrible job. I should have said no from the beginning—or no from the middle. I just wasn't smart at all." It was a feeling he would never shake off, long after the war. "I knew it wasn't right but I let myself get pressured into it. It was stupid. It could never have worked. It should never have been done. But everybody was ready to fight and win the war right there."

A later intelligence report, however, proved that the strike had had its fortunate side. The bodies of a North Vietnamese sapper team were found near the perimeter fence. The sappers had crawled there under cover of their own fire. They had been only minutes away from entering the compound and destroying the hootch when they were killed by the wall of CBU dropped by the misguided Phantom. An accurate tally of casualties inflicted by the short round on the friendlies was never arrived at, on the orders of Gen. Vang Pao. He refused to take action against any Air Force pilot or Raven for a mistake made in the heat of battle, and blamed the enemy. (Press reports of the incident claimed that thirty soldiers had been killed and sixty wounded.)[6]

It was a chastened group who sat down to dinner that night. Once again they had been driven from their base, and would stage out of Vientiane and "commute" back and forth to Long Tieng during the day. The base was a bomb site, the village partially destroyed, and the enemy left with the upper hand. Once more the Meo townspeople had been turned into refugees. And the trust between Americans and Meo had been strained to its limit.

Among the mail handed out to the Ravens over dinner were several Valentine cards. The irony did not go unremarked. The incident became known among the Ravens, and the men of the secret war, as the St. Valentine's Day Massacre.

11

WASTELAND

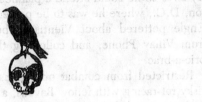

The fear, as in the previous year, was that the enemy would take Long Tieng and push on down to the capital, Vientiane. This meant the Vietnamese would have to battle their way through the resettlement area of Ban Son, where the Meo—ninety thousand of them wedged into a forty-mile-long dead-end valley sixty-seven miles north of the capital—would be forced to make a final bloody and hopeless stand. The refugees formed a human buffer between the government forces and the enemy, and neither side seemed inclined to go to any great lengths to avoid what would inevitably be a massacre.

There was a Pathet Lao raid on the American-run refugee relief center in early March, when guerrillas blew up warehouses and vehicles, but the attack was isolated and Ban Son was quickly back in operation.[1] As in the previous year, the enemy did not push their advantage and once again seemed to have achieved their strategic end. They were content to shell Long Tieng without moving into it. Two days after the St. Valentine's Day Massacre, between five thousand and eight thousand friendly reinforcements were moved into the base, now almost empty of civilians. Even Vang Pao's own family had been moved to a guarded compound in Vientiane.

After Grant Uhls's death, the Ravens began to take Chuck Engle's death wish very seriously. He continued to fly low and take unnecessary risks. "People were beginning to feel Chuck was hanging it out *too* much," Swedberg said. "Everybody began to believe he was going to die."

Engle, nearing the end of his tour anyway, was confined to flying in the area directly around the capital and kept away from the combat zone. The embassy was particularly anxious that he leave the country alive so he could attend a planned award ceremony in Washington, D.C., where he was to be presented with the Air Force Cross. Engle pottered about Vientiane, buying gold, ordering jewelry from Villay Phone, and collecting the usual last-minute souvenir bric-a-brac.

Restricted from combat operations, he limited himself to some risky rat-racing with fellow Ravens, a slightly absurd pastime in the underpowered O-1. It was a fighter pilot's game, and skill coupled with nerve always won out. Engle had a maneuver that never failed—the Split S. The maneuver requires the pilot to take the airplane onto its back, then pull the nose down through the vertical to level again—a half-roll followed by an inverted half-loop. The result is a reversal in the direction of flight at the price of a rapid loss of altitude—and the possible loss of both wings.

Bob Foster, the Head Raven, had resigned himself to the young Ravens' dogfighting, but ordered them not to play around below fifteen hundred feet, "because if you stall the stupid thing you can recover at that height." Naturally, Chuck Engle liked to fly in the face of authority and good sense and not only dogfight, but pull a Split-S at five hundred feet.

He was sent up to Alternate with Tom King to pick up two O-1s and ferry them back to Udorn for major maintenance, stopping off at Vientiane on the way down—a milk run with plenty of opportunity for a little rat-racing. Tom King immediately got on Engle's tail; Engle jinked the plane but could not shake him. He judged his moment, and as the two planes approached a small hill Engle dived to push his plane through the tall elephant grass on its crest and began to execute a Split-S, with less than five hundred feet between himself and the ground.

He cleared the hill and the plane completed the first half of the maneuver, but grass had jammed the elevator full up, so that the O-1 stalled and fell back on itself. For a moment it seemed frozen motionless in midair, then it dropped like a stone into a clump of trees at the bottom of the hill and burst into flames.

Craig Duehring, also approaching his DEROS date, had been spending his last days in Vientiane writing up awards and decorations citations for deserving people in Project 404. He had driven out to Wattay airport in a jeep with a stack of papers he needed to coordinate with Engle. Waiting for his colleague to come in, he heard that a Raven was down.

Almost immediately, King landed and explained what had happened: Chuck had crashed and burned, and there was not a chance he had survived. "I was stunned," Duehring said. He thought he had hardened himself against death, which he had seen so much of in his tour, including that of two Ravens. "But this was more than I could take." He walked out to the revetments to be alone and wept.

The death of Chuck Engle, the first Raven to be allowed the Air Force Cross, was a terrible blow to everyone in the program. At the hootch in Vientiane the cook's wife was inconsolable, and could be heard weeping in her room throughout the night. Chuck Engle had survived so much, only to kill himself in a silly stunt. It had not been an enemy bullet that had claimed him, but the last thing a man like Engle could have expected—pilot error.

Duehring volunteered to accompany his friend's body back to the United States. "But my offer was refused. So some unknown individual did the honors and laid Chuck to rest."

Craig Duehring worked out a few statistics relating to his six-month tour: 90 percent of the Ravens had been hit by ground fire, 60 percent had spent time on the ground as a result of enemy action, and 30 percent had been killed. This was unacceptable by any standards—particularly those of the Air Force, which considered a 2 percent casualty rate among its pilots too high.

In the eyes of the Air Force hierarchy, the Ravens were still nothing more than renegade Yankee Air Pirates, and their cheerful embrace of the image of Mexican *banditos* stuck in the craw of senior, rear-echelon officers. The recent run of deaths was seen as nothing more than a lack of proper Air Force procedures, and another concerted effort was launched to "put some structure in the program."

The Air Force had already attempted to inject more of a mainstream Air Force flavor into Project 404 by introducing a large number of Academy graduates—Zoomies—into the Ravens. This had not worked. The moment they had taken to the air in Laos they had turned into Yankee Air Pirates.

The Air Force decided to gain control by choosing a young, highly responsible, clean-cut officer from outside the program to go up to Long Tieng and take over as the Head Raven. Larry Sanborn was picked for the job. "I was more of a Downtowner personality than a renegade, a Blue Suiter rather than a soldier of fortune. I never did wear a beard."

Sanborn was briefed that the Mexican *bandito* era was over; the war was changing and the Air Force wanted to exert direct control over the Ravens. Sanborn arrived in Laos expecting to find a pretty ragged crew, but as he was checked out in the various military regions he saw that the Ravens were doing an exceptionally good job with very few men. He also understood why they interpreted orders rather than following them blindly. "They had the savvy—the trail-riders knowing what the trail was all about. You couldn't get *that* Downtown."

Sanborn tried to make the Ravens explain exactly what they were doing. One, sitting at the bar of the hootch, spoke for them all: "We're kicking ass and taking names."

Sanborn nodded. "Carry on."

He discovered the Ravens regularly worked eighteen-hour days—including time on the ground. "I was really concerned about the troops. Periodically I would have to send a couple of them out of country—just to get them off the line. Guys were logging twelve hours in the saddle a day. You didn't have to worry about motivation. A six-month tour, twelve hours a day, seven days a week, in a combat environment, getting shot at every day—I spent my time worrying about how to keep them from burning themselves out."

In answer to the complaint that the Ravens were flying too much, Sanborn demanded more men. The number of FACs working out of Long Tieng increased from seven to eleven. Instead of controlling the program, Sanborn unknowingly followed historical precedent and became the buffer between the Downtowners, forever expanding the regulations, and the Ravens, increasingly hard pressed in a losing battle.

The Air Force also felt that the tradition of the "nubie night"—when a new Raven was taken out drinking and whoring—was several notches below the conduct becoming an officer, but Sanborn saw it as a fascinating psychological test of newcomers. "The Ravens operated a blackball system. Which meant that you could be a Raven up to a point on the official level, but the final decision was really with the other Ravens. It was important to know what a new guy was really like, and nubie night helped figure out the sort of stuff the other guy was made of. Was he belligerent when drunk? Was he concerned for his soul when he found himself in a whorehouse? The plain fact of the matter was, we had to depend on each other. If there was something about a fellow that made you real nervous, you needed to face that up front.

"One guy turned around halfway through his nubie night and said, 'Weird stuff—I don't want anything to do with you guys.' We were not trying to teach him a new set of manners—we were trying to find out who he was. When all the restraints are removed, he is going to revert to his natural self. When nobody was there to give him orders, he would have to operate all by himself. And I thought about it a lot, and in the end I have to say there was a mystical side to the Raven camaraderie."

This was not what the Air Force had hoped from Sanborn, but as hard as it tried it could never quite exert the degree of control over the Ravens it felt it needed. "Why did they want control?" Sanborn said. "Just because they wanted it. They were singularly unsuccessful."

By the time Sanborn left Laos he had notched up seven hundred combat missions, and had protected the program from the ravages of his superiors. The fundamental trouble with the program, the Air Force might have concluded, was that every time they sent a good officer across the river to clean it up, he became a goddam Raven.

Given the feelings of the Air Force hierarchy by mid-1971, the last person they would have chosen to return to Laos was Mike Cavanaugh. The contemporary Ravens, on the other hand, looked forward to meeting someone who had become something of a legend in FAC circles. The word went along the grapevine: "One of the old bunch, the wild bunch, and he's coming back."

Cavanaugh had been back in the States for a year, during which time he had organized the Forward Air Controllers' International to help wives and families of POW/MIAs in California. His activities had attracted the attention of H. Ross Perot, whose interest in the POW/MIA issue had never slackened. Cavanaugh received a call at his home from the Texas billionaire asking him to fly to Dallas and talk. "He had a big bulldog and a big silver telephone," Cavanaugh said. "It was nice to be around wealth."

Perot wanted him to undertake a mission of a diplomatic nature. The Texan handed him a custom-built, gold-plated .45 revolver with a hand-tooled Western belt and two boxes of ammo, a present for Gen. Vang Pao. "I want to get the general's attention," Perot said.

"I've got a fix on some guys who are in a POW camp in Laos. See if VP knows anything about it and I'll finance a mission to go in there and pluck some guys out."

Cavanaugh flew into Laos two days before he was supposed to start work, and went directly up to Long Tieng to pay a courtesy call on Vang Pao. Burr Smith greeted him warmly and took him to the general, who received the gun with amused fascination. Cavanaugh pitched Perot's idea of a POW raid to the general, and one of the case officers took a few pictures.

Cavanaugh returned to Vientiane, where he made a visit to the embassy. He was amazed at the growth in the bureaucracy. He had been assigned to Laos to work in the air attaché's "Frag" shop, the office that picked and planned targets for each of the military regions and also designated the number of planes to be sent on each mission and the type of ordnance they would carry. (It was a far cry from being a Raven, but Cavanaugh felt that with his previous experience he could do an especially good job.) "The whole shop used to be run by one man. Now they had four guys—a lieutenant colonel, a major, and two captains. I would have been the lowest-ranking member of the team, destined to spend a year working at a desk in a room without windows, across from this guy who had a hair transplant that looked like a ricefield."

But it was not to be. When word of Cavanaugh's connection with billionaire civilians harboring free-lance military plans, the success of which could only embarrass and humiliate the administration, reached the embassy he was given twenty-four hours to leave the country. He eventually managed to land himself a job back in Vietnam as a FAC. "Tame stuff," Cavanaugh said. "After the Ravens it was like being sent to a Triple A team after playing for the Yankees. It was a letdown."

Gen. Vang Pao launched his annual monsoon offensive at the end of June 1971. Backed by Thai battalions, he took back the critical hilltop position of Ban Na, captured by NVA troops two months earlier. Using helicopters, his men leapfrogged across the Plain of Jars in a plan aimed at destroying enemy supplies. The operation was similar in essence to that of About-Face in 1969, but less ambitious, using small, helicopter-mobile units while avoiding major confrontation. The NVA fell back to hilltop positions, where they harassed Vang Pao's troops with mortar and rocket fire, while friendlies captured thirty tons of food supplies.

At the opening of the operation, the general and his CIA advisers had planned no more than hit-and-run, spoiling tactics, and had no intention of digging in. But after the reoccupation of Muong Soui in September they became convinced that the Plain of Jars was defensible and the NVA should be made to pay a high price to retake it. Five Thai artillery positions were dug in and supplied, forming the backbone of the defense plan, while the Meo positioned themselves for the inevitable NVA counterattack.

B-52s were now used routinely on the plain against enemy base camps and dumps, but nothing could stop the North Vietnamese—and even Gen. Vang Pao was forced to accept the limits of air power. The general had exacted a price from the enemy in men and supplies, but it was one they were prepared to pay.

The Plain of Jars now looked like a desert. John Wisniewski was flown up there for the first time toward the end of 1971 on his checkout ride in the backseat of an O-1 piloted by Mike Butler. As they flew in a zigzag pattern over trails and mountains, slowly climbing toward the plain, Wisniewski was struck by the extraordinary beauty of the country.

"Look ahead, John," Butler said. "There it is—that's the Plain of Jars."

Wisniewski had heard so many stories of the fabled plain he expected symphonic music to well up as they flew onto it. "It was so dramatic, the most dramatic moment I had in flying there." At first glance it seemed that the plain was shaped like a human heart, but as he grew closer he was exposed to a different sight.

"Everything was bombed out. *Everything* was worked over with bombs. I couldn't believe it! Anyplace you would go on the PDJ would be pockmarked with bomb craters. There were burnt-out C-47s, abandoned tanks, destroyed trucks—the hulks of years of war, just left lying around."

The first time Wisniewski flew over Xieng Khouang on his own he thought it looked like a miniature postwar, bombed-out Berlin. "Jesus," he said to his Backseater, "that place is all beat to hell."

"Yes," the Backseater said flatly, pointing a finger at himself. "I live there one time. Me Xieng Khouang boy."

By December the enemy were threatening Long Tieng again. Although the Ravens were sleeping there once more, they now lived in ramshackle quarters patched together from the leftover debris of the previous year. They still flew long combat days, and landed back at the base grateful to have survived, but any thought of victory had long since receded.

"We knew we couldn't win," Terry Murphy said. "All the career majors and lieutenant colonels who had never made it to the war were coming over to Vietnam to fill a square in their career development sheet. They didn't give a damn. It had made me very disgruntled, very cynical, to see that. If they had let the lieutenants run the war it would have been over in a hurry. But they don't let the lieutenants run the war—except in the Ravens, which was a real morale booster. Even if we couldn't win, we couldn't just let these guys go to the wall."

A warning came through the CIA that the NVA planned to send suicide sapper squads onto the ramp to blow up aircraft. "Don't get too drunk tonight, guys," the senior Raven, Marv Keller, said. "There may be NVA coming across the fence."

He told the Ravens to split the six O-1s up and move three to another part of the ramp. Wisniewski moved his and then went back to the operations shack. A Meo soldier was sitting on the steps, no more than thirteen years old. He had attached a bayonet to his M-16, making the rifle taller than he was. It amused Wisniewski, and he grinned at him. The boy flashed back a warm, open smile.

Wisniewski returned to the hootch, ate dinner, and sat around afterward drinking Singha beer. The movie that night was *The Dirty Dozen*—an unfortunate choice in the circumstances. It could not help but remind the Ravens of the suicide sapper squad, a Vietnamese dirty dozen, somewhere out there beyond the base perimeter, hidden in the jungle and the night.

Wisniewski drank another Singha beer and went to bed in the narrow, miserable room he shared with fellow Raven Bill Kozma. At 3:00 in the morning he was awakened by a series of booming explosions somewhere nearby in the valley. "Koz, are you there?" he called out in the dark. "Koz?"

Kozma had opened all the windows and was standing beside one with a CAR-16, looking toward the runway.

"What's going on, man?" Wisniewski asked.

"I think we're being invaded."

"Oh shit," Wisniewski said, climbing out of bed. "I don't want to be invaded."

Both men felt powerless as incoming shells exploded somewhere in the valley. It was impossible to know from which direction the fire was coming, or where to go to escape it. They stood by the window, waiting.

The incoming soon stopped, and at first light they went down to the ramp. The sappers had made their way onto the strip as warned, and the first, loud explosions had been of satchel charges blowing up aircraft. The artillery fire that followed was supposed to cover the team's exit, but Meo soldiers had caught them and been merciless.

Burr Smith had hurried to join the Meo guards in the dark and found they had not only killed the sappers but cut their hearts out. A soldier handed one to the CIA man—to hold the beating heart of your enemy was good *phi*, a way to ingest his courage.

Wisniewski saw the hulks of several aircraft on the ramp and walked over to the operations shack to find out the extent of the damage. The enemy had destroyed the three O-1s the Ravens had been at such pains to move. The other three were untouched. A filled body bag lay on the ground outside the building.

"Who's in the bag?" Wisniewski asked.

He was told it was the soldier he had seen the previous day. The boy had been on guard duty on the ramp when the sappers had come across, and they had cut his throat on their way. Wisniewski stood looking at the body bag. "Shit. He was dead. He was in a body bag. Thirteen fucking years old! Smaller than his rifle and there he was. I remembered looking at him and smiling, and him just smiling back. I couldn't understand it. What was going on? How could he be a soldier? He was thirteen years old, for Christ's sake."

The raid by the sappers was seen as the overture for a concerted NVA attack, and yet another evacuation of the base was organized. A few CIA case officers were to remain with a skeleton force of the Meo, and there was a feeling among those chosen to stay behind that they were dead men. The Ravens who no longer had planes to fly boarded the last Air America transport of the day, mostly reserved for case officers.

John Wisniewski, who had been in Long Tieng only a week, was delighted to be leaving and took his seat on the Air America transport. He was disturbed by the sight outside the window, witnessed by the Ravens for the past two years in Long Tieng, as Meo refugees clamored around the plane. "It was like the movies where the Germans are invading France and you see the people in Paris getting on these trains. It was the same thing around these airplanes, because they knew the Vietnamese were coming. They were trying to get on and get out—but there was no room."

George Bacon—Kayak—was accompanied by the young wife and child of a Meo lieutenant, ordered to remain and defend the base. One of the senior CIA officers boarded and began counting heads. "George, this airplane is for case officers and Americans only," he said. "She has to get off."

"I told her husband I'd get her out," Kayak said.

"George, she has to get off," the CIA man insisted. "Get her off!"

"If she gets off, I get off."

"Okay—get off!"

George Bacon stood up and left the plane. Wisniewski had watched the exchange in awe. "Holy shit, he's going to die," he thought to himself, deeply impressed. As the plane took off he looked out the window and saw Kayak trudging away from the runway, followed by the woman and child.

Long Tieng became a hell over the next few days. The base was shelled repeatedly by the long-range 130mm artillery pieces the Vietnamese had brought into the country. These had an effective range up to thirty kilometers, and the enemy fired them at night, pushing the guns back into caves during the day to conceal them. As more and more troops massed on Skyline Ridge, a B-52 Arclight strike was put in on them, the first time the bomber had been used in such close vicinity to Alternate itself.

The Arclight was given the credit of saving Long Tieng, although as before, the enemy might never have planned to take it. They had achieved their objective by rendering it inoperable. The Ravens no longer even staged out of Alternate, as the enemy offensive grew stronger; they flew out of Lima Site 272, twenty miles to the southwest.

By March 1972, the NVA had seven divisions in Laos, and for the first time in a decade they moved down Route 13 toward Vientiane. Another 130,000 refugees had been created, and the Laotian government did not want them either in Vientiane or anywhere on the plain surrounding the capital. They were forced into the horribly overcrowded Ban Son settlement.

In April there was another battle for Skyline Ridge when enemy tanks were spotted in the area for the first time. The enemy 130mm artillery pieces continued their long-distance work, and a U.S. TV film crew were allowed into Long Tieng for the first time to film the action. (Stateside Ravens were disgusted, when they saw the film, to hear one of their colleagues call the reporter "sir.")

And as the situation deteriorated the air attaché's office responded by saddling the Ravens with a flurry of new rules and regulations. It was getting to be like the old days in Vietnam. Terry Murphy had friendly troops under attack in his area and desperately needed antipersonnel ordnance to help them out. At the same time and in the same area, a colleague had a set of fighters under his control pre-planned to hit a nearby bridge. The fighters showed up carrying CBU, useless against a hard target.

"I can't use it—give it to Terry," the fellow Raven reported to Cricket, the orbiting command post.

The change in plan was refused. The ordnance was dropped on the bridge, which remained standing and intact, while the troops were left to fend for themselves without air support. Furious, Murphy flipped out the code wheel provided to the Ravens to enable them to encode coordinates before passing them over the air. They rarely used it, as they could usually validate their own targets, so when Murphy got through to Cricket with a coded coordinate and a request for both target validation and special ordnance, it was unusual enough to attract attention throughout the chain of command.

Cricket passed the encoded information through to the computer at Blue Chip, the Air Force HQ in Saigon, and also to the embassy in Vientiane. In the radio room of the air attaché's office an excited operator called over an assistant air attaché: a Raven had logged a coded request for highly unusual ordnance to be used on a controversial target which would need to be cleared with the ambassador himself—maybe even the president. The request was rapidly decoded: Murphy had asked for permission to hit the U.S. embassy in Vientiane with a nuclear weapon.

PART V

PARTY

12

DOWN SOUTH

The Ravens were sent to the south, during the earlier years of the war, to relax and enjoy the calmer atmosphere of the so-called country-club postings. But while there could be long periods of inactivity in the panhandle, where troops from the Royal Lao Army were happy to conduct the war in a lackadaisical manner, there were also times of furious battle.

The principal preoccupation of the war in the south was the Ho Chi Minh Trail, which came out of North Vietnam into Laos and snaked through its mountains along the border of South Vietnam. Aerial reconnaissance and bombing missions over the Trail were not the province of the Ravens, who were ordered to keep well to the west. Their mission was to support the government troops on the ground, the CIA tribal irregulars, and a growing number of Thai mercenaries dressed in Lao army uniforms.

These were the only troops who could be relied on to fight in the south. "They were paid regularly by their case officers, who black-bagged the money in," a senior CIA officer said. "At my base I paid them once a month in cash, and I was there to see they got paid. They were fed and taken care of. If they were wounded they were air-evaced immediately." In the Royal Lao Army, corrupt senior officers banked most of the money earmarked for their men, sold rations on the black market, and bought expensive foreign cars and houses, which they rented to Americans.

The CIA also operated road-watch bases of 70 to 150 men, and teams were flown out in helicopters or Pilatus Porters to count the number of trucks and troops coming down the Trail. Case officers flew over them to pick up their reports by radio, and a significant target would be "boxed" for a B-52 strike. "Of course, you never knew who was telling the truth and who wasn't," a CIA man admitted. For the Ravens, the war waxed and waned in the panhandle according to enemy activity on the Trail.

Throughout most of the war, the North Vietnamese denied that their soldiers infiltrated South Vietnam, and even that the Trail existed. Troops and supplies poured down this elaborate skein of roads and paths, sometimes no more than a narrow mountain ledge or rickety bamboo bridge capable of taking men on foot, but wide enough in other places for two trucks to pass abreast. The Communist leadership in Hanoi understood that the Trail was vital, having used it in their struggle against the French, and created Group 559 in 1959 to enlarge the traditional infiltration route into the south.

From primitive beginnings it was endlessly expanded and improved until it became a complex communication network capable of providing men and provisions to every area of the front. Despite massive and relentless bombing, it would eventually contain underground repair shops and barracks, and could carry the largest trucks and tanks.

The cycle of escalation greatly increased on the Trail once the wider war in Laos had been contained by the 1962 Geneva Accords—which supposedly denied the North Vietnamese the use of the Trail. In the early days, when all of the supplies were carried by human porters either on foot or bicycle, the journey tapped the stamina of the most resolute troops. By 1964 it still took a hellish six months; men trudged along narrow jungle paths and crossed bamboo bridges swaying over deep ravines. Even before the bombing, those who traveled down the Trail had to endure malaria, amoebic dysentery, blood-sucking leeches, and venomous snakes.

By 1964, U.S. intelligence estimated that the infiltration rate was tripling each year, and U.S. fighter jets were secretly ordered to support Lao T-28s on interdiction and strafing missions code-named Steel Tiger. In 1965 the North Vietnamese set up a special unit, Group 565, to secure the Trail from ground attack, while 36,000 troops passed along it into South Vietnam; in 1966, 90,000 troops were fed through the system. Two years of round-the-clock bombing failed even to slow down the enemy.

In reality, no amount of bombing could ever close the Trail. The North Vietnamese needed to deliver only sixty tons of supplies a day to maintain their operation in the south—the equivalent of just twenty truckloads. With North Vietnam as the open mouth of a funnel for limitless supplies of provisions and ammunition from the Soviet Union and China, it became clear to anyone who studied the problem that bombing could never work.

The military were itching to cut the Trail once and for all, and in 1966, General Westmoreland prepared detailed plans to invade far enough into Laos to block it permanently with a corps-sized force of three divisions. The plan was opposed by Ambassador Sullivan, and turned down by Washington, which calculated that the resulting casualty rate and the risk of escalation would be too high. This is when Westmoreland, stymied yet again by Laos's ambassador, dubbed the Trail "the Sullivan Freeway."

The United States reverted to ever-increasing bombing, but the B-52 proved to be an inadequate weapon against the bicycle. The network continued to be improved. By mid-1967 the idea of invading Laos and cutting the Trail was once again raised, this time by the American ambassador to South Vietnam, Ellsworth Bunker. He believed that if the Vietcong were denied supplies, weapons, and ammunition they would "wither on the vine." The idea was again emphatically rejected by President Johnson, who ordered that there should be no further discussion of invading Laos.

More bombing was ordered, and sorties increased from three hundred to nine hundred a day. The tonnage dropped staggered the imagination—more than two million tons by the war's end—but not the enemy, who continued to improve the road network. Although U.S. intelligence claimed to have "every crossroad and gully" of the seven thousand kilometers of the Trail covered by photo reconnaissance and logged in its computers, the enemy later disclosed that in actuality the network extended over thirteen thousand kilometers.

By far the greatest majority of the bombs were delivered by B-52, but it was estimated that it took three hundred bombs for every infiltrator killed. This in turn translated into less than one in a hundred infiltrators, which meant that in the peak year when 150,000 men moved down the Trail, only 1,500 would have been killed by the bombing, at a cost in excess of two billion dollars.

Richard Helms, director of the CIA, explained the realities of the situation in June 1968 to a colleague who asked him about the effectiveness of the bombing. "Look: before the bombing they used to send three men south to get two in place," Helms explained. "Now they have to send five. We're willing to lose planes, they're willing to pay in manpower. So it doesn't make a particle of difference. There are more dead bodies. But in terms of net result, it doesn't make a damned bit of difference."[1]

Between 1966 and 1971 the Trail had been the route used by Hanoi to infiltrate 630,000 troops into South Vietnam, as well as 100,000 tons of foodstuffs, 400,000 weapons, and 50,000 tons of ammunition. The total failure of the bombing to cut the Trail did not go unnoticed in Washington. One report, from the Defense Communications Planning Group—a top-secret think tank containing every type of expert—concluded that by 1967 no amount of bombing, not only of the Trail itself but even of North Vietnam, would halt the flow of supplies. Another independent report, this time from the U.S. Strategic Bombing Survey Group, confirmed that even the wholesale devastation of North Vietnam was no means of cutting off the Trail's supply source. North Vietnam was actually making money on the bombing—economic damage was estimated at $100 million, while replacement aid received by Hanoi was several times this amount.

As the bombing continued to escalate, so the Trail burgeoned. It now had a permanent, elite guard 25,000 strong manning checkpoints and artillery positions. "Volunteer" pioneers, made up of boys as young as fifteen years old and young women, formed a dedicated cadre for a coolie work force of 50,000. Ten thousand antiaircraft pieces were moved into position, and as many trucks were spaced throughout the road network. A Special Forces commando who saw the Trail close-up reported, "At times the Ho Chi Minh Trail was so busy it was like the Long Island Expressway—during rush hour."[2]

A program using electronic gadgetry was devised in the hope that technology could prevail where military might had failed. This remote-control interdiction campaign—"beep and bang" warfare, as the military called it—was code-named Igloo White when the U.S. wired the Trail like a pinball machine. Tens of thousands of expensive seismic and acoustic sensors were dropped into the jungle. These were supposed to pick up the enemy's every movement, the location of which could then be accurately transmitted to orbiting drone aircraft, which would pass them on to fighter-bombers, which would hit the coordinates. The primitive Vietnamese were not expected to outwit such highly sophisticated equipment as infrared scopes capable of magnifying moonlight fifty thousand times, or personnel detectors—"people sniffers"—that were operated from helicopters and registered body heat or smell. (The enemy countered this particular marvel of electronic wizardry by hanging bags of buffalo urine along unused sections of the Trail, and retreating before the inevitable B-52 strike was put in. Similarly, they registered their contempt for the sensors by urinating on them.)[3]

The "antenna farm" for Igloo White was situated in Nakhon Phanom in Thailand, where it sat incongruously alongside the obsolete weaponry of the Air Commandos, one of whose principal jobs was to bomb the Trail. Using transport planes modified into gunships and slow-moving propeller fighters and bombers, the commandos actually scored a much higher ratio of truck "kills" than the sophisticated Igloo White operation. (Eight Douglas A-26 Invaders, veteran bombers of World War II, flown by the Air Commandos out of Nakhon Phanom on night hunter-killer missions against truck convoys, accounted for 50 percent of all truck kills, although they only flew 4 percent of night sorties.) But nothing could keep the supplies from getting through.

The idea men were getting desperate. A whole range of ordnance was specially designed for use against the Trail. Dragonseed, the pill-sized button bombs intended to blow out tires, maim foot soldiers, and activate sensors, were dropped in their millions. There were toxic defoliants that killed vegetation, and one plan, which did not work, involved dropping a chemical agent onto the soil to turn it into grease. There was a plan to use homing pigeons with bomblets attached to their legs, and even a harebrained scheme to drop Budweiser beer (which the North Vietnamese apparently loved) to slow the enemy down with drink.

The invasion of Cambodia in May 1970 denied the enemy the use of the port of Sihanoukville, through which 85 percent of the heavy arms used by the Communists in South Vietnam had come. But this short-term success on the part of the Americans was later to boomerang badly on the South Vietnamese. Hanoi, now forced to rely entirely on the Trail, allocated massive resources into widening the network still further, building all-weather roads which could take even tanks, and bringing down SAM missiles to protect them.

By the end of 1970 the U.S. finally decided to support a limited invasion into Laos with the objective of cutting the Trail. U.S. troops were returning home in large numbers, and Congress had imposed a legal prohibition on the expenditure of funds for U.S. ground forces operating outside of Vietnam. This meant the South Vietnamese would have to undertake the operation, at best a risky gamble, without even the aid of U.S. advisers. Code-named LAMSON 719, after a famous Vietnamese victory over the Chinese, the operation was intended to seize the Laotian city of Tchepone, about fifty kilometers from the border, which dominated the most important junction of the Trail. Once this had been completed—in an estimated four or five days—the plan was to use the following two months before the dry season to block the Trail completely. Success would mean delaying North Vietnamese plans to invade the south by at least two years.

The invasion was a closely kept secret in Washington, where only a handful of people in the Pentagon and State Department were aware of it, while detailed plans were drawn up in Vietnam on a strictly classified need-to-know basis. It seems that considerable effort was also made to keep knowledgeable people who might be critical of the operation in the dark—including the former ambassador to Laos, William Sullivan. "I won't say they waited until I was out of town, but I was not invited to the briefing," he said.

When he returned to Washington and heard about the planned invasion, he was so concerned that he insisted the Pentagon give him the briefing that had been given to the president. "It turned out they had used a map that showed no topography. I thought that was totally unfair and told Henry Kissinger they ought to do it over the topographic maps, which would show that all the ridgelines ran north and south—and that our people coming in from Vietnam would have to go over these ridgelines, while the North Vietnamese reinforcements would come right down the valleys. Which is exactly what happened."

But Kissinger's problem was to persuade all the U.S. principals involved of the wisdom of the undertaking, not to sow doubts. "It was a splendid project on paper," he wrote in his memoirs.[4] By 1971 Kissinger's power was at its height. He had practically usurped the responsibilities of the secretary of state, had encroached upon areas usually controlled by the secretary of defense, and was for all practical purposes the chairman of the joint chiefs.[5] Through skillful maneuvering he managed to bring everyone into line, whatever their initial misgivings, finally obtaining the agreement of the prime minister of Laos, Prince Souvanna Phouma, through Ambassador McMurtrie Godley (although Souvanna's son, Prince Mangkhra Phouma, insists his father was presented with a *fait accompli*).

Despite the rigorous attempts to keep the planned invasion secret, there were leaks in Washington. As early as the end of December 1970, staff members who worked for Sen. Edward Kennedy on the refugee committee told journalist T. D. Allman—who had exposed the existence of Long Tieng and reported the first B-52 raid on the Plain of Jars—that they had heard the administration was going to invade Laos. "That's ridiculous," Allman said, dismissing the invasion as a wild rumor, and simultaneously passing up the story of a lifetime. Six weeks later he was to read of the invasion in the world's press. Later he reflected philosophically, "Knowledge of Laos could be a disadvantage."[6]

But the secret got out anyway. Incredibly, Military Assistance Command, Vietnam, briefed the Saigon press corps on the invasion five days before it was launched, imposing an embargo on the story until the operation was actually underway. The news was immediately widely leaked, the first time many senior U.S. officers to be involved in the invasion heard of the plan. The North Vietnamese, well prepared in any event for such an attack on a route upon which they had become totally dependent, were now specifically forewarned.

"The operation, conceived in doubt and assailed by skepticism, proceeded in confusion," Kissinger wrote, using a sentence with a Churchillian cadence to describe a military gamble cursed with ill fortune from the moment it was launched.[7] Everything went wrong.

The South Vietnamese committed their very best soldiers to the invasion, which jumped off on schedule on February 8, 1971. The lack of U.S. troops was to be compensated for by tactical air support, assault and armed escort helicopters flown by U.S. Army pilots, and massive B-52 strikes. But terrible weather limited the tactical air support, and there were periods of fog so bad that even the helicopters could not operate. A continuous downpour of rain turned the main invasion route into a quagmire.

The incursion stalled far short of Tchepone within twelve days, while the enemy counterattacked in strength. Communication links between South Vietnamese infantry and artillery broke down. Some troops fought well, but they were no match for the experienced NVA, and even the elite units broke under sustained assault.

In Washington the debacle was viewed in horror. "Kissinger willingly assumed a field marshal role when things went well," Gen. Bruce Palmer, Jr., later wrote, "but, not understanding the nature of war and its treacherous uncertainties, became irritable and upset when LAMSON 719 stalled. . . . At the climax of the crisis Kissinger could stand it no longer and sent his trusted 'deputy field marshal' Haig to assess the situation personally."[8]

The report Haig brought back from Vietnam destroyed the last of the White House's illusions of what the invasion might achieve. Kissinger railed that the operation deviated from the original plan— an armchair critique unencumbered by the realities of the battlefield.

On March 9, President Thieu called off the invasion, and the surviving troops withdrew over a twelve-day period that became a nightmare. Although they had made some gains—the enemy had sustained twelve thousand dead and their lines of communication had been temporarily disrupted, factors that would delay their next major offensive—none of the original objectives of the invasion was achieved.

At the end more than five thousand of a South Vietnamese assault force numbering seventeen thousand were killed or wounded; more than a hundred U.S. Army choppers were lost in combat, with another six hundred damaged, many of them so badly they would never fly again. The USAF also lost seven fighter-bombers. American casualties in this non-American assault totaled 176 dead, 1,042 wounded, and 42 missing in action.[9] Most significantly, even at the height of the fighting, the North Vietnamese maintained a sufficient flow of supplies to their forces inside South Vietnam.

Critical weaknesses of the South Vietnamese Army had been put in sharp relief: principally, an overdependence on U.S. firepower and air support, and a measurably poorer performance because of the absence of American advisers. The rout shook the Saigon high command, which now took a pessimistic view of their chances of surviving a future without the Americans.

In public the White House put a brave face on things. President Nixon endorsed Kissinger's assessment of the operation: "If I had known before it started that it was going to come out exactly the way it did, I would still have gone ahead with it."[10] But in his memoirs Kissinger admitted, "The Laos incursion fell far short of our expectations."[11]

In a televised speech on April 7, 1970, President Nixon declared, "Tonight I can report Vietnamization has succeeded." Benefit of hindsight led him to modify this extravagant claim in his memoirs, although he still maintained the invasion had proved worthwhile because there was no Communist offensive in 1971. "The net result was a military success but a psychological defeat . . . in South Vietnam where morale was shaken by media reports of the retreat."[12] The reports, which included TV film of panicked soldiers clinging to the skids of American evacuation helicopters, might not have told the whole story, but they provided a graphic account of the rout and hell which LAMSON 719 became.

The verdict outside the White House was more outspoken. "A totally irresponsible exercise" was William Sullivan's judgment. The current ambassador, G. McMurtrie Godley, said, "I never thought it would be the failure that it was—with the terrible loss of life."[13]

Once again the war was viewed from Washington through distorting mirrors, and it was thought that the careful use of words could transform defeat into victory. In Laos itself it was increasingly difficult to sustain the illusion.

The war in Laos had moved south in earnest after the invasion of Cambodia in 1970, when part of the Communist supply route into South Vietnam was cut off. Later still, in 1971 when the South Vietnamese Army invaded Laos in an attempt to cut the Trail, the panhandle again became the principal area of activity. The main base for the Ravens was Pakse, a sleepy place on the banks of the Mekong with the atmosphere of a Mexican border town. Situated on the edge of the Bolovens Plateau—the panhandle's geographical and strategic equivalent to the Plain of Jars—it controlled the gateway to the south.

When the plateau was in friendly hands, Thai artillery and roadwatch teams on the Bolovens were able to help control the roads which ran beneath it. During 1965, increased use of the Trail led to greater food requisition and impressment of the local population, and there was an escalation in military activity as the enemy extended their control westward. As the war dragged on and the North Vietnamese improved the Trail, they also made efforts to control the Bolovens, and January 1968 marked the beginning of three years of sporadic and sometimes bitter fighting.

North Vietnamese military strategy in the Laotian panhandle was to isolate the towns in the Mekong valley, and by the end of 1969, Communist troops had most of them surrounded and also controlled the roads. As in the north, towns and territory changed hands on a seasonal basis; similarly, the deficiencies of the Royal Lao Army were made up by tribal irregulars and Thai mercenaries led by U.S. Special Forces officers seconded to the CIA.

Deprived of the Cambodian port of Sihanoukville in March 1970 because of the U.S. invasion of the country, the North Vietnamese began to use the Se Kong River as a main waterway route. This meant disposing of the Royal Lao Army's garrison at Attopeu, which threw down its arms and retreated rapidly when the enemy announced their intended attack.

After a series of battles, the Communists gained control of the eastern rim of the Bolovens in August 1970. In 1971, regular units of the NVA replaced the Pathet Lao, and the nature of the war became fierce. The Laotian standoffs and gentlemanly agreements became a thing of the past. The CIA attempted to counter the new threat by fielding more Thai troops.

But by early April 1971, the enemy took Paksong, one of the small towns on the Bolovens and the closest to Pakse (a particularly cruel loss to the Ravens because it was the strawberry capital of the country). A plan to recapture it was greeted by the Ravens with pessimistic skepticism. Instead of relying on the Royal Lao Army, a young CIA firebrand—call sign Sword—was going to lead an attack with his irregulars—Bataillon Guerrier 403. He arrived in Pakse prior to the upcoming battle, and the Ravens were not impressed.

"This guy had driven sixty miles to see the war," said Frank Kricker, one of the Pakse Ravens. "We were really leery having someone come from another place to show us how to fight the war." Kricker took one look at the newcomer, who seemed to be fifteen years old, and nudged his friend Bill Lutz: "I can't believe this."

Sword stood up at the briefing and spoke quietly to the assembled Ravens, who lounged disrespectfully at the back of the room. "I will need air cover at a quarter after five tomorrow morning—our troops are going in to take Paksong. That's what we came here for and that's what we are going to do."

Sword left the room. The Ravens looked at one another, certain the newcomer had no idea of what he was up against. The NVA had barricaded themselves into the houses of the town, and it would take brutal house-to-house street-fighting to move them. "Getting his battalion off its dead ass at five in the morning is going to be a good one," Frank Kricker said.

But at exactly five the following morning, Sword stood in front of his tribal irregulars and led them down the road in a forced march on Paksong. Using automatic weapons, grenades, and even knives in hand-to-hand combat, the troops fought their way through the town until by the end of the day it was in their possession. The soldiers returned to Pakse grinning, some carrying human ears as grisly war trophies. Sword looked as fresh-faced and youthful as the previous day, but the Ravens now saw him in a different light.

But only a few days later the enemy moved back into Paksong. Frank Kricker flew over the town on his way to see what he could find for a three-ship of Navy A-7s that had just checked in with him. Normally the NVA positioned heavy artillery or antiaircraft guns on the outskirts of a town, but flying overhead at three hundred feet Kricker found himself eye to eye with the gunner of a dual-mounted 12.7mm antiaircraft gun. The gun was parked beside a building right in the middle of the town. Kricker was so close that he could see the gunner's face. "I would recognize him now if I saw him again. I knew right then it was all over."

The gunner opened up at point-blank range. Kricker felt the plane coming apart around him as the shells ripped into it. The Lead A-7 saw the Bird Dog fly into the fire. "FAC's hit—I see him going in," he radioed to his wingmen. "I'm in."

The plane dived toward the town, followed by his colleagues. The engine on the O-1 had been hit and was overspeeding and the oil pressure had gone, but Kricker somehow managed to turn the plane and pull off. The Navy jets spread CBU and Rockeye, a thermite charge used to burn trucks, over the gun and destroyed it.

Some short distance from the town, Kricker's engine quit. He was flying so low he had only moments to act. He slammed the plane down in a coffee plantation, where the trees snapped off the wings. "I thought my Backseater was hurt because I knew that somebody in the airplane was bleeding to death and I was hoping it was him."

Kricker turned and saw his Backseater staring at him wide-eyed. Although he felt no pain, a bullet had taken off Kricker's left toe and gone on to tear open his right hip. His jeans and left shoe were burned by the bullet. Almost immediately an Air America chopper was on the scene, and he was medevaced to the hospital in Udorn, where forty stitches were put into his leg in an emergency operation.

The Ravens visited the hospital, presenting Kricker with a tiny urn full of cigarette ash, supposedly the remains of his cremated left toe. CIA man Kham Sing (Gold Lion) brought him the sight from the 12.7, which a team of his men had gone into the town to retrieve. But alone in his hospital bed, Kricker knew he had gone through a transformation. "I had been hosed down before—lots of times, regularly. But suddenly my mind had been changed about them never getting me."

By May 16, 1971, the last of the government forces were defeated and driven from the plateau, giving the enemy complete control. In the meantime, Jim Hix, still ragged and unnerved by his experiences in the north, had been sent south to relax. He had extended for a second tour just before he was shot down, and had then taken a much-needed thirty-day leave. He spent the time wandering all over Europe, and on his return his hair had grown so long he looked like a hippie. But he felt like a new man after his vacation, eager as ever to fly in the war. In the meantime the war had heated up in the panhandle, and no one called it a country-club posting anymore.

Arriving back at Udorn, he heard that Kricker was in the hospital. He went over to visit his friend, who was mending nicely and able to hobble around on crutches. Hix convinced a formidable head nurse to allow him to take Kricker to dinner at the O club, and took a solemn oath that they would both behave impeccably. The two friends had a lot to talk about, and before either of them noticed it they were hopelessly drunk. At the end of the evening, Kricker, a neophyte in the art of walking with crutches, was so inebriated he might as well have been on skis. He stumbled and tripped, banged into doors, and fell down steps.

Hix flagged down the air police, who helped him load his friend into the back of their jeep. They dropped the Ravens off at the hospital, where the door was opened by the head nurse. Kricker collapsed in a heap at her feet, once again unable to master the conflicting dual nature of his crutches. The head nurse's eye fell on Hix, whose nerve failed him entirely. He ran from the hospital and hid across the street behind a tree. "I figured she was going to kill me."

The next day he flew to Laos. The weather was awful during the first part of June 1971, and the NVA made the occidental mistake of trusting their forecasters' predictions in their plan to launch a big push toward Pakse. They set out in the middle of the night with three Soviet tanks leading hundreds of troops down the main route into Pakse. Troops of the Royal Lao Army defending a fortified position in their path heard the ominous rumble of the approaching tanks, fired one salvo from their 105mm howitzers, and fled.

The NVA plan had been to push the attack home the following day, when the friendlies would be denied air support because of thick cloud cover. With the advance position already abandoned with scarcely a struggle, the next prize was to be a Thai artillery position—the only effective force between the enemy and Pakse itself. But the Thais held firm in a fierce firefight that continued through the night.

The next morning, June 11, broke clear as a bell, and the enemy were caught in the open. The Ravens—Jim Hix, Larry "Pepsi" Ratts, and Lloyd Duncan—were in the air in their O-1s at dawn, and could see the Thai position surrounded on three sides, with enemy troops as close as fifty meters to their eastern flank. "The whole damn area was alive with bad guys," Hix said.

The battle raged throughout the day, but with the NVA in the open it was a turkey shoot. Hix alone destroyed four howitzers, eight trucks, several mortar pits, and caches of ammunition. "I was having a hell of a good time blowing this stuff up."

Duncan and Ratts began to search for the tanks, which the NVA had hastily moved under cover. It had been a great day for Duncan, capped during the midafternoon when he found and destroyed a tank—every combat FAC's dream. He looked down on the burning hulk with enormous satisfaction, and then realized he would have to return to Pakse to reload with gas and rockets. He was so excited he abandoned all caution and began a slow, lazy climb. Despite having been hammered with air strikes throughout the day, the enemy still had antiaircraft along the road—three 12.7mms on the south side and seven on the north. They bracketed the target hung invitingly above them in a continuous torrent of antiaircraft fire.

"Dunc's going in!" Pepsi Ratts screamed into the radio, as he saw the plane rocked by gunfire.

He took his own plane down low and pulled out his CAR-15 and M-79, which he fired through the window in an attempt to push the enemy away from the coffee plantation where his colleague's plane had crashed. Furious and upset, he held the stick with his left hand and fired his weapons using his right, aiming behind them—reversing the technique of taking a bead on a bird. "Dunc's dead," he yelled into the radio, as he lobbed high-explosive shells from the M-79 at running NVA soldiers.

Duncan had always been a casual, fatalistic type, the kind of Raven who left his survival vest hanging from the back of the seat and never wore his shoulder straps. The moment the enemy guns had opened up on him he had lost the engine, and a shell had hit the main bone in the calf of his left leg and shattered it. He had successfully managed to crash-land the plane, but was unable to move as the enemy closed in. The Backseater hauled him a hundred meters from the plane and dragged him into cover. Duncan was in shock, but astute enough to tell the man to return to the plane and bring back the radio from the survival vest. He returned, carrying the vest and Duncan's floppy hat, which was Day-Glo orange inside. Duncan turned it inside out and put it on his head.

Jim Hix had flown into the area, and he spotted the flash of color near the downed plane. "Hey, Pepsi," Hix called. "Dunc isn't dead—he's over here."

Ratts changed his tactics and began making low passes half a mile from the crashed plane to lure the enemy away from the downed Raven's actual position. Duncan came up on the radio for the first time to say his leg seemed to be broken and he was badly hurt. Hix gave him the standard SAR spiel: move farther away from the wreckage, don't panic, drink water—Air America is on the way.

A Lao T-28 arrived and made low passes over the area, raking the ground with its guns to keep the enemy pinned down. Once again the gunners, situated about two kilometers away, opened fire. Hix pushed his O-1 into a slip, which he would have liked to be supersonic, to avoid the gunfire. "It was like the Fourth of July—pretty red tracers everywhere."

Fighter-bombers had been diverted to the area from all over Laos and South Vietnam, until Hix had them stacked in layers above him. Endless strikes silenced the three guns on the south side of the road, but those to the north were putting out so much fire the fighters were forced to pull off high. A flight of Navy A-7s loaded with Rockeye CBU came on station, and Hix ordered Lead to fake a pass and come off dry to draw their fire. "Two—just go for the flashes as Lead starts to pull and hit anything you see down there. Cleared in hot."

The A-7 laid the CBU down in a football-field pattern and shut down half the remaining guns. At the same time an Air America H-34 attempted a pickup under heavy fire. The pilot complained that there was more action than made him feel comfortable, and could a Raven do something about it?

Hix diverted a set of fighters to drop bombs on the north side of the road between Duncan's position and the guns, setting up a screen of smoke and fire. It was almost dark and difficult to see when the Air America H-34 approached the crash site along a gorge that dropped into a river. The pilot saw Duncan sitting in his orange Day-Glo hat and quickly snatched him to safety.

It was the end of the war for Lloyd Duncan.[14] An athlete who had played football for the Air Force Academy, he was medevaced back to the States, where he was told his leg was so badly damaged he would never walk again. (But within a year he was walking and back on flying status—another example of Raven willpower.)

Jim Hix and Larry Ratts flew back to Pakse, where they celebrated by making quite a night of it. Ratts, known as "Pepsi" after his favorite tipple, was a music major and entertained his colleagues on the squeeze box and tuba (the natives called him "Songboy Kip" because he would sing them a song for a *kip*). He was also a very funny man, and his inspired imitation of country holy rollers was exquisite, a required tour de force at any *baci*. He was a gentle person, had never

Captured Russian guns lined up on the Plain of Jars after the success of Operation About Face in 1969. *(Morrison collection)*

Captured Russian tanks on the PDJ after Operation About Face. *(Morrison collection)*

Captured enemy antiaircraft guns decorate the front of Gen. Vang Pao's house in Long Tieng. *(Morrison collection)*

Captured 12.7mm antiaircraft gun that nailed many Ravens. *(Swedberg collection)*

The road outside of the Raven hootch after the St. Valentine's Day Massacre. (*EAPLS Archives*)

The aftermath of the St. Valentine's Day Massacre—the Raven hootch. (*EAPLS Archives*)

Pakse control tower. (*Private collection of Chuck Hightower*)

The face of the future—the enemy in Vientiane. *(Kouba collection)*

The writing on the wall. *(Kouba collection)*

A typical party suit worn to the Raven reunions at Randolph Air Force Base, Texas. *(EAPLS Archives)*

Craig Morrison and baby son Trey, born just before he went to war in Southeast Asia. Beneath the smiles, there were psychological scars that took years to heal. *(Morrison collection)*

The Meo mass for the final American evacuation of the war in May 1975. Only a fraction of their number could be taken out by the C-130 and two C-46s (one of which is shown here) manned by ex-Air America personnel. *(Kouba collection)*

Raffish armorers beside the bomb dump in Pakse. *(Hightower collection)*

Thai 155mm battery at KM 21 on the road toward Paksong. *(Hightower collection)*

Left and above: The war devoured the young Meo men until there were only children left. *(AP/Wide World Photos)*

An unidentified American inspects the M-16 automatic rifle of a Laotian boy soldier. *(AP/Wide World Photos)*

The Meo were first organized by the French into bands of *maquisards* who fought behind the lines of the Vietminh. A group of Meo soldiers lead a pony carrying supplies across the Plain of Jars. *(AP/Wide World Photos)*

A boy holding an M-16 rests against a tree while a water buffalo grazes nearby.

Cheerful boy soldiers rest beside a bamboo hut, eagerly awaiting the next battle.

Overleaf: A Vietnamese antiaircraft gun inside Laos—their camouflage was superb. (*AP/Wide World Photos*)

been known to swear, and was a teetotaler, but in a rare moment of combat celebration Pepsi actually broke his own strictly held rule and drank a cold beer.

After two weeks in the hospital, Frank Kricker returned to the war, but his heart wasn't in it any longer. "It was like falling off a horse. I was really afraid." It now became an act of will to drag himself to his plane each morning to fly in combat, and he began to wonder if he would always be equal to the mission.

The needs of the men on the ground, and the quiet peer pressure exuded by fellow Ravens and CIA men like Sword and Kham Sing, kept him in the cockpit. He flew a support mission to watch over the two CIA men as they flew in two Air America H-34s to put a road-watch team on Muong Mai, a mountaintop overlooking Route 7 where it entered the Bolovens. The main body of troops was to be flown by Air Force H-53s once the CIA and their seven-man squads had secured the landing area.

The mountain was thought to be sterile—the quaint military term for free of enemy—and Kricker flew behind the Air America chopper expecting a milk run. As the first chopper approached the landing area it was hit by a remote-controlled rocket, which sprayed the copilot with shrapnel. Kham Sing and his men jumped down into withering fire, while the chopper managed to lift off despite a damaged gearbox. Kricker escorted it safely to a nearby road, where it made an emergency landing, but the copilot was to die of his wounds.

The Air Force helicopters, which had been monitoring the operation over the radio, heard that the helicopters had been driven off. Thinking the mission had been aborted, they wheeled around and flew back toward Udorn. The team left on the ground had secured the landing area but could not hope to hold it without the support of the main body of troops.

Kricker got on the radio to the Air Force choppers. "Listen, the guys are on the ground—the mission's on. Nothing's changed. Turn around and come back."

The choppers turned and headed for the mountain, while the team on the ground held on as best they could. They would certainly have been destroyed if Kricker had not taken his O-1 down between them and the enemy to direct air support from T-28s and A-7s. The second team landed under heavy fire but beat the company of NVA back to the edge of the mountain.[15]

Kricker had averted disaster, but he felt his courage was now a dwindling asset. He could imagine the day when he had nothing left to draw upon, and he would no longer be able to face the ground fire. And he dreaded the consequences that such hesitation might invite. "I wasn't worth a shit after I got shot. I recognized that I wasn't doing them any good and I wasn't doing me any good. I was afraid and I was tired and I didn't want to do it anymore. I wanted to go home."

The Royal Lao Government fought to regain control of the plateau throughout the second half of 1971—The Bolovens Campaign—but failed.[16] After a punishing six months, Dick Defer, who had been Head Raven in Pakse during most of this time, had gone on thirty days' leave. Almost immediately after his return he went up to Alternate for a day to fill in. Taking Scar as his Backseater, he flew out to the Plain of Jars to check an area the CIA needed intelligence on. Diving low, he flew into a hail of small-arms fire. He was too badly wounded to fly the plane; it was left to Scar to crash-land the O-1 from the backseat. Defer was thrown forward against the instrument console and knocked out.

Air America was at the scene within moments, but by the time the helicopter landed back at Alternate, Dick Defer was dead. Raven Greg Wilson gently lifted his motionless body from the chopper. "It was the very first person I knew, face to face, who I had seen die. We all felt immortal, but when you take a friend off a helicopter it brings it home to you."

The atmosphere at the Raven hootch that night was dismal. "It got so that you really didn't want to get too close to people," Frank Kricker said. "You tried not to get too friendly. But it was impossible. Those circumstances make for the closest of comrades. And when a guy got killed, it was devastating—really devastating. It would tear you up."

The Ravens sat around the dining-room table, and unthinkingly the maid laid a place for the missing man. Nobody ate. The Ravens said nothing, unsuccessfully fighting back tears. "We just sat there and cried," Kricker said. "Five grown men in tears."

It was decided to send Frank Kricker back to the States as a returning hero, rather than keep him on as a liability. Dr. Robert C. Seamans, the secretary of the Air Force, was visiting Laos, and Ambassador Godley invited Kricker—as an Air Force pilot with 2,700 hours of combat, the Silver Star, and the Purple Heart—to dinner at the embassy. "They wanted some dusty, dirty Raven—a field speci-men—to look at," Kricker said. He put on his best jeans and flew up to Vientiane. He expected the ambassador to be a pompous, formal figure, but was immediately put at his ease when Godley appeared wearing his garish Mobutu shirt and spectacles held together with tape. The ambassador seemed to favor the warriors in Laos, rather than his own State Department people, which also endeared him to Kricker.

Steak was served at dinner, accompanied by what Kricker took to be a curious lily-pad soup. "It was a damned finger bowl." The secretary of the Air Force suggested that instead of flying home in some dirty troop transport, Kricker should accompany him on Air Force Two. "Tom will meet you in Bangkok and see to everything," the secretary said. Tom turned out to be an Army full colonel who picked up Kricker at the Bangkok airport in a large black staff car and obligingly drove him to the Siam Hotel downtown. The following day Kricker was aboard Air Force Two, sitting alongside the secretary of the Air Force as they headed back to Andrews Air Force Base, lunching on lobster and contemplating the peculiarities of modern war.

Jim Hix had only a month to go and now flew into battle each day exercising the utmost caution. "I had a pistol, a sackful of grenades, a sackful of smoke cans, and three radios, which I checked every other day. And I had my Buddha with me too."

As he was flying back across the Bolovens at one hundred feet beneath cloud, the engine of his O-1 quit. His Backseater, Pontee, pointed toward a big rice paddy, and Hix nodded. He slowly lowered the flaps, and as he came across the edge of the jungle and began to set the plane down, the engine caught. With the flaps down to almost sixty degrees he had no maneuverability—"like having a barn door hanging there"—and no option but to chop the throttle. The plane went skidding across the top of the paddy and into the jungle on the far side.

Apart from a badly bent prop and a hole in the windshield, there was little damage done to the airplane. Hix had been wearing his shoulder straps and was unhurt, and so was Pontee. He climbed out of the plane and looked around. There was no sign of the enemy. This time both of his radios were working, and the flares were good. He called in an Air America chopper and was back in Pakse within half an hour.

But caution had truly become the better part of valor for Jim Hix, who now felt he had experienced enough adventure for one war. He had already decided he was not going to extend again, and he lived every day of the final weeks with the nervous expectancy of a man walking across thin ice. He hardly dared hope that his luck would hold, but Buddha was watching over him, and he made it through to the end without mishap. On his last day he bought two cases of Hennessy cognac for the Lao fighter pilots and gave a party. He then hopped an Air America flight and flew to Udorn. "I was damn glad to be going home."

13

ATTRITION

The country-club posting was now using up Ravens just as the war in the north was: killing them, wounding them, or just burning them out. And as in the north, somehow the right man always seemed to materialize to fill another's shoes. Chad Swedberg had been sent south, flying down in the back of a T-28 with his dog, Princess Hamburger, on his lap, and was joined by Greg Wilson, Chuck Hightower, and Al Galante. (Galante, one of the few New Yorkers in the program, had developed a taste for flying at the age of five when he sat on his uncle's lap in the backseat of a J3 Piper Cub flown by his father, a New York City fireman who had gained his pilot's license flying old biplanes.)

The enemy had opened a new offensive in Laos and Cambodia in December 1971, and by the beginning of 1972 the NVA and Pathet Lao had moved from the Bolovens Plateau down Route 23 and into the valley and were advancing on Pakse. The Ravens found new roads cut on the edge of the Ho Chi Minh Trail along which convoys of trucks were moving massive amounts of supplies, including gasoline and ammunition. Wilson, Galante, and Hightower flew up to the area—a stretched ride from Pakse. They climbed high, pulling the power back so the enemy could not hear the plane engines, waiting for trucks to show up. They were destroying as many as fifteen vehicles in a single strike, with so much smoke and flame coming from the secondary explosions the sky was black with it.

"It began to sink in that with all this activity, moving all these supplies in broad daylight, something was going to happen someplace," Greg Wilson said. In fact the enemy were moving into position for their massive Easter offensive in South Vietnam. Wilson peered through his binoculars and thought he saw the debris of Fan Song radar—the type used to guide SAM missiles. He reported it to CIA intelligence, which passed it on to the 7th Air Force, which scoffed. The Americans did not officially recognize the presence of SAM missiles that far down the Trail until May.[1]

But the buildup of conventional antiaircraft weaponry alone made it an impossible environment for Ravens to work, and from now on Ravens flew exclusively to direct close air support for troops defending the towns at the base of the Bolovens Plateau. With the enemy so close to town there was also the constant danger of a night sapper attack on the airstrip, so a number of O-1s were always kept at PS 18, a base to the north of Pakse where the CIA had a training camp and there was also a field hospital run by Filipino doctors.

As the enemy increased their presence on the Bolovens Plateau, they began to stockpile ammunition and supplies and move artillery pieces into the various small towns. One of the principal storage places was a town near Paksong, where the king had a summer palace. "We found out the enemy had moved into it because they knew we didn't want to bomb the town," Al Galante said. "So we bombed the town."

The Laotian pilots were particularly reluctant to hit towns, but the first bomb that struck set off multiple secondary explosions of enemy ammunition. Numerous flights were directed onto the town, which was so stacked with ammunition that the pillar of flame and smoke from explosions could be seen fifty miles away. Native pilots sat in the Raven hootch that night drinking heavily and weeping that Laotian towns in the panhandle were now targets in the war.

The NVA continued to creep closer and closer to Pakse. Chuck Hightower was shot down around Saravane, but managed to deadstick his airplane into a rice paddy and walked south to avoid capture.

There was a choke point where Route 23 came down off the Bolovens and the road passed between steep cliffs on either side, and as Greg Wilson flew overhead he saw the Lao troops digging a pit in front of their compound. "What are they doing, building a swimming pool?" he asked the Backseater.

"They build tank trap."

Wilson chuckled. The soldiers were terrified of tanks, and it was enough for the enemy to rev their engines within a kilometer of a friendly position for the troops to turn tail. The tank trap was so obvious and the Lao troops so halfhearted it seemed ludicrous. But a week later a Raven flew over the spot and saw beneath him, neatly filling the trap, a tank turned turtle.

The boundary of land held by the friendlies was marked by a gun position known as Klick 11, because it was eleven kilometers outside of Pakse down Route 23. It was generally accepted, but unspoken, that when the enemy took Klick 11, Pakse would fall. And they were expected to make a move on the outskirts of the town at any time.

One rumor that circulated was of an enemy gun emplacement beyond Klick 11, which no one had been able to locate from the air, preparing to shell the town. Late one night after an evening spent drinking *lau lao*—the most potent of which was said to be laced with opium—Greg Wilson and Al Galante decided to steal a jeep and drive out into the countryside to find the gun and blow it up.

They drove out along Route 23, drunkenly harmonizing the obscene duets for which they had become famous around the hootch piano. Somewhere along the road they came upon a bamboo barricade, but a sleepy Laotian soldier raised it and waved them through. They were too drunk to know they had passed through Klick 11, and they must have been ten kilometers down the road when they hit a command-detonated C-4 charge, which blew up directly under the jeep's gearbox. The transmission took the full force of the mine's blast, but the Ravens were thrown into the air, and their eardrums were ruptured, temporarily rendering them stone-deaf.

They crawled back to the jeep to collect CAR-15s and bandoliers of grenades. The vehicle's canvas top had been blown open and the tires were flat, but somehow the headlights were still shining. It was only when they were back on the far side of the road, lying in a culvert with their weapons at the ready and grenades heaped beside them, that the mortars opened up.

The men could see the shells exploding around the jeep, but neither could hear a thing. They watched the world erupt in front of them, a war movie without a soundtrack. When the shelling stopped, a squad of NVA soldiers came out of the treeline, and the Ravens saw the flashes of their guns as they sprayed the jeep.

The NVA dropped back into the treeline and never crossed the road. Wilson and Galante lay where they were until sunup, and then made their way slowly across country back to Klick 11. A bus was waiting beside the barricade, where locals carrying live chickens and loaded with enormous bundles were boarding for the journey into the market at Pakse. The Ravens boarded the bus and rode back into town.

They reported to Dick Green, the Head Raven in Pakse, that they had misplaced a jeep. The ruptured eardrums meant there would be no more flying for a while, and there was the usual talk at the air attaché's office of court-martial, but Green quickly kicked them out of the country before worse punishment could be meted out.

Although the enemy did not attack Pakse directly, the war in the panhandle continued to intensify, and the CIA now concentrated air power there. The military objectives in Laos were now reduced to interdicting the enemy's progress along the Trail and tying up as many of their combat troops as possible (according to CIA estimates, between six and ten divisions were involved in the war in Laos).

In September 1972, a CIA-planned operation was launched—Black Lion IV—that involved moving two thousand men into the field around Saravane. The USAF was to supply H-53 helicopters, but pulled out of the operation on the first day, claiming the landing zone was too hot. Air America filled the gap, and paid the price when a chopper was lost and a CIA adviser was killed.

The men put into the Saravane operation were tribal irregulars and Thai mercenaries led by CIA case officers, and they moved their position each night as the enemy lobbed a thousand rounds of artillery shells into their camp. In between firefights the guerrillas seeded the roads with mines. By October the friendlies had pushed the NVA from the town, taken the airstrip, and established a defensive perimeter. Ravens were able to fly in to refuel and rearm, in order to direct close air support in the areas surrounding the town throughout the hours of daylight.

Each Raven was flying up to two hundred hours a month, an exhausting and punishing routine. The NVA made a concerted effort to retake Saravane one night in November and pushed the defending troops out to the south of the town and recaptured the airstrip. The enemy then moved onto the friendlies' eastern flank, driving them into the mountains to pin them against the Trail. Although the NVA attack was a success, many of the mercenaries slipped through their lines and escaped.

As the enemy hunted down the Thai mercenaries they began to maneuver in daylight. They were spotted spread out along a creek bed by Ravens Mike Stearns and John Rhodes, who called for air. Because of bad weather in South Vietnam they were sent a total of fifty sets of fighters, which they directed onto the enemy throughout the day. "With all the flying I was too exhausted and too crazy to consider the loss of human life," Stearns said. "My attitude was, 'Man, I got them! That'll teach them to come down here with their rifles on their shoulders.'"

The next day when he returned to assess the damage inflicted he ran into a cloud made up of hundreds of black buzzards, some with five-foot wingspans, which had gathered to feed off the corpses. The impact of the bombs had blasted the soldiers and thrown their body parts into the trees, where they hung like so many bloody rags. "You could smell the dead bodies from a thousand feet."

Ravens were getting wounded at such a rate that Lew Hatch, who was only a lieutenant, kept finding himself the senior Raven. Knife, one of the mercenary Thai forward air guides, had been killed when he threw himself onto an enemy grenade to save three other men squatting in a foxhole with him. He had seen the grenade come in and scrambled to reach it in the mud, but when he knew it was impossible he threw himself upon it. Such clear-cut heroics would have earned an American the Medal of Honor, but Knife received nothing.

Less than a week later, H. Ownby and Chuck "Buddha" Hines were in the O club at Udorn having lunch. Ownby had long hair, and both men were in dirty, casual clothes, so the Thai waitress, a dumpy, homely woman, immediately spotted them as Ravens. She went across to their table.

"You know Knife?"

"Yeah, works with Mule," Ownby said.

Great tears appeared in the waitress's eyes, and she tried clumsily to wipe them away with the order pad she held in her hand. "Knife—him die, him dead."

"Yeah," Chuck Hines said. "Got it up on the ridge at night."

The waitress said that Knife was her husband, and his death had left her alone with three young children. Ownby mumbled his regrets. The waitress stood with red eyes, waiting to take their order.

"Hamburger, fries, and a Coke," Hines said.

"BLT and a 7-Up," Ownby said. And that was the extent of Knife's memorial service, except for the twenty-dollar tips the Ravens always left on the table when the dumpy Thai waitress was on duty.

In early November the CIA called in Lew Hatch to say they had intercepted some disturbing enemy plans. "I don't want to spread panic and alarm," the CIA officer told him, "but the enemy are sending some assassins into town to get you guys."

A radio intercept had revealed that the enemy had assigned six assassins—one for each of the four Ravens, and one for each of the Laotian flight leads. The CIA told Hatch that the NVA had an official USAF photograph of him, which must have come from the Soviets, who built up dossiers on all U.S. military officers. Hatch was impressed: "I was just a fucking lieutenant!"

While the CIA attempted to discover who might be used for the assassination attempt, each of the Ravens was told to carry a handgun at all times and was assigned a Lao bodyguard. In less than a week after the warning the first assassination attempt was made. Lew Hatch was at the wheel of the jeep driving into downtown Pakse, with Mike Stearns and Jay Johnson as passengers, when he ran into what seemed to be a riot outside the Chinese theater. The road was blocked off and Hatch found himself being funneled into side streets which would take him out of town. A brick came through the windshield and there were shots, and Hatch quickly turned the jeep around in the middle of the road and headed for the safety of the Thai officers' club. Later, in a separate incident, a hand grenade was rolled next to the Raven hootch, but no one was hurt. But for the next fortnight the Ravens returned from a full day of combat to the fear of personal assassination.

Two months after the attack on Saravane, a thousand Thai mercenaries were air-assaulted onto the Bolovens Plateau, where they set up an artillery firebase. The assault threatened vital NVA supply lines, and the enemy responded by fielding more and more troops until it was estimated they had three divisions committed to the regions around Saravane and Paksong. The new offensive meant the Ravens had to direct air support for three separate areas of operation in the panhandle alone. There were not enough airplanes, and certainly not enough men. "We had opened a three-front war," Lew Hatch said. "We started it and we were fixing to get our asses kicked."

During the second air assault on Paksong, Mike Stearns crashed his plane on the edge of the Bolovens when the engine quit. A badly cut foot meant he was unable to fly, and he was sent home. Hal Mischler, who was soon to leave and had already sent his personal belongings home, was sent to Pakse as a replacement—the fourth senior Raven Lew Hatch had served under.

Jack Shaw arrived in Vientiane on December 10, 1972, flown up from Udorn by Skip Jackson, and then moved down to Pakse two days before Christmas. H. Ownby, Terry Pfaff, and Ed Chun had already been sent south from Long Tieng and Luang Prabang as Christmas help.

Most of the Ravens' rooms were basic but Shaw, who had a reputation as a ladies' man, immediately set about converting his into a bachelor's seduction pad, complete with heavy curtains, black satin sheets, and light dimmers. He had been intrigued by the Ravens for more than six months, since he first met Al Galante in the bar of the O club at Ubon. "A big guy, a really cocky son of a bitch in civilian clothes acting as if all these fighter pilots were scum. His attitude was that if you were gracious enough he would talk to you—and that you were extremely lucky to be allowed to talk to him. I can't say I was *favorably* impressed, but I was impressed."

The decision to transfer to the Ravens was finally made after Shaw had been grounded by his commander as a punishment for losing an airplane—he had been shot down in an OV-10 by a shoulder-fired heat-seeking missile. His best friend, Hal Mischler—who had been his roommate back at the Air Commando base in Florida and also at Nakhon Phanom, where they were both Nail FACs working the Trail—had joined the Ravens a month ahead of him.

When Shaw left Nakhon Phanom to become a Raven he was presented with two Buddhas by Nupal, the O club's Thai bartender. They had been blessed by monks in a temple for seven days, and the Thai wanted Shaw and Mischler to have one each (Mischler's parting gift to Nupal had been more temporal—his ten-speed bike). Nupal explained the nature of the Buddhas' power. "This Buddha only good for stopping you get shot. No good for fights or against knives. Only getting shot."

"How does Buddha know about guns?" Shaw teased. "They weren't around when Buddha was."

Nupal lowered his voice: "Buddha knows all."

Shaw threw the presents in his briefcase and gave Mischler his Buddha the moment he joined up with him in Pakse. Mischler smiled, touched that the barman should have thought of him. He told Shaw that he would have the Buddha put on a gold chain and wear it around his neck. Shaw said he was taking no chances, and attached it to a gold bracelet he wore around his wrist so that he would have the Buddha's protection against antiaircraft fire on his first day in combat over Laos.

A massive air campaign had been launched against North Vietnam—the so-called Christmas bombing—with the result that there was no air available for the Ravens by December 23. Heavy air strikes against military targets in Hanoi and Haiphong had been launched on December 18 after the North Vietnamese had broken off the peace talks in Paris, and the entire U.S. air effort was now temporarily concentrated against the north. "Great," Lew Hatch told the CIA. "We don't have to fly today."

"No, you still have to fly."

"Why?"

"We need to know how many trucks they're running down the Trail without U.S. air to interdict them."

"I can tell you that," Hatch said. "Take their normal daily average and multiply it by four—and that's how many trucks they'll move down."

On the morning of December 23, the Bolovens Plateau was held by friendly forces, but the enemy had Saravane under siege. It was decided that Mischler would direct Laotian T-28s against the forces attacking Saravane while Lew Hatch, who had been in the area longer and knew the countryside better, would take Jack Shaw out for a check ride.

Shaw flew the plane and Hatch sat in the backseat. Flying out toward the Trail, they suddenly heard a transmission from Hillsboro, the panhandle's orbiting command post: "Stand by—a Raven's down." There was a pause, and then Hillsboro came back up on the air. "Raven 40—Saravane."

Raven 40 was Hal Mischler. Shaw turned the O-1 around and headed toward Saravane, some fifty miles to the east of them. As it was his first day on the job, he handed the FM radio to Lew Hatch, who was used to working with Lao troops on the ground. Hatch asked the ground commander in the area what had happened to the downed Raven and was told that Mischler had been trolling for guns with the intention of directing artillery onto them when he was nailed. Khammane, his Backseater, shared his fellow countrymen's terrible fear of fire, and as smoke seeped into the cockpit he threw himself from the plane at two hundred feet and was cut in half when he hit a jagged brick wall. There was no report on Raven 40, but the commander said he intended to send out a platoon of commandos to bring him in.

It took the Ravens some time to find the wreckage of the plane. The moment they spotted it they immediately launched a SAR operation. With an American airman down, U.S. fighters were diverted as a priority, and Shaw directed them on the suspected gun emplacements. Antiaircraft fire was fierce—the NVA had moved two 37mm, one 23mm, a 14.5mm quad ZPU, and at least five 12.7mm guns into the area. Shaw took the O-1 lower and lower, trying to get below the 37mm so he could work the crash site.

He was unused to the O-1 and being shot at, and thought the sound he heard outside the cockpit—as if people were snapping their fingers—was the noise the plane made when the engine backfired. But when the Lao ground commander screamed into the radio that they were taking a massive concentration of ground fire he realized it was the sound of spent bullets.

"Yeah," Hatch said calmly, "I can hear them."

A couple of the rounds found their mark, and as Shaw put the power up to maneuver the plane there was suddenly no response from the engine. The choice now was whether to crash the plane halfway home or put it down on an unused airstrip in disputed territory. Shaw began a slow spiral to earth, putting out a Mayday call as he went down.

Ed Chun flew onto the scene and took over the SAR, redirecting the Air America choppers already in flight to stand by and pick up the Ravens about to crash-land in enemy territory.

"Lew, you've had more time in this thing," Shaw said. "You land it."

"I got it," Hatch said, taking over the controls. The problem with landing from the back was that it was like sitting in a bucket and the pilot could see nothing. The runway on which he was about to land was a grass strip built by the Japanese in World War II, and had been used occasionally by the Ravens as a forward base when in friendly hands. Now it was littered with crates and engine parts, and pockmarked with holes made by mortar and artillery shells. One end of the runway had been bombed, while a burned-out T-28 lay at the other.

Lew Hatch, unable to see over the nose of the airplane, lowered full flaps and came down blind in the middle of the runway. "Let me know where the debris is."

Shaw yelled directions from the front. A pile of abandoned crates lay on the runway directly across the path of the plane, and Hatch punched the rudder to veer around them. The O-1 left the strip and hurtled through undergrowth. "A stack of boxes the size of a desk went under the right wing," Shaw said. "This was not good. All I could see in front of us was a wall of elephant grass."

Hatch had lost control of the plane, which had blown a tire somewhere on landing; he kept punching the rudder but it refused to turn. Both men simultaneously stabbed their feet at the brakes, and the plane ground-looped and spun to a halt thirty feet from a lake.

Shaw grabbed his CAR-15 and scouted around the plane to see if there were any enemy in the vicinity. There was no apparent movement, and he returned to help Hatch haul himself out of the backseat. They gathered up their weapons, maps, and code sheets and waited for the Air America chopper, which was only five minutes behind them, to come in. Hatch had already radioed the chopper's pilot, Mel Cooper, where he was going to land, but because of the ground loop he had ended up on the opposite side of the runway.

"Waiting for that chopper seemed to be like a lifetime," he said. "Everything seemed to be in slow motion." He could hear shooting from what he took to be a position five hundred yards away, but circling above them Ed Chun could see that the enemy were much closer and moving from every direction through the bushes toward the crashed plane.

The chopper landed some distance away, kicking up a small dust storm. Hatch and Shaw gathered up their stuff and began walking toward it, unaware of the immediate danger. Ed Chun spoke to Mel Cooper over the radio: "They're *walking!* Just like on a picnic. They're just *walking!*"

Cooper was furious, and began shouting at the Ravens to hurry. They clambered aboard, and as the chopper lifted off they began to take fire. Hatch and the crew chief knelt at the door and fired into the elephant grass. Once in the air, Shaw lit up the first cigarette from the pack he would smoke over the next hour.

The crew chief yelled over the roar of the rotors into Hatch's ear that the pilot wanted to talk to him, and he handed the Raven a helmet with earphones. Cooper wanted to know if he should stop off at a nearby landing zone for a pickup. There were some wounded there, the pilot said—and the body of the downed Raven. Hatch looked across at Shaw, but he had heard nothing. "Let's go in and get the body."

When they landed at the firebase, four of the Thai walking wounded, swathed in bandages, climbed aboard the helicopter. The dead body of the Raven, wrapped in white parachute material because of a lack of body bags, was carried aboard. As the chopper lifted off, a soldier ran toward it and clung to the skids. Cooper hovered six feet off the ground while the crew chief shouted at the man to let go. But he hung on, prepared to ride the skids for as long as it took to get away from the firebase. The crew chief unholstered his .45, chambered a round, and waved the gun toward the soldier, gesturing to him to let go. The man scowled before dropping in a heap to the ground.

The ride to Pakse took thirty minutes. Hatch spoke on the headset to the Customer in the operations shack to tell him that they were bringing in the body of a Raven and that he wanted an American flag to cover it. Officially, the clandestine nature of the Ravens' activity in Laos forbade them this traditional dignity, but the CIA officer said he would find one somewhere. Shaw could hear nothing of the conversation over the noise of the engine, and sat mute in the back of the chopper smoking cigarette after cigarette, unaware of the identity of the body lying in front of him.

"I could see the back of the head, which looked gray, and the hair was singed," Shaw said. "I sat there thinking, 'This poor sucker's dead—I wonder what happened to him? I made it—this poor sucker didn't.' "

The chopper flew nose down, and a large flow of blood ran from the body and collected in a pool against the bulkhead. It made the wounded soldiers uncomfortable, and they moved to huddle together in the rear of the cabin away from the blood. The pool deepened, until a stream trickled to the side of the helicopter and out through the open door into the slipstream. "I wonder who this guy is," Shaw thought, "spilling his blood over Laos?"

The chopper landed briefly at PS 18 to let off the wounded to be treated at the hospital there, and then flew on to Pakse. The Customer was there to meet them, accompanied by a small group of Americans, and in one hand he clutched the folded square of a flag. The body was lifted down and laid on a stretcher and carefully covered with the Stars and Stripes.

"What the hell is this?" Jack Shaw asked, turning to Lew Hatch. "Some CAS guy get blown away on the firebase out there? Who is this?"

"Jack, that's Hal," Hatch answered awkwardly.

Jack Shaw tried to take the information in. Hal. He's dead. That's his body. "I'd been thinking all these philosophical thoughts about this poor fucker who died in the war—about him not making it and me being alive—and it was my goddam roommate. I was just stunned."

Two men picked up the stretcher on which Hal Mischler lay covered with the flag and loaded it onto another helicopter, a Chinook bound for Udorn. Jack Shaw walked toward it and stood at the base of the ramp underneath the rotors, staring up at the body lying before him. Tears ran down his face. "Nobody said a word to me. I think they knew what was going on. The sun was going down, and it was dim inside that chopper. The lights were on and they had put down the stretcher crosswise with the American flag on it. There was nothing else inside. Then a guy walked over there and stood looking at me across Hal's body. I heard the engine crank up, the ramp close, and it just took off. And I stood there and I watched that chopper until it had gone over the horizon. Until the sun went down."

When Jack Shaw returned to the hootch he found Lew Hatch sitting at a table with two bottles of Johnny Walker Black Label in front of him sent over by the Air America helicopter crew. "We're supposed to buy them Scotch," Shaw said. "They saved our lives."
"No, they said we didn't make as much money as they did today." Hatch took the top off one of the bottles and poured two large drinks. Together, the men drank to the memory of Hal Mischler. They did not move from the table until they had finished the bottle.
"The other bottle was Hal's," Jack Shaw said. "And every time we started thinking about Hal we took it down and drank some of it. It didn't last long." After the men had finished the first bottle they fell into bed, asking colleagues to wake them at 6:00 the following morning. Lew Hatch was scheduled to fly the dawn patrol, while Shaw had to fly to Udorn to pick up a replacement O-1.

On Christmas Eve, Jack Shaw was sitting on his own at the bar of the Air America club at Udorn. A man drinking next to him struck up a conversation and asked him what he did. Shaw said he was a Raven.
"Sorry to hear you lost a guy today."
"Yesterday. Over Saravane."
"Yeah, yesterday over Saravane," the man said uncomfortably. "And today. Over the PDJ."
Skip Jackson, who had flown Shaw into Laos when he first arrived, had been run over by a Navy jet. He had been directing a set of A-7s over the Plain of Jars when one of the fighters had clipped a strut under the wing of the O-1. It plummeted to the ground and pancaked. The pilot of the A-7 remembered a flash, then suddenly his plane became unstable and he punched out—only to be captured and imprisoned by the enemy.
Jack Shaw returned to Pakse after Christmas. The casualty officer was in the hootch going through Mischler's property (a discretion the

Air Force afforded a pilot who had been killed so nothing offensive
would be returned to his wife or family). Laid out on the dining-room
table was a small collection of worthless but painfully intimate possessions: shaving cream, razor blades, toothpaste, after-shave lotion.

"This is Mischler's stuff," the casualty officer said. "Want any of it?"

"Throw it away!" Shaw said in a voice that was quiet but deadly. He
turned and walked from the room.

Later he explained: "You were so hurt you just buried your feelings. The guys at the hootch never talked about it. And I couldn't talk
about it for years and years. I had flown with the Nails for ten months,
and guys got shot down but no one was killed. Everybody got picked
up. It was humorous almost—you earned the right to tell your own
war story. I'd been in Laos just a couple of days and all of a sudden
everybody seemed to be dying. I thought it wasn't a joke anymore—
this is war."

14

PEACE

They made a wasteland and called it peace.
—Tacitus
(*c*. A.D. 55–120)

The Paris Agreement on Vietnam was signed on January 27, 1973. Laos had not been a negotiating party at the peace talks between the United States and North Vietnam—excluded along with South Vietnam and Cambodia—at which the United States had quickly dropped its demand for a truce encompassing the whole of Indochina. The Royal Lao Government had wanted the United States to conclude a Laotian cease-fire as part of the Vietnam settlement but was rebuffed.

One of the issues during negotiations was the withdrawal of North Vietnamese troops from Laos. Hanoi continued to maintain the fiction that it had no soldiers in the country, but did confirm in writing that North Vietnamese would be considered "foreign" troops in respect to the agreement's call for the withdrawal of such forces.

Souvanna Phouma chose to interpret this as a defeat for the North Vietnamese, and believed that he would at last be able to work out a political settlement with the Pathet Lao that would be a nationalistic, Laotian solution free of foreign interests. In reality it was Hanoi that stood to gain from an early cease-fire in Laos, one of the terms of which included the cessation of all U.S. air support.

It was as if America had learned nothing from its previous negotiations over Laos. The mistakes of earlier agreements—1954 and 1962—were not only repeated but compounded. Laos and Cambodia were disposed of in the Paris Agreement by Article 20, a paragraph of 185 words of diplomatic waffle in which the United States and North Vietnam agreed to respect Laotian and Cambodian neutrality and to end military intervention. But there was no deadline laid down for any such intervention to cease, and no means to enforce it.

The North Vietnamese Communists had blatantly violated the two previous agreements, and it took optimism on the level of an act of faith to believe that they would now abandon the ambitions and struggles of thirty years because of a clumsily drafted afterthought in a document they had no intention of honoring anyway.

It is hard to accept that the U.S. negotiators were not cynical in regard to Laos, ignoring the fate of a small, irrelevant power in their anxiety for a quick exit from an unpopular war. But it is a charge that is denied by William Sullivan, who as a deputy assistant secretary and head of the State Department's Vietnam Working Group acted as Kissinger's deputy in the peace negotiations: "We were skeptical but not cynical. In retrospect we had hypnotized ourselves with our own mythology on this, because this is what we had been attempting to do from the very beginning—to contain the North Vietnamese back in the area that had been allocated them in the 1954 agreements. The underlying assumption was that we had pushed them into a position where they would have to truncate their ambitions. Maybe we were kidding ourselves."[1]

Ambassador Godley is more severe. He feels that Prime Minister Souvanna Phouma was treated shabbily. "He was a great man," he said. "I respected him tremendously—his honesty, consistency, and personal courage. He was never consulted. We led him down the garden path. Let's face it, we were cutting and running. We pulled the rug from under him. But once we were out of Vietnam the only way we could have protected Laos was with an Army corps. It was totally out of the question and we knew it. We were licked. There was nothing to be done."[2]

Dr. Henry Kissinger arrived in Vientiane on his way to Hanoi thirteen days after the Paris agreement was signed. He dined with Souvanna Phouma at the prime minister's villa, which struck Kissinger as so modest he recorded its simplicity in his memoirs: "It looked like the residence of a French junior minister, without the trappings usually associated with presidential palaces."

After dinner Souvanna Phouma made a moving appeal to Kissinger: "The very survival of Laos rests on your shoulders. But your shoulders are broad. We are counting on you to make our neighbors understand that all we want is peace. We are a very small country; we do not represent a danger to anybody. We count on you to make them know that the Lao people are pacific by tradition and by religion. We want only to be sovereign and independent. We ask that they let us live in peace on this little piece of ground that is left to us of our ancient kingdom.

"If pressure is kept on the North Vietnamese to understand the risk they run from violating the Agreement, then perhaps they will respect the Agreement. . . . Therefore we must count on our great friends the Americans to help us survive. We hope, we dream, that this wish will be granted."

"What a touching hope," Kissinger wrote, and publicly responded in kind. "We have not come all this way in order to betray our friends."[3] But behind closed doors the Americans were exerting enormous pressure on Souvanna Phouma to sign, telling him bluntly that unless he accepted whatever settlement was being offered he stood to lose everything.

According to the prime minister's son, Prince Mangkhra Phouma, who filled the position of director of the cabinet in the Ministry of Defense at the time, his father was presented with a *fait accompli*. "We had to sign the agreement because of the menace from Mr. [sic] Kissinger. He threatened to cut off all aid to Laos if my father refused. He signed, so that the Americans would continue to help Laos. But as soon as we signed the help stopped."[4]

This view is supported by Maj. Gen. Oudone Sananikone, the Army chief of staff, who said that John Gunther Dean, the U.S. chargé d'affaires involved in the Laotian peace negotiations, made thinly veiled threats to the Royal Lao Government in order to obtain concessions for the enemy. The pressure became so intense that the Communist Pathet Lao believed Souvanna Phouma "would agree to anything" and considered the Americans so keen on a peace settlement that they were, "in effect, in their [the enemy's] corner." The pressure exerted by the Americans was not subtle. "We would find that the weekly shipments of American-supplied rice for the army would not arrive," Sananikone said, "or that the American-supplied money to pay the army would be delayed, or that only part of the fuel needed to run the army's vehicles would be delivered."[5]

On the day Kissinger was in Vientiane, the official news agency, Lao Presse, issued a dignified, heartfelt editorial that was pathetic in the circumstances. "America . . . has ended its suffering, but it cannot forget that in international morality, peace has the same value for all people, small or large."[6]

This small, gentle voice went unheeded in the hard world of international realpolitik. To power brokers with the muscle of Henry

Kissinger, Laos was very small beer indeed. Critics have suggested that a better cease-fire agreement might have been negotiated over Vietnam, giving the allies a greater chance of survival, had a permanent, senior negotiator been given the job, rather than relying almost exclusively on the overextended skills of Kissinger, who was committed to an exhausting round of worldwide shuttle diplomacy. (During the extended Vietnam talks, Kissinger was also involved in negotiations regarding Salt 1; the Four Power Agreement on Berlin; the India-Pakistan war; the treaty between the two Germanys; various treaties with Chile, Cuba, and countries of the Middle East; opening contact with China; secret talks with President Sadat over his plans to expel the Soviets from Egypt; and the beginnings of the Panama Canal Treaty.)[7]

Prime Minister Souvanna Phouma had written to his half brother Prince Souphanouvong in July, proposing yet another new effort at negotiating a peace agreement between the warring Laotian factions. Peace negotiation between the Royal Lao Government and the Pathet Lao had opened in Vientiane on October 17, 1972.

Souvanna Phouma genuinely sought conciliation, hoping nationalist interests would bring the two sides together, but there was a desperate edge in his search for peace once he understood the U.S. position that any agreement was better than none. In principle, both sides agreed on neutralization, a coalition government, and an end to foreign intervention. In reality, the talks in Laos were tied to the coattails of events in Vietnam.

The subsequent Vientiane Agreement between the Pathet Lao and the Royal Lao Government bowed to almost every demand made by the Communists. In his desperation to reach an understanding that would avoid further bloodshed, Souvanna Phouma made even more concessions than those favored by Washington.

The Pathet Lao retained complete control of their own zone, while gaining a half-share in the national government. Worst of all, the North Vietnamese were allowed to remain for sixty days after the formation of a new coalition government, while U.S. air support was to be closed down within twenty-four hours of signing the truce. The Royal Lao Government received the news of the agreement with profound dismay. "This is the worst defeat we have suffered," Sisouk Na Champassak, Lao defense minister, said.

The Pathet Lao were naturally delighted with the terms of the agreement. But these are now only of interest to students of Laotian history, for events were soon to prove that even the most generous agreement was seen by the Communists as nothing more than a stopgap to the total takeover of the country. Laotian sovereignty was violated everywhere by the North Vietnamese. On the other hand, the removal of U.S. and Thai military elements and the disbanding of the CIA irregulars was to go ahead according to the letter of the agreement. The ineffective International Commission for Supervision and Control, a body that had proved a complete failure in its oversight of the previous agreements, was brought back into being.

The same miscalculation made by Averell Harriman in 1962, when he underestimated Hanoi's independence of Moscow and Peking as well as its territorial ambitions, was repeated by Kissinger. It was a major strategic mistake. "I cannot, even today, recall Souvanna Phouma's wistful plea without a pang of shame that America was unable to fulfill his hopes for our steadfast support against a voracious enemy," Kissinger wrote in his memoirs.[8] It is a shame that is not out of place.

The Ravens would be required to fight to the last minute of American involvement in Laos. They too had learned of the terms of the peace agreement with shame, and could not share in the euphoria that was sweeping America at the news of the end of the war. The general public in the United States, who knew little about the war in Laos and cared even less, could have no knowledge of the terrible sacrifice the Meo had made on America's behalf and the tragic fate to which they had been abandoned. But for the few Americans intimately involved, the end of the war was no cause for celebration.

Gen. Vang Pao's 1972 monsoon offensive northeast of the Plain of Jars had kicked off in August with the understanding that USAF helicopter support was crucial. The plan was to insert a 2,400-man force in the northern plain to the enemy's rear, but it faltered because of bad weather, and restrictive Air Force rules limited the use of CH-53 helicopters without escort. Only half the intended assault group was deployed, and the force was no match for enemy artillery and tanks. Survivors were split up and forced to make their way overland through enemy lines, a ragged retreat that went on for several weeks.

Despite dwindling support, Vang Pao continued to launch attack operations. The last major combat assault using USAF helicopters took place on January 20, 1973, when seven CH-53s and two Air America Chinooks flew in a thousand men to reopen the Vientiane–Luang Prabang highway. Four choppers were hit, but the road was successfully reopened prior to the cease-fire.[9]

The enemy, meanwhile, kept up the pressure in the panhandle, while the United States piled on the last of its air power. From the end of January until the cease-fire, sorties flown in Laos averaged 350 a day and totaled 8,900.[10] With the war over in South Vietnam—for the Americans, at least—massive air support now became available for use over Laos during the last days of the war there. Hillsboro, the orbiting command post in the panhandle, called Jack Shaw and asked if he had a target. Shaw said he had seen a truck in a river, but was not sure if it was stalled there or had been previously destroyed.

"Okay, you got air."

"Wait a minute," Shaw argued. "I don't know if this truck is any good."

"You've got air," Hillsboro insisted. "You've got the only target in the war."

The entire afternoon launch from a carrier arrived in relay, and Shaw directed the mixed bag of twenty-five fighters onto the truck, stacking them up and putting them onto the target as fast as possible. It was a hectic period of furious activity which was nothing more than battlefield make-work. "I can't remember if we got the truck," Shaw said. "It was probably dead anyway."

On the last official day of the war in Laos, February 22, 1973, Gen. Vang Pao received an unsigned, typed communication at his HQ in Long Tieng, part of which read: "1. In accord with the terms of the cease-fire agreement between the Royal Lao Government and the Neo Lao Hak Sat (Pathet Lao) that established 1200 22 February as the time armed action between those forces would cease, the United States is honoring this agreement.

"2. As we discussed previously, USAF air support would cease as of 1200 22 February. . . . USAF were under instructions to clear Lao air space by 1200 this date."[11]

One of the outposts defending Long Tieng duly fell at 2:30 that afternoon, while others were being heavily shelled in preparation for direct attack. Vang Pao shook his head and told reporter Arnold Isaacs of the *Baltimore Sun*, who was standing beside him, that he did not see how his positions could be held without American support. "We are not like South Vietnam. South Vietnam, the Americans have given all means, thousands of tanks, trucks, airplanes . . ."[12] He left the sentence unfinished; Laos was to be abandoned with scarcely anything to defend it.

The Ravens were ordered to be back on the ground by midday, and were threatened with the most dire consequences if they were not. The objectives of the war in the previous couple of months had changed, from tying up NVA troops and interdicting traffic on the Trail to a frantic last-minute scramble for territory before the cease-fire went into effect. On the day before the cease-fire, friendly troops were told to hoist Royal Laotian flags, specially made up and dropped by the CIA, to mark their positions.

The final morning of the war was fought in dismal weather. In the north, H. Ownby, Darrel Whitcomb, and Craig Dunn flew three missions apiece in support of a surrounded enclave of Meo battling for their lives. "I had taken off before dawn," Ownby said, "and worked some U.S. air and Laotian T-28s. Then, starting about ten o'clock, it was like the world quit. The planes started disappearing and it got real quiet on the radio. It was eerie."

He put in his last set of fighters and turned the plane around to head for home by the noon deadline. The battle still raged on the ground, and as he flew away he felt he was ignoring every instinct in his being. "I felt like a coward. If I'd had more guts I would have said screw the diplomats, screw my boss, and screw the president—I'll do what I know needs to be done. But I was young and believed that somebody knew more about it than I did."

The war on the Bolovens Plateau was furious, and Jack Shaw kept begging Hillsboro, "Send us air, send us air." He had flown out of Pakse with CIA case officer Sword sitting illegally in his backseat. They fired M-16s and M-79 grenade launchers from the windows of the plane. The enemy had opened up on Paksong with mortars and had the town under siege, and seemed to be on the move everywhere. "No more air after the next ten minutes," Hillsboro radioed. "Everybody has to be out of Laos and west of the Mekong by noon. That's it, buddy."

The last fighters dropped their bombs at 11:50, and Shaw turned the plane around and flew home during what he knew to be the height of the battle. Paksong fell at 12:30.

"We knew damn well the North Vietnamese would not recognize the cease-fire," Lew Hatch said. "As we left, the tanks started rolling. In four days they overran four positions on the Bolovens. The thousand-man Thai artillery post was cut off and they had to walk out through the enemy lines. And we had to sit there and watch the Lao fly."

Back on the ground the Ravens went through the ritual that all combat pilots who had completed a tour in Southeast Asia experienced: a bottle of champagne was opened, and the pilot was hosed down with cold water while a photograph was taken of him beside his plane. But on the last day of the war in Laos it was an empty ritual acted out with an absolute lack of spirit. Shamefully, they handed their planes over to Lao FACs, who turned them around and flew into battle to direct the hopelessly inadequate squadrons of T-28s.

Their frustration mounted as they watched their old allies return to the war without them. "We've got to help those guys," Shaw said to an officer from the air attaché's office. "Those fuckers on the ground are getting their shit blown away."

"The war's over, lieutenant—and that's official."

The Ravens stationed in Vientiane went out for dinner that night at Chez Hélène and tried to celebrate. "Everybody felt shitty," Ownby said. "We had a real good dinner and we all still felt shitty. The life had gone out of everybody."

In the panhandle the Ravens went out drinking with Air America and CIA personnel and suffered a similar dispirited evening. Doug Mitchell, the last Raven to be sent to Laos, stayed at home in the hootch in Savannakhet. After three years of flying combat in Southeast Asia, the sudden release from tension was overwhelming. "I got a case of the total shakes. Total, uncontrollable shaking, and I felt cold as ice. And I was shaking like that for an hour."

Enemy activity after the cease-fire was so blatant that the prime minister, Souvanna Phouma, was forced to accept the cynicism of the Communists. The next morning he told reporters that instead of honoring the cease-fire, the Communists had planned all along to wait until the skies were clear of American bombers to mount a general offensive to grab more land. Dejected and emotionally distraught, Souvanna Phouma stated, "We had faith in this agreement and we have been tricked. Our faith has been violated."[13]

He declared that unless the Communist attacks stopped he would request further air strikes from the Americans. Almost indifferent to the threat, the Pathet Lao spokesman said accurately that they had successfully withstood American bombing until then, and would continue to do so. That night the Americans reacted to the request and nine B-52s struck near Paksong.

But the post-cease-fire conflict continued. "The goddam International Control Commission in Pakse was living in a downtown hotel which they never left, logging every T-28 that took off as a cease-fire violation," Lew Hatch said. He appealed to the Canadian delegate, offering to fly him and his colleagues around the panhandle to see exactly what the situation was. "The Canadian wanted to do it but he was perpetually outvoted by the Polish and Indian delegates. A large part of the country which we controlled was overrun after the cease-fire."

The war went on, but there was less of it. Government weekly casualties dropped to a quarter their previous number.[14] Serious violations that could not be overlooked brought the B-52 back in April 1973, when the final strike of nine years of USAF bombing was put in south of the Plain of Jars.[15] It is symbolic that the last raid of the war, made by one of the most awesome weapon systems on earth, was nothing more than an empty and impotent gesture.

A contingent of Ravens remained stationed in Vientiane, supposedly to act as a reminder to the Communist Pathet Lao that USAF personnel were on hand to resume air operations if the necessity occurred. The enemy saw this for what it was—an empty bluff. The countermeasures threatened if they broke the agreement were nullified when the power of the U.S. president, the chief executive of the administration, was frozen by the inquiry into the Watergate break-in. The Ravens were not allowed to fly or even move out of Vientiane. "Sadly, we were there doing absolutely nothing," Chad Swedberg said.

Time passed slowly in a city where, without the war, there was nothing to do. The Ravens rose at 10:00 and passed the mornings taking language classes from a local who came to the house. The afternoons seemed endless. In the evening there was dinner and a movie, after which everyone went down to Charlie's to drink beer and play darts until the early hours of the morning. The Purple Porpoise had closed after its owner, Monty Banks, suffered a stroke and returned to Australia. Madame Lulu too closed up shop and returned to Paris after spending the greater part of a lifetime in the Far East.[16]

Half of the Ravens were duly sent home.[17] Chad Swedberg left, after a specially chartered Air America plane had flown down to Pakse to pick up Princess Hamburger. The mongrel returned with him to America, her regal title enabling her to be listed on the airplane's manifold as "Priority Passenger—Do Not Bump." One by one the Ravens were sent from the country, until by the end of September 1973 only H. Ownby was left. "I was housemother, so it was my job to close up the hootch. The saddest part was figuring out what to do with Mr. Van and Mr. Tung—the cook and the housekeeper." Van was someone who would always fall on his feet, and he left for Bangkok;

Tung was a less adaptable character, and the Americans remaining in Vientiane collected two thousand dollars to enable him to take his family and settle across the Mekong in Thailand.

"The house was closed as a typical military operation. I went through it with the property officer, checking off an inventory. It was eerie—a great big empty house. I turned out the lights, locked up, and walked away."

The last of the O-1s had been flown out of Vientiane in a four-ship. They took off from Vientiane and executed the traditional "missing man" formation, usually done as a fly-past at a military funeral when one plane pulls up and out of the formation in a symbolic act of remembrance. "It was a tribute," Jack Shaw said. "To Hal, and the Ravens who had died. To the Lao we left behind, and the Meo we abandoned and betrayed. To the American POWs left in the country. It was our way of saying we might have been made to go, but we would never forget."

15

AFTER THE WAR

Well, the tragedy is over. The failure is complete. I turn my head and go away. I took my share in this fight for the impossible.

—Albert Camus,
Notebooks: 1942–1951

"See you next war, baby." This was the traditional sign-off radioed to Cricket after a Raven's final combat mission, and there was no one who did not feel some relief as he spoke the closing three words of his last radio transmission, "Alpha, Mike, Foxtrot" (Adios, motherfucker).

A Raven left the war after a round of quiet handshakes around the breakfast table, and then a jeep ride out to the airport through the sleepy streets of Vientiane, skirting the muddy brown Mekong. A brief flight took the retiring Raven across the river and into Thailand, and suddenly the war was over.

In Udorn the civilian-clad FAC was handed back his Air Force uniforms, ID tags, and private belongings and then took a taxi out to the terminal to board a C-130 for Bangkok. Most flew on to Clark Air Force Base in the Philippines, where they transferred to another Air Force transport and flew across the Pacific to Hawaii. And then, after an overnight stay, they flew on to Travis Air Force Base outside San Francisco—and set foot safely on the American mainland.

Returning to American soil with the war left behind was a moving experience for everyone. One of the first things Jack Shaw did on his return was to go into a McDonald's and order a hamburger, a milk-shake, and fries. Standing in line for a Big Mac, he was so overcome by emotion to be home and among fellow Americans he found himself unable to speak.

On the flight from Travis Air Force Base to his home in Ohio, Craig

Morrison had a few mementoes from the war in his bags: a Chinese SK bolt-action rifle with a foldout bayonet attached to it, some individual photographs of enemy soldiers (so young they looked like girls), and an enemy helmet, the inside headband of which was inscribed in Vietnamese lettering with the haunting prophesy, "Born in Vietnam—Die in Laos." He penned the last entry for the war in his journal: "So! It's over! And now no more war zone. Leaving FL 290 [Flight Level 29,000 feet] with 130 knot tail wind with the sierras off the right wing all covered with snow. *Good God is it good to be back in America!* I couldn't put it into words how I feel now if I were to write all the way to Chicago so I won't try, but I guess I'll admit I've got a lump in my throat and tears in my eyes, and I'm glad to be home, so damn glad."[1]

But the euphoria was to prove short-lived. America had been so deeply divided over the war, so shaken by its lack of success and disturbed by the endless bloodletting, that the country had turned in on itself. The men who returned from battle—American soldiers, sailors, and airmen—were shunned as if they were members of a despised occupying army. Men in uniform were shouted at, spat upon, and even physically assaulted. (French soldiers returning from an earlier, equally unpopular Indochina war faced an even worse reception: hospital trains carrying the wounded were stoned by French Communists as they stopped to unload men in their hometowns.)[2]

Ron Rinehart arrived at Travis Air Force Base proud to be back in uniform after a year of flying in civilian clothes. The realities of life in the United States were explained to him by an apologetic officer: "We think maybe you shouldn't wear your uniform from here down into San Francisco. Feelings run pretty high."

This was understatement. Fred Platt was forced to fight his way through an antiwar rally in San Francisco to the persistent chant of "Baby killer." "I got back to the States," Mike Byers said, "and, holy shit, I'm one of the bad guys. It really amazed me. I'd been one of the good guys for quite a while—one of the *really* good guys—at least that's what everybody in the village at Long Tieng thought."

Bob Foster, who had returned to the States and retirement after a stint as air attaché to the U.S. embassy in Singapore, felt the country's mood was eloquently expressed by the fact that 20 percent of all active-duty enlisted men were so badly paid under the Carter administration that they qualified for food stamps. "There were a few people out there who really carried the burden—the guerrillas who fought alongside us, the Ravens, the Air America guys. And I felt very sorry for the younger people who fought a damn good battle and then came home and found they were not liked.

"And I got upset by the stories of psycho Vietnam veterans—a tiny percentage that got all the publicity. Most of the veterans were nice young men who got sold down the river by their own people. The poor guy who had to come back to the States to his wife and family, to find a job and make a new life, is the one who deserved the credit."

Bewildered servicemen faced similar experiences in all of the large cities, and from the student population—even the black draftees who had taken the places of more fortunate white contemporaries who had been granted a privileged exemption, or simply run away. But in small-town America, where the population did not have the connections, the cunning, the money, or the inclination to organize draft avoidance for their sons, or in the south, where military service was still considered a duty, men returning from the war were more kindly treated.

Too often it seemed as if the United States needed to punish those who had been involved in the only war it had ever lost. When Ambassador G. McMurtrie Godley returned, having been nominated for the post of assistant secretary of state for East Asian affairs, the Senate Foreign Relations Committee, at the bidding of its chairman, Senator J. W. Fulbright, rejected him. The reason given was that Godley had been "too closely associated with U.S. policies in Indochina," which he had pursued with "enthusiasm." Fulbright also tried to block William Sullivan's nomination as ambassador to the Philippines, but failed to win adequate committee support after some strenuous lobbying by Averell Harriman.

The rejection of Godley was unprecedented, the first time a career diplomat had ever been turned down for what was a routine appointment. No one questioned Godley's qualifications or competence, but tarred with the brush of U.S. defeat in Indochina, he became an ideal scapegoat.

But even a press that had wholeheartedly turned against the war felt the senator had gone too far. "To punish a career officer for faithfully executing unpopular policies established by higher authority, with which he may or may not agree, is a perversion of the 'advise and consent process,'" the New York Times stated in an editorial. The Washington Post agreed: "How could any ambassador to Laos fail to be 'intimately associated with Vietnam policy'? Should a diplomat whose competence is otherwise acknowledged be penalized because he was 'enthusiastic' about the policy he was obligated by his oath to carry out?" The editorial suggested Fulbright's spite was the result of personal bitterness, an example of McCarthyism through the looking glass.

But the knife was in, and no amount of press outrage could help Godley. His appointment was "indefinitely postponed." Newspapers in the Far East understood the significance of the action and what it heralded. "Study carefully the handwriting on the Senate wall," the *Bangkok Post* advised its readers. America was about to turn its back on Southeast Asia as if it had never existed.[3]

The Americans went home from Laos leaving behind them a paper agreement they called peace. But however unsatisfactory the terms, it was welcome after a quarter of a century of war. Despite immediate cease-fire violations by the Pathet Lao, the conflict was relatively minor and there was no full-scale resumption of hostilities for a time. Things returned to the placid political muddle that passed for normality in Laos.

It also seemed in the first moments of peace that the Meo had finally earned their rightful place in Lao society as a result of the war. They could no longer be ignored and looked down upon by the lowland Lao; they had proved their worth and would have to be treated as equals. The Meo now demanded to be known as Hmong. "We have made more progress in fourteen years of war than we have in fifty years of peace," said Dr. Yang Dao, the first of his people to earn a Ph.D. Even Gen. Vang Pao believed early in 1974 that an accommodation with the Pathet Lao was possible.[4]

At least the bombing had stopped—although such a massive tonnage had been dropped it was said that there was enough unexploded ordnance in northern Laos and on the Trail to fuel another war. In excess of 6,300,000 tons of bombs rained down on Indochina, more than all the explosives dropped in both the European and Pacific theaters in World War II. Less than a tenth (about 600,000 tons) of the total tonnage dropped in Southeast Asia fell on North Vietnam, and despite both press reports and USAF claims that the country had been devastated by the bombing, visiting journalists found Hanoi and Haiphong almost completely unscathed after the war, and the surrounding countryside barely touched. The bombing of North Vietnam was mostly concentrated around the area directly above the 17th parallel, where troops and supplies were massed to move south.[5] It is one of the supreme ironies of the war that it was South Vietnam, the allied country being defended, that bore the brunt of the U.S. bombing—a staggering 3,900,000 tons.

Laos took second place. More than 1,100,000 tons of bombs were dropped on the Ho Chi Minh Trail, with a further 500,000 tons in northern Laos (which means that a considerably greater tonnage was dropped on Laos than on Germany—which was devastated by 1,360,000 tons in World War II). The 1,600,000 tons of bombs dropped on Laos would have amounted to seventeen tons every square mile—had the tonnage been spread evenly across the country—or was equal to six-tenths of a ton of bombs for every man, woman, and child.[6]

Such figures are almost impossible to imagine and need to be put in perspective. The devastating cannonade fired by Napoleon's eighty-gun Grand Battery in the Battle of Waterloo would not have exceeded 20,000 *rounds*. The 21,000 tons of shells fired during the Battle of the Somme took 50,000 gunners, working around the clock, seven days to discharge.[7] A total of only 543 tons of explosives was dropped from the air by the British during the whole of World War I, while in World War II it was estimated that a British bomber would deliver 40 tons of bombs during its lifetime.[8] In the first Indochina war the French dropped only 834 tons of bombs during the whole of 1949—although this figure climbed to 12,800 tons during the last seven months of the war during the battle of Dien Bien Phu.[9] In the ten-year war the British waged in Malaya they dropped only 33,000 tons of bombs.[10] Even in the Korean War the United States dropped only 1,000,000 tons of bombs.[11]

There would be no more bombing, but the killing was to continue unabated. The peace agreement soon proved to be as illusory as the previous international arrangements made in regard to Laos, and the temporary lack of hostilities merely a respite before the final bloodbath. When U.S. reconnaissance flights over Laos—monitoring preparations for the Communist offensive—halted on June 4, 1974, the North Vietnamese enjoyed the unimpeded use of the Trail for the first time. Large numbers of their troops moved in and out of Laos at will. None of the landmarks called for in the peace protocol, to show the division of control between forces, had been put in place. Pathet Lao troops placed flags forward of their own positions along Route 7 on the PDJ, and when Vang Pao's soldiers removed them the Communists charged him with violating the cease-fire, but refused the International Commission for Supervision and Control permission to investigate. "War is difficult, peace is hell," Vang Pao concluded.

In Vientiane the Communists coiled themselves around the machinery of government in preparation for a takeover. They also made military preparations, in concert with the North Vietnamese, for the Communist conquest of Indochina. On March 27, 1975, after the NVA had launched their offensive in South Vietnam, the Pathet Lao attacked Vang Pao's forces. Prime Minister Souvanna Phouma ordered the general to defend himself as best he could, but refused to authorize air strikes against the enemy.

On May 9, the Pathet Lao openly declared their future intentions toward the Hmong for the first time when they published an article in their newspaper: it was necessary to exterminate the hill tribesmen "to the last root," and Vang Pao's Military Region II would be taken by force.[12] Without air support, U.S. advisers, or Thai reinforcements, Vang Pao was cornered at last. His ragtag children's army did not even have sufficient ammunition or supplies.

"I will never leave my people," the general declared as his advisers tried to persuade him to pull out. But as the enemy encircled Long Tieng, he finally agreed reluctantly to a CIA plan to extract him from the base with as many of his followers as a hastily put-together airlift could manage. After disastrous defeats in March and April of 1975, the general was forced to accept that further armed resistance was futile, and the CIA argued that he would be more effective as his people's leader in exile than as a martyr on the battlefield.

The task of organizing the airlift fell on Gen. Heinie Aderholt, the last remaining general officer in Southeast Asia. As it was not possible to use official Air Force assets, the general looked around him for old Air America–type pilots to undertake what would in effect be the last mission of the war. Almost everyone had gone home, and the single C-130 pilot left in Southeast Asia was on his way to Bangkok airport on the very morning the airlift was mooted. Aderholt sent an Air Commando aide to try to stop him. "The son of a bitch is about to leave the country and we need him to fly one mission," Aderholt said.

Matt Hoff was standing in line with his wife, about to check in his luggage for the flight home to Houston, when the breathless Air Commando found him. Hoff was eager to go home and was psychologically finished with the war. He was extremely reluctant to fly yet another mission, which struck him as unnatural and unlucky. But he was persuaded to telephone the general, who was a hard man to turn down.

"How much are you going to pay me?" Hoff growled.

"Hell, Matt, name your price. I don't really care. Make it good. It's the last one—the last U.S. mission of the war."

A fee of five thousand dollars was agreed upon, and Hoff loaded his bags into a taxi and drove back into Bangkok. Three former Air America pilots and a Continental Air Services captain were contacted in Vientiane, and the airlift was complete—Les Strouse and Al Rich would fly C-46 transports as backup to the C-130 in the refugee airlift, Dave Kouba would fly a STOL Pilatus Porter, and Jack "90" Knotts would fly a helicopter in the operation to extract Gen. Vang Pao.

The Porter and the helicopter left Vientiane to arrive in Long Tieng at 6:30 A.M. on the morning of May 14, 1975. "Long Tieng was a sea of refugees—thousands of them," Jack Knotts said. He set down his chopper by the unmanned tower and waited for Kouba, who parked his Porter on the ramp on the other side of the runway. Together the men went up to the old CAS operations shack, where they met Jerry "Hog" Daniels, Gen. Vang Pao's CIA case officer.

Daniels began to outline how he felt the evacuation should be handled, and also told them how Gen. Vang Pao was to be taken out. If Vang Pao was seen to leave from the airfield it would cause untold panic and anarchy among those who would be left behind; the general could not be accompanied by Daniels, either, for this too would arouse suspicions. The plan was for Vang Pao to be picked up by Knotts, once the refugees were being loaded into the transport planes, and taken to a nearby deserted strip. Knotts would then return for Daniels, fly back to the strip, pick up the general, and fly on to a third strip, where he would rendezvous with the Porter.

As the men discussed the details of the plan, Gen. Vang Pao entered the room. The men were silent for a moment, but the general ignored them and sat down without saying anything. He stared ahead of him, expressionless and without life. When the plan was explained to him he contributed nothing, merely nodding indifferently.

Jack Knotts returned to the strip and sat waiting in his chopper for the go-ahead. The C-130 came in and landed, and Matt Hoff waved to him from the cockpit. The C-46, flown by Les Strouse, followed close behind. Refugees swarmed the planes. "It was a chaotic scene, absolutely chaotic," Jack Knotts said. "The planes couldn't even taxi to the parking area. It was just a mass of thousands of Meo all fighting to get in." The transports were to fly half a dozen trips in and out of Long Tieng, fired at continuously by enemy on the surrounding ridgelines. Thousands of refugees, packed so tightly into the planes they had to stand, were flown to Nam Phang, a remote airstrip south of Udorn, Thailand.

To Knotts, sitting on the strip in the chopper, the wait seemed endless. Finally, he saw Jerry Daniels's Ford Bronco drive onto the ramp. The CIA man handed Knotts a slip of paper with the location and exact time of Vang Pao's pickup written on it. "Okay, Jack, off you go."

Knotts cranked up the helicopter, nervous that the Meo might mob him. He saw small groups of refugees eyeing the helicopter inquisitively, and he was worried that they might run toward it and hang on to the skids. But he lifted off without incident and headed out of the valley bowl, circling for twenty minutes in a diversion until it was time to rendezvous with Vang Pao. At 9:45 he set down by a small pond half a mile from the town. The general stood holding a reflecting silver signal panel, accompanied by only two bodyguards.

Once the chopper was on the ground, Vang Pao boarded, loading a large heavy machine gun that scarcely fitted into the cabin. The general said nothing as they flew to Site 103. He was clearly depressed but in control of his emotions. His lack of expression was unnerving. A family of Meo were crossing one end of the small dirt strip as the helicopter landed, and they respectfully gave the general the *wai*, the traditional greeting of hands clasped together as if in prayer.

Jack Knotts flew back to Long Tieng to pick up Jerry Daniels. He set down on a predetermined spot behind the king's house where the road widened. There was no sign of the CIA man, and Knotts waited anxiously. A group of Meo soldiers eyed him suspiciously as they trudged out of town. Eventually, Jerry Daniels turned the corner in the Bronco and drove toward the chopper.

Daniels walked unhurriedly to the rear of the vehicle and opened the back to take out a briefcase. Knotts wished he would move faster. Hog seemed to slump momentarily against the Bronco, leaning his head against it. Then he straightened himself and, with his back to the chopper, looked off into space and slowly raised his right hand in a final salute. The action brought a lump to Jack Knotts's throat: he was watching a man bid farewell to fifteen years of dangerous work which had turned to nothing. Daniels turned and walked briskly toward the helicopter and climbed in. He said nothing, as silent and expressionless as the general.

As the chopper eased off, Knotts saw two of the Meo soldiers take their M-16s from their shoulders and begin to raise them, drawing a bead on the slowly rising bird and preparing to fire. "Oh-oh, here it comes," Knotts thought.

But the men did not shoot, and Knotts flew without incident to Site 103. He picked up the general and his bodyguard and their ungainly weaponry, and flew on to the second strip, Site 113, coordinating the landing with Dave Kouba over the radio. Almost the moment he set down the Porter was raising dust at the far end of the strip.

His passengers jumped down without a word and walked toward the Porter, which was already turning. "There wasn't anything to be said. I was sad as hell, but occupied my mind by concentrating on accomplishing the mission in the correct manner. This was the end."

Jerry Daniels helped Vang Pao's bodyguards load the heavy machine gun into the Porter. The general seemed to hesitate for a moment before climbing into the plane. Then he jumped in and closed the door. The Porter was in the air within seconds.

It was an uneventful flight. As the Porter crossed the Mekong into Thailand, Gen. Vang Pao left his mountain kingdom behind him forever. He would never return to Laos again.[13]

With the infiltration of Communist cadres into all walks of Laotian life and their seizure of positions in the coalition government, Souvanna Phouma lost control and resigned as prime minister on November 28, 1975. The king was forced to abdicate—a terrible blow to the majority of Laotians, for whom he embodied the country's spiritual and temporal soul. The six-hundred-year-old system of village autonomy, which even the French had not tampered with, was abolished. Laos became a Communist state.[14]

The year's upheavals led to a massive exodus from the country that would eventually number more than 300,000.[15] Of those who chose to stay, at least twenty thousand "officials" were sent to remote jungle camps for "reeducation."[16] At the same time more and more Vietnamese moved into the sparsely populated regions of northern Laos (a form of colonization the Vietnamese have used many times as a prelude to actual annexation), while fifty thousand soldiers of the NVA remained scattered all over the country, which now became increasingly totalitarian.

Once the bases of Long Tieng and Sam Thong were finally overrun, following the flight of Vang Pao, approximately sixty thousand Hmong fled to the heights of Phu Bia massif, south of the Plain of Jars, where they established new mountaintop settlements fortified against attack. Another group headed south on a journey in which thousands died, but 25,000 survived to cross the Mekong into Thailand and begin the sad life of the refugee, confined to a camp that was to grow to the size of a city, surrounded by barbed wire.

Then in 1977 Phou Bia massif was besieged by Vietnamese troops and shelled by 130mm artillery. When the Vietnamese found themselves unable to penetrate the defenses from the ground, napalm, gas, and—possibly—poisons such as yellow rain (trichothecane mycotoxins) were dropped.[17] In the month of December 1977, one group of 2,500 Hmong refugees reached Thailand, the remnants of a band originally numbering eight thousand, culled by the rigors of the journey, which included capture or death at the hands of the Pathet Lao. By the end of 1979 the exodus reached its peak when three thousand Hmong were crossing into Thailand each month.

The fate of the Hmong is nothing less than tragic. The years of war, and the numerous dislocations throughout it, followed by an active policy of extermination and genocide by the new Communist government, have virtually destroyed them as a significant ethnic group in Laos. No one knows the precise number of Hmong who have died, but a figure around 100,000 is probable—an equivalent of 48,000,000 Americans killed, with most of the remaining U.S. population being forced to flee across the border to Mexico.[18]

Back in the United States, no one paid much attention to the fate of a scarcely known hill tribe in a distant country that had never succeeded in capturing the attention of the American public for long. Refugees brought news from Laos to the Ravens, who felt a profound sense of shame coupled with anger. "We packed our bags and went home," Greg Wilson said, "and for the next ten years we read stories about the people we fought *with*—not for—being massacred. And we weren't doing a damn thing about it.

"We gave them our word. I gave them my word. We betrayed them, and I felt betrayed too. Our government, our leaders, our country, said we had done this long enough—it's not working out. Let's just sell them out. And so we did.

"It made me a hell of a cynic. I was going to wrap up all of the DFCs, Purple Hearts, and Air Medals and mail them back to the Air Force and say, 'Keep these. People who lose a war should not be decorated for it.'"

"The Hmong believed that we would stay with them—go to the end with the last man," Frank Kricker said. "They figured if there was one Hmong left there would be an American there at his side. We really let them down—a low, awful thing."

"We turned them out like lambs to the slaughter," H. Ownby said. "It has cost us a lot since then. Nobody will trust us anymore. And rightfully so."

"We did our thing and went back to the States," Mike Byers said. "The Hmong had to stay and fight until they were dead. And that always bothered me. The U.S.A. abandoned them. Our politicians said, 'Nobody likes the war in Southeast Asia—and we want to get reelected. Okay, the war is over.' So fuck you, Hmong."

It was left to a tiny minority of individual Americans to continue active support for the abandoned peoples of the region. Larry "Pepsi" Ratts returned to Laos after the Communist government took over, supporting himself by running a combination travel agency and bicycle shop in Luang Prabang. He walked a fine line, careful not to provoke the new regime, while secretly running a one-man escape center for Hmong refugees and other Laotians destined for the reeducation camps. He remained until an American reporter, who was begged not to write of his activities, filed a story that ran in U.S. newspapers and triggered an expulsion order.

Once Jerry Daniels had resettled Gen. Vang Pao in Missoula, Montana, he too returned to work in Bangkok, Thailand, attached to the State Department's refugee program. His work earned him the department's Superior Honor Award. He continued his efforts until his death on April 29, 1982, when he was asphyxiated by gas from the extinguished pilot light of the bathroom water heater in his apartment. Conspiracy theorists linked Daniels's death to his supposed skepticism over reports of yellow-rain attacks on the Hmong, but there is no evidence to support the claim. Lengthy investigations in Thailand by journalists confirm he died as reported, possibly after an evening of drinking.[19]

Pop Buell also stayed in Laos until the last minute when the Rev. Luke Bouchard and other friends persuaded him to leave. He was flown out by Les Strouse of Continental Air Services on May 10, 1975, on the last Porter flight from Vientiane to Bangkok. Strouse dared not look at the old man or say anything, but stared straight ahead, certain that if he made eye contact he would break down. Pop set up base in a cramped one-and-a-half-room apartment in Bangkok, spending half of his meager pension to help refugees emigrate. "We didn't carry through, that's all," he said. "Had we won, it would have been one of the greatest things we ever accomplished against communism, but the way it panned out, it would've been a hell of a lot better if we'd never fired a shot."

He never returned to live in the United States. "We have got an obligation to these people," he said, meaning the U.S. government had an obligation. "There's no question we used them. How in the goddam hell can you use people and then one day tell them, 'Goodbye, it's been nice knowing you'? The least goddam thing somebody could do is to come back and say, 'I'm sorry.' "[20]

To those pilots still jagged from combat, the peacetime Air Force was not much of a place—an organization dominated by REMFs that seemed to offer a future only to those aspiring to be bureaucrats. "One day you were there in the jungle being shot at," Mike Cavanaugh said, "and the next you are in San Francisco being told to clean up your act by some REMF. It happened so quickly it was devastating."

Various promises had been made along the line, vaguely worded and ill-defined, that Ravens would be given choice assignments as a reward for volunteering for hazardous duty. The opposite was often the case. They were offered the backseats of fighters, a pilot slot in a transport, or worse, an office job.

"I ended up in a shitty job behind a desk," John Wisniewski said. "I was in the command post at Andrews Air Force Base answering the phone. I was totally disillusioned and depressed. It was the worst year of my life. I came to the conclusion that in peacetime the military really doesn't need people who are skilled in combat. They get in the way of a smooth operation."

Greg Wilson asked for a fighter assignment on his return. He was told over the phone by the officer in charge of military personnel control, "We're trying to purge the Vietnam FAC experience from the fighter corps because we have moved into an era of air combat where the low-threat, low-speed, close air support you did in Southeast Asia is no longer valid. And we don't want these habits or these memories in our fighter force."

Whatever the problems of adapting to the peacetime Air Force, they were nowhere near as complex as those of grappling with peace itself—settling back into civilian life. The difficulties almost always came as a surprise. "I just thought, I'm going to get out of the service, go back and pick up my life where I left off," Craig Morrison said, "and that everything was going to be great and I was going to jump right back into being a civilian."

But there was a recession, the airlines had a surfeit of pilots and were not hiring, so Ravens were forced to take any job they could.

Morrison went to work for Procter and Gamble, selling soap powder. "It was kind of tough, after being a Raven and flying in combat, to have to worry suddenly about how many feet of shelf space you had in the supermarket. Selling soap—the ultimate bad deal. It was awful. Really awful."

Worse still, everyone thought the returning Vietnam veteran should be happy to be back from the war. Morrison moved through his new life as if in a dream, disconnected from everyone around him. His wife was expecting a new baby and was anxious to forget about the war and move on. "I didn't know what the problem was—how could she know?" Morrison said. "She wanted to put it behind her, sweep it under the rug—just like the rest of the civilians. It didn't happen, did it? Now you're an executive like everybody else on the block."

He had bought a house in Terrace Park, a pleasant, unspectacular suburb of Cincinnati, and went to work every morning in a three-piece suit, carrying an attaché case. Sooner or later he would be promoted to vice-president of the department, join the local country club, and play golf on weekends. "I hated it. *Hated it!* I was going crazy."

It was a perplexing, muddled time. "I used to take these long walks in the summer in Cincinnati, where it is supposed to be hot and humid, but compared to Vietnam it was lovely. I would walk around this new neighborhood on my own trying to sort my feelings out about what was going on. Inside I was in turmoil. Essentially, it was a lonely time mixed with some anger. But the anger was not directed. I didn't know who the hell to get angry at. I was just generally pissed off."

Gerald Greven, the Raven whose conscience had been so troubled by the secret nature of the war, testified before a Senate committee on the secret bombing raids on Cambodia and the routine targeting of hospitals. As a prospective pilot on probation with an airline, his controversial stance led to his dismissal. Some of the Ravens objected to his action, feeling that he had betrayed their mission, while others—especially those who had known him in Laos—admired his stand.[21]

But in the end by far the largest group of Americans were neither for nor against the war in Vietnam, merely bored by it. "It was not that they didn't understand, it's that they weren't interested in understanding," Mike Cavanaugh said. "They were talking about their investments, their houses, and their kids, and nobody had a feel for it. I don't blame them. It was four minutes on the evening news. Americans like something to have a lot of pizzazz if it's going to keep them interested. If the ratings go down you are out of there. The ratings went down on the war—same old plot."

In Morrison's case there had been a brief report in the local paper when he had been awarded the Silver Star. "Most people I knew just ignored it," he said. "I got a letter from a retired colonel—'Well done, son'—which was nice. But a lot of people who saw it looked at me like I was an asshole. Most people just weren't interested. It wasn't going on in the streets of Cincinnati—it wasn't *their* war."

Suburban life seemed so unimportant. His wife would ask him about social plans for the weekend, and he was singularly unenthusiastic. "There were guys dying out there in the jungle—who gave a fuck where we went on Saturday night?"

Part of the problem was that the war was still going on when most of the Ravens returned home, and the lack of interest over its progress was crushing. At any party the Vietnam veteran was treated at best like a bore, and often avoided as possibly dangerous. The Ravens became defensive, aggressive, or humorless.

Ironically, the people who were most aware of what was happening in Vietnam were those most opposed to the men who fought the war. Unable to adjust to the world of detergent, Morrison went to work for Merrill Lynch as a stockbroker. As part of the training program he was sent to New York for three months, and for the first time public indifference was replaced by hostility. A great many young people lived in his building at 37th Street and Lexington Avenue, and late one night he was awakened and invited to party in a nearby apartment. A Canadian had gathered a group of antiwar people together for a discussion, and it was thought it would be interesting to bring in someone who had been in the military to broaden the argument.

"I was half asleep and thought I was going to a party, but when I walked through the door about fifteen of them jumped on my ass. The war was immoral—people should refuse to fight it. The military were killing innocent civilians—the usual line of shit everyone back from Vietnam got.

"I tried to tell them about Laos and about the Meo, but they were *absolutely* not interested in what I had to say. I was outnumbered, and every time I spoke somebody would scream, 'Bullshit!' They *knew* it was wrong—end of debate. After that I was shunned and referred to as 'the fascist down the hall.' "

* * *

The delayed effects of combat—recognized as a genuine psychological malady by the American Psychiatric Association in 1980, and dubbed post-traumatic stress disorder—are more subtle and less dramatic for the pilot than for the infantryman on the ground, but no less real. The stress of working long hours over hostile enemy territory waiting to be shot at, and the fear of being killed, all take their toll. But for the flyer the business of war is somewhat antiseptic and removed—"like stepping on ants" is how one Raven described it—although a difficult period of adjustment is inevitable for anyone returning from battle proper. The military did nothing to prepare its people for this, and an unsympathetic civilian population exacerbated the problem. In addition, the American corporate style of war was impersonal and demoralizing, with none of the supportive camaraderie of belonging to a regiment or squadron that traveled and fought together: a young American joined the unit in which he would serve his time in the war alone, was sent to Vietnam alone, and returned home alone.

Unprepared for the psychological aftermath of combat, Ravens dealt with problems as they came. Emotional numbness, nervousness, depression, insomnia, and difficulty with relationships overwhelmed many. Noises bothered them excessively. They woke up in the night for no reason, and everyone had dreams. "I had the same nightmare every night for years and years after I left," Tom Shera said. "I am flying along a road in Laos in an O-1 and all of a sudden I look up and there is nothing but high-tension and telephone wires above me. And yet there were no such wires in Laos. I must have had that dream a thousand times, and was having it at least once a week after I quit flying—up until five years ago. A real nightmare."

Sometimes the delayed reaction to an extended period exposed to combat was physical. Art Cornelius had been back from the war for only a week when he took his family to the Los Angeles County Fair. As they walked among the various outdoor stands a helicopter passed overhead. "The sound of a Huey is very similar to what you hear when you are taking heavy automatic-weapons fire—whop, whop, whop. That is how a 14.5 sounds through the open window of an O-1. This guy flew over, and I guess I thought I was being shot at. I acted nuts." In view of his family and the crowd around them, he began to pull into himself, desperately looking around for somewhere to dive under cover. His wife and children looked on helplessly, until one of them blurted, "What's going on with Dad?" It took Cornelius three years before he was entirely free of the anxiety of combat.

A problem that several Ravens took home with them was drink. In Laos it seemed the most natural thing in the world, after a day of combat, to unwind with a few stiff drinks. There was nothing else to do. The secret war was a world without women, family, outside interests, or even television, and the only diversions were two movies a week, a dart board, and cheap booze.

The extent of the problem ranged from those who looked on their drinking as little more than an expensive habit—"Surprisingly, what worried me most about having to adjust to a drinking problem when I left was whether I would be able to afford it," Chad Swedberg said—to chronic alcoholism. "Once I started drinking [at that time] I wouldn't stop until I passed out," one Raven said. "I was in conflict— part of me felt I should keep up the fight and go to Angola, and not be reading law books. The other side said it was clearly wrong to be an international outlaw, and I was just being macho. And it was a conflict I couldn't handle. I was in the pits when I got out of law school and would be in an alcoholic haze all weekend. An endless, meaningless groping around, trying to find something."

But mostly, the problem of readjustment was psychological. "The U.S.A. was like a foreign country to me," John Wisniewski said. "I was totally lost, I didn't know what the hell I was doing. I felt so different from everybody around me, in a different world. They had no idea what I was going through, and I didn't expect them to. I would talk with ordinary people who had stayed at home and feel I had nothing in common with any of them. So I was remote, didn't give a shit about anybody, and couldn't care less whether they loved or hated me. I just built a wall around myself."

Ignored or reviled by the general public, the men who returned from the war became excessively defensive, and this often expressed itself in exaggerated behavior and extremist views. They fed the popular image of the psycho Vietnam vet in order to anger and offend those who angered and offended them. "You played it to the hilt," Mike Byers said. "They expected you to be a napalm-dropping, baby-murdering, dope-smoking Vietnam veteran, so of course you had to do it. Fuck them if they couldn't take a joke."

Combat humor is callous and deliberately unfeeling, and does not translate into everyday life. Ravens burned plastic straws in bars, and looked dreamy when people complained, saying it reminded them of napalm on human flesh (in reality a gagging mixture of burned pork and gasoline). Air America chopper pilots told of dropping candy to children in villages and then banking sharply to cut the infants to ribbons with the aircraft's tail rotor. The stories were tasteless and obnoxious, and meant to be. They were also untrue, but it is a measure of the division among Americans at the time that noncombatants almost always believed them.

Fred Platt had a business card printed, the flip side of which carried the illiberal sentiment:

> The greatest happiness is to scatter your enemy and drive him before you, to see his cities reduced to ashes, to see those who love him shrouded in tears, and to gather to your bosom his wives and daughters.
>
> Genghis Khan 1226
> Fred Platt 1969

Platt enjoyed handing them out to people and waiting patiently for their reaction. (He did not know it, but the joke was on him: the Vietnamese are one of the few nations ever to defeat the Mongols on the field of battle, and routed Kublai Khan, the grandson of Genghis, in 1278.)

"If people asked what I thought of the war, I'd say I thought I had a damn good time," Platt said. Some people, on learning he had crashed eleven airplanes, argued that his good time had cost a great many dollars of American taxpayers' money. "To have a ready answer I looked up the figure going around which said the U.S. spent half a million to kill a single North Vietnamese. I was flying fifteen-thousand-dollar planes upgraded to forty thousand—so even if I had written off all eleven it would be less than half a million at the very outside." Platt enjoyed this argument and carefully led fellow drinkers and cost-conscious citizens in Texas bars into his trap. When they complained about his profligate use of tax money to subsidize his fun, he would trot out the figures. "You bastards owe me a couple of billion dollars," he would conclude triumphantly, banging his fist on the bar. "And I want my fucking money!"

Fred Platt had paid a higher price in the war than could be accounted for in tax dollars. After leaving Udorn he had bought a round-the-world ticket on Pan Am and returned to the States via Katmandu, Penang, and Hong Kong. He had been on a heavy dosage of morphine in pill and injection form in the Air Force hospital, but on the journey home attempted to endure the constant pain without narcotics. "I could stand it because I really believed I was going to heal."

On his return to the States he slowly began to regain the use of his legs and felt progress was being made, despite nonstop pain. A drug had been introduced onto the market called Talwin, a synthetic morphine touted as a nonaddictive painkiller. He was given a phial of tablets and told to use them when the pain became unbearable.

He was at home, lying on the couch watching television, when he first felt the need to take one of the tablets. He was surrounded by war mementos, including enemy weapons and a collection of hats he had placed on wig stands on top of the bookshelf. One had belonged to a Chinese artillery officer working on the Chinese road in Laos, another to a North Vietnamese engineering officer stationed on the Ho Chi Minh Trail, one to a Pathet Lao tank driver, and another to a NVA infantry captain—souvenir booty from men killed in battle.

As he lay on the couch, he began to feel horribly uncomfortable. The television blurred and the voices of the people on the screen became distorted and unintelligible—it was as if they were talking Vietnamese. The wooden wig stands with the enemy caps on them became human forms and began to talk. When arms sprouted from the babbling faces and reached to grab him, Platt rose from the couch, grabbed a loaded 9mm pistol, and emptied a full clip at the figures on the bookshelf. The wig stands splintered, the hats flew off and fell to the ground, and the enemy retreated. Platt fell back onto the couch exhausted.

He had suffered an extreme hallucinogenic reaction to the drug, a side effect he had not been warned about. The following morning, when he saw what he had done, he threw the remaining tablets away and decided to face the pain without them.

Although he was not fit to fly, either physically or psychologically, he managed to outrun his own records and confuse the authorities sufficiently to be put back on flying status. Incredibly, he managed to bluff his way through an Air Force physical. But after initial improvement, he was regressing and beginning to stiffen. It was necessary for airmen to lift him in and out of the cockpit of the T-33 jet trainer he was flying on the Inspector General team. The procedure was witnessed one morning by the surgeon general of the Military Airlift Command. Waiting on the run-up pad, the general watched speechless as a pilot was carried to a plane and lifted into the cockpit. As a result there was an investigation into Platt's records, which revealed he should have been under permanent medical supervision. "They put me back into the medical system, and I never got out."

He was readmitted to hospital, where it was noted on his admission record that he was allergic to Talwin. In an attempt to relax the severe muscle spasms he was experiencing he was put on a daily dosage of eighty milligrams of Valium. Despite this high dose, and perhaps as a result of a combination of drugs, Platt became manic. He thrashed about in his bed and raved. Hospital staff strapped him down and gave him a shot—a large dose of Talwin.

He does not remember much about the next twenty-one days. Throughout this time he remained strapped to the bed, and was injected with Talwin every eight hours. He experienced occasional semilucid moments and remembers one incident when the chief of the orthopedic service stood at the foot of the bed, surrounded by interns and nurses, and discussed his condition in the third person: it was Udorn Air Force hospital all over again. "I tried to join in the conversation, but they wouldn't listen. Maybe I was babbling through the drug. To get their attention I grabbed the full bedpan from the bed next to me and covered them with it."

He was strapped to a litter and medevaced to Wilford Hall Air Force Hospital in San Antonio, where he was left lying in a corridor for three hours. The neglect proved beneficial—no one administered any Talwin, so the effects of the drug began to diminish. Strapped to the litter, abandoned in the receiving hall but increasingly lucid, he stopped anyone who would listen to him. "What am I doing here? Please tell me where I'm at."

He was moved to a ward. "Am I in the loony ward?"

"No, you're in the neurosurgery ward," a doctor told him. "We need to check you out and see what's wrong. We think it's an organic problem, but we don't know what to do about it yet." The doctor examined the chart. "It says here that you're allergic to Talwin."

"Yeah. I get an extreme hallucinogenic reaction to it."

The doctor nodded, and it was only later that Platt discovered he had been regularly injected with the drug. He was taken off all medication for three days. "Can you unstrap me?" Platt asked.

The doctor ordered the restraints to be removed, and after three days Platt was transferred to a new ward. Built to accommodate eight patients, it was jammed with a dozen and the beds almost touched one another. He was bitter that all the single or double rooms in the hospital seemed to be filled with colonels' wives with headaches, while combat cases were crowded together.

"The guy whose bed was directly across from me was a sergeant who was an Indian. He had brain cancer, and rather than let the poor sucker die they had scooped out half his brain so that there was this big concave dish beneath the skin of his skull. He sat there and screamed unintelligible things in some Indian language, and had no control of his body so he peed in the air and lay in his own shit. I was surrounded by people who were vegetables, except they were in extreme distress."

He stayed in the ward for three months. His original X-rays had been mislaid, and new ones failed to reveal the hairline fractures along his spine. "My basic problem was Catch-22. They knew something was wrong but they couldn't find what it was. If they can't find out what it is there is nothing wrong. If there's nothing wrong he must be faking it. So they sent me to the shrinks."

An Air Force psychiatrist at Brook's School of Aerospace Medicine, San Antonio, put him through a series of psychological tests. He asked Platt to talk about his experiences in Laos and listened attentively. He gave him paints and canvas and asked him to express himself visually. Platt daubed pictures of O-1s suspended over burning jungle.

Being attached to the Air Force, the doctor knew the type—bright, egocentric, highly motivated and opinionated, hostile to authority and individualistic to a troublesome degree: fighter-pilot material. He testified before the Air Force medical review board at the hospital that Platt was "as sane as any fighter pilot." When asked to be more specific he said, "I would classify him as 'eccentric.' "

The pain did not go away. Platt would continue to be in and out of hospital for years, although his experience with the Air Force and Veterans Administration medical programs made him opt for expensive private care. "It was a horror show. I came out hating Wilford Hall so bad that for the next five years my palms would sweat when I drove past it on the highway to San Antonio."

He has been in varying degrees of pain every day since January 12, 1970. He wore a neck and back brace for five years until in 1975 the trainer of the Houston Oiler football team designed a special exercise program, using the team's facilities for five days a week, and eventually he was able to put the braces aside for lengthy periods. In 1977 he began to use a transcutaneous electrical nerve stimulator, a type of external spinal pacemaker (a device that masks an unbearable pain with a controlled pain by shooting electrical impulses into the painful area to overload the nerve stimuli and circuits to the brain). Some days are worse than others. Platt is never heard to complain, although close friends can tell when the pain is bad, but he bears it with stoicism and a supply of Royal Ages, his favorite Scotch.

In the bars around Houston, Platt likes to joke about being certified "eccentric" and to tell people that he had a "damn fine time" in the war, but he does not mention the sixteen years of pain with no remission in sight. Could it possibly be worth the price he paid? It is not as easy a question as it sounds, and one he finds very difficult to answer directly.

"I never expected to come back until the war was over. And I expected that to mean we won. We chickened out, we lost the war. So in a sense I was short-changed. In addition, I fully accepted that if the war went on too long, something was going to kill me. Being injured and coming home crippled was never an alternative that entered my mind. I thought it would be black and white—I forgot about gray.

"And if I could do it all over again? I would do it all again except for the last flight." It is only a part answer, but the evasion comes out of the genuine difficulty Platt has in deciding for himself whether he would trade in his year in Laos for his health. To an outsider this seems extraordinary, but it gives an idea of the intensity of the Raven experience. "It's hard to say. I've had sixteen years now to learn to live with the pain. And to accept the fact I'm medically unfit and can't get a license to fly. I've also accepted that I can't jump in parachutes. Getting on a horse to ride one hundred feet is so painful I've only put myself through it once. I can't ride motorcycles. A lot of the things I like to do I can't do.

"Would I trade that experience to be able to have all the other experiences? It's a tough question for me to answer, because I was very much committed to what I did. Give me the infirmities . . . but let me have one more year there, maybe two. I think the answer is—I wish we had won."

Today some 52,000 Hmong are in refugee camps in Thailand, the majority living in Ban Vinai, a tantalizingly short distance from the Mekong and the border with Laos. Groups of young guerrillas periodically cross the river to continue waging the hopeless battle against an enemy that is strong and settled, and backed by the might of the Soviet Union. For some, even life in the refugee camp is to be envied. Before dawn on Sunday morning, March 15, 1987, Thai security forces raided the Ban Vinai refugee camp detaining "illegal" Hmong, who were then forcibly repatriated to Laos. Yang Tong Khai, who had fought for Gen. Vang Pao in the war and as an anti-communist guerrilla since, told a reporter, "If they send me back, I am dead."[22]

Many thousands of Hmong have begun new lives in strange lands. Two thousand are scattered throughout Canada, Australia, Argentina, and French Guyana; six thousand are in France; the largest number, over fifty thousand, are in the United States. Those who arrived in America came without either practical or psychological preparation. A people who had always farmed with hand tools, who still maintained a belief in the presence of spirits in all things, and who had developed a written language only in recent memory, some of the Hmong brought hoes and crossbows with them. American city dwellers were alarmed to see orientals with crossbows trudging through the mean streets, hunting pigeons for their supper.

The complexity of the new life has been daunting. In the mountains of Laos a generation of Hmong endured almost perpetual war, but rules and regulations were at a minimum, the land was free, they paid no taxes, and there was virtually no crime. Each of the twenty-four Hmong clans enjoyed a strong social structure, and it was a point of honor that no one was without work or a place to live. No Hmong ever begged. Life was simple despite the war.

In America they hoped to live together, but the authorities had other ideas. The Hmong—most of whom had never visited a real town, let alone a modern city—were scattered throughout the United States and dumped into some of the country's toughest urban neighborhoods. "They were spread like a thin layer of butter throughout the country so they'd disappear," an officer for Refugee Resettlement said.

They traded their mountain villages for yet another war zone, the stark landscape of America's urban poor: ramshackle tenements, potholed streets littered with stripped automobiles, burned-out buildings. "It was a kind of hell they landed into," Eugene Douglas, the president's special ambassador to the refugees, said. "Really, it couldn't have been done much worse."

For the Hmong, ignorant of modern technology, city life, or even the language, the battle with the problems of daily existence replaced the war. A number of new Hmong proverbs came into being, one of which is "If you think it's easy, you don't know America."

They are not adapting well, and federal officials who work with the Hmong say no other group of refugees has had more difficulty. Since they are isolated from their clan and its leaders, cut off from cultural and spiritual traditions, this is no surprise. One official described them as "emerging from the mists of time," adding, "Whether they make it or not is anybody's guess."

Their exile has also given them new songs, a favorite of which is the bittersweet "Remember Long Tieng." Phang Vang, a former lieutenant in Gen. Vang Pao's Backseater Corps, walked hundreds of miles to cross the Mekong, braving Communist bullets and famine on the way. He was the first Hmong to be settled in Providence, Rhode Island—where the Hmong community now numbers some 2,500. When he saw snow for the first time, he thought with dread of his grandfather's warning "Snow means death." He was too frightened at first to leave his apartment, a bare third-floor walk-up without heating, hot water, or furniture, and was almost as scared to remain indoors, where he could not understand the incomprehensible, ominous banging of radiator pipes he mistook for evil spirits —bad *phi*. "Nobody knows inside our hearts and minds how much we hurt."

Teng Thao, a Backseater who flew fifteen hundred missions with Ravens during the war, found himself being dunned for bills he could not pay. "I have never been so frightened." Moua Tong, who joined Gen. Vang Pao's forces in 1970 at the age of fifteen, finally fled the country on foot in 1976. After years in a refugee camp he was resettled in West Philadelphia: "I was so unhappy, so afraid in the city. I never knew how to do things, where to go. The people don't seem nice. I was so worried that all of America was like this." Maj. Wang Seng Khan, a former battalion commander now living in Providence, is forced to rely on his wife's earnings and on his children to translate English for him. "We have become children in this country."

But many Hmong have managed to regroup, sometimes traveling thousands of miles to join with clan members. There are more than 10,000 in St. Paul, Minnesota, and another 27,000 scattered throughout California, with increasing numbers finding their way to the rural Central Valley area.

"For many years, right from the start, I tell the American government that we need a little bit of land where we can grow vegetables and build houses, like in Laos," Gen. Vang Pao said. "I tell them it does not have to be the best land where we can live . . . maybe like your Indians."

Instead of being given a piece of land to work, the Hmong have been given welfare—another baffling part of their new life. Many have become victims of the welfare trap—discovering they receive more money for not working, often receiving twice as much as they could earn at a minimum-wage job. Those who took up farm work found they lost their welfare checks if they worked more than a hundred hours a month, however little money they earned. This means that any Hmong working the land—which is what most of them do best—automatically loses his welfare payment, his principal source of income.

"All this money," Vang Pao says of the welfare payments made to his people, "this could buy us the land. Now it is just wasted—it gives us bad morale. Give us money for the land and in three years the Hmong will be off welfare."

They have also become the easy victims of crime, a bewildering experience they find difficult to understand. Their apartments have been burgled and their cars stolen, and Hmong children are often beaten on their way home from school. They do not go to the police because they think of themselves as "guests" in America.[23]

Arrests of the Hmong for crime are almost nonexistent, but the exceptions have been harrowing. Theng Pao Yang settled with his wife and children in a small bungalow provided as a temporary home by members of the First Baptist Church of Fairfield, Iowa, a small community that went out of its way to be friendly and helpful to the bewildered refugees. But Theng Pao was miserable and homesick, and often sobbed.

Volunteer church workers tried to comfort the Yangs, but could not hope to reach the core of such a deeply felt misery. People dropped in on them all the time to try and cheer them up. One day in January 1980 one of the members of the Baptist congregation drove over to the Yangs' bungalow to drop off a load of laundry his wife had washed for the family.

When he entered the house he found Yi Li, the wife, hysterical. Theng Pao and his six-year-old daughter, Bay, were suffering from serious injuries and groaning in the bathroom. Lying on the living-room sofa was the eight-year-old son, So, and he was dead. At first it was unclear what had happened, but later Yi Li took the Baptist visitor's wife into the basement of the bungalow. The paraphernalia of some sort of ritual was littered about the floor, including a shattered Hmong flute, a knife with a broken blade, and five one-dollar bills that had been shredded with scissors. Hanging from a pipe were six nooses.

The Yangs had attempted a family suicide. The parents had intended to hang the children too young to hang themselves, and then put their own heads in the noose. At the last minute Yi Li had changed her mind and cut everyone down, but it had been too late to save So. Theng Pao's reasons for his actions were contradictory and bordered on the hallucinogenic: his dead sister had asked him to join her; Jesus had given him orders; one of his children had broken the church tape recorder and they were afraid they would no longer be loved by their patrons; a death threat had been delivered from other refugees belonging to the lowland Lao.

The county attorney did not know what to believe, or whether Theng Pao and Yi Li should be prosecuted at all—the irony of a felony conviction being that it would bring automatic deportation. In the course of his investigation he studied a paper by a psychologist on "trauma syndrome," which cited cases of stress suffered by refugees throughout the world. The county attorney emphasized this in his presentation of the case to the grand jury, which returned no indictment. The Yangs were resettled with other Hmong elsewhere in the state.

A number of down-to-earth citizens of Fairfield, Iowa, understandably thought the Yangs got off lightly, and wondered what might have happened had it been an American couple who had attempted to hang their children. "Trauma syndrome" sounded too big-city slick for some, who felt that merely giving a fancy title to an unfathomable act did not adequately explain the motivation of a man who set about the calculated killing of his children.[24]

But there is evidence of other, equally mysterious deaths throughout the Hmong refugee community in America. Thirty-four of them have died from unknown causes in recent years, mostly in their sleep. Each case defies western logic, and has left doctors, psychologists, and police investigators baffled. The federal Centers for Disease Control, responsible for investigating such deaths, say they have not ruled out "emotional triggers" caused by stress, and it has been suggested that the unfortunate Hmong have succumbed to severe cultural shock, an extreme form of the psychologist's "trauma syndrome." Which is all to say, no one knows why the Hmong are dying.

As animists, the Hmong—who believe everything contains a spirit—were connected to their mountain world by a thousand invisible threads, and followed an elaborate calendar of ritual to propitiate the spirits. Daily reality edged into dream. But how to propitiate the alien spirits of modern America?

Who can imagine how painful, disturbing, and unhappy are the dreams of the Hmong, confounded and made miserable by daily life? In the Far East, death from nightmare is known and accepted (the Filipinos even have a word for it: *bangungot*). Perhaps some of the Hmong suffer from a homesickness so profound, generated by living in a modern world to which they are unable to adapt, that in the lonely and desolate small hours before dawn dream and reality merge to overwhelm the spirit. In a simpler age it would have been said that the Hmong are dying of a broken heart.

As time has passed the Ravens have adjusted to life back in the United States. Many decided to stay in the Air Force, with varying degrees of success: several retired as majors—fighter pilots defeated by paperwork—but a good number are now reaching the rank of full colonel, while Tom Richards—the Steve Canyon look-alike—has gone to the very top of his profession and is a four-star general.[25]

A good number of ex-Ravens fly for the airlines; others fly in small bush outfits or pilot private jets. Most have worked out the early problems and let go of their initial bitterness. But sparks can still fly, especially, it seems, when veterans meet up with antiwar protesters at high school reunions.

Karl Polifka went to his twenty-fifth high school reunion in Hawaii, fifteen years after the war, when he met up again with a classmate who had been an active antiwar protester. The woman remarked how strange it was that they had taken such different paths—Polifka had gone to Southeast Asia and the war, and she had stayed at home to protest it. "But all is forgiven and forgotten."

Polifka remembered the comrades who had died, and the Hmong who had been destroyed as a people and who had lost their country. "Don't ever make that mistake again," he said harshly. "It is certainly not forgiven and will never be forgotten."

The Ravens who died in Laos are not forgotten. But as their deaths were classified and went unremarked, it fell to colleagues who served beside them to honor their memory and keep it alive. Refused permission to travel back to the United States with his friend Chuck Engle's body, Craig Duehring made a special journey to Lynn, Indiana, Engle's hometown. "The grave was well tended," Duehring said. "I have visited it twice now and will go again whenever I travel the east-west interstate."

Christmas is the worst time of all for the survivors of the Ravens who were in Laos at the very end of the war. Three Ravens were killed over the Christmas period in 1972 just before the end of the war, and those who had been kept in Southeast Asia held the first annual "Dead Raven Drunk" at the Udorn O club the following year. "Since then I do it every year," H. Ownby said. "I had known Hal for a year over in Laos. I had roomed next to Skip at the Academy, and we were both involved in the boxing program. Tom Carroll left a wife and two little boys, Skip Jackson a widowed mother, Hal Mischler's folks were Kansas farm people. Tom's wife didn't want to talk to anybody after the war, she was just mad at the world. Christmas is a very melancholy time for me."

Just before Christmas, on December 23 every year, Jack Shaw and Lew Hatch get drunk on Johnnie Walker Black Label and remember Hal Mischler. They get drunk over the telephone if they are unable to meet in person. When Shaw returned from the war he flew to Upton, Kansas, to see his friend's parents. They had been told of their son's death on Christmas Eve, and in a macabre coincidence Hal's belongings, which had been shipped home a month earlier, arrived by truck thirty minutes later. The combination made the news more terrible still.

Shaw visited Hal's grave and stayed with his parents for three days. "His mom was a big old farm lady, and his dad was this little old wispy guy. Hal was their only son. They were devastated." The couple adopted Shaw as their own, and still send him boxes of homemade candy and fudge on his birthday and at Christmas. When he left at the end of his first visit, Hal's father presented him with his son's boyhood .22 rifle. "Hal's old rabbit gun—he don't need it anymore."

Ron Rinehart had been back in the States for three years and gone into the U-2 program, where the camaraderie among the pilots was equal to that among the Ravens. He had put the war behind him and was at home in Tucson, Arizona, when he received a telephone call at 8:00 in the evening from an officer with Graves Registration at the Pentagon. He said that the MIA status of Cookie 2, the F-105 Thud pilot who had crashed into the mountain back in 1969, remained unresolved. The wife and father of the pilot would like to talk to the FAC who directed him, the officer said, if it would not make Rinehart uncomfortable.

Papa Fox understood that the family wanted more than the government version of events and needed to speak to someone who had seen it happen. He called them immediately and described the terrain in Laos and what he remembered of the mission. The pilot's father and wife listened in silence as Papa Fox spoke. Finally the pilot's father asked if Papa Fox was 100 percent sure that his son was dead.

"Personally, I think he went in with the airplane and there is no way that he is alive today. I watched it happen."

There was a moment's silence on the end of the line. "Thank you very much," the father said. "It takes a burden off my mind."

Papa Fox put the phone down. He had been out of the war for four years, but the brief call had taken him back. "It really hit me. It was a little bit moving. It takes you right down in that low area—the feeling in the stomach area." For a moment he felt like having a damn good cry, but poured himself a large drink instead and toasted the Thud jock he never knew, who had gone to his death in the secret war the United States had lost in Laos.

Epilogue

REUNION

> Here's to us.
> Who's like us?
> Damned few—
> And they're all dead.
>
> —Toast of the Highland regiments

It is Saturday night and there is a formal dining-in at the officers' club at Randolph Air Force Base outside San Antonio, Texas. An honor guard of Air Force military police in highly polished boots, gleaming helmets, and white gloves and puttees present arms as senior officers in dress uniforms emerge from a line of staff cars. They salute smartly and enter the club. Inside, the atmosphere is subdued, as groups of bemedaled men make polite, almost hushed small talk, and club servants move deferentially among them with trays of drinks. Later there will be an elaborate dinner with speeches by generals, and loyal toasts to the president and the flag—this is the United States Air Force at its most formal and self-satisfied.

On the same night as the dining-in, the club is also host to the annual Raven reunion—possibly the USAF at its most informal. Before the officers retire to the main dining room, and the Ravens plunge down into their subterranean bunker known fondly as the Augur (sic) Inn, there is a brief mingling of the two groups. The result is a scene which might have been taken from a Marx Brothers' movie.

The Ravens are not in dress uniforms but sport irreverent party suits made up by the Sikh tailor Amarjit in Udorn, Thailand. These are based on the standard flight suit but come in a variety of colors, from jet black through jungle green to powder blue. They are embroidered with an array of fighter squadron patches from Vietnam and the peacetime Air Force. These make many of the party suits look like quilts, and each one follows its own pattern, but all include "Yankee Air Pirate," "Air Commando," and, of course, "Raven," whose patch consists of the bird perched on a bleeding skull, against a background of the legend "Nevermore," although another version is a drunk raven collapsed in a martini glass. Some of the Ravens have the word "Mister," stitched in a delicate shade of pink, in place of an officer's shoulder bars.

There are those among the group in dress uniform who smile indulgently at the presence of the Ravens—old fighter pilots, mostly, who had been stationed in Thailand or Vietnam—but there are also those who are not at all amused. The latter glower at the ragged, semi-intoxicated rabble that have infiltrated their ranks. They clutch their glasses defensively, set their lips in a line, and adopt a ramrod-rigid posture as they stare fixedly into the middle distance.

To make matters worse, some of the Ravens could be fairly described as of a nonmilitary demeanor—or even as dressed for Halloween. Greg Wilson, known as "the Growth," a musclebound figure almost bursting out of his party suit, sports a waxed handlebar mustache and shining shaved head; J. Fred Guffin wears a solid gold bracelet weighing three pounds, each individual link of which is the size of a half dollar; Jack Shaw is wearing a Zorro hat and cape, while Ed Gunter sports a gorilla mask. H. Ownby is mincing through the room in a woman's wig, and Col. Mike Cavanaugh, a popular and well-known figure from his time as protocol officer at Randolph, lies on the floor in a state of advanced inebriation, hands folded over his chest clasping a lily.

The Air Force certified eccentric, Fred Platt, is leaning on a silver-topped cane and chewing on a cigar, the bands of which have his name printed on them. His party suit has "Magnet Ass" printed across the top right-hand pocket and a portrait of Mao Zedong stitched into its seat. He has a thick black beard, and around his neck hangs a jade Buddha in a silver setting, alongside the Star of David. Before he moves on to chat to another group he hands out his Genghis Khan visiting cards. One of the officers looks at it—"Capt. Fred Platt, Legend Lane, Houston, Texas"—and mutters to a companion, "Either that's the *oldest* captain in the Air Force, or with that beard he's a goddam *sea* captain!"

As the dining-in is announced and the officers begin to file into dinner, leaving the ragtag collection of strangely dressed mavericks behind them, one colonel cannot contain himself. "Good God," he explodes, "are these men really officers in the United States Air Force?"

"Ravens," an old fighter pilot says with a grin, as if that were explanation enough.

The Raven reunion is held every year in mid-October, when varying numbers of Ravens, under the auspices of the Edgar Allan Poe Literary Society, turn up at the Carriage Inn outside of San Antonio for a get-together. "War," jokes Fred Platt, "is the only adult activity which spawns alumni associations." The motel is a modest, no-frills establishment backing onto the Santa Fe railroad, along which mile-long freight trains rattle and strain throughout the night. But the place is opposite Randolph Air Force Base, and the management is tolerant, blocking off a wing of rooms for its rowdy guests each year.

On Friday afternoon the first Ravens begin to arrive—in campers, pickup trucks, personal and rented cars, and taxis from the airport. They not only come from all over the United States, but from as far afield as Korea, Hawaii, Great Britain, West Germany, and Saudi Arabia. There is no bar at the Carriage Inn, so the Ravens wander in and out of each other's rooms and congregate in the motel parking lot, where they pop the tops off cans of beer from an endless supply of six-packs. The empties are crushed underfoot and tossed into a corner, and by the end of the weekend will form a mountain. "We thought of staying in a nice hotel somewhere," Craig Morrison said. "Then we thought, perhaps not."

It is chic among the Ravens to arrive in a T-shirt expressing some sentiment designed to outrage or depress the civilian population. One wears a shirt with the picture of a T-28 in a dive with its guns blazing, and the logo "Fly the Friendly Skies of Laos"; others say things like "Shot at and Missed—Shit at and Hit" or "Fuck You, the Horse You Rode In on, and the Colonel Who Sent You."

Many of the Ravens make extraordinary efforts to return to the reunion each year. "It's important to get the batteries recharged and wipe the bullshit off the windscreen," Greg Wilson said. As they gather, the simple act of getting together generates an atmosphere of extraordinary energy and camaraderie that is affecting even to outsiders. The hallmarks of every reunion are noise, bad behavior, and alcoholic acrobatics, yet behind the sophomoric high spirits, the fraternity food fights, and obligatory rowdiness, there is a genuine bond that is very real and very deep. The Raven reunion is not just some Top Gun club or fellowship of the Right Stuff, but a gathering of men who went through a tragedy together and emerged forever changed.

Ravens who never encountered one another in the war meet at reunion for the first time and form lifelong friendships, made possible by a shared experience known only to the few. "It's a pleasant memory of good guys who were not afraid," Frank Kricker said. The reunions are festive weekends when the Ravens are able to relive the intensity of their time in Laos. "The other eleven months of the year you go out and deal with all the assholes and REMFs and all that sort of shit," John Wisniewski explained, "and once a year you get back."

The Ravens have been holding reunions since 1972, when there were still FACs on active duty in Laos. "They came in and hadn't seen each other for a long time," Bob Foster said. "They actually went up to one another and started touching each other—the face, the hair. Like a mother seeing her firstborn child. It was really something to see—very moving."

The reunions have since settled into an annual ritual. Friday evening, throughout which the Ravens continue to flock, is spent at the O club disco. On Saturday morning there is a late hungover brunch at Leon's Mexican Restaurant, across the road from the Carriage Inn. It is Mike Cavanaugh's life's ambition to be the last surviving Raven, and to brunch alone on *huevos rancheros* in melancholy triumph.

After brunch and beer, the Ravens make their way to a room in the O club for their annual business meeting. For years the Ravens—who in Texas are obliged to operate under the name of the Edgar Allan Poe Literary Society, the state's founder, Sam Houston, having monopolized his nickname of Raven—have raised and contributed significant sums of money for a refugee fund, which helps Hmong families settle in the States, or buys food and medicine for the refugee camp of Ban Vinai in Thailand.

The greatest success story is the help given to one family that settled in Atlanta, Georgia. The husband had been sent to a reeducation camp by the Communist regime and never returned, so the family swam the Mekong, pushing their belongings before them on homemade rafts. Unable to speak English, the mother brought her daughter and two sons to the United States, where the boys found jobs as bricklayer's assistants. In less than two years the family has been able to put down the deposit and take up a mortgage on a sixty-thousand-dollar house. Several Ravens have lent houses to Hmong families, and all have offered to act as sponsors, although the proud Hmong prefer to sponsor their own.

Various points of order are discussed at the business meeting, such as the yearly attempt to preserve a bottle of *lau lao* in a teak box as the

Last Man Bottle (presumably to be enjoyed by Cavanaugh with his *huevos rancheros*). Somehow, at some time during each reunion someone manages to drink at least half of the bottle. Each year efforts are made to obtain a new bottle of *lau lao* to put back in the box.

There are a number of Ravens who do not like to attend the reunions. They find the spectacle of men fast approaching middle age behaving like young combat fighter pilots fatuous. There is also a generation gap—the last Ravens were in Laos eight years after the first—and a cultural gap—the soldier-of-fortune faction tends to dominate and outnumber the blue-suit brigade. (Perhaps the true decadence of the Ravens can be dated from the arrival in Laos of Fred Platt, a personality who automatically leaned toward the CIA and away from the Air Force hierarchy, and who adopted the sartorial affectations of Air America.) "You can't please everyone," Craig Morrison said philosophically. "No rank is recognized at any reunion. And no Raven has ever allowed another to finish a sentence or take himself too seriously."

The Raven banquet is held on Saturday night. Three long tables are set for dinner and grouped facing a podium upon which stands a raven perched upon a skull, the flag of the Royal Lao Government, an American Legion memorial flag, and other memorabilia. To the left of the podium a makeshift stone fireplace has been constructed. Carafes of wine and bottles of White Horse whisky are dotted along each of the tables.

The Ravens begin to drift in to their banquet and stand at the bar where Moss, a black mess sergeant dressed in a Raven T-shirt, will serve drinks to the early hours of the morning. When the group is complete the barman begins to open bottles of champagne, and each Raven takes a glass for the memorial toast. The room falls silent. "We're all thinking the same thoughts but we don't say it," Jack Shaw said. "The toast is a tender moment."

In earlier reunions individual Ravens toasted personal friends killed in action, but this cast such a maudlin pall over the group that the mood was difficult to shake. Then at one reunion a poem was shoved into Craig Morrison's hand, and it has become a ritual ever since to read it in memory of the Ravens who never returned. The poem was written by Art Cornelius after the death of his friend Sam Deichelman. Unashamedly emotional, and written immediately after the loss, the knowledge that it is not the work of a poet but the heartfelt tribute of a warrior to a fallen comrade gives its words a poignant authenticity:

In my memory I carry
The twinkle of your eye, the delight of your laugh,
And the courage that was life, as we expected every day to die.
The red mud stuck
To our boots and tires, the dust to our bodies,
And silver wraiths of mist swirled over and around,
Green mountains.
Smaller men stood taller and larger than our size,
But you towered over us all, your grin, your tears,
Every orphan was your child, every life a part of yours.
When Chou held on to the thread of his life,
You'd have bled for him, breathed for him,
You'd have given your life for him, if you could.
We lived each day in fire and air,
And every dawn life's croupier spun the wheel again,
And I'd have been a better friend, but I trusted time.
There never was a man more strong, more peaceful,
More fierce, more fair,
And we were all proud to love you.
Perhaps one day when the fire is out,
Green mountains will show a flash of gold,
I'll see the twinkle of your eye
And smile again

The Ravens listen to the poem staring directly in front of them with unfocused eyes, or look down at the floor. When it is finished Morrison reads the honor roll of "Everlasting" Ravens, which seems to go on for a very long time. It also includes those men closely identified with the Ravens who lost their lives: Lee Lue and Pop Buell; and the CAS guys: Will Green—Black Lion—who died of a liver fluke in 1972; George Bacon—Kayak—who died in action in Angola in 1976; Frank Odum—the Bag—who died in Zaire; Burr Smith—Mr. Clean—who died on his return to the United States. A toast is drunk, and Craig Morrison, having drained his glass, walks halfway across the room and hurls it into the makeshift fireplace. This is a ritual enacted ever since Park Bunker was killed after Christmas in 1970 and the Long Tieng Ravens drank to his memory. The other Ravens follow suit, and glasses arc across the room and shatter on the stone.

The Ravens take their places at the tables, and Al Galante stands to say grace. He folds his hands before him and bows his head: "The Lord giveth, and the Lord taketh away—if that's not a square deal I'll kiss your ass." A china bedpan—once belonging to H. Ownby's grandmother—is filled to the brim with White Horse whisky and passed up and down the tables throughout dinner.

The president, Craig Morrison, seated at the top table beside the visiting speaker, amuses the guest of honor by eating his wineglass. (The trick is to take a clean bite, and grind the glass between molars until it is very fine and can be swallowed without danger—finely ground glass, despite the conventions of numerous murder mystery writers, is nothing more than sand. Both Morrison's doctor and his dentist have declared his odd habit unwise but harmless.)

The waiters at the banquet have developed their service into an art, having learned the hard lessons of previous experience. The secret is to get all of the food onto the table fast and run like hell for the kitchen before somebody throws something. Dinner is eaten in a general murmur of conversation, interrupted by the occasional Raven rising to risk a toast.

There is usually a guest speaker, who at this stage in the proceedings has turned a pale shade of gray. Sometimes the Air Force sends an officer to talk on the current MIA/POW situation, a subject guaranteed to raise blood pressure. It is a hapless task for the unfortunate speaker to try to convince the Ravens that either the Air Force or the U.S. government is doing all it can to ensure the return of Americans who might still be held captive in Vietnam or Laos. Whether such men still survive today or not, the Ravens believe the government has withheld vital information and been less than forthright in its dealings—a view shared by many veterans.

But expressions of outrage are restricted by making the Ravens who take the floor to speak plunge one hand into a bucket of melting ice cubes and water—it is beyond human endurance to talk for long.

There is one guest speaker, however, who is treated with reverential respect—Gen. Vang Pao. A small, unremarkable, round-faced oriental in a well-cut gray suit, he is perfectly at ease among the Ravens and beams at even their most excessive behavior, for he has seen it all before at *bacis* in Long Tieng.

Since his departure from Laos in 1975 he lived briefly in exile in Thailand and then moved to Missoula, Montana, where the mountain landscape bears some resemblance to his native land, accompanied by his CIA case officer, Jerry Daniels, whose home was in Missoula. He divorced five of his six wives and settled down with his twenty-six children to a life of farming, together with the first group of Hmong refugees to arrive in America. Today, as the acknowledged leader of the Hmong in exile, he is based in Santa Ana, California, and spends most of his time traveling around the United States to various Hmong refugee settlements.

He is accompanied to the reunion by his son Vang Chong, an earnest, bespectacled, and Americanized thirty-year-old whose education at West Point was interrupted by the collapse of his people's military resistance. The CIA kept the general under wraps for many years after the war, and meetings with him took on a clandestine and melodramatic nature, and had to be arranged from Montana phone booths at remote crossroads.[1]

The Ravens listen to the general's short speech in broken English with great attention. There is more than a smattering of propaganda in it, and his heartfelt invitation to join him in an uprising to free Laos is more emotional than feasible. But whatever life holds for the Hmong in the United States, the general makes it plain that his people mostly desire to return to their mountaintops in Laos. He knows this is an unrealistic dream at present, although sporadic guerrilla fighting still continues in the interior of Laos. But he is patient, and his will matches that of his enemy. Perhaps in ten years, he says, or twenty—or even a hundred—the Hmong will have another chance to regain their mountains and live among them without interference. Perhaps the Russians will tire of supporting their difficult and expensive client, the Vietnamese; perhaps the Chinese, who have already set up a training camp for Lao dissidents and actively begun supporting anti-Vietnamese guerrilla movements, will make a move into Laos to stem the expansion of an age-old and traditional enemy who will have a population of 90 million by the year 2000.[2] Who knows what the future has in store? But when the times comes and the opportunity arises, the Hmong will make yet another effort to win back what was theirs.

When the general sits down the Ravens give him a standing ovation, a reaction no one else is likely to receive from this irreverent and skeptical group. The waiters return to clear the tables. They place them end to end, remove the tablecloths, and cover them with crushed ice. Lighted candles are placed along their edges.

These are the preliminary preparations for simulated carrier landings. The idea is to imitate bodily the perils of landing a jet on a carrier at night. A Raven takes a run toward the table from the far side of the room and dives onto it, attempting to keep between the lighted candles as he skids along a surface made slick by the melting ice. Two other Ravens take up positions at the far end of the tables, where they stretch Fred Platt's cane about a foot and a half above the surface.

This is the "snag," to catch the speeding body in the crick formed behind raised legs, before it hurtles off the end.

Newcomers to the practice are given the following advice: Don't run too fast or you'll break your legs on the edge of the table; don't jump too hard or you'll break your ribs when you land; for God's sake remember to crick your legs as you speed along the surface or you'll zip beneath the cane and brain yourself on the bar—best of luck.

There are accidents, and casualties. One Raven spins out of control and rockets off the side of the table, smacking his face on the floor in a crash landing. His bleeding wounds are bathed with whisky. H. Ownby attempts a landing blindfolded and runs into the corner of the table, and the pain is shared by onlookers, who let out a sympathetic groan. Fred Platt—who should not be participating in such an activity anyway because of his weak back—gathers such momentum as he screams down the length of the joined tables, that the cane fails to stop him and he knocks himself out on the bar.

As the carrier landings continue, a group of Ravens gather around a piano, played by Jim Roper, to sing selections from the Raven Song Book, a collection of violent and obscene ballads constituting the only publication of the Edgar Allan Poe Literary Society to date. Craig Morrison begs a light for his cigar, and Greg Wilson obligingly unzips the front of his party suit and sets fire to his chest. Morrison calmly draws on his cigar until it is alight, and Wilson smothers the crackling wall of flame moving up his torso with his left arm.

At the end of the evening when almost everyone is half or completely crocked, and the high spirits, acrobatics, and disco dancing have done their work, the Ravens sit in quiet groups and Jim Roper sets up his slide show—snapshots of a secret war. The lights are dimmed and the slides are projected onto the wall, accompanied by a synchronized soundtrack. The Ravens fall silent.

The soundtrack is made up of rock songs in vogue at the time, snatches of cheerful radio banter between Ravens and Hmong pilots, the rattle of a T-28's machine guns, the scream of an F-4's jet engine, and the dull boom of exploding bombs. The photos are of children on the ramp at Long Tieng, the dilapidated exterior of Madame Lulu's Rendezvous des Amis, and the CIA bears receiving a can of beer through the bars of their cage. There are pictures of Hmong pilots in the cockpits of their fighters, the CAS guys in their golfing clothes, and paramilitary types loaded with weapons scowling into the camera. A rocket hurtles toward its target, smoke billows from a cave mouth, and napalm blazes orange against a green hillside. A flight of Skyraiders fire tracer across a blue sky, a T-28 drops in a vertical dive, while the Raven war-horse itself—the O-1 Bird Dog—hangs everywhere over Laotian landscapes of jungle valleys, river mists on the Mekong, and fantastic rock formations.

There is also a collection of portraits of Ravens, sitting in their planes or relaxing in the hootch, hamming it up for the camera. They all look so young. And occasionally there is a picture of a Raven who did not return: jaunty, smiling, seemingly immortal.

When the show is over Jim Roper begins to pack up his slide show. Most of the Ravens remain quiet, sunk into a nostalgic reverie that is tinged with sadness. The feeling throughout the room is that they would all go back in a heartbeat, but they probably wouldn't—held back by family commitments, mortgages, and middle-aged spread.

They eventually drift back to the Carriage Inn where they wander in and out of one another's rooms for a final drink. Late on Sunday they begin to straggle back to the O Club for another hungover breakfast, after which they bid each other farewell and go their separate ways. For another year, until the next reunion, everything fades once again into legend, a hazy, half-remembered war story known only to a few veterans of Vietnam.

"The Ravens. Yeah, I remember—a weird bunch of guys who lived and fought out there in the jungle in the Other Theater somewhere. Hell, what was the name of the country?"

ACKNOWLEDGMENTS

The source for the greater part of this book has been the Ravens themselves. Their agreement to cooperate—on the understanding that the author should have complete freedom to write what he wanted as long as the Ravens were allowed to review the manuscript for factual errors—resulted in hundreds of hours of interviews. None of the Ravens received payment, although the author has agreed to contribute a tithe of the book's earnings toward the Edgar Allan Poe Literary Society's refugee fund.

It has been necessary to be brutally selective in telling the story, which could have run into several volumes if each individual Raven had been given his due. The author decided it could best be told by following the experiences of those Ravens posted to work with Gen. Vang Pao in Military Region II.

Space and continuity forbid a description of the Ravens' activities in the other theaters of war that ran concurrently in Laos. The author recognizes that this is grossly unfair to those men who served in other military regions during different periods of the war, and the resulting lacunae have meant that some Ravens, who might have warranted a book to themselves in other circumstances, have received short shrift or not been mentioned at all: Frank Birk, for example, who was stationed at Luang Prabang, and whose heroic rescue of a CIA team cut off to the north of the Chinese Road and given up as lost deserved the Air Force Cross (he was hit forty-three times by ground fire during his tour as a Raven, and in one case took more than twenty hits when the glass and radios were shot up in his O-1, the fire extinguisher blew up in the Backseater's face, and one gas tank exploded, ripping the wing three inches out of the fuselage—but he flew the plane back to base); or Al Daines, the teetotal Mormon also posted to Luang Prabang, who impressed the Air Commando site commander as the bravest pilot he had ever known.

And while the panhandle of Laos was known as a country-club posting during the early years of the war, there were periods of intense battle and Ravens were killed there throughout. Early Ravens, like Bill Sweeney and Huey P. O'Neal, who served in the panhandle, certainly saw their share of action and might justifiably wonder where the "country club" was—while later in the war the panhandle became the worst area of all. In Laos everything is relative and needs to be qualified.

The account here is not about the bravest or the best Ravens, but about the sort of men they were and the type of war they fought. A definitive history would have to include many more names than is possible in this book. For example, John Swanson is cited by his peers as the most competent FAC of his period; or the quiet and self-effacing Ed Chun, who is mentioned only briefly, is unreservedly acknowledged to be a pilot of exceptional skill, quite apart from his three thousand hours of combat flying. "I've got to admit it," one Raven said grudgingly, "he's even better than me."

Research has been an exercise in piecing together a large, faded jigsaw, of which many of the pieces have been lost forever. Recounting recent history is always a treacherous exercise, and even participants and eyewitnesses are subject to the inevitable distortions of time and memory. And then there is the transmutation from reality to war story, as anecdotes are polished and retold. Great pains have been taken to avoid the excesses and exaggerations to which a book based on first-person accounts is vulnerable. Details of events have been cross-checked with as many people taking part as possible, as well as with whatever declassified documents are available. Many of the Ravens spent a large amount of their time alone in the cockpits of their planes over remote jungle, but smuggled their small, green notebooks recording strike information, bomb damage assessment, hours logged each day, and so on, out of Laos with them. These have proved invaluable *aide-mémoires* and kept people honest.

The author—who is not a pilot, has been unable to visit the areas of Laos described in this book, and has never been to war—was obliged to go back to basics in his research. Ravens who spent hours answering his endless questions about flying and the art of being a forward air controller include Craig Morrison, who as president of the Edgar Allan Poe Literary Society helped locate Ravens scattered around the world; Fred Platt, who drove the author all over Texas to interview colleagues; Michael Cavanaugh, who gave the author valuable pointers at the Alfred F. Simpson Historical Research Center, Maxwell Air Force Base, Montgomery, Alabama, the staff of which extended patient and courteous assistance throughout; and Karl Polifka, who gave the author help at the Historical Research Branch, Center of Military History, the Pentagon, Washington, D.C.

Ravens other than those mentioned above who reviewed the manuscript for accuracy include Michael Byers, Craig Duehring, Al Galante, Carl Goembel, Jim Hix, Tom Richards, Jim Roper, Larry Sanborn, and Bill Williams.

Other Ravens interviewed by the author include Jim Baker, Victor Bonfiglio, Art Cornelius, Mark Diebolt, Jack Drummond, Robert Foster, Gerald Greven, Lew Hatch, Melville Hart, Charles Jones, Frank Kricker, John Mansur, Harold Mesaris, Douglas Mitchell, H. Ownby, John Wisniewski, Ron Rinehart, Don Service, Jack Shaw, Tom Shera, Michael Stearns, Chad Swedberg, Richard Welch, Darrel Whitcomb, Greg Wilson, and Tom Young.

Others who kindly granted an interview include ambassadors William Sullivan and G. McMurtrie Godley III; air attaché Col. (ret.) Paul "Pappy" Pettigrew and assistant air attaché Col. (ret.) William Keeler; Air Commandos Brig. Gen. Harry "Heinie" Aderholt, Lt. Col. (ret.) Wayne Landen, Lt. Col. (ret.) Howard Hartley, and Lt. Col. (ret.) Robert Zimmerman; former Air America personnel Jack "90" Knotts, David Kouba, and Stanley Wilson; and C. M. Sgt. Patrick Mahoney.

Valuable background information was provided by T. D. Allman; Asa Baber; Douglas Blaufarb; Jane Merritt Brown; Dr. Yang Dao; Alan Dawson; Ed Dearborn, Continental Air Services; Arthur Dommen; Jinny St. Goar; Col. Martin Kaufman, USAF; C.A.S.H. Helseth, Commander China Post 1; Douglas Hulcher, Institute of Foreign Policy Analysis and American Refugee Committee; Col. (ret.) Tom Henry, Green Berets; A. R. Isaacs; Dr. Gene Kirkley, USAF medic at Long Tieng; Leon LaShomb, secretary of the Air America Club; Prince Mangkhra Phouma; Paul and Helen McCloskey; Thomas Powers; H. Ross Perot; Lt. Col. (ret.) John Clark Pratt, USAF Project CHECO; Sir Robert Thompson; Don Schanche; Col. Jack Schlight, Office of Air Force History, the Pentagon; the late

Robert Six, Continental Air Services; Calvin Trillin; Col. (ret.) Roger Trinquier; and Monsieur et Madame Max Varner.

I would also like to thank my literary agent in New York, Jane Cushman, for her support throughout; my editor at Crown, James O'Shea Wade, for his work on the manuscript; and my in-house critic and confidante, Mary Agnes Donoghue, without whom this book would not have been possible.

THE RAVENS

Wayne T. Abbey, Walter E. Ackerlund, Ernest B. Anderson, William W. Angliss, James D. Baker, Frank T. Birk, Robert M. Blackman, Jr., William M. Blaesing, Victor J. Bonfiglio, Craig S. Bradford, Charles W. Brewer, Michael R. Butler, John M. Byers, James E. Cain, Don Carlisle, Terry M. Carroll, Jr., Michael E. Cavanaugh, Randall J. Chenevy, Edmund B. W. Chun, James E. Cochran, Jimmie C. Coombes, Arthur B. Cornelius, Alan R. Daines, Roger W. Daisley, Timothy E. Danforth, Peter K. W. Dang, John A. Davidson, Ramon E. Dearrigunaga, Mark T. Diebolt, J. Briggs Diuguid III, Robert E. Drawbaugh, Jack Drummond, Craig W. Duehring, Arthur A. Dulaney II, Robert H. Dunbar, Lloyd F. Duncan, Craig T. Dunn, Kenton R. Elley, Mark D. Elliott, Jr., David J. Erickson, Stanley L. Ersted, Robert E. Foster, John H. Fuller, Jr., Jerry D. Furche, Albert R. Galante, Carlos D. Goembel, Richard C. Green, Melvin L. Greene, Gerald J. Greven, J. Fred Guffin, Edwin D. Gunter, Jr., Gene D. Hamner, Theodore L. Hanson, Jerry N. Hare, Thomas A. Harris, Melville D. Hart, Jr., Lewis M. Hatch IV, Charles D. Hightower, Charles W. Hines, James H. Hix, Jr., Allen D. Holt, Jr., Max N. Hottell, Jay D. Johnson, Charles L. Jones, Robert A. Kain, John J. Keeler, Marvin R. Keller, Marsdeng G. Kelly, Jr., Thomas L. King, Jerome Klingaman, William J. Kozma, Frank M. Kricker, Waldemar D. Krueger, Blake M. Lancaster, Edward W. Lauffer, James F. Lemon, J. Ross Leonard, Ted H. Liebig, Raymond A. Liss, William J. Lutz, Stephen B. Maddox, Anthony P. Mahoney, John W. Mansur, Burton

E. McKenzie, Jr., J. Lee McKinley, Richard M. Meeboer, Paul A. Merrick, Harold L. Mesaris, Jerry W. Milam, Douglas J. Mitchell, Donald R. Moody, D. Craig Morrison, Norman D. Munsey, Terance P. Murphy, Steven J. Neal, Ellis T. Nottingham, Huey P. O'Neal, Harrold K. Ownby, Thomas H. Palmer, Vincent J. Pastore, Robert H. Passman, Andrew L. Patten, Richard B. Patterson, Terry L. Pfaff, Alfred G. Platt, William E. Platt, Karl R. Polifka, Claude S. Puckett, Jay R. Puckett, Larry J. Ratts, Thomas D. Redford, William H. Rees, Stephen H. Reich, E. Jerry Rhein, Jr., Thomas C. Richards, Dale F. Richardson, Ronnie O. Rinehart, James E. Roper, Frederick E. Roth, Mervin E. Roussell, Larry K. Sanborn, John R. Sanderson, Joseph M. Scheimer, Don W. Service, Jack W. Shaw, Thomas L. Shera, Prescott N. Shinn, Richard E. Shubert, Ernest M. Skinner, Hal C. Smith, Joseph A. Smith, Niles E. Smith, James J. Stanford, Michael L. Stearns, Richard L. Stewart, James E. Struhsaker, John F. Swanson, Chad L. Swedberg, William L. Sweeney, Jeff E. Thompson, Kenneth R. Thompson, John F. Urban, Lloyd E. Van Zee, Thomas J. Verso, Brian E. Wages, Richard E. Welch, Darrel D. Whitcomb, John W. White, George B. Williams, Paul E. Williams, Victor M. Williams, Jr., Warren E. Williams, G. Steven Wilson, S. Greg Wilson, John W. Wisniewski, James R. Withers, James A. Yeager, William H. Yenke, Thomas O. Young, Robert L. Zbornak.

IN MEMORIAM

Robert L. Abbott, Henry L. Allen, John J. Bach, Jr., Charles D. Ballou, Danny L. Berry, Park C. Bunker, Joseph K. Bush, Jr., John L. Carroll, Joseph L. Chestnut, James E. Cross, Daniel R. Davis, Richard H. Defer, Samuel M. Deichelman, David A. Dreier, Richard G. Elzinga, Charles E. Engle, John J. Garritty, Jr., Richard W. Herold, Paul V. Jackson III, Edward E. McBride, Harold L. Mischler, Dennis E. Morgan, Joseph W. Potter, Gomer D. Reese III, John W. Rhodes, James Rostermundt, Charles P. Russell, Marlin L. Siegwalt, George H. Tousley III, W. Grant Uhls, Truman R. Young.

CHRONOLOGY: LAOS TO 1960

1373 Laos becomes a recognizable entity and unified state for the first time. Ancient Lan Xang, the Kingdom of a Million Elephants, reaches from the crest of the Annamite Mountains on the east to the watershed division between the Mekong and Menam rivers in the west, and from China in the north almost as far as Angkor Wat in the south. It includes Chiang Mai and much of the Korat plateau in what is modern Thailand, and portions of present-day northern Cambodia.

1479 Lan Xang is threatened with extinction when Vietnamese troops invade from Annam, capture Luang Prabang, and drive out the king. His son rallied his subjects and expelled the Vietnamese from the kingdom.

1641 A Dutch merchant, Gerrit van Wuysthoff, becomes the first recorded European to arrive in Laos.

1694 The reigning monarch dies leaving no sons.

1700 The country splits in two after a period of coup and counter-coup, and infighting among the royal family. Two minor grandsons of the late king capture Luang Prabang and proclaim it the seat of a separate kingdom made up of the northern provinces.

1713 Territories in the panhandle group themselves into the Kingdom of Champassak, further weakening Lan Xang which is now split into three separate kingdoms. Debilitating warfare between the rival princes continues throughout the eighteenth and nineteenth centuries.

1827 A Siamese army sacks Vientiane after its ruler unsuccessfully attempts a march on Bangkok. Thousands of Lao from the Korat plateau are forcibly resettled on the right bank of the Mekong.

1872 France dispatches military forces to the Red River delta, defeating Vietnamese troops and Chinese mercenaries, and imposes Treaty of Protectorate over the court of Hué.

1885 Siam launches a large-scale military expedition into Northern Laos fearful that the Vietnamese will use French military power to expand.

1886 Siam grants France the right to post a vice-consul to Luang Prabang.

1887 Auguste Pavie, French vice-consul, persuades the king to give up the worthless Siamese protectorate in favor of the French—the beginning of French colonial rule in Laos.

1889 Vientiane is officially declared the administrative capital of French Laos. The country comes under complete French control in 1893.

1895–1897 The boundaries of modern Laos are drawn: Auguste Pavie carefully maps the border with Vietnam; a joint survey with the British establishes the border with Burma at the Mekong; the border with China is established in agreement with the Chinese.

1940 Japan occupies the whole of Indochina in September, but leaves French colonial administration intact.

1943 The Royal Road, linking Luang Prabang to Vientiane, completed by the French (work overseen by the future Prime Minister, Souvanna Phouma).

1944 Vo Nguyen Giap forms Vietminh army.

1945 Japanese take over French administration throughout Indochina in March.

King Sisavang Vong defies the Japanese and proclaims independence of Laos in April.

Japanese transfer power in Indochina to the Vietminh in August.

British forces land in Saigon in September and soon return authority over Indochina to France.

Ho Chi Minh proclaims Democratic Republic of Vietnam in Hanoi in September.

1946 Constitutional monarchy proclaimed in Luang Prabang in April.

The French regain control over the whole of Laos by September.

Outbreak of first Indochinese war in December.

1949 Chinese Communists complete the conquest of China on October 1.

1950 The term Pathet Lao (Land of the Lao) used for the first time by those Lao forces that refused to accept the previous year's accommodation by the government with the French.

1951 Four Vietminh battalions are stationed in Laos, and while ordered to avoid contact with French forces, remain until 1953 to train Pathet Lao troops.

Marshal Jean de Lattre Tassigny, commander-in-chief of French forces in Indochina, creates a service which recruits and organizes the Meo into *maquisards*, guerrilla units to fight the Vietminh.

1952 Dwight D. Eisenhower elected president of the United States in November.

Vietminh guerrillas continue to infiltrate Laos.

1953 Vietminh forces invade Laos in March. Sam Neua is abandoned by the French and falls into Communist hands in April. Prince Souphanouvong establishes his seat of government there.

Vietminh advance through northeastern, central, and southern Laos in May.

French sign treaty with Royal government in October which obliges them to protect the country from invasion.

The French commander sends telegram to his government in November that he intends to reoccupy Dien Bien Phu to cover the approach to Luang Prabang.

1954 Battle of Dien Bien Phu begins in March and after a three-month siege the French are defeated in May.

Geneva Conference opens in May. Agreements are reached by July calling for cessation of hostilities in Vietnam, Cambodia, and Laos. Vietnam is divided into South and North at the 17th parallel.

1958 Prince Souvanna Phouma dissolves first neutralist government in July and is succeeded by Phoui Sananikone, favored by America as a military strongman and anti-Communist.

1959 The North Vietnamese create Group 559 to enlarge the Ho Chi Minh Trail through Laos, the traditional infiltration route into the south.

The U.S. State Department sets up a disguised military mission, known as the Program Evaluation Office (PEO), the members of which wore civilian clothes and were described as "technicians," even the U.S. Army general who headed it. Its task was no less than to create and train a viable Laotian army.

NOTES

Ravens interviewed are listed in Acknowledgments. When the source of information is a Raven mentioned in the text, no numbered endnote has been thought necessary.

Prologue: Myth

1. Many of the documents, oral histories, and end-of-tour reports requested by the author, but not released to him, are covered by the whole gamut of the classification system: Top Secret, Secret, Confidential, Air Force Eyes Only, No Foreign Dissemination, Especially Sensitive Information, etc. Others have been declassified only very recently. *The War in Northern Laos* by Maj. Victor B. Anthony has no date for its release. "It is unlikely it will be published in our lifetime," said Col. John Schlight, USAF historian at the Pentagon. Both the State Department and the CIA have opposed the publication of the Air Force history because of its intensely critical view of their role in the war.

1. Chance

1. Monopoly briefing: Col. Robert Foster, interview with author, Lompoc, Calif., January 16, 1985. Only the later Ravens received this briefing.
2. Steve Canyon's biographical data from *Milton Caniff's Steve Canyon Magazine* (Kitchen Sink Comix, a division of Krupp Comic Works, Inc., 1983).

3. USAF FAC policy in Vietnam: William M. Momyer, *Airpower in Three Wars* (Washington, D.C.: U.S. Government Printing Office, 1978), pp. 266–68.
4. USAF Project, Contemporary Historical Evaluation of Combat Ops (CHECO) reports, "Evolution of the ROE for South East Asia 1960–1965; 1966–1969; 1969–1972." Declassified by Defense Secretary Caspar Weinberger at the request of Senator Barry Goldwater and placed in the *Congressional Record*, March 1985.
5. Capt. D. C. Morrison, FV3176367, Journal. The first entry is made on April 18, 1969, and entries continue sporadically until April 19, 1970, covering seventy-seven pages of blue-lined paper. The journal is a slim black leather book with the Vietnam FAC badge stuck to the cover—Snoopy in his First World War flying helmet holding the joystick of his shot-up kennel, with "Vietnam" written underneath. Quoted with permission.
6. USO show at Pleiku: Craig Morrison, interview with author, Santa Monica, Calif., December 6, 1983.

2. Across the Fence

1. Welcoming speech: Capt. Karl L. Polifka, interview conducted by Lt. Col. Robert G. Zimmerman for the USAF Oral History Program, December 17, 1974, Washington, D.C., classified Secret. Declassified on December 31, 1982.
2. Blank on form: Col. Larry Sanborn, interview with author, San Antonio, Texas, October 18, 1985.
3. Col. Tom Shera, interview with author, Hurlburt Field AFB, Florida, March 15, 1985.
4. Hmong and Meo: Dr. Yang Dao, conversation with author, April 11, 1987.

3. The Secret City

1. Almost all of the Ravens stationed at Long Tieng interviewed by the author compared the base to Shangri-La. An invention of James Hilton in his 1933 novel *Lost Horizon*, the paradise was conceived as an ageless retreat of peace and prayer. However, the name has been used before by Americans with warlike intentions. Franklin D. Roosevelt called his mountain refuge in Maryland Shangri-La, and the "base" from which the U.S. planes flew in the Tokyo air raid in 1942—an aircraft carrier—was also code-named Shangri-La.

4. The Sacred Mountain

1. Lockheed engineers: Ambassador William H. Sullivan, interview with author, Columbia University, New York, N.Y., May 21, 1985.
2. 150 tons of equipment: Ray L. Bowers, *Tactical Airlift: The United States Air Force in Southeast Asia* (Washington, D.C.: Office of Air Force History, 1983), p. 455.
3. A garbled account of the air action was reported in the *Far Eastern Economic Review* and its yearbook in 1969. For a sanitized version, see William Colby, *Honorable Men* (New York: Simon & Schuster, 1978), p. 200.
4. A Top Secret Air Force report on the incident, written in August 1968, remained classified until 1986, when it was released to Ann Holland, the widow of T. Sgt. Melvin Holland, who lost his life on the Rock. The testimony of Maj. Stanley Sliz, given in a closed hearing before the U.S. Senate Foreign Relations Subcommittee on May 8, 1970, remains classified, but was made available to the *Sunday Oklahoman*, which published excerpts on October 5, 1986.
5. Seesaw and change in enemy tactics during this period: Douglas S. Blaufarb, *The Counterinsurgency Era: U.S. Doctrine and Performance 1950 to the Present* (New York: Free Press/Macmillan, 1977), pp. 158–60.
6. *The Pentagon Papers*, Senator Gravel edition (Boston: Beacon, 1971–72), vol. 4, p. 595.
7. Charlie Jones (one of the original Butterflies), interview with author, Fort Walton Beach, Fla., March 15, 1985.
8. Patrick Mahoney, interview with author, Washington, D.C., May 15, 1985.
9. Samuel M. Deichelman, missing in action, September 6, 1968.
10. Lt. Col. Howard K. Hartley, Secret interview #K239.0512–746, USAF Oral History Program. Declassified December 31, 1984.
11. The note, written in blue ballpoint pen on a lined sheet of paper from a yellow legal pad, was kept by Jim Baker as a memento.
12. Marlin L. Siegwalt, killed in action, October 30, 1968.
13. Charles D. Ballou, killed in action, November 7, 1968. The official explanation for his death is "Fuel exhaustion—crash-landed."
14. Don A. Schanche, *Mister Pop: The Inside Story of the American Involvement in Laos* (New York: McKay, 1970), p. 298.

15. Edward E. McBride, killed in action, November 27, 1968. Details of his last flight: Wayne Landen, interview with author, Fort Walton Beach, Fla., March 16, 1985; and Jim Baker, interview with author, San Antonio, Texas, October 18, 1986.

5. The Big Picture

1. Stanley Karnow, *Vietnam: A History* (New York: Viking, 1983), p. 124; P. J. Honey, *Communism in North Vietnam: Its Role in the Sino-Soviet Dispute* (Cambridge, Mass.: MIT Press, 1963).
2. No record of the Jungle John briefings exists, as Garritty did not use written notes. The reader will have to settle for the more prosaic descriptions of Laos and its history presented here.
3. Norman Lewis, *A Dragon Apparent: Travels in Cambodia, Laos, and Vietnam* (London: Jonathan Cape, 1951), p. 284. The book gives a lyrical description of Laos in the early 1950s, before it was engulfed by the brutalities of modern war.
4. "The Hmong of Laos: No Place to Run," *National Geographic*, January 1974, p. 86.
5. Quotes from Col. Roger Trinquier are from interview with author (unless noted otherwise). Vence, France, September 29, 1985.
6. G. Linwood Barney, "The Meo of Xieng Khouang Province," in Peter Kunstadter, ed., *Southeast Asian Tribes, Minorities, and Nations*, Vol. 1 (Princeton, N.J.: Princeton University Press, 1967), p. 292.
7. And continues to be so today even under a puritanical, Vietnamese-controlled Communist government. For a detailed account of the history of the narcotics industry in Laos and in Southeast Asia in general, see Alfred W. McCoy, *The Politics of Heroin in Southeast Asia* (New York: Harper & Row, 1972). Although well documented, McCoy's book ignores early attempts by the Air Commandos to curb the trade—see Secret oral history of Lt. Col. Howard K. Hartley, declassified December 31, 1984—or later efforts by CIA station chief Hugh Tovar and Ambassador G. McMurtrie Godley. Indeed, when the CIA promoted the use of herbicides against opium poppy fields, after a 1971 government ban, there was a furious backlash from the Meo.
8. Gen. Vang Pao's background: *Conflict in Laos*, p. 294; Don Schanche, *Mister Pop, passim; National Geographic, op cit*; author's interview with Trinquier.

9. Charges the author is guilty of promulgating in an earlier book, *Air America*. But in judging Vang Pao one should use the standards of his own people.

10. Bernard Fall, *Anatomy of a Crisis: The Laotion Crisis of 1960–61* (Garden City, N.Y.: Doubleday, 1969), p. 52.

11. Ibid., p. 53.

12. The anthropologist was Henri Deydier, whose findings were published posthumously: *Lokapala—Genies, Totems et Sorciers du Nord Laos* (Paris: Plom, 1954). References to Blind Bonze, pp. 164–84; quoted by both Fall and Dommen.

13. But British intelligence took a different view. Sir Maurice Old-field, who became director-general of M16 between 1973 and 1978, was posted to the Far East during the period directly before the French defeat in Indochina. He took a special interest in Laos, "one of my favorite countries in the whole world." Sir Maurice, a medievalist who spoke Latin in his sleep, studied the *I Ching*, the Egyptian *Book of the Dead*, and the Nine Star Ki system of Chinese astrology. See Richard Deacon, *"C": A Biography of Sir Maurice Oldfield, Head of M16* (London: Macdonald, 1985).

14. Fall, *Anatomy of a Crisis*, p. 57.

15. Bernard Fall, *Street Without Joy* (New York: Schocken, 1972), p. 116.

16. For a detailed account of the Vietnamese role in the genesis of the Pathet Lao and the Vietnamese control over the Laotion Communist movement, see Paul F. Langer and Joseph J. Zasloff, *North Vietnamese and the Pathet Lao: Partners in the Struggle for Laos* (Cambridge, Mass.: Harvard University Press, 1970).

17. George Ball's remark quoted in Walter Isaacson and Evan Thomas, *The Wise Men: Six Friends and the World They Made* (New York: Simon & Schuster, 1986), p. 606.

18. General Aderholt was made the senior air adviser to the CIA in Southeast Asia on January 1, 1960. Interview with author, Fort Walton Beach, Fla., March 15, 1985.

19. *Pentagon Papers*, Gravel ed., vol. 2, p. 646.

20. For detailed accounts of this extremely complicated period, see the books of Dommen, Toye, and Fall listed in the bibliography.

21. Kennedy briefed by Eisenhower: *Pentagon Papers*, Gravel ed., vol. 2, pp. 636–37.

22. Domino theory: Dwight D. Eisenhower, news conference, April 7, 1954.

23. "Kung Fu movie": Isaacson and Thomas, *Wise Men*, p. 607.

24. Highest-priority supply operation: Deputy Foreign Minister G. M. Pushkin to Averell Harriman, in Arthur M. Schlesinger, Jr., *A Thousand Days: John F. Kennedy in the White House* (Boston: Houghton Mifflin, 1965).

25. President Kennedy, television address, March 23, 1961.

26. Quotes from William Sullivan are from interview with author (unless noted otherwise).

27. Kennedy view: Arthur Schlesinger, *A Thousand Days: John F. Kennedy in the White House*, p. 368.

28. "Why take risks": Roger Hilsman, *To Move a Nation: The Politics of Foreign Policy in the Administration of JFK* (Garden City, N.Y.: Doubleday, 1967), p. 130.

29. Quoted in Arthur Dommen, *Conflict in Laos: The Politics of Neutralization*, rev. ed. (New York: Praeger, 1971), p. 287.

30. American view of king: Roger Hilsman, *To Move a Nation*, p. 109. King's choice of automobile: Don Moody, AOC commander at Luang Prabang, interview with the author, Fort Worth, Texas, April 12, 1985.

31. Quoted in Dommen, *Conflict in Laos*, pp. 183–84.

32. Quoted in Hilsman, *To Move a Nation*, p. 136.

33. Details of the road-building project first revealed in a dispatch from the New China News Agency on January 13, 1962. The agreement with North Vietnam was signed on March 10, 1962. Arthur Dommen, *Conflict in Laos*, pp. 229–30. Road work expanded in 1968, ibid., p. 284.

34. Henry Kissinger, *Years of Upheaval* (Boston: Little, Brown, 1982), pp. 58–59.

35. Revelations 13:18.

36. Quoted in Isaacson and Thomas, *Wise Men*, p. 618.

37. Editorial in *Nhan Dan*, official newspaper of the North Vietnamese Communist Party, on Geneva Agreement, July 24, 1962. Quoted in Gareth Porter, ed., *Vietnam: A History in Documents* (New York: Earl M. Coleman Enterprises, 1979), p. 232.

38. Blaufarb, *Counterinsurgency Era*, p. 157.

39. Ralph McGehee, *Deadly Deceits: My 25 Years in the CIA* (New York: Sheridan Square, 1983), pp. 83–84.

40. Hague Conference: Harry G. Summers, Jr. *On Strategy: A Critical Analysis of the Vietnam War* (Novato, Calif.: Presidio, 1982), pp. 106–107.

41. Curtis E. LeMay (with MacKinley Kantor), *Mission with LeMay: My Story* (Garden City, N.Y.: Doubleday, 1965), p. 565. The most recent biography of LeMay, *Iron Eagle: The Turbulent Life*

of General Curtis LeMay (New York: Crown, 1986), by Thomas Coffey, claims that the general never uttered the remark, but that it somehow slipped into his ghosted biography and LeMay failed to catch the phrase in reading the manuscript. Maybe he failed to catch it because it so completely encapsulated his views on air power.

42. Quoted in Charles A. Stevenson, *The End of Nowhere: American Policy Toward Laos Since 1965* (Boston: Beacon, 1972), p. 180.

43. William Sullivan, *Obbligato: Notes on a Foreign Service Career* (New York and London: Norton, 1984), p. 21.

44. Ibid., p. 21.

45. Ibid., p. 13.

46. General William Westmoreland, *A Soldier Reports* (Garden City, N.Y.: Doubleday, 1976), p. 92.

47. Sullivan, *Obbligato*, pp. 211–13.

48. Stevenson, *The End of Nowhere*, p. 217.

49. Westmoreland, *A Soldier Reports*, p. 238.

50. Air Force desire for jets: Robert Komer, "Was Failure Inevitable?" W. Scott Thompson and D. D. Frizzel, eds., in *The Lessons of Vietnam* (New York: Crane Russak, 1977), p. 269.

51. Sullivan's Air Force organized at Nakhon Phanom airport, Thailand, April 8, 1967. Redesignated as Special Operations Wing, August 1, 1968.

52. Roger Trinquier, *Les Maquis d'Indochine 1952–1954* (Paris: Sociéte de Production Littéraire, 1976), pp. 189–90.

53. The 316th was among the first five 10,000-man divisions created in 1950 from small guerrilla groups that had already evolved into battalions and regiments. (The 312th, also used in Laos, was another.) It was to the political commissars of the 316th that General Giap, a French history professor and member of the Indochinese Communist Party since 1930, presented his plan to defeat the French. "The enemy will pass slowly from the offensive to the defensive. The *Blitzkrieg* will transform itself into a war of long duration. Thus, the enemy will be caught in a dilemma: he has to drag out the war in order to win it and does not possess, on the other hand, the psychological and political means to fight a long drawn-out war." Exactly the same political and military philosophy was employed against the Americans. Fall, *Street Without Joy*, p. 34.

54. Project 404: Secret Air Commando briefing, declassified December 31, 1980.

55. U.S. Senate, Subcommittee on U.S. Security Agreements and Commitments Abroad, Kingdom of Laos, Hearings, October 1969.
56. United States Air Force, *Search and Rescue in Southeast Asia* (Washington, D.C.: Office of Air Force History, 1980), p. 48.
57. *Official History of the United States Air Force in Southeast Asia* (Washington, D.C.: U.S. Government Printing Office, 1977), p. 121.
58. USAF, *Search and Rescue in Southeast Asia*, pp. 48–49.
59. *The Washington Post*, June 14, 1964.
60. *Pentagon Papers*, Gravel ed., vol. 3, p. 264.
61. Ibid., vol. 3, pp. 253–54.
62. Senate Armed Services Committee Hearings, July 22, 1971, p. 4289.
63. Symington's outrage: Thomas Powers, *The Man Who Kept the Secrets: Richard Helms and the CIA* (New York: Knopf, 1979), pp. 178–79.
64. Ibid., p. 163.
65. Colby, *Honorable Men: My Life in the CIA*, p. 202.
66. David Atlee Phillips, *The Night Watch* (New York: Atheneum, 1976), p. 37.
67. Col. Robert Tyrrell, USAF Oral History Program, interview of Tyrrell by Lt. Col. Robert G. Zimmerman, May 12, 1975, Seattle, Washington, p. 58.
68. Blaufarb's liberalism: William P. Bundy in preface to Blaufarb, *Counterinsurgency Era*.
69. Douglas Blaufarb, letter to author, September 1985.
70. Blaufarb, *Counterinsurgency Era*, p. xvi.
71. Anthony Posepny, conversation with author, Bangkok, Thailand, February 1984. Talking to Poe was like being in the presence of a large grizzly bear who might pull off one's head at any moment—especially as he had just slammed the author's previous book, *Air America*, down onto the bar after looking himself up in the index: "That's all *goddam* classified!" Despite his fearsome reputation, which includes a much-advertised detestation of writers, Tony Poe proved to be amusing and rather endearing. He even signed the author's book.
72. The author was beginning to consider the stories of pickled heads to be Tony Poe folklore—very effective propaganda among primitive tribesmen and enemy troops—when Raven James Baker, who had served with Poe in 1968, said he had actually seen them.

73. Tony Pradith, Thai Special Forces commando and subsequent Air America pilot, conversation with author, Bangkok, Thailand, February 1984.

74. Theodore Shackley, *The Third Option: An American View of Counterinsurgency* (New York: Reader's Digest Press), p. xiii.

75. Ibid., p. 72.

76. Harry B. Rothblatt, "Why the Army Tried to Railroad the Green Berets," *True*, March 1970. Rothblatt defended the officers when they were charged with murder, but all charges were dropped by the Secretary of the Army a few days after the lawyer threatened to call Richard Helms as a witness in the case. Quoted in Powers, *Man Who Kept the Secrets*, p. 334.

77. Frank Snepp, *Decent Interval: An Insider's Account of Saigon's Indecent End Told by the CIA's Chief Strategy Analyst in Vietnam* (New York: Random House, 1977), p. 13.

78. Shackley as Western Hemisphere chief: Joseph Smith, *Portrait of a Cold Warrior* (New York: Putnam, 1976), pp. 11–13.

79. Snepp, *Decent Interval*, p. 13.

80. The extraordinary story of Ed Wilson is told in two books, *The Death Merchant: The Rise and Fall of Edwin P. Wilson* (New York: Simon & Schuster, 1984) by Joseph C. Goulden and Alexander W. Raffio, and *Manhunt: The Incredible Pursuit of a CIA Agent Turned Terrorist* (New York: Random House, 1986) by Peter Maas. Details of the Iran-contra affair have been published in the Tower report. For an idea of the complexity of the CIA's international network of CIA "cover" companies, see the author's book *Air America: The Story of the CIA's Secret Airlines*, which indicates that the revelations of Iranscam that continued to surface during the Iran-contra Hearings in session the time of writing, is little more than business as usual.

81. John Stockwell, *In Search of Enemies: A CIA Story* (New York and London: Norton, 1978), p. 136.

82. Church Committee, *Alleged Assassination Plots Involving Foreign Leaders* (New York: Norton, 1976), p. 21. Devlin goes under the alias "Victor Hedgman" in the report. Powers, *Man Who Kept the Secrets*, p. 340, n. 40.

83. CIA killers: *Alleged Assassination Plots*, p. 51.

84. Stockwell, *In Search of Enemies*, p. 237.

85. Ibid., p. 105.

86. *Alleged Assassination Plots*, p. 51.

87. For this view see Senate Judiciary Committee reports: Refugee and Civilian War Casualty Problems in Indochina. Staff report.

September 1970; War-Related Civilian Problems in Indochina. Pt. 2, "Laos and Cambodia," April 1971; War Victims in Indochina. May 1972; Relief and Rehabilitation of War Victims in Indochina. Pt. 3. "North Vietnam and Laos," July 1973.

88. See Schanche, *Mister Pop, passim,* Blaufarb, *Counterinsurgency Era,* pp. 128–68.

6. Air Power

1. Dommen, *Conflict in Laos,* p. 299.
2. U.S. Military Assistance Command, Vietnam, Office of the Assistant Chief of Staff J-2, "Current Summary of Enemy Order of Battle in Laos," December 15, 1967 (declassified February 17, 1982), August 15, 1968 (declassified February 12, 1982).
3. Langer and Zasloff, *North Vietnam and the Pathet Lao,* p. 91.
4. Rinehart was awarded the Silver Star for this mission.
5. Conversations between Pop Buell and Vang Pao: Schanche, *Mister Pop,* pp. 305–07.
6. CINCPACAF message, February 15, 1969.
7. Mike Heenan was shot down on February 18, 1969. Details from USAF accident report and Heenan and Rinehart interviews with author. Heenan received a Purple Heart. Rinehart was awarded the Silver Star, his second. The aircraft commander of the Jolly Green and the airman who was lowered into the gunfire were also awarded the Silver Star.
8. Quoted in John Clark Pratt, *Vietnam Voices: Perspectives on the War Years, 1941–1982* (New York: Viking/Penguin, 1984), p. 284.
9. *Official History of the USAF in Southeast Asia,* p. 127.
10. Sullivan's views at this time are quoted in Bowers, *Tactical Airlift,* p. 458.
11. John J. Bach, Jr., killed in action, April 20, 1969.
12. Don Service recommended the Thud pilots for the Silver Star.
13. Significance of capture of medical supplies: G. McMurtrie Godley, Interview #452, Project Corona Harvest, Oral History, Air Force, Eyes Only, January 27, 1970. Declassified.
14. Schanche, *Mister Pop,* p. 309.
15. This was not a problem peculiar to Americans in Vietnam. British fighter pilots in World War II were ordered to shoot down German rescue seaplanes—and these were clearly painted white and marked with eight large red crosses. Some pilots refused

to obey these specific orders as a matter of conscience. Len Deighton, *Fighter: The True Story of the Battle of Britain* (London: Jonathan Cape, 1977), p. 178.

16. Neither the author, nor researchers attached to the Biological and Medical Library at UCLA, could find any reference to *Panis Auritas* in any zoological encyclopedia or reference work.
17. *Official History of the USAF in Southeast Asia,* p. 127.
18. Polifka was awarded the Silver Star for these missions.
19. Mike Cavanaugh was awarded the Silver Star for this mission. He lobbied to get Moonface an award for saving his life, but the Backseater was given nothing. He was killed in 1971 while flying in the backseat of an O-1 with a Raven.
20. Bowers, *Tactical Airlift*, p. 458.

7. About-Face

1. Quotes from G. McMurtrie Godley are from interview with the author (unless marked otherwise), Morris, N.Y., May 22, 1985.
2. Background paper J-5 Joint Staff, "The Situation in Laos," August 2, 1969. State/Defense/CIA Coordinated Response, "Military Options in Laos," August 19, 1969.
3. House Judiciary Committee, "Bombing of Cambodia," Book II, Statement of Information and Hearings, Presidential Impeachment Investigation, 1974.
4. G. McMurtrie Godley, unpublished manuscript. Quoted by permission.
5. Fall, *Street Without Joy,* p. 282. The French dropped napalm—restricted by the Americans against structures—in Ban Ban village in May 1954. Fall, p. 110.
6. As opposed to the Allies in World War II when Lord Portal, onetime commander in chief of RAF Bomber Command, propounded the outright killing of 900,000 German civilians, the injury of a million more with 25 million made homeless. The aim was to turn Germany into a nation of refugees.
7. Senior CAS (CIA) official, interview, March, 17, 1970, by Ken Sams and Lt. Col. J. Schlight. The official, unidentified in the report, was CIA station chief Larry Devlin.
8. Ibid.
9. Security Agreement Hearings, 1979, p. 784.
10. Capt. Karl L. Polifka, interview, classified Secret, USAF Oral History Program, December 17, 1974, Washington, D.C. Declassified December 31, 1982.

11. Raphael Littauer and Norman Uphoff, *The Air War in Indochina* (Boston: Beacon, 1972), p. 79.
12. Meo outrun own intelligence: John Clark Pratt, interview with author, Fort Collins, Colo., November 29, 1984.
13. A-1s help Black Lion: Maj. Albert E. Preyss, transcript of tape recording sent home to his family, quoted in Pratt, *Vietnam Voices*, pp. 414–18.
14. Although nothing was said to Morrison at the time, he was later awarded the Silver Star for his day's work.
15. Craig Morrison, journal, December 20, 1969.
16. Details of Perot's Christmas trip: H. Ross Perot, letter to author, May 15, 1985.
17. Mahoney passed one rifle on to General Brown, and today it is in the Smithsonian Institution in Washington, D.C.

8. The War Turns

1. *Official History of the USAF in Southeast Asia*, p. 131.
2. The 21st Helicopter Squadron was flown to Long Tieng on January 4, 1970. Bowers, *Tactical Airlift*, p. 458.
3. In November 1968 there were 200 guns inside Laos; by the end of 1969 the figure had passed the 650 mark. Briefing notes, HQ 7th Air Force, Saigon, January 15, 1970. Declassified May 6, 1982. Ravens consider these "official" assessments very low.
4. Blaufarb, *Counterinsurgency Era*, p. 162.
5. *Official History of the USAF in Southeast Asia*, p. 131.
6. Henry Kissinger, *The White House Years* (Boston: Little Brown, 1979), p. 451.
7. Assessment of Laird: Bruce Palmer, Jr., *The 25-Year War: America's Military Role in Vietnam* (Lexington, Ky.: University Press of Kentucky, 1984), p. 107.
8. Kissinger, *White House Years*, p. 452.
9. Detailed memoranda were kept on the daily "Vietnamization" meetings held between Secretary Laird and his Pentagon staff. For Laird's view on Kissinger's military illiteracy, see William Shawcross, *Sideshow: Kissinger, Nixon and the Destruction of Cambodia* (New York: Simon & Schuster, 1979), pp. 212–13.
10. Kissinger, *White House Years*, p. 452.
11. Shawcross, *Sideshow*, p. 213.
12. Bowers, *Tactical Airlift*, p. 458.
13. Kissinger, *White House Years*, pp. 452–53.

14. DOCO contribution to Commander's End of Tour Report, HQ 7/13 AF, Udorn, RTAFB, Thailand. Col. Edward Kenny. March 1, 1970. Declassified 1982.
15. *Official History of the USAF in Southeast Asia*, p. 131.
16. The film was seen by Karl Polifka.
17. *New York Times*, February 19, 1970.
18. Kissinger, *White House Years*, p. 453.
19. *New York Times*, February 25, 1970.
20. Kissinger, *White House Years*, p. 451.
21. Ibid., p. 451.
22. Ibid., p. 455.
23. Seymour Hersh, *The Price of Power: Kissinger in the White House* (New York: Summit, 1983), p. 171.
24. Kissinger, *White House Years*, p. 456.
25. Ibid., p. 455.
26. Ibid., p. 456.
27. Ibid., p. 456.
28. Ibid., p. 455.
29. FBI wiretap: Hersh, *Price of Power*, p. 194.
30. Henry Kissinger, letter to Mel Laird, March 9, 1970, in Kissinger, *White House Years*, p. 456.

9. Long Tieng Besieged

1. Quoted in "The Pendulum of the War Swings Wider," Hugh D. S. Greenway, *Life*, April 3, 1970.
2. Morrison, journal, entry for March 21, 1970.
3. John Clark Pratt, *The Laotian Fragments* (New York: Viking, 1974).
4. Pratt, interview with author.
5. Quoted in Sams, Schlight, and Pratt, *Air Operations in Northern Laos*, November 1, 1969–April 1970 (HQ PACAF, Project CHECO, May 3, 1971), pp. 79–80.
6. Lt. Henry C. Allen, and Capt. Richard G. Elzinga, missing in action, March 26, 1970.
7. Morrison, journal, entry for April 1, 1970.
8. Dommen, *Conflict in Laos*, p. 305.
9. Sullivan, interview with author.
10. A series written by Jacques Decornoy was published in *Le Monde*, July 3–9, 1968.
11. T. D. Allman, quoted from interview with author (unless noted otherwise), Brooklyn, N.Y., December 5, 1985.

12. Daniel Southerland, "What U.S. Bombing Feels Like to Laotians," *Christian Science Monitor*, March 14, 1970; "The Laotians Caught in the Cross Fire," *Guardian*, March 14, 1970; "Laotian Refugees Want a Sanctuary," *Washington Post*, March 26, 1970; Robert Shaplen, "Our Involvement in Laos," *Foreign Affairs*, April 1970, pp. 488–89.

13. T. D. Allman, "Long Tieng Yields Its Secrets," *Bangkok Post*, February 25, 1970.

14. Story compiled from wire-service coverage of Associated Press and Reuters, April 21, 1970.

15. Godley, interview with author.

16. O-1 Altitude record held by Chuck Engle, confirmed by Craig Duehring in interview with author, London, July 5, 1985.

17. The citation for Chuck Engle's Air Force Cross, June 20, 1970, was written by Craig Duehring, based on sworn eyewitness accounts by himself and Ray Dearrigunaga. Dearrigunaga received the Silver Star for his part in directing the SAR.

18. John Fuller, Jr., wounded in action, May 25, 1970. He was medevaced to the Philippines, and only returned to flying status after lengthy hospitalization in the United States. It would be ten years, after repeated exertions by Bob Foster, before he was awarded his end-of-tour DFC from Laos.

19. Air Commando colonel: Col. Roland K. McCoskrie, Oral History, Washington, D.C., July 14, 1975. Unclassified.

10. Valentine

1. Chuck Engle was awarded the Silver Star for this mission of January 2–3, 1971.

2. 1st Lt. Grant Uhls, killed in action, February 11, 1971.

3. *Bangkok Post*, February 8, 1971.

4. Ban Son resettlement figures: U.S. Congress, Senate Committee on the Judiciary, War-Related Civilian Problems in Indochina, Part II: Laos and Cambodia, 92nd Congress, 1st sess., 1971, p. 48.

5. The Meo soldier was hit in the back of the head by a white-hot ball bearing and was to suffer blinding headaches for years. Later, as a refugee in Minnesota, he told welfare workers he had suffered his "industrial accident" as an employee of the CIA. The CIA disclaimed all responsibility, claiming that the Meo had technically worked for the USAF. The USAF also refused to do anything. The Meo was finally given an operation through the

good offices of the State of Minnesota, and the headaches went away. Karl Polifka, letter to author, December 22, 1986.
6. *Bangkok Post,* February 16, 1971.

11. Wasteland

1. Pathet Lao attack: *Far Eastern Economic Review Yearbook,* 1972.

12. Down South

1. Quoted in Powers, *The Man Who Kept the Secrets,* p. 177.
2. Ivan Delbyk, quoted in Michael Maclear, *The Ten Thousand Day War* (New York: St. Martin's, 1981), p. 182.
3. Details on Igloo White Program: Paul Dickson, *The Electronic Battlefield* (Bloomington: Indiana University Press, 1976), *passim.*
4. Kissinger, *White House Years,* p. 992.
5. Kissinger's power: Palmer, *25-Year War,* p. 107.
6. T. D. Allman, interview with author.
7. Kissinger, *White House Years,* p. 1002.
8. Palmer, *25-Year War,* p. 115.
9. *Official History of the USAF in Southeast Asia,* p. 116.
10. Richard Nixon, *RN: The Memoirs of Richard Nixon* (New York: Grosset & Dunlap, 1978), p. 498. Kissinger is quoted as saying this by Nixon, but does not record the remark in his own memoirs.
11. Kissinger, *White House Years,* p. 1010. Kissinger goes to some trouble in his memoirs to apportion blame on the U.S. military and the South Vietnamese, but does not share in it himself.
12. Nixon, *RN,* p. 499.
13. Sullivan and Godley, interviews with author.
14. Lloyd Duncan, wounded in action, June 11, 1971.
15. Frank Kricker was awarded the Silver Star for this mission.
16. The Bolovens Campaign, July 28, 1971. Prepared by Project CHECO, 7th Air Force. Classified Secret May 8, 1974. Declassified December 31, 1982.

13. Attrition

1. Earl H. Tilford, Jr., *Search and Rescue in Southeast Asia, 1961–1975* (Washington, D.C.: Office of Air Force History, USAF, 1980).

14. Peace

1. Sullivan, interview with author.
2. Godley, interview with author.
3. Henry Kissinger, *Years of Upheaval* (Boston: Little Brown, 1982).
4. Prince Mangkhra Phouma, interview with author, Paris, October 12, 1985.
5. Oudone Sananikone, *The Royal Lao Army and U.S. Army Advice and Support* (Washington, D.C.: U.S. Army Center of Military History, 1981), pp. 149–50.
6. Lao Presse editorial quoted in Arnold Isaacs, *Without Honor: Defeat in Vietnam and Cambodia* (Baltimore and London: Johns Hopkins University Press, 1983), p. 153.
7. Kissinger's critics: Palmer, *25-Year War*, pp. 186–87.
8. Kissinger, *Years of Upheaval*, pp. 22–23.
9. Bowers, *Tactical Airlift*, p. 462.
10. *Congressional Record*, May 9, 1973, p. 14991.
11. Quoted in Isaacs, *Without Honor*, p. 179.
12. Quoted in ibid., p. 179.
13. Quoted in ibid., p. 179.
14. Senate Foreign Relations Committee: Thailand, Laos, Cambodia, and Vietnam: April 1973. Staff report. June 11, 1973, p. 12.
15. *Official History of the USAF in Southeast Asia*, p. 135.
16. Madame Lulu died in Paris in 1985.
17. The last time the Ravens were ever in Vientiane as a group was when they were cleared for an overnight visit from Udorn for the wedding of Carl Goembel to his fiancée, Margaret. Briggs Diuguid, Davy Dreier, Al Galante, Doug Mitchell, H. Ownby, Jim Roper, and Chad Swedberg duly arrived in town. In the hours before the ceremony they bought gold—Galante and Guffin were vying to own the largest Raven ID bracelet—and visited old haunts. During the wedding reception the groom was divested of his attire. The following morning the Ravens left via the windows of the Vientiane Hotel when a Pathet Lao patrol made a spot check for passports, which Ravens never carried.

15. After the War

1. Morrison, journal, April 19, 1970.
2. Fall, *Street Without Joy*, p. 257.

3. Many newspapers ran editorials defending Godley and criticizing the Senate committee's decision, including the *New York Times*, July 21, 1973; the *Washington Post*, July 15 and 21, 1973; the *Baltimore Sun*, July 15, 1973; the *Washington Star News*, July 17, 1973; the *Detroit News*, July 13 and 23, 1973; the *Oregonian*, July 13, 1973; the *Christian Science Monitor*, August 3, 1973; *Newsday*, July 16, 1973; *Chicago Daily News*, July 13, 1973. Only the *Boston Globe* and the *Detroit Free Press* supported the action.

4. W. E. Garrett, "The Hmong of Laos—No Place to Run," *National Geographic*, January 1974.

5. Karnow, *Vietnam: A History*, pp. 41, 415.

6. *Pentagon Papers*, Gravel ed., vol. 5, pp. 280–81. Cambodia received 200,000 tons of bombs.

7. John Keegan, *The Face of Battle* (New York: Viking Press, 1976), *passim*.

8. Max Hastings, *Bomber Command* (London: Michael Joseph Ltd., 1979), *passim*.

9. Fall, *Street Without Joy*, p. 261.

10. "Symposium on the Role of Airpower in Counterinsurgency and Unconventional Warfare: The Malayan Emergency," edited by A. H. Peterson, G. C. Reinhardt and E. E. Conger, Rand Corporation, 1963, p. 49.

11. Littauer and Uphoff, *Air War in Indochina*, p. 9. In Indochina, American counterinsurgency experts were against the overuse of air power—and even of artillery—from the very beginning of the war, arguing that it was militarily counterproductive in a guerrilla war; the inevitable civilian casualties alienated the local population.

12. Quoted by Dr. Yang Dao in "The Coalition Government," in Al Santoli, *To Bear Any Burden* (New York: Dutton, 1985), p. 263.

13. Extraction of Vang Pao from Laos: Author interviews with Harry Aderholt, Fort Walton Beach, Florida, 1985; Howard Hartley, Navarre Beach, Florida, March 18, 1985; Jack Knotts, Bangkok, Thailand, February 12, 1984; Dave Kouba, Stuart, Florida, March 11, 1987. Directly after the mission, Kouba, Knotts, and Matt Hoff made an hour-long tape, which Kouba kindly lent the author.

14. Laos after the peace: Arthur Dommen, *Laos: Keystone of Indochina* (Boulder, Colo.: Westview, 1985), pp. 96–115.

15. *Bangkok Post*, November 25, 1980.

16. MacAlister Brown and Joseph Zasloff, eds., *Communism in Indochina: New Perspectives* (Lexington, Mass.: Lexington Books, 1975), p. 103.

17. Yellow rain has become a controversial subject with its advocates—see Sterling Seagrave, *Yellow Rain: Chemical Warfare—The Deadliest Arms Race* (New York: Evans, 1981); and Jane Hamilton-Merritt, "Gas Warfare in Laos," *Reader's Digest*, October 1980—and its detractors—see Matthew Meselson and Joan W. Nowicke, "Yellow Rain—A Palynological Analysis," *Nature*, vol. 309 (May 17, 1984). The U.S. government has certainly played the issue up as propaganda. The ensuing debate over the Soviets' possible use of biological weapons has clouded the more mundane but undisputed annihilation of the Hmong through conventional weapons.

18. The total number of U.S. servicemen killed in Vietnam was 57,709.

19. The author studied Daniels's death certificate (No. 26/25 Local Registry Office, Pratumwan District) in Bangkok, checking the Thai original against the U.S. embassy statement by the Thai mortician who embalmed the body and reported no irregularities. A visit by the author to the deceased's apartment block at 76/1 Soi Lung Suan confirmed that each apartment was equipped with a large, antiquated water heater, the pilot light of which was a small gas burner and could indeed cause asphyxiation. Such deaths are not unknown in Bangkok. A friend of Daniels, a Thai youth, survived the gas leak but was taken to the hospital unconscious. For a more sinister interpretation of events, see "Mystery in Bangkok: Yellow Rain Skeptic Found Dead," *Covert Action Information Bulletin*, No. 17, Summer 1982.

20. Pop Buell in Bangkok: Arnold R. Isaacs, in *Baltimore Sun*, February 22, 1977. Pop died in the Philippines, aged seventy-two, on December 30, 1985. He is buried in Edon, Ohio.

21. Gerald Greven's testimony before the Senate Armed Services Committee, Bombing in Cambodia, July and August 1973, pp. 275–333.

22. *New York Times*, March 18, 1987. "Illegal" Hmong are those who remained in Ban Vinai after 1983 when the camp was officially closed to new arrivals.

23. Hmong in Providence, R.I.: Stephen P. Morin, in *Wall Street Journal*, February 16, 1983. Hmong in West Philadelphia: Marc Kaufman, in *Philadelphia Enquirer*, July 1, 1984.

24. Calvin Trillin, "Resettling the Yangs," in *Killings* (New York: Ticknor & Fields, 1984), pp. 160–78.
25. Tom Richards was awarded his fourth star in 1986 after commanding the Air War University at Maxwell Air Force Base, Montgomery, Alabama.

Epilogue: Reunion

1. Although the general is always available to give interviews on yellow rain or the plight of his people, he is still loath to speak about the CIA-run war. Endless written or telephoned requests by the author for a taped interview were politely sidestepped. "How you?" the general always asked cheerfully, before announcing regretfully that he was about to leave on a three-month trip on the morning of the proposed interview.
2. Indian journalist Nayan Chanda interviewed one such Lao dissident in Peking in February 1982, who confirmed the existence of a training camp for anti-Vietnamese Lao resistance in south China. Nayan Chanda, *Brother Enemy: The War After the War—A History of Indochina Since the Fall of Saigon* (San Diego, New York, London: Harcourt Brace Jovanovich, 1986), p. 380.

GLOSSARY

A-1 Douglas A-1 Skyraider, two-place or single-seat single-engine land- or carrier-based multipurpose attack bomber, capable of carrying up to 8,000 pounds of external ordnance, and equipped with four fixed forward-firing 20mm cannon. Considered obsolete by 1950, it was more appreciated by 1970 after its performance in Indochina.

A-7 Vought A-7 Corsair II, single-seat jet attack plane first used by the Navy and launched from carriers, and later used by the Air Force for support of friendly Laotian forces.

ABCCC AB Triple C was the orbiting airborne command and control center that sent fighter-bombers to Ravens in Laos (*See* Cricket *and* Hillsboro).

abort To suddenly cancel a flight or mission.

ADF Automatic direction finder, a receiver that detects signal strength and provides bearings to low- and medium-frequency transmitters.

air Air power—usually used in the context of fighter-bombers.

AIRA Air attaché's office, Vientiane.

Air America The name of the CIA's proprietary airline operating throughout Indochina, particularly in Laos.

Air Force Cross America's second-highest medal for bravery, awarded in the name of the president for extraordinary heroism while engaged in an action against the enemy.

Air Medal Awarded in the name of the United States of America to recognize single acts of merit or heroism, or for meritorious service while participating in aerial flight.

AK-47 The Soviet Avtomat Kalashnikova 1947 automatic assault rifle used by the North Vietnamese. It fired a 7.62mm bullet, was easy to maintain and use, and was a very effective weapon. Hmong forces used a number of captured AK-47s.

Alley Cat The orbiting command center that took over from Cricket at night.

AOC Air operations center, usually made up of a commander, maintenance man, radio operator, and medic, which worked with the native fighter squadrons in Laos.

Arclight Code name of B-52 bombing missions.

Article 15 A formal reprimand, well below a court-martial but serious enough to hinder an officer's career.

auger in Crash; a term used among military pilots.

AWOL Absent without leave.

AWOL bag Slang expression for an overnight bag.

B-52 The Boeing B-52 Stratofortress came under the Strategic Air Command. First flown in 1952, it was designed to deliver nuclear bombs. The aircraft had a range of 7,500 miles unrefueled. After the Big Belly modification its bomb load was approximately 60,000 pounds. It is one of the supreme ironies of the war that this strategic bomber should have been used so widely in tactical air operations.

baci Traditional Laotian party given to welcome or bid farewell to honored guests.

Backseater The Meo officer—also known as a Robin—who sat in the backseat of the O-1 and, as a Lao national, was able to validate targets for a Raven and authorize strikes. They constituted a small, trained corps in Gen. Vang Pao's forces.

Barrel Roll The code name for the operations and area in which USAF planes bombed in Northern Laos.

BDA Bomb damage assessment, made by the FAC after a strike, measured in terms of troops killed, buildings or trucks destroyed, secondary explosions, etc.

Bingo Radio shorthand for "out of gas."

bird dog O-1 reconnaissance plane.

black Clandestine, in the sense of "black money," "in the black," etc.

blood chit A 10-inch-wide, 19½-inch-long piece of white nylon with an American flag covering the top quarter and the words written underneath in English: "I am a citizen of the United States of America. I do not speak your language. Misfortune forces me to seek your assistance in obtaining food, shelter, and protection. Please take me to someone who will provide for my safety and see that I am returned to my people. My government will reward you." Beneath the English were translations in Burmese, Thai, Laotian, Cambodian, Vietnamese, Malayan, Indonesian, Chinese, Modern Chinese, Tagalog, Visawan, French, and Dutch. A controlled serial number was printed on the bottom so the carrier could be identified.

Bullpup Early type of guided bomb steered via radio control by the pilot, who visually tracked it onto its target. Used in Laos against caves (see **Walleye**).

buy the farm A favorite euphemism for death.

CAR-15 Short version of the M-16, much used by FACs who could not use the larger weapon from inside an airplane.

Caribou C-7 was a twin-propellor-driven 32-passenger STOL aircraft used by Air America in Laos.

CAS Controlled American Source, the term used for the CIA in Laos. (Also refers to the covert action branch of the Saigon office of the CIA.)

CBU Cluster bomb unit. These deadly antipersonnel bomblets came in a variety of forms. In the Laotian language they were called *bombi*.

Chapakao Call sign used by the Hmong T-28 fighter pilots.

CHECO Contemporary Historical Evaluation of Combat Operations. In 1962 the Air Force, using rated officers with research skills, launched an extensive effort to collect documents and write accounts of its role in the conflict in Indochina.

Chinook CH-47 twin-engined, transport helicopter with rotor blades fore and aft.

CIA Central Intelligence Agency.

CINCPAC Commander in Chief Pacific Command, based in Honolulu, Hawaii.

Commando Hunt The term used after 1968 to describe operations aimed at interdicting the Ho Chi Minh Trail.

Company "The Company" was an insider's term for the CIA.

Continental Air Services A privately owned airline operating alongside Air America—although not a wholly owned CIA proprietary—created to serve the needs of the Agency.

Country Team Council of senior U.S. officials in the embassy, which in Laos included the ambassador, air attaché, military attaché, CIA station chief, U.S. AID chief, etc.

Cricket The radio call sign for the orbiting command center that controlled U.S. air in northern Laos during the day (redesignated as Alley Cat at night).

Customer Air America always referred to the CIA as the Customer.

DASC Direct air support center in Vietnam, the ground-based control center that was responsible for sending fighters to FACs.

DEROS Date of eligible return from overseas.

DFC Distinguished Flying Cross, first authorized in 1926, is awarded in the name of the president of the United States for heroism or extraordinary achievement while participating in aerial flight. The performance of the act of heroism has to be voluntary, above and beyond the call of duty.

Divetoss Computerized bomb aiming device sometimes used in Laos in the F-4.

Downtowner A term of contempt used by combat people to describe embassy personnel based in "downtown" Vientiane who were remote from the war.

ER Effectiveness Report. Written at the end of each man's tour.

Erawan The three-headed white elephant that is the symbol of Laos.

F-4 McDonnell Douglas F-4 Phantom II. Two-seat all-weather long-range attack jet fighter. Although designed as an air-to-air combat fighter, it became one of the principal bombers of the war, even though it was not equipped for accurate level bomb delivery from medium altitudes.

F-105 Republic F-105 Thunderchief. Single-seat jet fighter-bomber armed with 20mm Gatling gun and 6,000 pounds of bombs. Suffered the most losses of the war. Known as the Thud.

FAC Forward air controller.

FAC-U The so-called forward air controllers' "university" at Phan Rhang.

FAG Forward air guide, either American or native, who help direct fighters onto targets from the ground.

FNG Fucking new guy.

Frag In the Air Force the Frag was the daily plan for the number of fighter-bombers and the type of ordnance they would carry. (On the ground officers who were "fragged" by their own men were murdered with a fragmentation grenade.)

GCA Ground-controlled approach, in which a ground controller, using a radar landing system operated from the ground, talks the pilot to a landing; the pilot flies on instruments and follows the instructions.

glory hole A break in an overcast sky which the FACs could use to bring fighters through and onto a target.

Golden BB The single bullet with the pilot's name on it, destined to kill him.

Guard Special radio frequency pilots use in emergency conditions.

gunships A tactical innovation of the Vietnam War, the first gunship was a modified World War II C-47 Gooney Bird cargo plane, redesignated as AC-47 and known as Dragonship, Puff, or Spooky. Used to support Gen. Vang Pao's troops in Laos, under the auspices of the Lao Air Force, and the 14th Special Operations Wing of the Air Commandos. AC-119 Flying Boxcars were also modified, using aerial parachute flares to operate at night. C-130 cargo planes were later converted to AC-130 gunships and were used extensively over the Ho Chi Minh Trail and became the best truck-killer of the war.

H-34 Sikorsky H-34 Choctaw was the dated (deliveries to the U.S. Army began in early 1955) work horse of Air America used all over Laos.

HE High explosive, as in HE rocket.

Helio-courier The first of the Short Takeoff and Landing (STOL) aircraft used by the CIA in Laos, mostly superceded by the Pilatus Porter.

Hillsboro Code name for the orbiting airborne command and control center which operated in the Laotian panhandle in the day (designated Moonbeam at night).

Ho Chi Minh Trail The trail used by the North Vietnamese to move men and supplies down through Laos and Cambodia into South Vietnam.

Huey Most widely used helicopter of the Vietnam War, the small UH1 was employed in Laos by Air America.

in-country Vietnam—used in the sense of the in-country war (the out-country war was in Cambodia, Laos, and Thailand).

intervalometer Equipment in the cockpit of a fighter for selecting ordnance and rate of fire or bomb dropping.

JCA Joint chiefs of staff.

jink Maneuver the aircraft sharply and continuously to avoid ground fire.

Jolly Green Giant The nickname for the armored Sikorsky HH-3E helicopter, specially modified for rescue operations and flown by the Air Rescue Service of the USAF.

karst The ragged limestone mountain ridges of Laos.

khene Laotian stone-age gourd wind instrument used in much of the country's music.

KIA Killed in action.

King Airborne rescue center, operating out of a C-130 and controlling the majority of SARs over Laos.

kip Laotian currency, of which both sides in the war printed their own. The CIA forged Pathet Lao *kip* and dropped notes by the million over enemy lines.

L-19 The Army designation for the O-1.

laser-guided bomb The most sophisticated of the "smart" bombs. A laser beam designates the target; the bomb detects the reflected light and follows it to the target. Mostly used in Laos to guide a bomb into the mouth of a cave suspected to house supplies or enemy troops.

Lima Site Landing site, usually a small, unimproved dirt strip.

M-79 grenade launcher A break-open shotgun-style weapon that fired a 40mm grenade cartridge to an effective range of 375 yards. The grenade exploded on impact and had a casualty radius of five yards. Also fired a buckshot projectile that could be used at short range.

medevac Medical evacuation, usually undertaken by a helicopter.

MIA Missing in action.

MiG Russian jet fighter flown by the North Vietnamese.

mixture The fuel-and-air combination that enters the cylinders of a reciprocating engine for combustion. A "rich" mixture has more fuel in the combination, a "lean" mixture has less. The richness can be adjusted, to a large extent, in the cockpit.

MSQ Radar.

Nail FAC based in Nakhon Phanom, flying OV-10s over the Trail—occasionally used on missions in Laos.

negative objective The code used over the radio to announce that a pilot had been found dead.

Neutralists In the military sense, the forces who followed Capt. Kong Le after his coup attempt in 1960, and who originally sought to oust all foreigners—American and North Vietnamese—from the country. After a brief allegiance to the Communist Pathet Lao, they later sided with the Royal Lao forces—except for a small group, calling themselves the Patriotic Neutralists, who fought with the North Vietnamese throughout the war.

Nixon Doctrine Part of the strategy to remove U.S. forces from Vietnam, the part of U.S. policy that supported Vietnamization. On July 25, 1969, the president reaffirmed the United States would honor its treaty commitments and would continue to provide a nuclear shield and military and economic assistance as appropriate. However, the nation directly threatened would continue to assume the primary responsibility of providing the manpower for its defense. U.S. air power would now substitute for U.S. manpower.

NKP Nakhon Phanom, the town just across the border in Thailand that housed the secret base of the Air Commandos.

NVA North Vietnamese Army.

O-1 Spotter plane used by FACs in Laos.

O-2 Specially designed spotter plane that replaced the O-1 in Vietnam.

out-country Anywhere not in Vietnam, but used specifically—as in "out-country war"—to mean Laos, Cambodia, and Thailand.

OV-10 North American Bronco, specially designed for FAC use, a latecomer to the war and used widely over the Trail.

Pathet Lao Generic term used throughout the book for the various Lao Communist movements. First used in 1950 within Laos to describe the forces that followed the Communist Vietminh. Later gained international currency at the Geneva Conference of 1954 (although no Pathet Lao representatives were present, and a Vietminh general signed the cease-fire with the French on their behalf). Lao Communist movements included: the People's Party of Laos (Phak Pasason Lao—PPL); the Lao Patriotic Front (Neo Lao Hak Sat—NLHS), the central committee of which commanded the armed forces known as the Lao People's Liberation Army; and the Patriotic Neutralists. But by any name, these groups were little more than front organizations manipulated by Hanoi.

PDJ Plain of Jars, the fertile, rolling plain to the northeast of Long Tieng, named after the mysterious ancient stone funeral urns dotted throughout it. The French named it the Plaine de Jarres. Also known as the J.

PEO Program Evaluation Office. A disguised military mission set up by the State Department in 1959 to create and train the Royal Lao Army. Headed by a general from the U.S. Army, its members wore civilian clothes and were described as "technicians."

Phantom See F-4.

phi The spirits that the Meo believed inhabited everything, from rocks to humans, from trees to airplanes.

pickle Term used by pilots to describe a bomb coming off the plane. They could either "clean the wing"—pickle off all bombs at the same time—or drop them in pairs, or one at a time.

Pilatus Porter A Swiss-built short-takeoff-and-landing (STOL) airplane used by both Air America and Continental Air Services.

pipper A dot in the gunsight placed on the target.

Project 404 The code name of the secret Air Force operations in Laos and Thailand.

PSP Pierced steel planking, the perforated metal planks used to construct runways in remote strips.

Purple Heart Medal awarded to troops wounded in action.

ramp The area at an airport where airplanes are parked.

R&R Rest and recreation—leave from the war.

REMF Rear-echelon motherfucker—the name given to all people stationed away from the combat areas.

Robin The call sign used later in the war for a Meo Backseater.

ROE Rules of Engagement, by which the U.S. military sought to control and limit the war.

Romeos Slang for the ROE.

RON Remain overnight.

RTB Return to base.

SAC Strategic Air Command, under which the B-52 bombers were flown.

SAR Search and rescue. An elaborate procedure under Air Force rules involving the suppression of ground fire by fighters before Jolly Green helicopters attempt a pickup.

SEL Suspected enemy location.

SGU Special Guerrilla Unit. The most effective of Vang Pao's troops, using helicopters, were organized into these small combat units.

short Term used to describe someone with only a few days left in his tour.

shortitis The psychological condition which goes with the above, ranging from the reckless to extreme anxiety.

Sikorsky See H-34.

Silver Star America's third-highest medal for bravery awarded in the name of the president for gallantry in action against the enemy.

Skyraider See A-1.

smart bombs Bombs capable of homing in on their target during flight. Introduced late in the war, they cost four or five times more than conventional "iron" bombs and in 1971 accounted for less than 1 percent of the total weight of munitions dropped on Indochina.

sortie One attack, or operational flight, by a single military aircraft or single formation of aircraft.

Split-S A maneuver combining a half-roll followed by an inverted half-loop, making the lower half of the letter S. The result is rapid loss of altitude and a reversal in the direction of flight.

stall At high altitude or in bad weather the wing of a plane can no longer generate sufficient lift to support it. Not an engine failure.

Steel Tiger Code name for the area and operations of the U.S. Air Force over the northern portion of the Laotian panhandle aimed at interdicting the Ho Chi Minh Trail (*see* Tiger Hound).

STOL Short takeoff and landing—used to designate various aircraft and strips used in Laos.

strategic air warfare The *Dictionary of U.S. Military Terms* defines this: "Air combat and supporting operations designed to effect, through the systematic application of force to a selected series of vital targets, the progressive destruction of the enemy's war-making capacity to a point where he no longer retains the ability or will to wage war. Vital targets may include key manufacturing systems, sources of raw material, critical material, stockpiles, power systems, transportation, communication facilities, concentration of uncommitted elements of enemy armed forces, key agricultural areas, and other such target systems." (*See* tactical air warfare.) War proper—especially a war with no front line and a large guerrilla element—never falls quite so neatly into either category; strategy and tactics often overlap and sometimes blur to the point of becoming metaphysical.

T-28 North American Nomad, a two-seat armed counterinsurgency airplane, extensively modified from the Trojan Trainer. Maximum level speed 360 mph, cruising speed 276 mph. The principal attack plane of the Royal Lao Air Force. First flown in 1949; the T-28s used in South Vietnam all carried the tail-number prefix O, meaning obsolete. They were extremely effective in the war in Laos.

TACAIR Tactical Air Command. (See next entry.)

TACAN Tactical air and navigation control system, developed by the military to enable a pilot to pick up a radio bearing providing directional and distance-measuring information.

tactical air warfare Operations carried out in coordination with ground or naval forces in a direct relationship to the conflict on the battlefield and against military forces in being. (*See* strategic air warfare.)

TDY Temporary duty, the status of all Ravens in Laos.

Thud See F-105.

Tiger Hound Code name for the area and operation of the U.S. Air Force in the lower portion of the Laotian panhandle. The term was not used after 1968 when operations against the Trail were renamed Commando Hunt.

trash hauler Transport airplane or pilot.

TWIX Military cable.

U-17 Cessna with side-by-side seating and with greater range than the O-1, but less serviceable as a FAC aircraft.

USIS United States Information Service, generally referred to by warriors and reporters alike as "useless."

Uzi Israeli-manufactured sub-machine gun.

Vietnamization An integral part of Nixon's strategy to bring the Vietnam War to a close, where the war was gradually turned over from the control of U.S. forces to the South Vietnam armed forces. Meanwhile, U.S. forces would gradually be withdrawn. The term was coined by Defense Secretary Melvin Laird and was officially initiated by Nixon on June 8, 1969.

Volpar Light, general-purpose aircraft used by Air America in Laos to carry passengers (fifteen) or cargo.

Walleye A "smart" bomb, carrying a TV camera, that can be set on release to home in automatically on a selected visual feature.

Waterpump The code name of the Air Commando program to train native fighter pilots.

White Star The White Star Mobile Training Team replaced the PEO (*see* PEO) and was the U.S. Special Forces group responsible for training the Royal Lao Army—particularly Gen. Vang Pao's military forces. Withdrawn after the signing of the Geneva Accords in 1962.

WIA Wounded in action.

Willy Pete White phosphorous rocket used by FACs to mark a target.

Winchester Out of bullets or bombs.

zoomies Nickname applied to graduates of the Air Force Academy.

ZPU "Zeep," a rapid-firing, small-caliber antiaircraft gun extremely effective at low altitudes.

BIBLIOGRAPHY

Adams, Nina S., and Alfred W. McCoy, eds. *Laos: War and Revolution*. New York: Harper & Row, 1970.

Agee, Philip. *Inside the Company: CIA Diary*. Stonehill, 1975.

Barney, G. Linwood. "The Meo of Xieng Khouang Province." In Peter Kunstadter, ed., *Southeast Asian Tribes, Minorities, and Nations*, Vol. 1. Princeton, N.J.: Princeton University Press, 1967.

Berval, René de. *Kingdom of Laos: The Land of the Million Elephants and of the White Parasol*. Saigon: France-Asie, 1959.

Blaufarb, Douglas S. *The Counterinsurgency Era: U.S. Doctrine and Performance 1950 to the Present*. New York: Free Press/Macmillan, 1977.

Bowers, Ray L. *Tactical Airlift: The United States Air Force in Southeast Asia*. Washington, D.C.: Office of Air Force History, 1983.

Branfman, Fred, ed. *Voices from the Plain of Jars*. New York: Harper & Row, 1972.

Brown, MacAlister, and Joseph Zasloff, eds. *Communism in Indochina: New Perspectives*. Lexington, Mass.: Lexington Books, 1975.

Chanda, Nayan. *Brother Enemy: The War After the War—A History of Indochina Since the Fall of Saigon*. San Diego, New York, London: Harcourt Brace Jovanovich, 1986.

Church Committee. *Alleged Assassination Plots Involving Foreign Leaders*. New York: W.W. Norton, 1976.

Coffey, Thomas M. *Iron Eagle: The Turbulent Life of General Curtis LeMay*. New York: Crown, 1986.

Colby, William. *Honorable Men: My Life in the CIA*. New York: Simon & Schuster, 1978.

Deacon, Richard. *"C": A Biography of Sir Maurice Oldfield, Head of M16*. London: Macdonald, 1985.

Deighton, Len. *Fighter: The True Story of the Battle of Britain*. London: Jonathan Cape, 1977.

Deydier, Henri. *Lokapala—Genies, Totems et Sorciers du Nord du Laos*. Paris: Plon, 1954.

Dickson, Paul. *The Electronic Battlefield*. Bloomington: Indiana University Press, 1976.

Dommen, Arthur J. *Conflict in Laos: The Politics of Neutralization*, rev. ed. New York: Praeger, 1971.

———. *Laos: Keystone of Indochina*. Boulder, Colo.: Westview, 1985.

Doolittle, Jerome. *The Bombing Officer*. New York: Dutton, 1982.

Drury, Richard S. *My Secret War*. Fallbrook, Calif.: Aero Publishers, 1979.

Fall, Bernard. *Anatomy of a Crisis: The Laotian Crisis of 1960–61*. Garden City, N.Y.: Doubleday, 1969.

———. *Hell in a Very Small Place: The Siege of Dien Bien Phu*. Philadelphia: Lippincott, 1966.

———. *Last Reflections on a War*. Garden City, N.Y.: Doubleday, 1967.

———. *Street Without Joy*. Harrisburg, Pa.: Stackpole, 1964.

———. *The Two Vietnams: A Political and Military Analysis*. New York: Praeger, 1967.

———. *Vietnam Witness, 1953–1966*. New York: Praeger, 1966.

Garrett, W. E. "The Hmong of Laos—No Place to Run." *National Geographic*, January 1974.

Gelb, Leslie H., and Richard K. Betts. *The Irony of Vietnam: The System Worked*. Washington, D.C.: Brookings, 1979.

Goulden, Joseph C. and Alexander W. Raffio. *The Death Merchant: The Rise and Fall of Edwin P. Wilson*. New York: Simon & Schuster, 1984.

Halberstam, David. *The Best and the Brightest*. New York: Random House, 1972.

Hamilton-Merritt, Jane. "Gas Warfare in Laos: Communism's Drive to Annihilate a People." *Reader's Digest*, October 1980.

Harvey, Frank. *Air War—Vietnam*. New York: Bantam, 1967.

Hastings, Max. *Bomber Command*. London: Michael Joseph Ltd., 1979.

Hersh, Seymour M. *The Price of Power: Kissinger in the White House*. New York: Summit, 1983.

Hilsman, Roger. *To Move a Nation: The Politics of Foreign Policy in the Administration of JFK*. Garden City, N.Y.: Doubleday, 1967.

Honey, P. J. *Communism in North Vietnam: Its Role in the Sino-Soviet Dispute*. Cambridge, Mass.: MIT Press, 1963.

Isaacs, Arnold R. *Without Honor: Defeat in Vietnam and Cambodia*. Baltimore and London: Johns Hopkins University Press, 1983.

Isaacson, Walter, and Evan Thomas. *The Wise Men: Six Friends and the World They Made*. New York: Simon & Schuster, 1986.

Karnow, Stanley. *Vietnam: A History*. New York: Viking, 1983.

Keegan, John. *The Face of Battle*. New York: Viking Press, 1976.

Lewis, Norman. *A Dragon Apparent: Travels in Cambodia, Laos and Vietnam*. London: Jonathan Cape, 1951. Reissue, London: Eland Books, 1982.

Kissinger, Henry A. *The White House Years*. Boston: Little, Brown, 1979.

———. *Years of Upheaval*. Boston: Little, Brown, 1982.

Langer, Paul F., and Joseph J. Zasloff. *North Vietnam and the Pathet Lao: Partners in the Struggle for Laos*. Cambridge, Mass.: Harvard University Press, 1970.

LeMay, Curtis E. (with MacKinlay Kantor). *Mission with LeMay: My Story*. Garden City, N.Y.: Doubleday, 1965.

Littauer, Raphael, and Norman Uphoff, eds. *The Air War in Indochina*. Boston: Beacon, 1972.

Maas, Peter. *Manhunt: The Incredible Pursuit of a CIA Agent Turned Terrorist*. New York: Random House, 1986.

Maclear, Michael. *The Ten Thousand Day War*. New York: St. Martin's, 1981.

McCoy, Alfred W. *The Politics of Heroin in Southeast Asia*. New York: Harper & Row, 1972.

McGehee, Ralph W. *Deadly Deceits: My 25 Years in the CIA*. New York: Sheridan Square Publications, 1983.

Menger, Matt J. *Valley of the Mekong*. Vientiane: Catholic Mission, 1969.

Meselson, Matthew, and Joan W. Nowicke. "Yellow Rain—a Palynological Analysis." *Nature*, Vol. 309 (May 17, 1984).

Momyer, William W. *Air Power in Three Wars*. Washington, D.C.: U.S. Government Printing Office, 1978. (WWII, Korea, Vietnam.)

Moran, Lord. *The Anatomy of Courage*. London: Constable, 1945.

Nixon, Richard. *RN: The Memoirs of Richard Nixon*. New York: Grosset & Dunlap, 1978.

Official History of the United States Air Force in Southeast Asia. Washington, D.C.: U.S. Government Printing Office, 1977.

Palmer, Bruce, Jr. *The 25-Year War: America's Military Role in Vietnam*. Lexington, Ky.: University Press of Kentucky, 1984.

The Pentagon Papers. Senator Gravel edition. 5 vols. Boston: Beacon, 1971–72.

The Pentagon Papers. New York: New York Times Company, 1971.

Phillips, David Atlee. *The Night Watch*. New York: Atheneum, 1976.

Porter, Gareth, ed. *Vietnam: A History in Documents*. New York: Earl M. Coleman Enterprises, 1979. (Abridgement of 2-volume work, *Vietnam: The Definitive History of Human Decisions*.)

Powers, Thomas. *The Man Who Kept the Secrets: Richard Helms and the CIA*. New York: Knopf, 1979.

Prados, John. *Presidents' Secret Wars: CIA and Pentagon Covert Operations Since World War II*. New York: William Morrow, 1986.

Pratt, John Clark. *Vietnam Voices: Perspectives on the War Years, 1941–1982*. New York: Viking/Penguin, 1984.

———. *The Laotian Fragments*. New York: Viking, 1974.

Robbins, Christopher. *Air America: The Story of the CIA's Secret Airlines*. New York: Putnam, 1979.

Sananikone, Oudone. *The Royal Lao Army and U.S. Army Advice and Support*. Indochina Monograph Series. Washington, D.C.: U.S. Army Center of Military History, 1981.

Santoli, Al. *To Bear Any Burden*. New York: Dutton, 1985.

Schanche, Don A. *Mister Pop: The Inside Story of the American Involvement in Laos*. New York: McKay, 1970.

Schlesinger, Arthur M., Jr. *A Thousand Days: John F. Kennedy in the White House*. Boston: Houghton Mifflin, 1965.

Seagrave, Sterling. *Yellow Rain: Chemical Warfare—the Deadliest Arms Race*. New York: Evans, 1981.

Shackley, Theodore. *The Third Option: An American View of Counterinsurgency*. New York: Reader's Digest Press, 1981.

Shawcross, William. *Sideshow: Kissinger, Nixon and the Destruction of Cambodia*. New York: Simon & Schuster, 1979.

Smith, Joseph B. *Portrait of a Cold Warrior*. New York: Putnam, 1976.

Snepp, Frank. *Decent Interval: An Insider's Account of Saigon's Indecent End Told by the CIA's Chief Strategy Analyst in Vietnam*. New York: Random House, 1977.

Souvanna Phouma, Mangkhra. *L'Agonie du Laos*. Paris: Plon, 1976.

Stevenson, Charles A. *The End of Nowhere: American Policy Toward Laos Since 1965*. Boston: Beacon, 1972.

Stockwell, John. *In Search of Enemies: A CIA Story*. New York and London: Norton, 1978.

Summers, Harry G., Jr. *On Strategy: A Critical Analysis of the Vietnam War*. Novato, Calif.: Presidio, 1982.

————. *Vietnam War Almanac*. New York and Oxford: Facts on File Publications, 1985.

Sullivan, William H. *Obbligato: Notes on a Foreign Service Career*. New York and London: Norton, 1984.

Thompson, W. Scott, and D. D. Frizzel, eds. *The Lessons of Vietnam*. New York: Crane Russak, 1977.

Tilford, Earl H., Jr. *Search and Rescue in Southeast Asia, 1961–1975*. Washington, D.C.: Office of Air Force History, USAF, 1980.

Tower, John, Edmund Muskie, Brent Scowcroft. *The Tower Commission Report: President's Special Review Board*. A *New York Times* Special, Bantam-Times, 1987.

Toye, Hugh. *Laos: Buffer State or Battleground?* London: Oxford, 1968.

Trillin, Calvin. *Killings*. New York: Ticknor & Fields, 1984.

Trinquier, Roger. *Les Maquis d'Indochine 1952–1954*. Paris: Société de Production Littéraire, 1976.

————. *Modern Warfare: A French View of Counterinsurgency*. New York: Praeger, 1964.

United States Air Force, Office of Air Force History. *Search and Rescue in Southeast Asia*. Washington, D.C.: Office of Air Force History, 1980.

Westmoreland, General William C. *A Soldier Reports*. Garden City, N.Y.: Doubleday, 1976.

Wolfe, Tom. *The Right Stuff*. New York: Farrar, Straus & Giroux, 1979.

Zasloff, Joseph J., and MacAlister Brown, eds. *Communism in Indochina: New Perspectives*. Lexington, Mass.: Lexington Books, 1975.

INDEX